THE THIRD AND FOURTH
BOOKS OF MACCABEES

Dropsie College Edition

JEWISH APOCRYPHAL LITERATURE

SOLOMON ZEITLIN
Editor-in-Chief

ABRAHAM A. NEUMAN
Chairman, Editorial Board

MOSES HADAS
Secretary, Editorial Board

JOSHUA BLOCH
MORTIMER J. COHEN
SOLOMON B. FREEHOF
THEODOR H. GASTER
SOLOMON GOLDMAN
ROBERT GORDIS
CYRUS H. GORDON
FELIX A. LEVY

RALPH MARCUS
JULIAN MORGENSTERN
HARRY M. ORLINSKY
DAVID DE SOLA POOL
JOSEPH REIDER
SOLOMON L. SKOSS
SIDNEY TEDESCHE
HARRY A. WOLFSON

FRANK ZIMMERMANN

THE
THIRD AND FOURTH BOOKS OF
MACCABEES

Edited and Translated
by
MOSES HADAS

KTAV PUBLISHING HOUSE, INC.
NEW YORK

Library of Congress Cataloging in Publication Data

Bible. O. T. Apocryphal books. 3-4 Maccabees.
  Greek. 1976.
  The third and fourth books of Maccabees.

  Greek and English.
  Reprint of the 1953 ed. published for the Dropsie
College for Hebrew and Cognate Learning by Harper,
New York, in series: Jewish apocryphal literature.
  Includes bibliographical references.
  I. Bible. O. T. Apocryphal books. 3-4 Maccabees.
English. Hadas. 1976. II. Hadas, Moses, 1900-1966.
III. Title. IV. Series: Jewish apocryphal literature.
[BS1823.H2 1976]   229'.75'077   76-56119
ISBN 0-87068-425-6

FIRST PUBLISHED 1953

PUBLISHED BY SPECIAL ARRANGEMENT WITH

DROPSIE UNIVERSITY, PHILADELPHIA, PA.

Copyright, 1953, by Harper & Brothers

Printed in the United States of America

FOREWORD

ABRAHAM A. NEUMAN

The Dropsie College for Hebrew and Cognate Learning presents *The Third and Fourth Books of Maccabees*, edited and translated by Professor Moses Hadas, as the third volume of the series, Jewish Apocryphal Literature.

It was deemed expedient to publish the two books in one volume for purely external reasons without regard to the accidental circumstance of their numerical succession. A similar procedure will be followed in a number of other cases, where it will be found convenient to combine two or more of the smaller books into one volume.

If it is a truism that history illumines the present, it is equally true that the experiences of the living generation act as a commentary on the historic past. This fact is mirrored in the present work. Following Doctor Hadas' brilliant and persuasive interpretation, III Maccabees exposes the evil of race hatred and its preordained doom. In IV Maccabees, the spirit of the man of faith is portrayed in triumph over tyrants and their death-wielding instruments. For greater than the terrors of death is the victorious faith of martyrdom.

Thus while the two books are not consciously interrelated, these literary compositions are mutually complementary in voicing a truth to which Jewish history is the eternal witness. What generation bears fuller testimony to the evil course of human hatred and the swift punishment that descended upon the arch-conspirator? When, indeed, did free men crave so desperately for the assurance that the will of tyrants is brittle and that man is glorified in faith, victorious in the ability to rise above death in martyrdom?

To Mr. Harry Starr and The Lucius N. Littauer Foundation which he heads, we are grateful for having made possible for our time this literary gift of hope and faith in its present form.

PREFACE

To the degree that each employs Greek literary forms to convey edifying doctrine to a Greek speaking Jewish audience, III and IV Maccabees are related; but their relationship is nothing like that, say, between I and II Kings, for they are totally disparate works. Their inclusion in a single volume is only a matter of tradition and convenience. The difference in the character of the two books (and perhaps the circumstance that the editor approached the second three years after completing his work on the first) explains certain differences in treatment in the present edition.

For permission to reproduce the Greek text from Alfred Rahlfs' *Septuaginta*, grateful acknowledgement is due to the Württemberger Bibelanstalt of Stuttgart. The writer wishes to extend his personal thanks to Professor Solomon Zeitlin, editor of the present series, for his careful and helpful scrutiny of his work, and to President A. A. Neuman of Dropsie College, the sponsors of the series, for his unfailing courtesy and generosity. Thanks are also due to Mr. David H. Scott, of Harper and Brothers, for his courteous collaboration.

Moses Hadas

Columbia University

THE THIRD BOOK OF MACCABEES

⊷§ CONTENTS §⊶

Foreword: Abraham A. Neuman	vii
Preface	ix
Introduction	1
I. Summary of Contents	1
II. Prospectus of Critical Conclusions	2
III. Factors Which Render Historicity Suspect	3
Title	4
Rhetorical elements	5
Jewish parallels	6
1. Esther	6
2. Septuagint Esther	7
3. Aristeas to Philocrates	8
4. Josephus	10
5. II Maccabees	11
6. The Apocalyptic Technique	12
Pagan parallels	13
1. Greek Romances	13
2. Aetiological Histories	15
IV. Verisimilitude of the Account of Ptolemy Philopator and His Policy	16
V. Evidence of Later Composition	18
VI. *Laographia* in the Ptolemaic and Roman Periods	19

VII.	Date of Composition	21
VIII.	Language and Style; Place of Composition	22
IX.	Religious and Ethical Implications	23
	1. Affirmation of Faith in Providence	23
	2. The Aetiological Element	24
	3. The Internal Partisan Element	24
X.	Religious Premises	25
XI.	The Text	26
XII.	Editions	27
	Text, Translation, Commentary, and Critical Notes	29

⇜§ INTRODUCTION §⇝

The book called III Maccabees is a noncanonical work found in many, but not all, manuscripts of the Septuagint. Its seven chapters present an account of events involving Egyptian Jewry which are purported to have taken place under King Ptolemy IV Philopator (221–204 BCE). The book has left fewer traces in literature and art than others of its class, and is not generally familiar. It will be convenient, therefore, to preface the present discussion with a brief summary of its contents.

I

SUMMARY OF CONTENTS

After Ptolemy defeated Antiochus III the Great at Raphia he visited various neighboring cities and made offerings at their shrines, to confirm the loyalty of his subjects (1.1–8). At Jerusalem he admired the Temple greatly, conceived a desire to inspect its interior, and would be deterred by no expostulations (1.9–29). The High Priest Simon prayed that the desecration might be averted (2.1–20), whereupon the king fell in a swoon and his attendants carried him out (2.21–24). On his return to Egypt the king determined to avenge the affront by degrading the civic status of the Jews and branding them with the ivy leaf, the emblem of Dionysus; those accepting the cult were promised citizenship equal to the Alexandrians' (2.25–30). Most of the Alexandrian Jews persevered in their faith (2.31–33) and this angered the king, who ordered all the Jews in his dominions to be brought to Alexandria and put to death (3.1–30). They were brought together with great cruelty (4.1–13);

after forty days the registration of their names was left incomplete, because writing materials were exhausted (4.14–21). The king ordered the Jews to be trampled by infuriated elephants, but was providentially lulled into a deep sleep and the execution was postponed to the following day (5.1–22). But on that day God effaced his memory of the order and instead caused him to remember the Jews' loyalty (5.23–35). On this day, when the sentence was finally to be executed (5.36–51), the aged priest Eleazar offered prayer (6.1–15), and two angels descended from heaven, visible to all but the Jews, terrified the king and soldiers, and caused the elephants to trample their own party (6.16–21). The king was now filled with anger against his counsellors and benevolence toward the Jews (6.22–29), and ordered that they be lavishly entertained at the spot of their deliverance; the Jews determined to perpetuate the memory of the miracle by an annual festival (6.30–41). The king addressed letters of protection for the Jews to the provincial governors (7.1–9), and the Jews returned to their homes, slew the apostates, and celebrated their new security by inaugurating another festival (7.10–23).

II

Prospectus of Critical Conclusions

Of the events related in III Maccabees we have no direct knowledge from other sources, nor have we specific testimony concerning the date or the circumstances of the composition of the book, or of the literary and religious background out of which it grew. For all such information, essential to a proper appreciation of its historical, literary, and religious values, we must resort to the evidence supplied, usually unintentionally, by the book itself. The determination of its background and purpose depends largely on inference; and apportionment of space in the pages that follow must be governed by the availability of material rather than by the relative importance of the factors under discussion. It may therefore serve clarity if

INTRODUCTION 3

we state at once the major conclusions of our study, and then indicate the course of the arguments that lead to these conclusions.

In the view here taken, then, III Maccabees was written *ca.* 25-24 BCE, when the civic status of Egyptian Jewry was jeopardized by the new Roman administration. There had indeed been a similar crisis under Ptolemy Philopator almost two centuries before, concerning which our author has sound information; but the ancient crisis is used only as an effective analogue to an immediate situation. Similarly, the tale of the elephants, like other embellishments, if it belonged to history at all, did not belong to the history of Ptolemy Philopator or of the Romans, and was added for its effectiveness. The author probably had no expectation that his work would be read as literal history; it is intended rather as a historical romance of an edifying character and perhaps also as masked political criticism. His immediate motives may have included one or more of the following: To provide encouragement and strengthen faith in the face of a specific calamity; to supply historical justification for the legitimacy of a certain festival; to combat divergent views on the proper attitude for Egyptian Jews to take to their non-Jewish environment.

III

FACTORS WHICH RENDER HISTORICITY SUSPECT

The title of III Maccabees, the circumstantial indications of date and background in the opening verses, and the use of what purport to be official documents in the body of the book, would suggest that the work was intended as history, however biased in the direction of edification—on the analogy of the earlier books of the Maccabees and of other "historical" books in the corpus of the Septuagint. But the historicity of III Maccabees is rendered suspect, not only by exaggerations which tax credulity, but also by the fact that similar stories and analogous literary approach occur in other books, and by historical discrepancies and anachronisms within this book. This need not imply that the book is wholly fictional, for it surely reflects a crisis (perhaps, indeed, two crises) in Egyptian Jewish life, told quite directly; and the decorative element may be explained as dictated by the genus to which the book belongs and the uses for which it was intended.

Analysis of III Maccabees makes it plain that the crisis which is at its core was one in which the civic status of Egyptian Jewry was imperilled. Enough is known of the character and policy of Ptolemy Philopator and of the conditions of the Egyptian Jews during his reign to make it quite probable that some such crisis as is here reflected actually took place under Philopator. The episode of the Temple (not improbable in itself) and of the elephants (which appears to have been a floating literary commonplace) may have been included to heighten the religious interest, which is very pronounced in this book; it is to be noticed that in the king's decree setting forth his penalties for the Jews' rejection of his offer nothing is said of elephants. But if the status of Egyptian Jews was imperilled shortly after Raphia, it was imperilled even more gravely after Egypt became a Roman province (30 BCE); and it seems most likely that the book was written in response to this later crisis, employing the history of almost two centuries before, decorated with edifying miracles as ancient history may be decorated, to mask criticism of new oppressors and afford encouragement to the oppressed. We proceed now to examine the factors which make it difficult or unnecessary to accept the book as it now stands as a veracious account of actual events.

TITLE

III Maccabees purports to describe events which took place shortly after the battle of Raphia (Spring of 217 BCE), or precisely half a century before the Maccabean uprising. Only in a general sense, therefore, as providing background for conditions out of which the uprising grew, is the title of "Maccabees" appropriate. It is true that our Greek text opens with an

INTRODUCTION 5

illative particle which presupposes one or more preceding sentences; that the definite article at 1.2 ("*the* plot which he had conceived"), as well as the use of "aforementioned" at 2.25, seem to allude to material which has gone before, and that there is an abruptness about the opening verses which contrasts with the smooth transitions in the remainder of the book; and it may be that a whole introductory chapter has fallen out and that this chapter would better justify the title. Indeed, the applicability of the title of "Maccabees" even to the other books so named is dubious.[1] On the basis of its contents a proper title for the book would be something like "On Providence" (extant treatises of Seneca and Plutarch bear similar titles, but they are "philosophic" and do not tell a unified story as our book does); it is even conceivable that such a title as "Maccabees" became attached to such a title as "On Providence" on the analogy of the rhetoricians' use of double titles, as for example, Dio Chrysostom's *Diogenes or on Kingship*, or *Diogenes or On Virtue*. There is also some indication that the book was referred to as *Ptolemaica*,[2] which is not inappropriate.

But for our book as it stands the title is surely a misnomer. The title, further, may explain the presence of the book in the Septuagint. The impression of historical intent which derives from the book's title and its inclusion in the Septuagint may therefore be without proper foundation.

RHETORICAL ELEMENTS

The extraordinary events which thwarted the execution of the king's decree against the Jews (ch. 5) may be accepted as miracles which the author and many of his readers might credit, but there are a number of purple patches whose aim is patently mere rhetorical enhancement. In this category are the pathetic and exaggerated accounts of the brides who forsake their bridal chambers and the infants who are deserted (1.17–

[1] See Dr. Zeitlin's Introd. to II Maccabees in this series.
[2] See E. Schürer, *Geschichte des jüdischen Volkes im Zeitalter J. C.*, (Leipzig, 1909), 3.492.

20); of the brides, again, and their grooms and the elders who are dragged from their homes (4.4-10); of the cessation of the registry because the manufactures of writing materials were exhausted (4.20); of the incredibly large number of elephants (5.2); and similar exaggerations. In a somewhat different category, but in keeping with ancient rhetorical practice, is the insertion of formal epistles attributed to the king (3.12-29, 6.1-22), and of prayers put into the mouths of priests (2.1-20, 6.1-15). That the royal epistles observe correct chancellory form and the prayers are manifestly Jewish in language and content does not affect their present use as being dictated by the rules of rhetorical composition.

JEWISH PARALLELS

Perhaps the most compelling argument against the validity of III Maccabees in its present form as history is the existence of closely similar stories attributed to other historical conjunctures.

1. *Esther*

Of these the most familiar is the story of Esther, where a foreign tyrant similarly decrees the destruction of his Jewish population, the plan is balked, the Jews are authorized to turn the tables on their enemies, and the day of deliverance is commemorated in an annual festival. Aside from the general similarity of the two stories there are parallels in nonessential details and in expressions. The conspiracy of Theodotus in 1.3 is like the conspiracy of the chamberlains in Esth. 2.21-23; the charge that the Jews are hostile to the laws of the king (3.19) is like Haman's accusation in Esth. 3.8; and in both books significant decisions are taken at royal banquets. There are also important divergences in details and in tone. Esther has nothing to correspond to the battle of Raphia, the visit to the Temple, or, most significantly, the question of citizenship; and III Maccabees has nothing to correspond to the repudiation of Vashti and the choice of Esther, or the elevation of Haman and his hatred for Mordecai. The differences in tone, with respect to religion and to the relations of the Jews to their neighbors, are more striking and more relevant to our purpose. On the surface the Hebrew Esther appears to be a secular book.[3] There are no prayers, and the deliverance is effected by human means; God is not named. Esther shows no misgivings at marrying a non-Jew, and there is no emphasis on religious observance. On the other hand, the attitude toward the heathen is unqualifiedly hostile. When the tables are turned the Jews in Esther kill 75,000 Persians (9.16); in III Maccabees they kill only 300 *Jewish* renegades. Furthermore, III Maccabees repeatedly emphasizes the Jews' loyalty to the government, and makes a special point of the friendly connivance of their Greek neighbors, who are shocked at the injustice and folly of the persecution, to assist the Jews at their own peril (3.3–10). Some have indeed maintained the improbable view that even the Hebrew Esther was written in Egypt and is a masked allusion to events in that country; the author's familiarity with Persian usages and language is in itself sufficient to make such an hypothesis unlikely.

2. *Septuagint Esther*

But whatever the genesis of the Hebrew Esther, the Septuagint version seems to be in the Alexandrian tradition, and calculated to correct the secular tone of the Hebrew book.[4] The relationship of the Greek Esther to III Maccabees is patent.[5] There are verbal similarities between the Greek texts

[3] C. C. Torrey, "The Older Book of Esther," *Harvard Theological Review*, XXXVII (1944) 1–40, points out the pious elements in the book, and attributes its avoidance of theological terminology to its intended use at somewhat riotous festivals.

[4] E. Bickermann, "The Colophon of the Greek Book of Esther," *Journal of Biblical Literature*, LXIII (1944) 339–362, argues that it was written by a Jerusalemite [S. Lieberman, *Greek in Jewish Palestine* (New York, 1942) has shown that the Palestinians knew Gk.] and sent to Egypt to give authority to the celebration of Purim.

[5] See Bacchisio Motzo, "Il Rifacimento Greco di Ester e il III Mac.," in his *Saggi di Storia e Letteratura Giudeo-Ellenistica* (Firenze, 1924) 272 ff.

(in one manuscript tradition "Teresh" is given as "Theudeutos" or "Theudotos," which suggests the Theodotus in III Mac. 1.3), and the prayers attributed to Mordecai and Esther suggest those of Simon and Eleazar. A note at the end of the Septuagint Esther, unique in its kind, states that the "epistle" was brought to Egypt "in the fourth year of the reign of Ptolemy and Cleopatra by Dositheus, who declared himself a priest and a Levite." On cogent historical grounds it has been established[6] that the year in question must fall between 12 September 78 and 11 September 77 BCE, the fourth year of Ptolemy XII Auletes and Cleopatra V. From our author's failure to mention Esther in the catalogue of deliverances at 6.4–8 it has been argued that he was not aware of the existence of that book, and hence that III Maccabees must antedate the introduction of Esther to Egypt.[7] But the canonicity of Esther was long questioned, and the Alexandrian Jewish writers seem to have ignored it intentionally. It seems more probable that III Maccabees, like the Septuagint Esther, is a corrective of the Hebrew Esther. The motive may have been to present improved religious and social standards, or to offer an aetiological justification for dating a Purim-like festival in Epiphi (June–July) rather than Adar (February–March).

3. *Aristeas to Philocrates*

In this connection it is worth mentioning that the so-called Letter of Aristeas may in turn be regarded as in a sense a corrective of III Maccabees. In Aristeas the relations between the Jewish sages and their royal hosts are characterized by high mutual respect; the Jews are careful to observe their dietary laws, but they are enabled to do so by the king's courtesy and upon his own initiative. Aristeas seems specifically to suggest an alternative and superior *modus vivendi* with the Gentile authori-

---

[6] Bickermann, *op. cit.* Bickermann makes "Levite" in the passage a proper name, and translates ". . . Dositheus—who said he was a priest—and Levitas . . ." But the verb is in the singular.

[7] See J. Cohen, *Judaica et Aegyptiaca: De Maccabaeorum Libro III Quaestiones Historicae* (Groningen, 1941) 22 ff.

ties to that represented in III Maccabees.[8] In style, language, and general approach Aristeas seems closer to III Maccabees than any other of the noncanonical books. Both are conceived of as Greek books following traditional Greek forms,[9] and they share a number of unusual words and locutions found rarely or not at all elsewhere in the Septuagint.[10] Particularly significant is their common use of a number of terms of theological import.[11] A point of special interest, and a strong argument for the priority of Aristeas, is the similarity of Philopator's decrees at 3.12 ff., placing disabilities upon the Jews, and 7.1 ff., releasing them from persecution, to that of Ptolemy Philadelphus in Aristeas 22 ff., releasing the Jews of Egypt from slavery. The Aristeas passage is a decree (*prostagma*) in form, whereas our documents are circular orders in letter form; the similarities nevertheless seem closer than could be accounted for by the fact that both books follow correct chancellory usage. Like the Aristeas decree (and unlike Philadelphus' genuine decree on which we shall see the Aristeas decree was based) Philopator's hostile decree insists on the king's generally humanitarian motives, and it orders similar harsh punishment for recalcitrants—a punishment which is in fact virtually impossible, and which Josephus' paraphrase of Aristeas in *Ant.* 12 significantly omits. Philopator's favorable decree is in spirit very like the Aristeas passage, except that whereas in the latter the king's measures are motivated by enlightened statesmanship, in our book they are motivated by fear of God's retribution. The Aristeas decree has been pronounced on excellent authority either a genuine document of Philadelphus[12] or a

[8] See Sterling Tracy, "III Maccabees and Pseudo-Aristeas," in *Yale Classical Studies*, (1928) I 241–252.
[9] See below, and the present writer's Introduction to *Aristeas to Philocrates*, in this series.
[10] See H. G. Meecham, *The Letter of Aristeas* (Manchester, 1935) 323 f.; C. W. Emmet's Introduction to III Maccabees in R. H. Charles, *Apocrypha and Pseudepigrapha of the Old Testament* (Oxford, 1913) 1.157.
[11] The material is carefully assembled in Ralph Marcus, "Divine Names and Attributes in Hellenistic Jewish Literature," *Proceedings of the American Academy for Jewish Research* (1932) 43–120.
[12] U. Wilcken, *Archiv für Papyrusforschung*, XII (1937) 221 ff.

forgery[13] based on and closely following a decree of Philadelphus extant in papyri.[14] This would indicate that of the two books Aristeas is the older, and III Maccabees in a sense a reply to it. If the reply is assumed to be virtually contemporary, and if the date of ca. 100 BCE, which is at present most widely accepted for Aristeas,[15] is correct, we should have an argument against dating III Maccabees at ca. 25 BCE, as it is here proposed to date it. But the date of neither book is established with anything like certainty: good authorities date III Maccabees ca. 100 BCE,[16] and, on the other hand, there are plausible arguments for dating Aristeas near the beginning of the common era.[17] Even if (as the present editor believes) Aristeas was written ca. 130 BCE, it may well have become something of a classic in its kind, so that a book setting forth an opposing view might be written as a reply to it a century later. In any case the books are close enough in character to be mutually illuminating.

4. Josephus

More unmistakable is the parallel in Josephus, *Against Apion*, 2.53–55, which is short enough to quote:[18]

[13] W. L. Westermann, "Enslaved Persons Who Are Free," *American Journal of Philology*, LIX (1938) 1–30. Westermann argues from significant verbal parallels and equally significant alterations from the text cited in the note following.

[14] P. Rainer, 24.552, published by H. Liebesny in *Aegyptus*, XVI (1936) 257–291.

[15] Various opinions and the evidence on which they are based are conveniently summarized in H. G. Meecham, *The Oldest Version of the Bible* (London, 1932) 94–109. A date toward the end of the 2d century has been proposed, on the basis of epistolary formulae, by E. Bickermann, "Zur Datierung des Pseudo-Aristeas," *Zeitschrift für die neutestamentliche Wissenschaft*, XXIX (1930) 280–296; Bickermann's dating is widely accepted.

[16] Bickermann, in *Realencyclopädie*, ed. Pauly-Wissowa-Kroll, XIV 797–800 (1930).

[17] These are most fully and plausibly presented in J. G. Février, *La Date, la Composition, et les Sources de la Lettre d'Aristée à Philocrate* (Paris, 1924) 4–31.

[18] Trans. of H. St. J. Thackeray, in Loeb Classical Library.

For Ptolemy Physcon . . . had arrested all the Jews in the city with their wives and children and exposed them, naked and in chains, to be trampled to death by elephants, the beasts actually being made drunk for the purpose. However, the outcome was the reverse of his intention. The elephants, without touching the Jews at their feet, rushed at Physcon's friends and killed a large number of them. Afterwards Ptolemy saw a terrible apparition, which forbade him to injure these people. His favorite concubine (some call her Ithaca, others Irene) adding her entreaty to him not to perpetrate such an enormity, he gave way and repented of his past actions and further designs. That is the origin of the well known feast which the Jews of Alexandria keep, with good reason, on this day, because of the deliverance so manifestly vouchsafed to them by God.

The Physcon here referred to is Ptolemy IX (146–117 BCE). The incident referred to, whatever its historicity, is certainly identical with that of III Maccabees. It may be, as has been suggested,[19] a "memory" version of III Maccabees; on the other hand, though Josephus is certainly later than III Maccabees, his story is much more credible, and may be nearer history. If Josephus' attribution of date is correct, the author of III Maccabees may simply have pushed his story back half a century in order to motivate it by the Temple episode. In any case, the existence of a parallel by a reasonably well-informed and conscientious historian is a forceful argument against the validity of III Maccabees as history, and adds weight to the hypothesis that the story of the elephants and the deliverance had become a commonplace which might be adapted to various literary uses.

5. *II Maccabees*

In II Maccabees there are parallels, not indeed to III Maccabees as a whole, but to a number of leading ideas and incidents

[19] C. C. Torrey, *The Apocryphal Literature* (Yale University Press, 1945) 80.

in it, and also to verbal expressions, whose resemblance seems to be too close to be altogether fortuitous. Thus, Heliodorus' attempt to profane the Temple and his repulse (II Mac. 3.22-31) and Antiochus' punishment for his presumption (II Mac. 9.4 ff.) are like Ptolemy Philopator's (III Mac. 2.21-24). In both books there are miraculous visions of analogous character (II Mac. 3.25, 10.29, 11.8; III Mac. 6.18); stress on the sanctity of the Temple and prayers for its defense (II Mac. 3.15-22, 8.2-4, 14.34-36; III Mac. 1.11 ff., 2.1 ff.); attacks on religion (II Mac. 6.9 and elsewhere; III Mac. 2.27 ff., 3.21); attempts to enforce an alien citizenship (II Mac. 4.9; III Mac. 2.27-30); stress laid on commemorative festivals (II Mac. 10.6, 15.36; III Mac. 6.30-36); an aged and pious Eleazar appears (II Mac. 6.18; III Mac. 6.1); official letters are reproduced (II Mac. 9.18 ff., 11.16 ff.; III Mac. 3.12 ff., 7.1 ff.). The picture of horror in II Mac. 3.15 ff. is very like those in III Mac. in 1.16 ff. and 4.3-8. In style and language generally III Maccabees shows greater similarity to II Maccabees than to any other of the noncanonical books, with the possible exception of Aristeas.[20] Though in this case the resemblance is not as striking as the repetition of the incident of the elephants in Josephus, it is nevertheless clear that both books draw from the same reservoir of ideas, incidents, and linguistic expression. The date of II Maccabees cannot be placed earlier than the last quarter of the 2d century BCE.

6. *The Apocalyptic Technique*

If the view here taken that an event of 206 BCE is employed as a literary cover for an event of 25 BCE is correct, it may be relevant to notice a partial analogy to the regular Apocalyptic practice of dealing with contemporary events in the guise of a remote period of history. The analogy does not go on all fours, to be sure, for the visionary embellishments and the prophetic elements of the Apocalyptic are entirely wanting in our book.

[20] See Emmet, *loc. cit.*, 1.156.

INTRODUCTION 13

But at any possible dating of III Maccabees it is clear that an experience of the remote past, involving miraculous intervention, is employed to lend encouragement and resolution for a later crisis, and the parallel afforded by Apocalyptic writing is therefore suggestive.

PAGAN PARALLELS

Esther and III Maccabees are addressed to Jewish readers, to strengthen their faith and their pride in the face of the oppression or contempt of a dominant environment. Josephus, on the other hand, addressed himself to the outer world as well; and here it must be noticed that his and similar Jewish efforts to present the cultural claims of a depressed people to a politically dominant environment were not unique, and that there were also other non-Jewish forms of literature from which our author may have learned.

1. *Greek Romances*

Despite the external uniformity of Hellenistic culture, pride in disparate national traditions persisted; and among other peoples whose political independence had been suppressed there was felt a need, again bound up with motives of religion, to assert the antiquity and dignity of individual national traditions against competing traditions—chiefly, of course, the dominant Greek. Very early in the Hellenistic period the Babylonian Berossus, priest of Bel, dedicated his *Babyloniaca* to Antiochus I Soter, and Manetho, high priest at Heliopolis, his *Aegyptiaca* to Ptolemy Philadelphus. Such works as these, of which there appear to have been a considerable number, were a large factor in the development of the literary genre called Greek Romance.[21] The earliest of these is the so-called *Ninus*

[21] See Martin Braun, *History and Romance in Graeco-Oriental Literature* (Oxford, 1938); R. M. Rattenbury, "Traces of Lost Greek Novels," in J. U. Powell, *New Chapters in the History of Greek Literature*, 3d Series (Oxford, 1933) 211–219.

Romance (dated the 1st century BCE.), in which the eponymous hero of Nineveh, represented as a youthful king of bewildering prowess, is made the hero of a love story. Our earliest extant complete romance, the *Chaereas and Callirhoe* of Chariton (of which 2d-century CE papyrus fragments are extant) also employs a historical framework. The heroine is introduced as the daughter of "Hermocrates, general of Syracuse, the one who defeated the Athenians"; we know from Thucydides that Hermocrates was indeed the Syracusan leader, and allusions to the Sicilian war are fairly frequent in the book.

In a number of ways the literary technique of III Maccabees suggests the practice of Greek Romance. To begin with, there is (1) the introduction of a well-known character from a familiar period of history to give verisimilitude as well as background; the connection of the character with the body of the story is not essential. If III Maccabees does indeed belong to the literary tradition represented by Chariton it becomes unnecessary to assert the historicity of Ptolemy Philopator's connection with the story. (2) It is virtually a fixed element in the romances that the denouement is presented before a large assembly, not infrequently in a hippodrome or theater (as, for example, in Heliodorus' *Aethiopica* or Dio Chrysostom's *A Euboean History*), where a hero or heroine is brought to the very brink of destruction and then by a sudden reversal—through an agency which seems providential—is not only delivered but gains the upper hand, to the applause of the multitude. (3) The interest in special religious cults, and the prominence given to prayer and the responses to prayer, are so marked in the romances that many scholars have regarded the religious element as paramount.[22] (4) The romances regularly employ fictive letters and other documents, and are rich in allusions to and echoes of "classic" literature. (5) Extravagant rhetorical coloring is so pronounced in the romances that their origin was long ascribed

---

[22] See K. Kerenyi, *Die griechische-orientalische Romanliteratur in religionsgeschichtlicher Beleuchtung* (Tübingen, 1927); R. Reitzenstein, *Hellenistische Wundererzählungen* (Berlin, 1906).

to the so-called Second Sophistic;[23] in particular, pathetic junctures in the stories are always heightened. Of all the non-canonical books III Maccabees is the most rhetorical, and it too heightens pathos at critical junctures by essentially irrelevant detail. A familiar rhetorical device is the exaggeration of numbers. In the rhetorical and exaggerated passages especially the reader of Greek romances finds himself on familiar ground in III Maccabees, and it is just such passages that make the reader looking for history uncomfortable. The author probably had no thought that his rhetoric would be accepted as literal truth, and would be surprised to find readers troubled by the physical improbabilities.

The factors that most obviously set III Maccabees apart from the romances, from the literary point of view, are the absence of a personal hero and an erotic element. A rather forced interpretation would see all Israel as the hero, and the brides wrested from their bridal chambers as a weak surrogate for the erotic element;[24] but it is plain that the ethical and religious intent of III Maccabees could find no place for a hero in love. Yet however tenuous its analogy to romance may be, III Maccabees exhibits sufficient resemblance to professed fiction to make it unlikely that it was intended to be accepted as literal truth.

2. *Aetiological Histories*

Another species of Greek work which is closer to history but which was still allowed a certain romantic latitude may be relevant. In the Hellenistic period many romanticized antiquarian histories of individual Greek communities, called *Aitiai* ("causes"; in Lat., *origines*) were written.[25] The best

[23] See E. Rohde, *Der griechische Roman und seine Vorlaüfer* (Leipzig, 1900).
[24] See M. Hadas, "III Maccabees and Greek Romance," in *Review of Religion*. XIII (1949) 155-162.
[25] See Christ-Schmid, *Geschichte der griechischen Litteratur*, 2, 1 (Munich, 1920) 109 ff.

known are the *Atthides*, dealing with the antiquities of Attica, but there were others which dealt with other cities. A principal concern of these works was to provide a "historical" explanation for the genesis of such institutions as religious festivals and other public usages. These works were much studied by the Alexandrian scholars, and are their chief source for local history and legend; they were imitated in Latin by Varro, and to a degree by Ovid in his *Fasti*. Our author's competence in Greek literature would suggest that he must surely have known of these ordinary tools of scholarship; and if one of the purposes of our book is to supply historical proof of the legitimacy of celebrating a certain festival at a certain date, the technique may have been suggested to him by the aetiological works of the Greeks.

IV

VERISIMILITUDE OF THE ACCOUNT OF PTOLEMY PHILOPATOR AND HIS POLICY

What has been said so far tends to cast doubt on the veracity of III Maccabees *in its present form;* whatever its degree of historical truth, it is unlikely that the story *as we have it* took place in the reign of Ptolemy Philopator. But the character and policy of Philopator as they are known from other sources[26] are accurately reflected, and his measures against the Jews as

[26] Documented accounts of Philopator's character and policy are to be found in *Cambridge Ancient History*, VII (1928) 727 ff.; M. Rostovtzeff, *A Social and Economic History of the Hellenistic World* (Oxford, 1941) 2.707 ff.; P. Jougouet, *L'Egypte Ptolemaique* (Paris, 1933) 61 ff.; J. P. Mahaffy, *The Ptolemaic Dynasty* (London, 1899) 142 ff.; E. Bevan, *A History of Egypt* (London, 1927) 217 ff. Mahaffy thought very well of Philopator's statesmanship; Bevan (whose work was intended to replace Mahaffy's as the 4th part of Petrie's *History of Egypt*) reverts to the views based on the ancient sources, which are uniformly hostile to Philopator. Sherman L. Wallace, "Census and Poll-Tax in Ptolemaic Egypt," *American Journal of Philology*, LIX (1938) 418–442, deals competently and at length with the aspects of Philopator's policy which concern us here. He accepts a favorable view of Philopator's statesmanship and efficiency, and sees a substratum of truth in the account of his relationship to the Jews as set forth in our book.

related in our book can be made to seem consistent and plausible. Thus, the account of the battle of Raphia with which the book opens is consistent in general (though not in detail) with the fuller accounts in Polybius (5.40 ff., 5.82 ff.), and probably derives from a good independent source, possibly Ptolemy Megalopolitanus.[27] Philopator's desire to inspect the Temple is correctly motivated; we know that he was an enthusiastic amateur of architecture. We also know that he was dissolute in his habits, a great drinker, and under the thumb of his courtiers— all of which is reflected in our book. Furthermore, unlike others of his dynasty, Ptolemy Philopator is known to have taken measures to grant some sort of official recognition to the non-Greek population of Egypt, as in his unique use of native Egyptians in his phalanx at Raphia. We know also that he was a devotee of Dionysus and identified himself with that god. His recognition of peoples other than Greek (possibly deriving from the philosophic instruction of his tutor Eratosthenes) and the current identification of Dionysus' name Sabazius with the Jewish Sabaoth, might very likely have suggested his plan to unite Jews and Greeks in Dionysus worship.

There seems to be external evidence, moreover, for a *laographia*, or census, involving liability to poll tax and hence distinctions among the population, in Philopator's reign. Philopator introduced the practice, which was continued into the Roman period, of taking censuses at fourteen-year intervals. Perhaps the poll tax was introduced with the first of these censuses, which was taken in 220–219; and the attempt to subject the Jews to *laographia* after the battle of Raphia (217), as recounted in our book (2.28), would show that they had not been included in the census of 220–219. The census of our book would then be that of 206–205, which involves a somewhat greater interval after the king's campaign at Raphia than is consistent with the impression of hasty anger given by our

[27] This historian was probably the Ptolemy who was Philopator's governor of Cyprus. The fragments of his work are to be found in Muller's *Fragmenta Historicorum Graecorum* 3.66.

book. Loss of citizen status would be a prime catastrophe to the Jews of Egypt, and the crisis and its passing would naturally be a memorable event in the Jewish community. A later writer dealing with it in a kind of *megillah*, perhaps for liturgical use at a Purim-like festival, might well decorate it with the floating tale of the elephants and the varied hues of the rhetorical palette.

Indeed, if the rather confused account in our book is analyzed, the course of events that emerges is quite credible: In pursuance of his policy to extend citizenship, the king first issued a decree that Jews (probably those in the army and administration) should be initiated into the mysteries of Dionysus and receive citizen rights (3.21). Some obeyed but most refused, hoping the decree would be rescinded (2.31–33, 3.22–23). The king grew angry and posted an edict (2.27–30; this passage may well follow the actual language of the decree); none who refused to sacrifice to Dionysus would be permitted to enter their own Temple; all were to be enrolled in the degraded native status and be branded with the Dionysus emblem; those who resisted were to be executed. The Jews tried bribery (2.32); thereupon the king ordered all those in the provinces to be assembled and executed (3.12–30). Mention of the king's repulse in Jerusalem in this connection is an unlikely addition, introduced for the purpose of giving a religious motivation to the whole procedure. The entire remainder of the book, which deals with the story of the elephants, is a longer literary addition of the same character; it may well be that the author added it, or, perhaps more accurately, found the historical narrative of a similar earlier event (which he distorted) appropriate and useful to insert, in order to give historical background to his edifying literary work.

V

Evidence of Later Composition

Although, as we have noticed, our author seems to have employed good sources for the material relating to Ptolemy

INTRODUCTION 19

Philopator, his book bears internal evidence that it was written long after Philopator's time, and perhaps even in the Roman period. At 6.6, for example, Daniel with its additions is cited, and in Daniel itself, at 11.11, we should expect but do not find an allusion to Philopator's attempt on the Temple; the date of Daniel is generally agreed to be Maccabean. At 7.2 Philopator speaks of his children; we know that he had only one son, born 209–208. Details of style combine to suggest a date not earlier than the 1st century BCE; perhaps the most conclusive point here is the use of epistolary formulae which came into use only after 99 BCE.[28] In favor of the hypothesis that the book was written during the Roman period, it may be argued that such forthright criticism of a king, even one almost two centuries dead, would not be ventured while his dynasty was still reigning. At 5.26, furthermore, the institution of the early morning *salutatio* or levee characteristic of Roman usage seems to be alluded to. But the most cogent argument for dating the book in the Roman period is the peculiar significance of the word *laographia* in its context in III Maccabees.[29]

VI

LAOGRAPHIA IN THE PTOLEMAIC AND ROMAN PERIODS

Etymologically the word *laographia* (which occurs at 2.28) simply means census; we know that Ptolemy Philopator introduced the practice of taking censuses at fourteen-year intervals. It is a natural surmise that these censuses were taken for the purpose of taxation; but in the Roman period we know definitely that *laographia* denoted a poll tax, and that liability to this tax denoted noncitizen status. It is possible that *laographia* meant a poll tax in the Ptolemaic period also, and that this tax was an index of noncitizen status; but we have no definite

[28] See E. Bickermann, *Realencyclopädie*, etc., ed. Pauly-Wissowa-Kroll.
[29] The argument that follows and the consequent dating is in general agreement with V. Tcherikover, *The Jews in Egypt in the Hellenistic-Roman Age in the Light of the Papyri* (Hebrew, with English Summary; Jerusalem, 1945) 91 ff., where full documentation is given.

evidence that this was so, and the first clear use of *laographia* to denote poll tax occurs in a document of 22 BCE.[30] The silence of the papyri on this point is impressive; the Ptolemaic bureaucracy loved form, and we have hundreds of Ptolemaic receipts for all kinds of taxation, but none for *laographia*. The explanation that receipts were not given for so widespread a tax as a measure of economy[31] is rather lame.

Now it is true that Philopator and his efficient minister Sosibius addressed themselves to regrading the population and reforming the tax structure, and hence that the issue of their citizenship must have been a burning question to the Jews. Our author surely had before him a sound tradition of the impact of Philopator's reforms upon the Jews. But if the account in our book is roughly applicable to the situation under Philopator, its applicability to the Roman period is much more clearcut. When, after the defeat of Cleopatra at Actium in 31 BCE, the Romans took over the administration of Egypt, they systematized citizen classifications very rigidly, for the purposes of control and of taxation. In Egypt as elsewhere those who did not possess full citizenship were subject to *laographia* (which in the Roman period definitely means poll tax), and liability to *laographia* was in turn a mark of lower status. Our book clearly contrasts liability to *laographia* with possession of citizen status (2.30). Under the Ptolemies the distinction had never been as sharp; it is because the position of the Jews was somewhat anomalous that our literary sources seem equivocal on the question of their citizenship. Apparently it had always been possible for deserving or wealthy or enterprising individuals, especially such as had been educated in Greek *gymnasia*, to have *de facto* if not *de jure* citizenship. But now there were to be no exceptions.

It is easy to imagine the overwhelming catastrophe of loss of

[30] *Griechische Ostraka der Universitätsbibliothek zu Strassburg* (1923), No. 38, cited in Tcherikover, *loc. cit.*
[31] Offered by Wallace, *loc. cit.*

caste, where caste was so important socially and politically, not only for the upper classes who had enjoyed *de facto* citizenship but for the whole Jewish community, which was directly touched by the degradation. The crisis may well have precipitated violent uprisings, such as were common in Ptolemaic and Roman Egypt, and must surely have occasioned defections from Judaism and reactions to these defections on the part of the faithful. It is probably some such situation that our author has in mind and expects his readers to recognize. The record of the analogous crisis under Philopator affords him a point of departure, a framework for a "romance" which can properly be embellished, and incidentally an opportunity to criticize Roman administrators indirectly without incurring the great danger of using Roman names.

VII

Date of Composition

By 24 BCE Egypt was fully organized as a Roman province, and in that year[32] a census was taken and liability to *laographia* determined. If we must move the date of composition of III Maccabees down to the 1st century BCE, no other date is as plausible as 25–24. The registration, which we are told lasted forty days (4.15), is most likely this census. The prominence given to the question of the census and citizen status, on the other hand, makes a later dating unlikely, for these questions did not arise again in Roman Egypt. If, as has sometimes been held,[33] the book were written under Gaius Caligula or Claudius, we should surely have had as its central theme the desecration of sanctuaries by the introduction of images of the Emperor.

[32] See S. L. Wallace, *Taxation in Egypt from Augustus to Diocletian* (Princeton, 1938) 97–116.
[33] *E.g.*, by H. Willrich, "Der historische Kern des III. Makkabäerbuches," *Hermes*, XXXIX (1904) 244 ff.

VIII

Language and Style; Place of Composition

There can be no question that the original language of III Maccabees is Gk. Its author is master of a large vocabulary, including rare and poetic words and unique compounds. Such Hebraisms as are found occur chiefly in the prayers, and had become standard usage in Jewish writings in Gk.; they are not due to the author's incompetence in Gk. Indeed, the author has perhaps the fullest control of that language of any of the noncanonical writers, and clearly pretends to an elegant style—however verbose, florid, or bombastic a modern reader may find it.[34] Its preciosity, it may be said, including the well-marked purple passages, is no worse than that of the run of "rhetoricians" of the Roman period. If the stones in his edifice are sometimes oddly chosen and over-curiously wrought, the structure as a whole is impressive. The story engages the reader's interest at once, and keeps him absorbed to the final "Amen." Furthermore, the dignity appropriate to a hagiographic work is maintained; the story is not only absorbing but conveys a sense of its high significance, not only for the generation involved but as a general demonstration of God's Providence.

Of the author's competence in Hebrew it is less possible to speak with certainty. But if he did not know the language, he clearly knew the literature. In the prayers in particular, Heb. idiom is unmistakable; though such perfectly familiar Heb. but non-Gk. expressions as "Let Thy compassion speedily overtake us" (2.20, ταχὺ προκαταλαβέτωσαν ἡμᾶς οἱ οἰκτιρμοί σου מהר יקדמונו רחמיך LXX Ps. 78.5) were probably ready to hand in our author's models.

The language of the book, both the literary and the standard

---

[34] Summary criticism of the style of III Maccabees is to be found in the editions of Emmet, Kautzsch, and Gaster (see 27), and more detailed analysis in Grimm.

INTRODUCTION 23

Heb.-translation Gk., as well as its contents and purpose, point to Alexandria, and it is hard to conceive that it could have been written elsewhere. Corroborative evidence that Alexandria was indeed the place of its composition is supplied by the linguistic and other parallels to II Maccabees and Aristeas as noted above.

IX
RELIGIOUS AND ETHICAL IMPLICATIONS

As a work of religious edification stressing God's providence III Maccabees has general validity, and might seem peculiarly appropriate to many conjunctures in Hellenistic or indeed in general Jewish history. Whether or not the book was indeed written in the conjuncture we have thought probable, it may be illuminating to review the specific issues which may have motivated its emphases. Three such issues have been touched upon above: (a) a political crisis involving civic rights; (b) a difference of opinion concerning the genesis and date of a religious festival; and (c) a difference of opinion concerning the appropriate attitude toward the non-Jewish environment.

1. *Affirmation of Faith in Providence*

If the occasion of III Maccabees was the threatened or actual deprivation of civic rights, its purpose is plainly to reassert the dignity of the Jewish people as the special object of Providence, to raise their self-esteem in the face of political degradation and their faith in ultimate justification, and perhaps also to impress upon Gentile readers that their position in history and as the wards of a special Providence made it unjust and possibly even dangerous to molest and injure them. The story of divine deliverance from a specific oppression which it tells is offered as a new link in the chain of divine deliverances of the past listed in Eleazar's prayer (6.1 ff.).

2. The Aetiological Element

It is a widely held view in regard to Esther that that book was written to provide a justification for the celebration of Purim, whose true origin and legitimacy were doubtful. Our book is equally explicit in the matter of providing justification for the origin and date of a festival. The fact that historical authority and dates are provided for *two* festivals (6.30 ff., 7.17 ff.) suggests that there may have been rival opinions on the subject and that our author is attempting to reconcile the views, or to give authority to an innovation by supplying comparable justification for both views. The pagan aetiological works alluded to above seem frequently to have offered alternative origins for the same institution, or to have explained more than one institution by the same "historical" events.

3. The Internal Partisan Element

We have noticed above that a special effort is made in III Maccabees to stress the amicable relations of the Jewish community to their neighbors and the mutual respect subsisting between the two groups. The crisis develops not out of a general antipathy to the Jews but as a result of a caprice of the king, who is abetted by a hostile court. But the amicable relations do not involve compromises in religious observances on the part of the Jews; on the contrary, there is no relaxation of observance, except, of course, on the part of weak apostates. The Jews even win the respect of their neighbors by their adherence to their religious injunctions. Comparison with Esther has suggested that (like the Septuagint Esther) III Maccabees may be regarded as a sort of corrective to the attitude of the Hebrew Esther, which premises a state of tension and latent hostility. Aristeas to Philocrates goes further in the same direction, by demonstrating the possibility of harmonious relationship not only with the community in general but even with the court. It is not unlikely that the question of the proper *modus vivendi* of the Jewish community with their neighbors and with the

INTRODUCTION   25

authorities was a real issue, exacerbated by the threat of disabilities, on which opinion was divided; and that our book supports a moderate view against more extreme views, possibly in either direction, tending to open hostility at one pole and to assimilation at the other. It is not unlikely, furthermore, that the party which advocated a specific attitude in this respect, also held a particular view on the character and date of a festival. The motives here cited, and others which may be suggested, are not mutually exclusive.

X

RELIGIOUS PREMISES

It is clear that the book seeks to inculcate and justify loyalty to Judaism; and a word must now be said concerning the concepts of Judaism implicit in the book. It is a striking fact that developments characteristic of post-Exilic Judaism are ignored. God's power is universal, though He has chosen Jerusalem and the Temple as a favored place on earth, just as the Jewish people are the special object of His care. But there is no reference to a future life, or to retribution in another world. The omission is remarkable, for in II Maccabees the martyrs regularly console themselves with a vivid hope of retribution in a future life; and as a Greek scholar our author must have been familiar with Platonic and other pagan ideas of a future existence. On the other hand, an eventual return of the Dispersion is contemplated, for the regulations concerning the festival specify that they shall obtain as long as the παροικία, which means "a sojourning in a foreign land," shall endure. There is no mention of, and there seems to be no desire for, proselytization. The almost complete omission of angels and other intermediate beings seems more clearly intentional. Post-Exilic Judaism has its angelology, and a number of supernatural apparitions make their appearance at critical junctures in II Maccabees; the notion of intermediate powers called *daimones* was very familiar to pagan thought. The one apparition of two angels which frightens the elephants in III Maccabees is obviously like those that perform similar services in II Maccabees, and yet our author curiously takes special pains to tell us that it was not visible to the Jews but only to those on the point of attacking them. God's Providence, which figures so largely, is not hypostatized, though it would be in keeping with a section of contemporary Jewish thought to represent it as a semi-independent entity. It seems unlikely that our author's conservatism in these matters was due to his ignorance of developments in religious thought. It is not too much to say that he deliberately preferred and promulgated what he regarded as pure religion, in keeping with the eternally true traditions of Judaism. Because of its adult clarity of religious concept and its manifest conviction, III Maccabees, despite its antiquated literary conventions, can still claim the attention of readers and offer them its burden of edification.

XI

THE TEXT

III Maccabees offers no great textual problems. It is found in only one of the three great uncial manuscripts of the Gk. Bible, the Alexandrinus—not in the Vaticanus or Sinaiticus. Of fundamental importance, to support or correct the Alexandrinus, is the Venetus; and a number of the minuscule manuscripts are also helpful. The minuscules of the so-called Lucianic recension are less reliable. The text exhibits a number of small variants, but no major divergences. There is a free expanded version in the Syr. Peshitto, and a loose but literary Armenian version. The book is not in the Vulgate, and hence does not appear in the Roman Catholic canon or in the Apocrypha of the Protestant churches. There are a very few allusions to the book in the early writers of the Eastern Church. It seems to have left no trace in Jewish literature.

The text here offered is reprinted from A. Rahlfs' *Septuaginta* (Stuttgart, 1935), and the slight apparatus is based on Rahlfs'.

INTRODUCTION 27

Only such variants have been recorded as would affect the form of the translation. Mere variants in spelling; the omission or insertion of an article, a particle, or a prefix; transpositions; even differences in tense, number, or case have not been noticed unless the variant would yield significantly different English. For a fuller record of variants the reader is referred to Rahlfs and to H. B. Swete, *The Old Testament in Greek*, III (Cambridge, 1899).

In the present apparatus the symbol A represents the Alexandrinus; V, the Venetus; the plus sign (+) the support of the minuscules; and L the Lucianic recension.

XII

EDITIONS

The standard texts of III Maccabees are those of Rahlfs and of Swete, mentioned in the preceding section. The latest translations and commentaries are:

C. W. Emmet, in R. H. Charles, *The Apocrypha and Pseudepigrapha of the Old Testament* (Oxford, 1913) 115 ff. Emmet's translation with brief notes is published separately as *The Third Book of Maccabees* by the Society for Promoting Christian Knowledge (London, 1918). It will be obvious that the present translator is heavily indebted to Emmet.

E. Kautzsch, in his *Die Apokryphen und Pseudepigraphen des alten Testaments* (Freiburg, 1898) 119 ff.

T. H. Gaster, in A. Cahana, *Hasepharim Hahizonim* (Tel Aviv, 1937) 2.232–257.

The fullest commentary remains that of C. L. W. Grimm, *Kurzgefasstes exegetisches Handbuch zu den Apokryphen des alten Testaments* (Leipzig, 1857) 211 ff. These works, the entries in standard works of reference and histories, and the notes in the present edition will direct the student to other literature.

TEXT, TRANSLATION, COMMENTARY, AND CRITICAL NOTES

ΜΑΚΚΑΒΑΙΩΝ Γ´

1 ¹Ὁ δὲ Φιλοπάτωρ παρὰ τῶν ἀνακομισθέντων μαθὼν τὴν γενομένην τῶν ὑπ' αὐτοῦ κρατουμένων τόπων ἀφαίρεσιν ὑπὸ Ἀντιόχου παραγγείλας ταῖς πάσαις δυνάμεσιν πεζικαῖς τε καὶ ἱππικαῖς καὶ τὴν ἀδελφὴν Ἀρσινόην συμπαραλαβὼν ἐξώρμησεν μέχρι τῶν κατὰ Ῥαφίαν τόπων, ὅπου παρεμβεβλήκεισαν οἱ περὶ Ἀντίοχον. ²Θεόδοτος δέ τις ἐκπληρῶσαι τὴν ἐπιβουλὴν διανοηθεὶς παραλαβὼν τῶν προϋποτεταγμένων αὐτῷ ὅπλων Πτολεμαϊκῶν τὰ κράτιστα διεκομίσθη νύκτωρ ἐπὶ τὴν τοῦ Πτολεμαίου σκηνὴν ὡς μόνος κτεῖναι

1 υπ) επ A+

1.1–5, *The battle of Raphia*.
1. PHILOPATOR: Ptolemy IV (222–203 BCE). Ancient sources are at one in describing him as a debauched voluptuary, indifferent to affairs of state, and helpless in the hands of selfish and intriguing favorites; of the ancients who disparaged Philopator, Polybius (V 34 and elsewhere) is the most respectable and only some 50 years removed, and Plutarch (*Life of Cleomenes* 32 ff.) perhaps the best known. But a closer study of his reign, on the basis of epigraphic and papyrological as well as literary evidence, reveals that Philopator (or his minister Sosibius) was a very shrewd and successful ruler; see Introd. 16, and notes. Interesting light on his relations to priests and army is revealed in the so-called stele of Pithom; see H. Gauthier and H. Sottas, *Un décret trilingue en honneur de Ptolemée IV* (1925); W. Spiegelberg and W. Otto, "Beiträge zur Erklärung des neuen dreisprachigen Priesterdekretes zu Ehren des Ptolemaios Philopator," *Sitzungber. d. bayr. Akad. d. Wissensch., philosoph-philolog. Kl.*, 1924, No. 4; trans. in E. Bevan, *A History of Egypt* (London, 1927), 388 f. A good portrait of Philopator appears on a coin figured in Pl. LXIX of M. Rostovtzeff, *A Social and Economic History of the Hellenistic World* (Oxford, 1941), 2.604. ANTIOCHUS: Antiochus III, later called the Great (224–187 BCE), younger son of Seleucus II. He was energetic and competent, and did much to restore the shattered kingdom he had inherited; his seizure of southern Syria from Egypt is the situation to which this passage refers. Philopator's success at Raphia (Spring of 217) was a surprising and very considerable achievement, due in large part to his innovation of using native Egyptians in his phalanx. The account of the

THE THIRD BOOK OF MACCABEES

1 ¹When Philopator learned from those who had come back that Antiochus had seized the places which he had himself vanquished, he issued orders to all his forces, foot and horse, took his sister Arsinoë along with him, and marched to the region near Raphia, where Antiochus and his people had encamped.
²But a certain Theodotus was minded to consummate the plot he had conceived, and so took the best of the Ptolemaic arms, which had previously been assigned to him, and went by night to Ptolemy's tent, to kill him single-handed and

---

battle here is in general agreement with the full account in Polybius (V 79–86), and probably rests on a good independent source, perhaps Ptolemy Megalopolitanus (see Emmet, in Charles, I 159). The slight discrepancies (e.g., Arsinoë encouraging the soldiers in the midst of the battle instead of before it) are probably due to the "pathetic" coloring of this second source; Polybius prided himself on his "pragmatic" historiography, and records his contempt of such "pathetic" historians as Phylarchus. Our author's preference for a "pathetic" historian would be of some significance. Dan. 11.11–12 is usually interpreted as an allusion to the battle of Raphia. Arsinoë was hardly adolescent at the time, and is correctly called "sister"; later, following the custom of Ptolemaic brother-sister marriage, she became Philopator's wife. Livy (XXXVII 3.9) calls her Cleopatra, and Justin (XXX 1.7) Eurydice. It appears to have been something of literary commonplace to represent exotic princesses as encouraging armies in battle; cf. Virgil, Aeneid 8.696, regina in mediis . . . vocat agmina. The abruptness of the opening sentence and its use of the connective particle δὲ when nothing has as yet been said suggests that some preceding matter has been lost.

2. THEODOTUS: Polybius devotes an entire chapter (V 81; cf. V 40.1–3) to the attempt of Theodotus "the Aetolian." BEST OF THE PTOLEMAIC ARMS: Some think the phrase should be rendered "bravest of the Ptolemaic soldiers," and perhaps rightly; the literal translation here given does sound odd, for any sharp sword would do. On the other hand, our author says "single-handed," which would make "soldiers" impossible; but Polybius (5.81.2) says that Theodotus took two others with him.

αὐτὸν καὶ ἐν τούτῳ διαλῦσαι τὸν πόλεμον. ³τοῦτον δὲ διαγαγὼν Δοσίθεος ὁ Δριμύλου λεγόμενος, τὸ γένος Ἰουδαῖος, ὕστερον δὲ μεταβαλὼν τὰ νόμιμα καὶ τῶν πατρίων δογμάτων ἀπηλλοτριωμένος, ἄσημόν τινα κατέκλινεν ἐν τῇ σκηνῇ, ὃν συνέβη κομίσασθαι τὴν ἐκείνου κόλασιν. ⁴γενομένης δὲ καρτερᾶς μάχης καὶ τῶν πραγμάτων μᾶλλον ἐρρωμένων τῷ Ἀντιόχῳ ἱκανῶς ἡ Ἀρσινόη ἐπιπορευσαμένη τὰς δυνάμεις παρεκάλει μετὰ οἴκτου καὶ δακρύων τοὺς πλοκάμους λελυμένη βοηθεῖν ἑαυτοῖς τε καὶ τοῖς τέκνοις καὶ γυναιξὶν θαρραλέως ἐπαγγελλομένη δώσειν νικήσασιν ἑκάστῳ δύο μνᾶς χρυσίου. ⁵ ⁵καὶ οὕτως συνέβη τοὺς ἀντιπάλους ἐν χειρονομίαις διαφθαρῆναι, πολλοὺς δὲ καὶ δοριαλώτους συλλημφθῆναι. ⁶κατακρατήσας δὲ τῆς ἐπιβουλῆς ἔκρινεν τὰς πλησίον πόλεις ἐπελθὼν παρακαλέσαι. ⁷ποιήσας δὲ τοῦτο καὶ τοῖς τεμένεσι δωρεὰς ἀπονείμας εὐθαρσεῖς τοὺς ὑποτεταγμένους κατέστησεν. ⁸Τῶν δὲ Ἰουδαίων διαπεμψαμένων πρὸς αὐτὸν ἀπὸ τῆς γερουσίας καὶ τῶν πρεσβυτέρων τοὺς ἀσπασομένους αὐτὸν

---

4 πλοκαμους) πολεμους A+

3. A Dositheus along with an Onias (by some identified as Onias IV, founder of the temple at Leontopolis, ca. 164 BCE) are mentioned by Josephus (*Against Apion* 2.49) as generals of Ptolemy Philometor and his Cleopatra. The passage in Josephus is, significantly, the parallel of our elephant episode, though Dositheus does not have in Josephus a role corresponding to the present passage. On the other hand, his thwarting of the plot against the king's life is parallel to Mordecai's role in Esth. 2.21–23, and perhaps a conflation of sources is to be suspected. But there actually was an important personage of the name in Philopator's time. In the Josephus passage Dositheus' father is not named, but a Dositheus "son of Drimylus" actually occurs in papyri (P. Hibeh 90 shows him to have been a priest of Alexander in 222 BCE); whence H. Willrich, Klio VII (1907) 293, argues that Dositheus cannot have been a Jew. But the point of mentioning him here at all appears to be that though he was an apostate (and our author abhors renegades: see ch. 7), he was nevertheless a Jew by origin and his patriotic deeds should be recorded; else there seems no need to bring him in at all. Dositheus (like other theophoric forms) seems to have been an accepted Jewish name; it was borne by the emissary mentioned in the colophon to the Greek Esther, and by one of the translators of the Septuagint (Aristeas 50). SOME UNDISTINGUISHED PERSON: Polybius gives this man's name as Andreas, the king's physician, and so not "undistinguished." Gaster (*ad loc.*) ingeniously and very plausibly

so put an end to the war. ³But Ptolemy was removed by Dositheus, called the son of Drimylus, who caused some undistinguished person to sleep in the tent, whom it then befell to receive the vengeance intended for Ptolemy; Dositheus was a Jew by birth who had subsequently changed his religion and become estranged from his ancestral laws.

⁴A fierce battle took place, and success was rather inclining toward Antiochus, when Arsinoë moved up and down the ranks energetically, her hair unbraided, and piteously and tearfully implored them to rally manfully for their own sakes and the sake of their wives and children, promising, if they should be victorious, to give each man two minae of gold.

⁵And thus it came about that their adversaries were destroyed in the action and that many prisoners also were taken. ⁶Now that he had mastered the aggression, Ptolemy decided to visit the nearby cities and encourage them; ⁷by doing so, and by distributing gifts to their shrines, he inspired his subjects with confidence.

⁸The Jews dispatched some of their Council and Elders to greet him and bring him presents and felicitate him on what

suggests that our author read ἄνδρα τινά for Ἀνδρέαν τινά. But possibly Andreas was reduced to an "undistinguished person" of our author's source for the sake of the melodramatic contrast dear to the "pathetic" historian. CHANGED HIS RELIGION: literal Gk. for המיר את דתו את דחו, and was doubtless an accepted expression in "Hebrew-translation" Gk. current in the Hellenistic Diaspora.

4. Pathos, again, to the point of making Arsinoë appear in the midst of battle instead of (as in Polybius) before it. Two minae of gold seems extravagant, but not impossible. Polybius speaks of Philopator and his sister moving along the ranks (5.84.1) and promising rewards (5.86.3), and the Pithom stele published in 1925 (see on 1.1) states that Philopator presented 300,000 gold pieces to his army. It is worth noting that Polybius' account makes much of the use of elephants in this battle.

5. Polybius (V 86.5–6) gives Antiochus' losses as nearly 10,000 footmen, more than 300 cavalry, and more than 4,000 prisoners; Philopator's as about 1,500 foot and 700 horse killed. Philopator's elephants, however, proved inferior and intractable, and disrupted their own lines (5.84.7); this may have some connection with their parallel behavior in our book.

6–7. Entirely consistent with what we know of Philopator's and Sosibius' policy. Polybius, V 86.7–11, speaks of the gifts and adulation the cities of Coele Syria heaped upon him.

καὶ ξένια κομιοῦντας καὶ ἐπὶ τοῖς συμβεβηκόσιν χαρισομένους συνέβη μᾶλλον αὐτὸν προθυμηθῆναι ὡς τάχιστα πρὸς αὐτοὺς παραγενέσθαι. ⁹διακομισθεὶς δὲ εἰς Ἱεροσόλυμα καὶ θύσας τῷ μεγίστῳ θεῷ καὶ χάριτας ἀποδοὺς καὶ τῶν ἑξῆς τι τῷ τόπῳ ποιήσας καὶ δὴ παραγενόμενος εἰς τὸν τόπον 10 καὶ τῇ σπουδαιότητι καὶ εὐπρεπείᾳ καταπλαγείς, ¹⁰θαυμάσας δὲ καὶ τὴν τοῦ ἱεροῦ εὐταξίαν ἐνεθυμήθη βουλεύσασθαι εἰς τὸν ναὸν εἰσελθεῖν. ¹¹τῶν δὲ εἰπόντων μὴ καθήκειν γίνεσθαι τοῦτο διὰ τὸ μηδὲ τοῖς ἐκ τοῦ ἔθνους ἐξεῖναι εἰσιέναι μηδὲ πᾶσιν τοῖς ἱερεῦσιν, ἀλλ' ἢ μόνῳ τῷ προηγουμένῳ πάντων ἀρχιερεῖ, καὶ τούτῳ κατ' ἐνιαυτὸν ἅπαξ, ὁ δὲ οὐδαμῶς ἐπείθετο. ¹²τοῦ τε νόμου παραναγνωσθέντος οὐδ' ὣς ἀπέλιπεν προφερόμενος ἑαυτὸν δεῖν εἰσελθεῖν λέγων Καὶ εἰ ἐκεῖνοι ἐστέρηνται ταύτης τῆς τιμῆς, ἐμὲ δὲ οὐ δεῖ. ¹³καὶ ἐπυνθάνετο διὰ τίνα αἰτίαν εἰσερχόμενον αὐτὸν εἰς πᾶν τέμενος οὐθεὶς ἐκώλυσεν τῶν παρόντων. ¹⁴καί τις ἀπρονοήτως ἔφη κακῶς 15 αὐτὸ τοῦτο τερατεύεσθαι. ¹⁵γενομένου δέ, φησιν, τούτου διά τινα αἰτίαν, οὐχὶ πάντως εἰσελεύσεσθαι καὶ θελόντων αὐτῶν καὶ μή; ¹⁶τῶν δὲ ἱερέων ἐν πάσαις ταῖς ἐσθήσεσιν προσπε-

---

9 μεγιστω) πιστω A+ / ευπρεπεια) ευσεβεια A+
11 εξειναι) A omits
14 αυτο) αυτον Grimm / τερατευεσθαι) πραττεσθαι L
15 διά τινα) Rahlfs suggests διὰ τίνα / παντως) –των A+, –τες V+

9–29. *Philopator attempts to enter the sanctuary at Jerusalem.*
9. GOD THE GREATEST, μέγιστος θεός, occurs frequently in this book (1.9, 16, 3.11, 4.16, 5.25, 7.22) and in II Mac. 3.36, probably as a rendering of הָאֵל הַגָּדוֹל; עֶלְיוֹן is rendered (as in the LXX) by ὕψιστος. So τόπος, "place," for the Temple, is commonly used in II and III Maccabees, Aristeas, and elsewhere. τῶν ἑξῆς is obscure, but its meaning is probably as rendered, "appropriate to."
10. Philopator's eagerness to inspect the interior of the Temple was doubtless motivated by his curiosity concerning its architecture, for he was an amateur of the arts; his admiration of the orderly conduct of the Temple looks like a pious addition of our author, and would not logically have induced Philopator to violate the rules. The case of Pompey (63 BCE, Jos., *Wars* 1.152) shows that it is entirely credible that a powerful visitor should insist on entering the Sanctuary; it is not beyond possibility, if the body of our book refers to Roman domination (see Introd. 19), that the definite allusion here is to Pompey. There is naturally no corrobo-

had transpired, whereupon he grew the more eager to visit them as promptly as possible. ⁹Arrived then at Jerusalem, he sacrificed to God the Greatest and rendered thank offerings, acting in some degree as is appropriate to the Holy Place. While he was at the Holy Place he was astonished at ¹⁰its refinement and elegance, ¹⁰and also admired the orderly arrangements of the Temple; thus he conceived a desire to enter the Sanctuary. ¹¹He was told that this could not be done, because it was not allowed to their own countrymen to enter, nor even to all the priests, but only to the High Priest who was chief of them all, and to him only once a year; but he would by no means be convinced. ¹²The Law was then read out to him; but even so he did not cease insisting that it was appropriate for him to enter, and said, "Even if those others are deprived of this honor it is not proper that I should be." ¹³He asked too why it was that when he entered the shrine at all, none of those present had hindered him. ¹⁴Thereupon someone thoughtlessly declared that it was wrong to speak ¹⁵of that as a portent. ¹⁵"But since it did for some reason so happen," said Ptolemy, "should I not then enter in any case, whether they wish it or not?"

¹⁶The priests in their holy vestments prostrated themselves

---

ration for the story of Philopator's desire to enter the Temple, and indeed the silence of Dan. 11.11–12 may be taken as negative evidence.

11. The fact that only the High Priest might enter is mentioned in the Josephus passage referred to, and the phrase "and to him only once a year" seems like a natural heightening of a source, though the rule is correctly cited (Ex. 30.10; Lev. 16.34).

13. The context seems to favor this rendering, which really requires $\tau\grave{o}$ between $\pi\hat{a}\nu$ and $\tau\acute{\epsilon}\mu\epsilon\nu o\varsigma$; an alternative version is "when he entered any other shrine." For a discussion of the famous inscription enjoining Gentiles to abstain from trespassing on forbidden areas of the Temple precinct, see Bickermann, "The Warning Inscription of Herod's Temple," *Jewish Quarterly Review*, XXXVII (1947) 387–405.

14. TO SPEAK OF THAT AS A PORTENT: Lit. for $\tau\epsilon\rho\alpha\tau\epsilon\acute{\upsilon}\epsilon\sigma\theta\alpha\iota$ which must here mean "to make much of it as an argument."

16–21 is very like the picture of popular distress at Heliodorus' entry into the Temple treasury in II Mac. 3.15–22, where, indeed, the picture is more appropriate. The turgid language makes it easy to see why the text of 18 and 19 should be confused.

σόντων καὶ δεομένων τοῦ μεγίστου θεοῦ βοηθεῖν τοῖς ἐνεστῶσιν καὶ τὴν ὁρμὴν τοῦ κακῶς ἐπιβαλλομένου μεταθεῖναι κραυγῆς τε μετὰ δακρύων τὸ ἱερὸν ἐμπλησάντων [17]οἱ κατὰ τὴν πόλιν ἀπολειπόμενοι ταραχθέντες ἐξεπήδησαν ἄδηλον τιθέμενοι τὸ γινόμενον. [18]αἵ τε κατάκλειστοι παρθένοι ἐν θαλάμοις σὺν ταῖς τεκούσαις ἐξώρμησαν καὶ ἀπέδωκαν κόνει τὰς κόμας πασάμεναι γόου τε καὶ στεναγμῶν ἐνεπίμπλων τὰς πλατείας. [19]αἱ δὲ καὶ προσαρτίως ἐσταλμέναι τοὺς πρὸς ἀπάντησιν διατεταγμένους παστοὺς καὶ τὴν ἁρμόζουσαν αἰδὼ παραλείπουσαι δρόμον ἄτακτον ἐν τῇ πόλει συνίσταντο. [20]τὰ δὲ νεογνὰ τῶν τέκνων αἱ πρὸς τούτοις μητέρες καὶ τιθηνοὶ παραλείπουσαι ἄλλως καὶ ἄλλως, αἱ μὲν κατ' οἴκους, αἱ δὲ κατὰ τὰς ἀγυιάς, ἀνεπιστρέπτως εἰς τὸ πανυπέρτατον ἱερὸν ἠθροίζοντο. [21]ποικίλη δὲ ἦν τῶν εἰς τοῦτο συλλεγέντων ἡ δέησις ἐπὶ τοῖς ἀνοσίως ὑπ' ἐκείνου κατεγχειρουμένοις. [22]σύν τε τούτοις οἱ περὶ τῶν πολιτῶν θρασυνθέντες οὐκ ἠνείχοντο τέλεον αὐτοῦ ἐπικειμένου καὶ τὸ τῆς προθέσεως ἐκπληροῦν διανοουμένου, [23]φωνήσαντες δὲ τὴν ὁρμὴν ἐπὶ τὰ ὅπλα ποιήσασθαι καὶ θαρραλέως ὑπὲρ τοῦ πατρῴου νόμου τελευτᾶν ἱκανὴν ἐποίησαν ἐν τῷ τόπῳ τραχύτητα, μόλις

---

18 απεδωκαν) σποδω και L / γοου τε) που γε A+

19 απαντησιν) απαν νυν AV / διατεταγμενους) -νην A+ / παστους L) A

omits / εν τη πολει) A+ omit

21 ανοσιως / -σιοις V+

23 υπερ) υπο A+

19. NUPTIAL CANOPIES: παστός is the regular Gk. rendering of the familiar חֻפָּה; so in LXX of Ps. 19.5.

22–26. Perhaps it is not too fanciful to see in the emboldened citizens who clamor for direct action, the restraint enjoined by the Elders, the suasions of the king's own attendants, and his disregard of them, allusions to some crisis under the Roman administration, and a reflection of the partisan views mentioned in the Introd. (24).

1–20. *The prayer of Simon.* This prayer is of classic Jewish form. Like the *Amidah*, for example, it first addresses God in terms of glory and power, then relates His great works, then makes its specific petition. Like the prayer of Eleazar at 6.1–15, but not quite so clearly, it follows the pattern of Ps. 105 and 106 in making a rehearsal of the historical deliverances of Israel a point of departure for supplication for present help. The phrasing follows Hebrew usage closely, and it is easy to suppose that it was translated bodily from a Heb. original. In any case the language is marked as

and implored God the Greatest to aid them in their impending trouble and to turn aside the onset of the man's wicked attack, and they filled the Temple with cries and tears, ¹⁷so that those who were left behind about the city were aroused and sprang forth, supposing that something strange was happening. ¹⁸Maidens who had been secluded in their chambers rushed out with their mothers; they strewed their hair with dust and ashes, and filled the streets with groans and lamentations. ¹⁹Others who had but just been introduced into their bridal chambers, leaving behind their nuptial canopies which had been made ready for congress, and the modesty suitable to their station, dashed disorderly through the city. ²⁰Their mothers and the nurses responsible for them left newborn infants behind untended, here and there, in houses and in the streets, and swarmed to the Temple, which towers above all. ²¹Varied was the supplication of those here gathered over what that man had impiously undertaken to do. ²²Along with these were emboldened citizens who would not endure the consummation of what he purposed nor his determination to carry out his project. ²³Their shouts to fly to arms and die manfully on behalf of the ancestral Law produced a great up-

"Jewish liturgical Greek" by its numerous Hebraisms. The style is noticeably less florid than what precedes and follows; if the author is reworking an earlier writing he refrained from tampering with this prayer. "The house of the abominations" (18) is of course incorrect in the mouth of a pagan boaster; perhaps this is another indication of the author's reluctance to edit this particular document. The language echoes Biblical phraseology throughout; the following expressions may be especially noted: παντοκράτωρ "Almighty," ה צבאות or שדי; ἀνοσίου καὶ βεβήλου, "unhallowed and profane," ערל וטמא; κρίνεις (for κατακρίνεις), "dost judge," תשפוט; ἀδικίαν ποιήσαντας, "those who wrought iniquity," עושי עולה; ὑπερηφανίαν ἐργαζομένους, "workers of insolence," פועלי זדון; πυρὶ καὶ θείῳ, "with fire and brimstone," באש וגפרית; ὄχλων πλήθει, "a multitude of people," ברב המון; ἔργα σῆς χειρός, "the works of Thy hand," מעשי ידיך; ἁγιάσας . . . εἰς ὄνομά σοι, "sanctify . . . for Thy name," לקדש את שמך; στενοχωρία, "straitness," מצוקה or צרה; διὰ τὰς πολλὰς . . . ἡμῶν ἁμαρτίας, "for our many . . . sins," בעוונותינו הרבים; τῷ ὀνόματι τῆς δόξης σου, "to the name of Thy glory," לשם קדשך; ἀπάλειψον τὰς ἁμαρτίας ἡμῶν, "Blot out our sins," מחה פשעינו; τάχυ προκαταλαβέτωσαν ἡμᾶς οἱ οἰκτιρμοί σου, "Let Thy compassion [plural] speedily overtake us" (LXX Ps. 78.5), מהר יקדמונו רחמיך; ποιήσας ἡμῖν εἰρήνην, "granting us peace," עושה שלום עלינו.

δὲ ὑπὸ τε τῶν γεραιῶν καὶ τῶν πρεσβυτέρων ἀποτραπέντες ἐπὶ τὴν αὐτὴν τῆς δεήσεως παρῆσαν στάσιν. ²⁴καὶ τὸ μὲν πλῆθος ὡς ἔμπροσθεν ἐν τούτοις ἀνεστρέφετο δεόμενον. ²⁵οἱ δὲ περὶ τὸν βασιλέα πρεσβύτεροι πολλαχῶς ἐπειρῶντο τὸν ἀγέρωχον αὐτοῦ νοῦν ἐξιστάνειν τῆς ἐντεθυμημένης ἐπιβουλῆς. ²⁶θρασυνθεὶς δὲ καὶ πάντα παραπέμψας ἤδη καὶ πρόσβασιν ἐποιεῖτο τέλος ἐπιθήσειν δοκῶν τῷ προειρημένῳ. ²⁷ταῦτα οὖν καὶ οἱ περὶ αὐτὸν ὄντες θεωροῦντες ἐτράπησαν εἰς τὸ σὺν τοῖς ἡμετέροις ἐπικαλεῖσθαι τὸν πᾶν κράτος ἔχοντα τοῖς παροῦσιν ἐπαμῦναι μὴ παριδόντα τὴν ἄνομον καὶ ὑπερήφανον πρᾶξιν. ²⁸ἐκ δὲ τῆς πυκνοτάτης τε καὶ ἐμπόνου τῶν ὄχλων συναγομένης κραυγῆς ἀνείκαστός τις ἦν βοή· ²⁹δοκεῖν γὰρ ἦν μὴ μόνον τοὺς ἀνθρώπους, ἀλλὰ καὶ τὰ τείχη καὶ τὸ πᾶν ἔδαφος ἠχεῖν ἅτε δὴ τῶν πάντων τότε θάνατον ἀλλασσομένων ἀντὶ τῆς τοῦ τόπου βεβηλώσεως.

2 ¹Ὁ μὲν οὖν ἀρχιερεὺς Σίμων ἐξ ἐναντίας τοῦ ναοῦ κάμψας τὰ γόνατα καὶ τὰς χεῖρας προτείνας εὐτάκτως ἐποιήσατο τὴν δέησιν τοιαύτην ²Κύριε κύριε, βασιλεῦ τῶν οὐρανῶν καὶ δέσποτα πάσης κτίσεως, ἅγιε ἐν ἁγίοις, μόναρχε, παντοκράτωρ, πρόσχες ἡμῖν καταπονουμένοις ὑπὸ ἀνοσίου καὶ βεβήλου θράσει καὶ σθένει πεφρυαγμένου. ³σὺ γὰρ ὁ κτίσας τὰ πάντα καὶ τῶν ὅλων ἐπικρατῶν δυνάστης δίκαιος εἶ καὶ τοὺς ὕβρει καὶ ἀγερωχίᾳ τι πράσσοντας κρίνεις. ⁴σὺ τοὺς ἔμπροσθεν ἀδικίαν ποιήσαντας, ἐν οἷς καὶ γίγαντες

---

24 εν) A+ omit
25 επιβουλης) VL omit επι
26 παντα) παντας A+ / προβασιν) A+ add ηδη
29 τοτε) τον L, V+ omit

II

1 omitted entirely in AV, found in L
2 σθενει) ασθενει A+
3 γαρ) A+ add ει

1. SIMON: The High Priest in 217 was Simon II; but perhaps our author's use of the name is intended to suggest Simon I, surnamed the Just (d. 270), the story of whose encounter with Alexander the Great (see Ralph Marcus' Loeb Classical Library ed. of Jos., VI, App. C) may here be dimly reflected. Zeitlin (*The History of the Second Jewish Commonwealth*,

roar in the Holy Place; they were with difficulty turned from their design by the old men and the Elders, and they joined in the same posture of supplication. ²⁴The multitude meanwhile continued praying as before, ²⁵but the Elders about the king endeavored in many ways to turn his proud mind from the purpose he coveted. ²⁶But he was now grown bold, and dismissed all restraints; and he was already striding forward, thinking to achieve his announced intention. ²⁷When those who were with him perceived this, they joined with our people in calling upon Him Who has all power to defend them in their present need, and not to overlook such lawless and arrogant behavior. ²⁸From the united cries of the crowds, incessant and vehement, there arose an indescribable uproar. ²⁹One might think that not only the people but even the walls and all the pavement gave voice, for indeed at that moment all preferred death to the profanation of the Temple.

2 ¹Then the High Priest Simon bent his knees before the Temple, calmly stretched his hands forth, and pronounced the following prayer: ²"Lord, Lord, King of the Heavens and Sovereign of all creation, holy among the holy ones, sole ruler, Almighty, hearken unto us who are grievously troubled by an unhallowed and profane man, puffed up with insolence and strength. ³For Thou art the Creator of all and holdest sway over all; Thou art a righteous ruler, and dost judge those who do aught in frowardness and pride. ⁴Thou didst destroy those who wrought iniquity aforetime; among these were the giants who trusted in strength and boldness, upon whom Thou didst

---

p. 18) maintains that Simon II was Simon the Just.
2. LORD, LORD: The repetition is characteristic of Jewish (cf. ה' ה' אל רחום וחנון), but not of pagan prayer.   HOLY AMONG THE HOLY ONES: The Gk. phrase is that used in the LXX Is. 57.15 for שכן עד.   SOLE RULER: Emphasis on the sole sovereignty of God is particularly appropriate in a prayer to allay the presumption of a mortal sovereign.   UNHALLOWED AND PROFANE: The Gk. words carry the sense of "religiously impure, uninitiated." Forms of βέβηλος are used in the LXX Lev. 21.4, 9 for sexual defilement, and in Ezekiel.
4. GIANTS: Cf. Gen. 6.4–7.   MEASURELESS WATERS: Cf. Gen. 7.

ἦσαν ῥώμῃ καὶ θράσει πεποιθότες, διέφθειρας ἐπαγαγὼν αὐτοῖς ἀμέτρητον ὕδωρ. ⁵σὺ τοὺς ὑπερηφανίαν ἐργαζομένους Σοδομίτας διαδήλους ταῖς κακίαις γενομένους πυρὶ καὶ θείῳ κατέφλεξας παράδειγμα τοῖς ἐπιγινομένοις καταστήσας. ⁶σὺ τὸν θρασὺν Φαραω καταδουλωσάμενον τὸν λαόν σου τὸν ἅγιον Ισραηλ ποικίλαις καὶ πολλαῖς δοκιμάσας τιμωρίαις ἐγνώρισας τὴν σὴν δύναμιν, ἐφ' οἷς ἐγνώρισας τὸ μέγα σου κράτος· ⁷καὶ ἐπιδιώξαντα αὐτὸν σὺν ἅρμασιν καὶ ὄχλων πλήθει ἐπέκλυσας βάθει θαλάσσης, τοὺς δὲ ἐμπιστεύσαντας ἐπὶ σοὶ τῷ τῆς ἁπάσης κτίσεως δυναστεύοντι σώους διεκόμισας, ⁸οἳ καὶ συνιδόντες ἔργα σῆς χειρὸς ᾔνεσάν σε τὸν παντοκράτορα. ⁹σύ, βασιλεῦ, κτίσας τὴν ἀπέραντον καὶ ἀμέτρητον γῆν ἐξελέξω τὴν πόλιν ταύτην καὶ ἡγίασας τὸν τόπον τοῦτον εἰς ὄνομά σοι τῷ τῶν ἁπάντων ἀπροσδεεῖ καὶ παρεδόξασας ἐν ἐπιφανείᾳ μεγαλοπρεπεῖ σύστασιν ποιησάμενος αὐτοῦ πρὸς δόξαν τοῦ μεγάλου καὶ ἐντίμου ὀνόματός σου. ¹⁰καὶ ἀγαπῶν τὸν οἶκον τοῦ Ισραηλ ἐπηγγείλω διότι, ἐὰν γένηται ἡμῶν ἀποστροφὴ καὶ καταλάβῃ ἡμᾶς στενοχωρία καὶ ἐλθόντες εἰς τὸν τόπον τοῦτον δεηθῶμεν, εἰσακούσῃ τῆς δεήσεως ἡμῶν. ¹¹καὶ δὴ πιστὸς εἶ·καὶ ἀληθινός. ¹²ἐπεὶ δὲ πλεονάκις θλιβέντων τῶν πατέρων ἡμῶν ἐβοήθησας αὐτοῖς ἐν τῇ ταπεινώσει καὶ ἐρρύσω αὐτοὺς ἐκ μεγάλων κακῶν, ¹³ἰδοῦ δὲ νῦν, ἅγιε βασιλεῦ, διὰ τὰς πολλὰς καὶ μεγάλας ἡμῶν ἁμαρτίας καταπονούμεθα καὶ ὑπετάγημεν τοῖς ἐχθροῖς ἡμῶν καὶ παρείμεθα ἐν ἀδυναμίαις. ¹⁴ἐν δὲ τῇ ἡμετέρᾳ καταπτώσει ὁ θρασὺς καὶ βέβηλος οὗτος ἐπιτηδεύει καθυβρίσαι τὸν ἐπὶ τῆς γῆς ἀναδεδειγμένον τῷ ὀνόματι τῆς δόξης σου ἅγιον τόπον. ¹⁵τὸ μὲν γὰρ κατοικητήριόν σου οὐρανὸς τοῦ οὐρανοῦ ἀνέφικτος ἀνθρώποις ἐστίν. ¹⁶ἀλλὰ ἐπεὶ εὐδοκήσας τὴν δόξαν σου ἐν τῷ λαῷ σου Ισραηλ ἡγίασας τὸν τόπον

---

5 διαδηλους) αδηλ. A+
9 απεραντον ... αμετρητον) V+ transpose / ονομα σοι) ον. σου V+, σον ον. σοι A+
10 του) VL omit / αποστροφη) VL prefix η / τουτον) ημων A+
11 ει) A+ omit
12 θλιβεντων) A+ prefix και

5. FIRE AND BRIMSTONE: Cf. Gen. 19.24.

bring measureless waters. ⁵Thou didst consume with fire and brimstone the men of Sodom, workers of insolence, who had become conspicuous for their wickedness, and didst make them an example to future generations. ⁶The overweening Pharaoh who enslaved Thy holy people Israel Thou didst visit with diverse and numerous punishments, and didst make known Thy mighty power. ⁷And when he pursued with chariots and a multitude of people Thou didst overwhelm him in the depths of the sea; but Thou didst conduct in safety those that put their trust in Thee, the Ruler of all creation. ⁸And when they saw the works of Thy hand, they praised Thee, the Almighty. ⁹Thou, O King, when Thou didst create the boundless and measureless earth, didst choose this city and sanctify this Holy Place for Thy name, though Thou hast need of naught, and didst glorify it by a magnificent manifestation, establishing in this place an expression of the glory of Thy great and honorable Name. ¹⁰And out of love for Thy House of Israel Thou didst promise that if there should be a turning away on our part and if straitness should overtake us, Thou wouldst hearken to our supplication if we should come to this Holy Place and pray. ¹¹And truly, Thou art faithful and true. ¹²Forasmuch as Thou didst oftentimes succor our fathers in their humiliation when they were oppressed, and didst deliver them from great perils: ¹³behold now, O Holy King, for our many and great sins we are grievously troubled, and we are made subject to our enemies, and in our weakness we are grown faint. ¹⁴In our fallen estate this insolent and profane man seeketh to do violence to the Holy Place which is dedicated on earth to the name of Thy glory. ¹⁵Thine abiding place, indeed, the Heaven of Heaven, is unapproachable to men; ¹⁶but this Holy Place Thou didst sanctify because Thy good pleasure was in Thy glory amongst Thy people Israel.

6. DIVERSE AND NUMEROUS PUNISHMENTS: *Cf.* Ex. 5–12.
7. OVERWHELM HIM IN THE DEPTHS OF THE SEA: *Cf.* Ex. 14.21 ff.
8. PRAISED THEE: *Cf.* Ex. 15.
10. THOU DIDST PROMISE: *Cf.* I Kings 8.33–34.
15. THE HEAVEN OF HEAVEN: *Cf.* I Kings 8.27 ff.

τοῦτον, ¹⁷μὴ ἐκδικήσῃς ἡμᾶς ἐν τῇ τούτων ἀκαθαρσίᾳ μηδὲ εὐθύνῃς ἡμᾶς ἐν βεβηλώσει, ἵνα μὴ καυχήσωνται οἱ παράνομοι ἐν θυμῷ αὐτῶν μηδὲ ἀγαλλιάσωνται ἐν ὑπερηφανίᾳ γλώσσης αὐτῶν λέγοντες ¹⁸Ἡμεῖς κατεπατήσαμεν τὸν οἶκον τοῦ ἁγιασμοῦ, ὡς καταπατοῦνται οἱ οἶκοι τῶν προσοχθισμάτων. ¹⁹ἀπάλειψον τὰς ἁμαρτίας ἡμῶν καὶ διασκέδασον τὰς ἀμβλακίας ἡμῶν καὶ ἐπίφανον τὸ ἔλεός σου κατὰ τὴν ὥραν ταύτην. ²⁰ταχὺ προκαταλαβέτωσαν ἡμᾶς οἱ οἰκτιρμοί σου, καὶ δὸς αἰνέσεις ἐν τῷ στόματι τῶν καταπεπτωκότων καὶ συντετριμμένων τὰς ψυχὰς ποιήσας ἡμῖν εἰρήνην.

²¹Ἐνταῦθα ὁ πάντων ἐπόπτης θεὸς καὶ προπάτωρ ἅγιος ἐν ἁγίοις εἰσακούσας τῆς ἐνθέσμου λιτανείας, τὸν ὕβρει καὶ θράσει μεγάλως ἐπηρμένον ἐμάστιξεν αὐτὸν ²²ἔνθεν καὶ ἔνθεν κραδάνας αὐτὸν ὡς κάλαμον ὑπὸ ἀνέμου ὥστε κατ' ἐδάφους ἄπρακτον, ἔτι καὶ τοῖς μέλεσιν παραλελυμένον μηδὲ φωνῆσαι δύνασθαι δικαίᾳ περιπεπληγμένον κρίσει. ²³ὅθεν οἵ τε φίλοι καὶ σωματοφύλακες ὀξεῖαν ἰδόντες τὴν καταλαβοῦσαν αὐτὸν εὔθυναν φοβούμενοι μὴ καὶ τὸ ζῆν ἐκλείπῃ, ταχέως αὐτὸν ἐξείλκυσαν ὑπερβάλλοντι καταπεπληγμένοι φόβῳ. ²⁴ἐν χρόνῳ δὲ ὕστερον ἀναλεξάμενος αὐτὸν οὐδαμῶς εἰς μετάμελον ἦλθεν ἐπιτιμηθείς, ἀπειλὰς δὲ πικρὰς θέμενος ἀνέλυσεν.

25 ²⁵Διακομισθεὶς δὲ εἰς τὴν Αἴγυπτον καὶ τὰ τῆς κακίας ἐπαύξων διά τε τῶν προαποδεδειγμένων συμποτῶν καὶ

---

22 περιπεπληγμενον) πεπαρμενον L, A+   25 επαυξων) επ αυτων A+ omit περι

18. ABOMINATIONS: Odd on the lips of a pagan, but no Jewish writer could refer to a pagan shrine otherwise; cf. I Mac. 6.7, ed. Zeitlin.
19. BLOT OUT OUR SINS: Cf. LXX Ps. 50.3, 11.
20. GRANTING US PEACE: The normal conclusion of prayer; cf. the *Kaddish*.
21–25. *The punishment of Philopator*.
21. THE PRIMAL HOLY ONE: The rather rare and poetic προπάτωρ is used exclusively of divine or deified ancestral founders of a line. The idea of God as Father is familiar in prayer, as in אבינו שבשמים; cf. Deut. 32.6, Is. 63.16.
22. PARALYZED: In II Mac. 3.22–30 (whose language is very similar to that in our passage) Heliodorus is repulsed by an apparition, and in 9.4 ff. Antiochus is punished by a stroke. Philopator's swoon is not inherently

¹⁷Punish us not by the defilement of these men, nor chastise us by their profane doing, lest the transgressors boast in their wrath or exult in their arrogance of tongue, saying, ¹⁸'We have trodden down the house of the Sanctuary as the houses of the abominations are trodden down.' ¹⁹Blot out our sins and scatter abroad our offenses, and manifest Thy mercy at this hour. ²⁰Let Thy compassion speedily overtake us, and put praises in the mouth of those that are fallen and crushed in spirit, granting us peace."

²¹Then did God, Who beholds all, the primal Holy One among the holy, hearing the entreaties of the prescribed form, scourge him who was greatly uplifted in violence and frowardness, ²²shaking him this way and that as a reed is shaken by the wind, so that he lay on the ground powerless and paralyzed in all his members, nor was he able even to utter speech, being smitten by a just judgment. ²³Thereupon his friends and bodyguards, seeing that the chastisement which overtook him was quick and sharp, feared lest he should yield up his life, and drew him out speedily, being overwhelmed by fright exceeding great. ²⁴After some time he gradually recovered himself; yet never came to repentance, punished though he had been, but departed with bitter threats.

²⁵Arrived then in Egypt, Ptolemy multiplied his wickedness, through his aforementioned boon companions and

---

improbable, for he is known to have been a superstitious man, and he may well have been stricken when he felt the horror his act had inspired.

25–33. *Hostile measures against the Jews of Alexandria.* This passage furnishes valuable evidence for the history of the period and also for the validity of our book.

25. WICKEDNESS: Poly. 5.35 gives an appalling account of Philopator's general wickedness. BOON COMPANIONS AND FRIENDS: Philopator was under the domination of his courtiers, especially Sosibius, who persuaded him to connive at the murders of his mother, his brother, and his uncle. AFOREMENTIONED: There is in fact no previous mention of these boon companions in our text, and the use of the phrase here suggest that an opening section has fallen out (see Introd. 5). Perhaps this passage alludes to the banquet in honor of the victory of Raphia mentioned in the Pithom stele (see on 1.1 above).

ἑταίρων τοῦ παντὸς δικαίου κεχωρισμένων ²⁶οὐ μόνον ταῖς ἀναριθμήτοις ἀσελγείαις διηρκέσθη, ἀλλὰ καὶ ἐπὶ τοσοῦτον θράσους προῆλθεν ὥστε δυσφημίας ἐν τοῖς τόποις συνίστασθαι καὶ πολλοὺς τῶν φίλων ἀτενίζοντας εἰς τὴν τοῦ βασιλέως πρόθεσιν καὶ αὐτοὺς ἕπεσθαι τῇ ἐκείνου θελήσει. ²⁷προέθετο δημοσίᾳ κατὰ τοῦ ἔθνους διαδοῦναι ψόγον· ἐπὶ τοῦ κατὰ τὴν αὐλὴν πύργου στήλην ἀναστήσας ἐκόλαψεν γραφὴν ²⁸μηδένα τῶν μὴ θυόντων εἰς τὰ ἱερὰ αὐτῶν εἰσιέναι, πάντας δὲ τοὺς Ἰουδαίους εἰς λαογραφίαν καὶ οἰκετικὴν διάθεσιν ἀχθῆναι, τοὺς δὲ ἀντιλέγοντας βίᾳ φερομένους τοῦ ζῆν μεταστῆσαι, ²⁹τούς τε ἀπογραφομένους χαράσσεσθαι καὶ διὰ πυρὸς εἰς τὸ σῶμα παρασήμῳ Διονύσου κισσοφύλλῳ, οὓς καὶ καταχωρίσαι εἰς τὴν προσυνεσταλμένην αὐθεντίαν. 30 ³⁰ἵνα δὲ μὴ τοῖς πᾶσιν ἀπεχθόμενος φαίνηται, ὑπέγραψεν

29 second και) V+ omit

26. SLANDERS: Preisigke, *Wörterbuch der griechischen Papyrusurkunden*, s.v. δυσφημία cites papyrus usage of this word to mean "slanderous discourses." TOWNS AND VILLAGES: Preisigke, s.v., gives authority for this translation of τόποι; elsewhere the word, whose literal meaning is "place," is applied to the Temple at Jerusalem. FRIENDS: a specific title for Ptolemaic courtiers. We know that the powerful Sosibius and Agathocles were themselves surrounded by a large number of friends and relatives. FOLLOWED HIS WISHES: Perhaps with reference to the cult of Dionysus, which is implied in the verses following. Philopator's devotion to the cult of Dionysus motivated certain of his measures (*e.g.*, giving the tribe of Dionysus paramount importance: *FHG* III 164, Satyrus 21), and perhaps in part explains his reputation as a wastrel. Clement of Alexandria says that Philopator was called "Dionysus"— by his intimates as a sort of nickname—not officially, as was the case with Ptolemy XIII. A series of didrachmas and drachmas of Philopator bear the head of Dionysus crowned with ivy. *Cf.* Perdrizet, *Revue des Études Anciennes*, XII (1910) 217 ff.

27. TO INFLICT A STIGMA: What is probably involved in Philopator's measure is an effort to unify all parts of the Egyptian populace, and imbue them with national feeling by making the cult of Dionysus, to which he was himself devoted, universal. His use of native Egyptians in his phalanx was a move in the same direction. See Cohen, *Judaica et Aegyptiaca* (Groningen, 1941) 8–12, and literature there cited. TOWER: Posting decrees on palace walls was a regular practice. The Ptolemaic palace on the peninsula of Lochias at Alexandria was a kind of citadel: Kubitschek in *PWK* s.v. "Alexandria," 1.1384 f.

28. THAT NONE . . . : The language sounds as if it were taken directly from

friends, who were utter strangers to all justice. ²⁶He was not content with numberless acts of wantonness, but mounted to such a pitch of insolence as to raise slanders in the towns and villages; and many of his Friends, observing the king's design closely, themselves followed his wishes. ²⁷He designed to inflict a stigma on the nation publicly, and erected a pillar on the tower at the palace and inscribed upon it:²⁸That none of those who did not sacrifice should be allowed to enter their temples; that all the Jews should be reduced to the popular-census and slave condition; that those who spoke against it should be carried off by force and put to death; ²⁹that those who were registered should be branded by fire on their persons with an ivy leaf, the emblem of Dionysus, and that they ³⁰ should be recorded in their former limited status. ³⁰In order

the inscription, by the author or his source. The use of indirect discourse would rather favor authenticity, in accordance with the practice of ancient historians, than otherwise. In 30 the final clause is subjoined in direct discourse. The decree itself seems to be the king's *second* measure: see on 2.30 ff.   THOSE WHO DID NOT SACRIFICE . . . THE JEWS: Though the Jews were doubtless the special object of the decree, it is likely that it was couched in general terms, and that "the Jews" is an addition by our author; "those who did not sacrifice" would apply only to the Jews, who sacrificed only at Jerusalem.   POPULAR-CENSUS: For the meaning of *laographia* and its bearing on the date of our book, see Introd. 19. It must be noticed that nothing in the decree suggests the punishment by trampling elephants which is subsequently brought into connection with it.
29. BRANDED . . . WITH AN IVY LEAF: The emblem of the ivy and the practice of branding or tattooing go back to the Thracian origins of the Dionysiac cult. It is likely that Philopator himself was so branded. A collateral idea involved in branding was the mark of the runaway slave. The verb here used, χαράσσεσθαι, is probably a Semitic derivative (חרש).
RECORDED IN: The regular meaning for καταχωρίσαι in the papyri (see Preisigke *s.v.*).   FORMER LIMITED STATUS: That before their liberation by Ptolemy Philadelphus, as recorded in Aristeas 22.
30. EQUAL RIGHTS: The question of the civic rights of the Jews of Egypt is much vexed; but it appears clear that those who enjoyed full citizenship did so as individuals and not by virtue of being Jews. In 3.21 (end) we read, "and we determined to introduce a change, in rating them worthy of Alexandrian citizenship and making them participants in our regular religious rites." This would make it appear that the king had first desired that those Jews who were soldiers or employed in the administration should be initiated into the mysteries of Dionysus and receive full citizenship. Thereupon—

'Εὰν δέ τινες ἐξ αὐτῶν προαιρῶνται ἐν τοῖς κατὰ τὰς τελετὰς μεμυημένοις ἀναστρέφεσθαι, τούτους ἰσοπολίτας 'Αλεξανδρεῦσιν εἶναι. ³¹"Ενιοι μὲν οὖν ἐπιπολαίως τὰς τῆς πόλεως εὐσεβείας ἐπιβάθρας στυγοῦντες εὐχερῶς ἑαυτοὺς ἐδίδοσαν ὡς μεγάλης τινὸς κοινωνήσοντες εὐκλείας ἀπὸ τῆς ἐσομένης τῷ βασιλεῖ συναναστροφῆς. ³²οἱ δὲ πλεῖστοι γενναίᾳ ψυχῇ ἐνίσχυσαν καὶ οὐ διέστησαν τῆς εὐσεβείας τά τε χρήματα περὶ τοῦ ζῆν ἀντικαταλλασσόμενοι ἀδεῶς ἐπειρῶντο ἑαυτοὺς ῥύσασθαι ἐκ τῶν ἀπογραφῶν· ³³εὐέλπιδές τε καθειστήκεισαν ἀντιλήμψεως τεύξασθαι καὶ τοὺς ἀποχωροῦντας ἐξ αὐτῶν ἐβδελύσσοντο καὶ ὡς πολεμίους τοῦ ἔθνους ἔκρινον καὶ τῆς κοινῆς συναναστροφῆς καὶ εὐχρηστίας ἐστέρουν.

3 ¹"Α καὶ μεταλαμβάνων ὁ δυσσεβὴς ἐπὶ τοσοῦτον ἐξεχόλησεν ὥστε οὐ μόνον τοῖς κατὰ 'Αλεξάνδρειαν διοργίζεσθαι, ἀλλὰ καὶ τοῖς ἐν τῇ χώρᾳ βαρυτέρως ἐναντιωθῆναι καὶ προστάξαι σπεύσαντας συναγαγεῖν πάντας ἐπὶ τὸ αὐτὸ καὶ χειρίστῳ μόρῳ τοῦ ζῆν μεταστῆσαι. ²τούτων δὲ οἰκονομουμένων φήμη δυσμενὴς ἐξηχεῖτο κατὰ τοῦ γένους ἀνθρώποις συμφρονοῦσιν εἰς κακοποίησιν ἀφορμῆς διδομένης εἰς διάθεσιν ὡς ἂν ἀπὸ τῶν νομίμων αὐτοὺς κωλυόντων. ³οἱ δὲ Ιουδαῖοι τὴν μὲν

---

31 επιπολαιως) some L have επι πολεως   III

2 εξηχειτο) εξεκειτο A+ / συμφρονουσιν) συμφοραν ουσιν A+

---

31. SOME ... DELIVERED THEMSELVES UP READILY: To obtain the benefits promised; but—
32. THE GREATER PART PERSEVERED: Attempting to procure release by bribery; and—
33. REMAINED RESOLUTELY HOPEFUL ... AND ... DESPISED THOSE WHO SEPARATED THEMSELVES: It is to this attitude that vv. 3.22–23 in the king's circular decree refer, and the inscribed decree of 2.28–30 is best understood as having been issued *after* the first tentative invitation to apostasy had miscarried. Hence the stringent punishment for recalcitrants; hence also the extension of the decree to cover the Jews in the interior as well as those in Alexandria (3.1).
1–10. *The Jews and their neighbors.* One of the objects of our book is to demonstrate that no compromise must be made with loyalty to Judaism.

not to appear an enemy to them all he subjoined, that if any of them should prefer to join those who are initiated in the mysteries, they would have equal rights with the citizens of Alexandria.

³¹Some, grudging the price of their city's religion, delivered themselves up readily, expecting to share in some high prestige from the association they would have with the king. ³²But the greater part persevered with stalwart spirit, and did not depart from their religion; offering money in redemption for life, they fearlessly endeavored to save themselves from the registration. ³³They remained resolutely hopeful that they would obtain relief, and they despised those who separated themselves from them, accounting them as enemies of their people and excluding them from social intercourse and the rendering of any service.

3 ¹When that impious man understood these things, he was so enraged that he was not only infuriated against those in Alexandria but was even more bitterly incensed against those in the interior, and ordered that they should all be speedily brought together to a single place and put to the most cruel of deaths. ²While these measures were being arranged a malicious report was noised abroad against the Jewish people by persons who were agreed to do them mischief, an opportunity offering for the pretext that they hindered them from the observance of the laws. ³But the Jews continued to preserve

The present passage shows that such loyalty wins rather than repels the friendly sympathy of the heathen.

1. NOT ONLY INFURIATED AGAINST THOSE IN ALEXANDRIA: But in 4.12 we read that "the Jews' compatriots from the city frequently went out secretly to bewail the ignominy and distress of their brethren," which would indicate that the Jews of Alexandria were *not* incarcerated. On the other hand, the parallel in Josephus (see Introd. 10) speaks only of the Jews *in the city*. It would seem that the ancient source dealt only with the fate of the Jews *outside* Alexandria, and that the scene of the elephant episode which our author attached was Alexandria; the discrepancy would therefore be due to unskilful mortising.   IN THE INTERIOR: Χώρα, "country," is regularly used of Egypt outside Alexandria.
2. MALICIOUS REPORT: *Cf.* Esth. 3.8.

πρὸς τοὺς βασιλεῖς εὔνοιαν καὶ πίστιν ἀδιάστροφον ἦσαν φυλάσσοντες, ⁴σεβόμενοι δὲ τὸν θεὸν καὶ τῷ τούτου νόμῳ πολιτευόμενοι χωρισμὸν ἐποίουν ἐπὶ τῷ κατὰ τὰς τροφάς, 5 δι' ἣν αἰτίαν ἐνίοις ἀπεχθεῖς ἐφαίνοντο. ⁵τῇ δὲ τῶν δικαίων εὐπραξίᾳ κοσμοῦντες τὴν συναναστροφὴν ἅπασιν ἀνθρώποις εὐδόκιμοι καθειστήκεισαν. ⁶τὴν μὲν οὖν περὶ τοῦ γένους ἐν πᾶσιν θρυλουμένην εὐπραξίαν οἱ ἀλλόφυλοι οὐδαμῶς διηριθμήσαντο, ⁷τὴν δὲ περὶ τῶν προσκυνήσεων καὶ τροφῶν διάστασιν ἐθρύλουν φάσκοντες μήτε τῷ βασιλεῖ μήτε ταῖς δυνάμεσιν ὁμοσπόνδους τοὺς ἀνθρώπους γίνεσθαι, δυσμενεῖς δὲ εἶναι καὶ μέγα τι τοῖς πράγμασιν ἐναντιουμένους· καὶ οὐ τῷ τυχόντι περιῆψαν ψόγῳ. ⁸οἱ δὲ κατὰ τὴν πόλιν Ἕλληνες οὐδὲν ἠδικημένοι ταραχὴν ἀπροσδόκητον περὶ τοὺς ἀνθρώπους θεωροῦντες καὶ συνδρομὰς ἀπροσκόπους γινομένας βοηθεῖν μὲν οὐκ ἔσθενον, τυραννικὴ γὰρ ἦν ἡ διάθεσις, παρεκάλουν δὲ καὶ δυσφόρως εἶχον καὶ μεταπεσεῖσθαι ταῦτα ὑπελάμβανον· ⁹μὴ γὰρ οὕτω παροραθήσεσθαι τηλικοῦτο 10 σύστεμα μηδὲν ἠγνοηκός. ¹⁰ἤδη δὲ καί τινες γείτονές τε καὶ φίλοι καὶ συμπραγματευόμενοι μυστικῶς τινας ἐπισπώμενοι πίστεις ἐδίδουν συνασπιεῖν καὶ πᾶν ἐκτενὲς προσοίσεσθαι πρὸς ἀντίλημψιν.

¹¹Ἐκεῖνος μὲν οὖν τῇ κατὰ τὸ παρὸν εὐημερίᾳ γεγαυρωμένος καὶ οὐ καθορῶν τὸ τοῦ μεγίστου θεοῦ κράτος, ὑπολαμβάνων δὲ διηνεκῶς ἐν τῇ αὐτῇ διαμενεῖν βουλῇ, ἔγραψεν

---

4 κατα τας τροφας) καταστροφας Α+ /
ενιοις) Α+ omit s
7 ψογω) φοβω Α+

8 ανθρωπους) ανδρας Α+
11 υπολαμβανων) –νειν Α+

---

4. HELD THEMSELVES APART: Jewish separatism and its effects are frequently alluded to in Hellenistic writings. It is a principal theme in IV Maccabees, and is vigorously defended in the speech put into the mouth of the High Priest Eleazar in Aristeas 128 ff., though the remainder of that book is more latitudinarian. For III Maccabees' partisanship in the question of the proper relation of the Jews to their neighbors see Introd. 24.

8. THE GREEKS IN THE CITY: The point seems to be that the separation caused by Jewish observance did not (as the partisans of a less rigorous

their good will toward the royal house and their unswerving fidelity; ⁴yet, revering God and regulating their lives according to His Law, they held themselves apart in the matter of food, and for this reason they appeared odious to some. ⁵But their intercourse they ordered by the good practice of righteousness, and so their good repute was established among all men. ⁶Of this good practice, however, which was bruited among all men concerning this nation, other peoples took no account. ⁷They in turn bruited the differences with reference to worship and food, alleging that these people were not bound to the king and his authority, but ill-disposed and utterly opposed to his interests; it was no slight reproach that they cast upon them.

⁸The Greeks in the city, who were in no way injured, when they saw the unforeseen tumult involving these people and unlooked-for concourses taking place, they were not strong enough, indeed, to help them, for they lived under a tyranny, but they did try to comfort them and were distressed for them, and they supposed the situation would change for the better: ⁹surely so great a community could not be thus abandoned when they had committed no fault. ¹⁰Some of their neighbors and friends and business associates drew some aside secretly, and offered pledges to protect them and to exert their utmost efforts to assist them.

¹¹The king was elated by his present success. Paying no regard to the power of the Greatest God, and assuming that he would always firmly abide by the same purpose, he wrote

---

view perhaps insisted it did) necessarily involve strained relations with non-Jews, who indeed, so far as they were able to do so, assisted the Jews despite the danger to themselves. Nevertheless, the hatred of the heathen for the Jews is assumed; *cf.* 4.1.

11–30. *Ptolemy orders the arrest of all the Jews in his kingdom.* Ptolemy's letter (3.12–29) shows on the whole correct chancellory style, but is not in its entirety as convincing as the decree of 2.28–30. The motivation of the king's attitude toward his rebuff in Jerusalem (3.14–18) seems an adventitious link contrived by the author to relate his disparate themes.

κατ' αὐτῶν ἐπιστολὴν τήνδε ¹²Βασιλεὺς Πτολεμαῖος Φιλοπάτωρ τοῖς κατ' Αἴγυπτον καὶ κατὰ τόπον στρατηγοῖς καὶ στρατιώταις χαίρειν καὶ ἐρρῶσθαι· ¹³ἔρρωμαι δὲ καὶ αὐτὸς ἐγὼ καὶ τὰ πράγματα ἡμῶν. ¹⁴τῆς εἰς τὴν Ἀσίαν γενομένης ἡμῖν ἐπιστρατείας, ἧς ἴστε καὶ αὐτοί, τῇ τῶν θεῶν ἀπροπτώτῳ
15 συμμαχίᾳ κατὰ λόγον ἐπὶ τέλος ἀχθείσης ¹⁵ἡγησάμεθα μὴ βίᾳ δόρατος, ἐπιεικείᾳ δὲ καὶ πολλῇ φιλανθρωπίᾳ τιθηνήσασθαι τὰ κατοικοῦντα Κοίλην Συρίαν καὶ Φοινίκην ἔθνη εὖ ποιῆσαί τε ἀσμένως. ¹⁶καὶ τοῖς κατὰ πόλιν ἱεροῖς απονείμαντες προσόδους πλείστας προήχθημεν καὶ εἰς τὰ Ἱεροσόλυμα ἀναβάντες τιμῆσαι τὸ ἱερὸν τῶν ἀλιτηρίων καὶ μηδέποτε ληγόντων τῆς ἀνοίας. ¹⁷οἱ δὲ λόγῳ μὲν τὴν ἡμετέραν ἀποδεξάμενοι παρουσίαν, τῷ δὲ πράγματι νόθως, προθυμηθέντων ἡμῶν εἰσελθεῖν εἰς τὸν ναὸν αὐτῶν καὶ τοῖς ἐκπρεπέσιν καὶ καλλίστοις ἀναθήμασιν τιμῆσαι ¹⁸τύφοις φερόμενοι παλαιοτέροις εἶρξαν ἡμᾶς τῆς εἰσόδου λειπόμενοι τῆς ἡμετέρας ἀλκῆς δι' ἣν ἔχομεν πρὸς ἅπαντας ἀνθρώπους φιλανθρωπίαν. ¹⁹τὴν δὲ αὐτῶν εἰς ἡμᾶς δυσμένειαν ἔκδηλον καθιστάντες ὡς μονώτατοι τῶν ἐθνῶν βασιλεῦσιν καὶ τοῖς ἑαυτῶν εὐεργέταις
20 ὑψαυχενοῦντες οὐδὲν γνήσιον βούλονται φέρειν. ²⁰ἡμεῖς δὲ τῇ τούτων ἀνοίᾳ συμπεριενεχθέντες καὶ μετὰ νίκης διακομισθέντες εἰς τὴν Αἴγυπτον τοῖς πᾶσιν ἔθνεσιν φιλανθρώπως ἀπαντήσαντες καθὼς ἔπρεπεν ἐποιήσαμεν, ²¹ἐν δὲ τούτοις πρὸς τοὺς ὁμοφύλους αὐτῶν ἀμνησικακίαν ἅπασιν γνωρίζοντες· διά τε τὴν συμμαχίαν καὶ τὰ πεπιστευμένα μετὰ ἁπλότητος αὐτοῖς ἀρχῆθεν μύρια πράγματα τολμήσαντες ἐξαλλοιῶσαι ἐβουλήθημεν καὶ πολιτείας αὐτοὺς Ἀλεξανδρέων καταξιῶσαι καὶ μετόχους τῶν ἀεὶ ἱερῶν καταστῆσαι. ²²οἱ δὲ τοὐναντίον

---

14 της) VL prefix εκ
15 ποιησαι τε ασμενως) ποιησαντες μεν ως AV+
21 τολμησαντες) A+ omit / V omits second και to end

---

12. PHILOPATOR: Though Ptolemy IV received this title after Raphia, papyri evidence indicates that the Ptolemies did not use their "divine" epithets in official documents until ca. 100 BCE; see Bickermann, in Pauly-Wissowa-Kroll, *Realencyclopädie* 14.797–800 (1930). GREETING AND GOOD HEALTH: The formula χαίρειν καὶ ἐρρῶσθαι seems to have come in

the following letter against the Jews: ¹²"King Ptolemy Philopator to his generals and soldiers in Egypt and its towns and villages, greeting and good health! ¹³I myself am in good health, and our affairs prosper. ¹⁴Our expedition to Asia, of which you too have knowledge, having been brought to its expected conclusion by the deliberate assistance of the gods, ¹⁵we thought to foster the peoples inhabiting Coele Syria and Phoenicia not by force of arms but by kindness and generous benevolence, bestowing benefits upon them gladly. ¹⁶After we had granted large revenues to the temples in the cities, we proceeded to Jerusalem also, coming to do honor to the temple of this accursed people, who never cease from their folly. ¹⁷Seemingly they welcomed our presence, but in fact their welcome was spurious; for when we were eager to enter their shrine and honor it with choice and beautiful offerings, ¹⁸they barred us from the entry, carried away by their inveterate absurdities; but they were not made to feel our strength, because of the benevolence we cherish for all men. ¹⁹Their ill will toward us they have plainly exhibited; quite unique among peoples, they stand stiff-necked against their kings and their own benefactors, and are willing to accept nothing as genuine.

²⁰"We accommodated ourselves to this folly, and returned to Egypt with victory, meeting all peoples with benevolence; we did as was meet for us to do. ²¹Among these measures we made known to all our amnesty of the Jews' fellow countrymen [in Egypt], because of our ties with them and the countless matters which had been freely entrusted to them from of old; and we determined to introduce a change, in rating them worthy of Alexandrian citizenship and making them participants in our regular religious rites. ²²But they received

---

at the same period. This would indicate that our document was composed after 100. TOWNS AND VILLAGES: See on 2.26.

21. ENTRUSTED TO THEM FROM OF OLD: The Elephantine papyri show that Jews had been settled as garrisons in Elephantine and Aswan by the Persians as early as the 5th century, and there is evidence that the practice continued under the Ptolemies; cf. 6.25, 7.7; Aristeas 36; Jos., Ant. 12.1.

ἐκδεχόμενοι καὶ τῇ συμφύτῳ κακοηθείᾳ τὸ καλὸν ἀπωσάμενοι, διηνεκῶς δὲ εἰς τὸ φαῦλον ἐκνεύοντες ²³οὐ μόνον ἀπεστρέψαντο τὴν ἀτίμητον πολιτείαν, ἀλλὰ καὶ βδελύσσονται λόγῳ τε καὶ σιγῇ τοὺς ἐν αὐτοῖς ὀλίγους πρὸς ἡμᾶς γνησίως διακειμένους παρ' ἕκαστα ὑφορώμενοι μετὰ τῆς δυσκλεεστάτης ἐμβιώσεως διὰ τάχους ἡμᾶς καταστρέψαι τὰ πράγματα. ²⁴διὸ καὶ τεκμηρίοις καλῶς πεπεισμένοι τούτους κατὰ πάντα δυσνοεῖν ἡμῖν τρόπον καὶ προνοούμενοι μήποτε αἰφνιδίου μετέπειτα ταραχῆς ἐνστάσης ἡμῖν τοὺς δυσσεβεῖς τούτους κατὰ νώτου προδότας καὶ βαρβάρους ἔχωμεν πολεμίους ²⁵προστετάχαμεν ἅμα τῷ προσπεσεῖν τὴν ἐπιστολὴν τήνδε αὐθωρὶ τοὺς ἐννεμομένους σὺν γυναιξὶ καὶ τέκνοις μετὰ ὕβρεων καὶ σκυλμῶν ἀποστεῖλαι πρὸς ἡμᾶς ἐν δεσμοῖς σιδηροῖς πάντοθεν κατακεκλεισμένους, εἰς ἀνήκεστον καὶ δυσκλεῆ πρέποντα δυσμενέσι φόνον. ²⁶τούτων γὰρ ὁμοῦ κολασθέντων διειλήφαμεν εἰς τὸν ἐπίλοιπον χρόνον τελείως ἡμῖν τὰ πράγματα ἐν εὐσταθείᾳ καὶ τῇ βελτίστῃ διαθέσει κατασταθήσεσθαι. ²⁷ὃς δ' ἂν σκεπάσῃ τινὰ τῶν Ιουδαίων ἀπὸ γεραιοῦ μέχρι νηπίου καὶ μέχρι τῶν ὑπομαστιδίων, αἰσχίσταις βασάνοις ἀποτυμπανισθήσεται πανοικίᾳ. ²⁸μηνύειν δὲ τὸν βουλόμενον, ἐφ' ᾧ τὴν οὐσίαν τοῦ ἐμπίπτοντος ὑπὸ τὴν εὔθυναν λήμψεται καὶ ἐκ τοῦ βασιλικοῦ ἀργυρίου δραχμὰς δισχιλίας καὶ τῇ ἐλευθερίᾳ στεφανωθήσεται. ²⁹πᾶς δὲ τόπος, οὗ ἐὰν φωραθῇ τὸ σύνολον σκεπαζόμενος Ιουδαῖος, ἄβατος καὶ πυριφλεγὴς γινέσθω καὶ πάσῃ θνητῇ φύσει καθ' ἅπαν ἄχρηστος φανήσεται εἰς τὸν ἀεὶ χρόνον. ³⁰Καὶ ὁ μὲν τῆς ἐπιστολῆς τύπος οὕτως ἐγέγραπτο.

---

25 κατακεκλεισμενους) -οις AV
27 υπομαστιδιων Schulze) -στιαιων AL, -σθιαν V+ / αισχ.) εχθισταις A+ / πανοικια) -κει L ; cf. Exodus 1.1

28 τη ελευθερια) Deissmann, on the basis of a single MS, της -ριας AV, to which L add τευξεται και / L add εις τον αει χρονον at end

24. AT OUR BACKS: This motive seems borrowed by our author from an earlier Egyptian king's justification for destroying the Jews; cf. Ex. 1.10.
28. REWARDED WITH FREEDOM: Probably with reference to the Egyptian populace, who did not enjoy full rights; an alternative rendering is "crowned at the Eleutheria" (a festival of Dionysus). If III Maccabees

this in a sense opposite to that intended, and in their inborn malice rejected the good, inclining, as they constantly do, to the base. ²³Not only did they refuse the priceless citizenship, but by their words and by their silence they show contempt for the few among them who are properly disposed toward us; in every case they secretly expect that through their infamous persistence we shall speedily alter our regulations. ²⁴Therefore, being well persuaded by the evidence that these people are evilly disposed towards us in every way, and apprehending lest, if ever some sudden tumult should be raised against us hereafter, we should have these impious people at our backs as treacherous and barbarous enemies, ²⁵we have ordained that as soon as this letter reaches you you shall immediately dispatch to us, with harsh and violent treatment, those that reside among you, along with their women and children, fettered in every way with iron chains, to meet inexorable and ignominious death, as befits malevolent enemies. ²⁶When these have been punished as a body, we anticipate that our government will be perfectly established for all future time in a sound and excellent state. ²⁷Whosoever shall shelter any Jew, from graybeard to infant to suckling babe, shall be bastinadoed to death, along with all his household, with horrible torments. ²⁸Whoso will may give information, on condition of receiving the property of him that incurs punishment and two thousand drachmae from the royal treasury, and he shall also be rewarded with freedom. ²⁹Any place where a Jew shall be detected receiving any shelter whatever shall be made anathema and burned with fire; it shall be rendered altogether useless for every mortal creature for all time." ³⁰Such was the form of the letter that was written.

---

and Aristeas are related to one another as exponents of opposite views (see Introd. 24), the reward promised here for information *against* the Jewish interest may have a direct connection with the reward promised by Ptolemy Philadelphus in Aristeas 25 for information *for* the Jewish interest.

4 ¹Πάντῃ δέ, ὅπου προσέπιπτεν τοῦτο τὸ πρόσταγμα, δημοτελὴς συνίστατο τοῖς ἔθνεσιν εὐωχία μετὰ ἀλαλαγμῶν καὶ χαρᾶς ὡς ἂν τῆς προκατεσκιρωμένης αὐτοῖς πάλαι κατὰ διάνοιαν μετὰ παρρησίας νῦν ἐκφαινομένης ἀπεχθείας. ²τοῖς δὲ Ἰουδαίοις ἄληκτον πένθος ἦν καὶ πανόδυρτος μετὰ δακρύων βοὴ στεναγμοῖς πεπυρωμένης πάντοθεν αὐτῶν τῆς καρδίας ὀλοφυρομένων τὴν ἀπροσδόκητον ἐξαίφνης αὐτοῖς ἐπικριθεῖσαν ὀλεθρίαν. ³τίς νομὸς ἢ πόλις ἢ τίς τὸ σύνολον οἰκητὸς τόπος ἢ τίνες ἀγυιαὶ κοπετοῦ καὶ γόων ἐπ' αὐτοῖς οὐκ ἐνεπιπλῶντο; ⁴οὕτως γὰρ μετὰ πικρίας ἀνοίκτου ψυχῆς ὑπὸ τῶν κατὰ πόλιν στρατηγῶν ὁμοθυμαδὸν ἐξαπεστέλλοντο ὥστε ἐπὶ ταῖς ἐξάλλοις τιμωρίαις καί τινας τῶν ἐχθρῶν λαμβάνοντας πρὸ τῶν ὀφθαλμῶν τὸν κοινὸν ἔλεον καὶ λογιζομένους τὴν ἄδηλον τοῦ βίου καταστροφὴν δακρύειν 5 αὐτῶν τὴν δυσάθλιον ἐξαποστολήν. ⁵ἤγετο γὰρ γεραιῶν πλῆθος πολιᾷ πεπυκασμένων, τὴν ἐκ τοῦ γήρως νωθρότητα ποδῶν ἐπίκυφον ἀνατροπῆς ὁρμῇ βιαίας ἁπάσης αἰδοῦς ἄνευ πρὸς ὀξεῖαν καταχρωμένων πορείαν. ⁶αἱ δὲ ἄρτι πρὸς βίου κοινωνίαν γαμικὸν ὑπεληλυθυῖαι παστὸν νεάνιδες ἀντὶ τέρψεως μεταλαβοῦσαι γόους καὶ κόνει τὴν μυροβρεχῆ πεφυρμέναι κόμην, ἀκαλύπτως δὲ ἀγόμεναι θρῆνον ἀνθ' ὑμεναίων ὁμοθυμαδὸν ἐξῆρχον ὡς ἐσπαραγμέναι σκυλμοῖς ἀλλοεθνέσιν· ⁷δέσμιαι δὲ δημοσίᾳ μέχρι τῆς εἰς τὸ πλοῖον ἐμβολῆς εἵλκοντο μετὰ βίας. ⁸οἵ τε τούτων συνζυγεῖς βρόχοις ἀντὶ στεφέων τοὺς αὐχένας περιπεπλεγμένοι μετὰ ἀκμαίας νεανικῆς ἡλικίας

IV
3 οικητος) οικτιστος AV+ / ουκ ενεπιπλωντο) A+ omit
5 γεραιων ... πολια) γερων πληρης

πολιας A+, but A also has πεπυκασμενων / επικυφον) –κουφ– AL, –φων V+
6 σκυλμοις) σκυμνοις A

1–21. *The Jews brought to Alexandria and imprisoned.* Beginning with ch. 4 the connection of our account with history seems vaguer, and the accentuated ornateness and hyperbole of the language (except for Eleazar's prayer at 6.21) corresponds to the more romantic and miraculous tone. The explanation may be that in these chapters the author is attaching the episode of the elephants to the older and more sober tradition of the measures of Philopator.
1. HATRED: Of the heathen for the Jews is assumed in III Maccabees;

4 ¹In every place that this decree reached, a feast was set up for the heathen at public expense with exultation and gladness, for the hatred which had long grown inveterate in their hearts was now given free expression. ²But for the Jews there was grief unceasing and lamentable and tearful cries; their hearts were altogether inflamed with groaning, as they bewailed the unforeseen destruction which had suddenly been decreed against them. ³What province or city, what inhabited place at all, or what byways were not filled with lamentations and groans for them? ⁴For with such cruel and pitiless spirit were they sent away, one and all, by the respective generals that their inordinate suffering made some even of their enemies, perceiving the common pity before their eyes, reflect on the uncertain revolutions of life and weep at their utterly ⁵miserable expulsion. ⁵For there was carried away a multitude of old men covered with hoary hair, forcing the sluggishness of their limbs, which were stooped with age, to a quick pace because of the shameless and violent driving. ⁶Young women who had but lately entered their bridal chamber for sharing wedded life, uttering cries of lamentation instead of joy, their myrrh-drenched locks sullied with dust, were driven on unveiled, and with one accord chanted a dirge instead of a marriage hymn, as if mangled by heathen whelps. ⁷In prisoners' bonds and exposed to view, they were forcibly dragged to the embarkation aboard ship. ⁸Their husbands too, in the

---

Aristeas represents a different view (see Introd. 24). It is noticeable that in this section feasts form a background not only for important decisions, but for setting forth significant reactions to decisions. For the analogy of Esther see Introd. 6.

2. BUT FOR THE JEWS THERE WAS GRIEF: *Cf.* Esth. 4.3: "And in every province, whithersoever the king's commandment and his decree came, there was great mourning among the Jews, and fasting, and weeping, and wailing; and many lay in sackcloth and ashes."

3–10. The full-blown pathos of this passage, culminating in the melodramatic disruption of marriage feasts, exhibits familiar commonplaces of the rhetorician's stock; see Introd. 5. From 4.18 it appears that the round-up was not nearly as ruthless as it is here described. The tone amounts almost to formal notice that the author is setting his pitch to romance, not history; see also on 5.2.

ἀντὶ εὐωχίας καὶ νεωτερικῆς ῥαθυμίας τὰς ἐπιλοίπους τῶν γάμων ἡμέρας ἐν θρήνοις διῆγον παρὰ πόδας ἤδη τὸν ᾅδην ὁρῶντες κείμενον. ⁹κατήχθησαν δὲ θηρίων τρόπον ἀγόμενοι σιδηροδέσμοις ἀνάγκαις, οἱ μὲν τοῖς ζυγοῖς τῶν πλοίων προσηλωμένοι τοὺς τραχήλους, οἱ δὲ τοὺς πόδας ἀρρήκτοις 10 κατησφαλισμένοι πέδαις, ¹⁰ἔτι καὶ τῷ καθύπερθε πυκνῷ σανιδώματι διακειμένῳ, ὅπως πάντοθεν ἐσκοτισμένοι τοὺς ὀφθαλμοὺς ἀγωγὴν ἐπιβούλων ἐν παντὶ τῷ κατάπλῳ λαμβάνωσιν.

¹¹Τούτων δὲ ἐπὶ τὴν λεγομένην Σχεδίαν ἀχθέντων καὶ τοῦ παράπλου περανθέντος, καθὼς ἦν δεδογματισμένον τῷ βασιλεῖ, προσέταξεν αὐτοὺς ἐν τῷ πρὸ τῆς πόλεως ἱπποδρόμῳ παρεμβαλεῖν ἀπλάτῳ καθεστῶτι περιμέτρῳ καὶ πρὸς παραδειγματισμὸν ἄγαν εὐκαιροτάτῳ καθεστῶτι πᾶσι τοῖς καταπορευομένοις εἰς τὴν πόλιν καὶ τοῖς ἐκ τούτων εἰς τὴν χώραν στελλομένοις πρὸς ἐκδημίαν πρὸς τὸ μηδὲ ταῖς δυνάμεσιν αὐτοῦ κοινωνεῖν μηδὲ τὸ σύνολον καταξιῶσαι περιβόλων. ¹²ὡς δὲ τοῦτο ἐγενήθη, ἀκούσας τοὺς ἐκ τῆς πόλεως ὁμοεθνεῖς κρυβῇ ἐκπορευομένους πυκνότερον ἀποδύρεσθαι τὴν ἀκλεῆ τῶν ἀδελφῶν ταλαιπωρίαν ¹³διοργισθεὶς προσέταξεν καὶ τούτοις ὁμοῦ τὸν αὐτὸν τρόπον ἐπιμελῶς ὡς ἐκείνοις ποιῆσαι μὴ λειπομένοις κατὰ μηδένα τρόπον τῆς ἐκείνων τιμωρίας, ¹⁴ἀπογραφῆναι δὲ πᾶν τὸ φῦλον ἐξ ὀνόματος, οὐκ εἰς τὴν ἔμπροσθεν βραχεῖ προδεδηλωμένην τῶν ἔργων κατάπονον λατρείαν, στρεβλωθέντας δὲ ταῖς παρηγγελμέναις αἰκίαις

---

11 απλατω) απλετω V / second μηδε omitted in AL   στρεβλωθεντας) στρεβλωθεντα A+, στρεβλωσαντες L, στρεβλωθεντες V+
14 καταπονον) κατα τροπον A+ /

---

11. SCHEDIA: A dock area 3 m. from Alexandria, the hippodrome was at the E. or Canobic gate of the city; a canal joined Schedia and the Canobic gate; Strabo, 17.1.10, 16. CLAIM TO BE WITHIN THE CIRCUIT: This seems to be clear evidence that our author's original dealt with measures directed only at Jews living outside Alexandria; and
12. COMPATRIOTS FROM THE CITY: shows that the Jews of Alexandria were not subjected to these measures.
13. HE WAS INCENSED, AND ORDERED . . . : This appears to be our author's not unskillful explanation of how the decree directed originally only against the Jews of the countryside came to be applied to the Alexandrians

flower of their youth, wore halters about their necks instead of garlands, and instead of feasting and youthful ease they spent the remaining days of their nuptials in dirges, seeing Hades at their very feet. ⁹They were embarked in the manner of wild beasts, driven under the constraint of iron bonds; some were riveted to the rowers' benches by their necks, others were made fast by the feet with unbreakable fetters. ¹⁰Their light was cut off by thick planks above, so that, their eyes being kept in darkness altogether, they might throughout the voyage receive the treatment due traitors.

¹¹When they were brought to the place called Schedia, and the voyage as decreed by the king had been completed, he ordered them to be thrown into the hippodrome before the city, a place of huge compass and very suitable for making them a conspicuous example to those going down into the city and to those from the city setting out to the country for a sojourn; for here they could neither communicate with the king's forces nor in any way claim to be within the circuit of the city. ¹²But when this had come to pass, and the king heard that the Jews' compatriots from the city frequently went out secretly to bewail the ignominy and distress of their brethren, ¹³he was incensed, and ordered that these should receive precisely the same treatment as the others, and that their punishment should in no detail fall short of the others'. ¹⁴The whole race, furthermore, was to be registered by names; not for the toilsome labor service, as briefly indicated above, but to be tortured by the torments which he had proclaimed, and then finally to be done away with in the space of a single day.

---

also; the elephant story, as has been noticed, was associated specifically with Alexandria.

14. REGISTERED . . . TO BE TORTURED: This is again puzzling. Perhaps the source's account of a registry for status (a reasonable and necessary procedure) is transferred by our author to a registry for a mass execution, which seems a preliminary by no means as necessary as the king's anger at its failure (4.19) would indicate. The registry is then made the subject of a miracle (4.20), which at the kindest estimate seems very odd. The awkwardness is patently due to clumsy adjustment of disparate elements.
AS BRIEFLY INDICATED: Presumably at 2.28.

15 τὸ τέλος ἀφανίσαι μιᾶς ὑπὸ καιρὸν ἡμέρας. ¹⁵ἐγίνετο μὲν οὖν ἡ τούτων ἀπογραφὴ μετὰ πικρᾶς σπουδῆς καὶ φιλοτίμου προσεδρείας ἀπὸ ἀνατολῶν ἡλίου μέχρι δυσμῶν ἀνήνυτον λαμβάνουσα τὸ τέλος ἐπὶ ἡμέρας τεσσαράκοντα. ¹⁶Μεγάλως δὲ καὶ διηνεκῶς ὁ βασιλεὺς χαρᾷ πεπληρωμένος συμπόσια ἐπὶ πάντων τῶν εἰδώλων συνιστάμενος πεπλανημένῃ πόρρω τῆς ἀληθείας φρενὶ καὶ βεβήλῳ στόματι τὰ μὲν κωφὰ καὶ μὴ δυνάμενα αὐτοῖς λαλεῖν ἢ ἀρήγειν ἐπαινῶν, εἰς δὲ τὸν μέγιστον θεὸν τὰ μὴ καθήκοντα λαλῶν. ¹⁷μετὰ δὲ τὸ προειρημένον τοῦ χρόνου διάστημα προσηνέγκαντο οἱ γραμματεῖς τῷ βασιλεῖ μηκέτι ἰσχύειν τὴν τῶν Ιουδαίων ἀπογραφὴν ποιεῖσθαι διὰ τὴν ἀμέτρητον αὐτῶν πληθὺν ¹⁸καίπερ ὄντων ἔτι κατὰ τὴν χώραν τῶν πλειόνων, τῶν μὲν κατὰ τὰς οἰκίας ἔτι συνεστηκότων, τῶν δὲ καὶ κατὰ τόπον, ὡς ἀδυνάτου καθεστῶτος πᾶσιν τοῖς ἐπ' Αἴγυπτον στρατηγοῖς. ¹⁹ἀπειλήσαντος δὲ αὐτοῖς σκληρότερον ὡς δεδωροκοπημένοις εἰς μηχανὴν τῆς ἐκφυγῆς συνέβη σαφῶς αὐτὸν περὶ τούτου 20 πιστωθῆναι ²⁰λεγόντων μετὰ ἀποδείξεως καὶ τὴν χαρτηρίαν ἤδη καὶ τοὺς γραφικοὺς καλάμους, ἐν οἷς ἐχρῶντο, ἐκλελοιπέναι. ²¹τοῦτο δὲ ἦν ἐνέργεια τῆς τοῦ βοηθοῦντος τοῖς Ιουδαίοις ἐξ οὐρανοῦ προνοίας ἀνικήτου.

5 ¹Τότε προσκαλεσάμενος Ἕρμωνα τὸν πρὸς τῇ τῶν

16 επι) απο VL / πεπλανημενη) πεπληρωμενη A+ / AL omit τον ... θεον; V+ omit εις δε to the end; L adds after λαλων, το ουκ οντα

18 τοπον) πορον L, probably correctly / επ) υπο V+, κατ L
19 πιστωθηναι) πεισθηναι V

16. REVELS AT ALL HIS IDOLS: Cf. Dan. 5.4.
17. IMMENSE NUMBERS: It is futile to inquire into the basis of the hyperbole of this passage. From Aristeas 27 (whose fictive date is a half century before the fictive date of III Maccabees) we gather that the Jewish population of Egypt was some 120,000. Philo, but with patent exaggeration, says (A. Flaccum 6) that there were a million in Alexandria. In any case, an uncountable number seems more appropriate to a date nearer Philo's than to the reign of Philopator.
18. THE GREATER NUMBER ... STILL IN THE COUNTRY ... ON THE JOURNEY: This seems an inadvertent admission that the picture in 4.3–10 is greatly overdrawn, and that what was in fact involved was a registration for

THE THIRD BOOK OF MACCABEES

¹⁵Their registration was therefore carried out with bitter haste and zealous diligence, from the risings of the sun until its settings, and, still uncompleted, was brought to an end after forty days.

¹⁶With exceeding and continuous joy was the king then filled, setting up revels at all his idols, with heart far astray from truth and mouth polluted, praising creatures dumb and impotent to answer or help, and uttering things unseemly against the Greatest God. ¹⁷But after the aforementioned interval of time the scribes reported to the king that they were no longer able to continue the registration of the Jews because of their immense numbers, ¹⁸although the greater number of them were still in the country, some yet remaining in their homes and others on the journey; the task was an impossibility for all the generals in Egypt. ¹⁹He menaced them with harsh threats, suspecting they had been bribed to contrive an evasion; but he was eventually convinced on the point, ²⁰when they declared and demonstrated that the paper factory and the writing pens which they used had given out. ²¹But this was the working of the invincible Providence of Him who aided the Jews from heaven.

5 ¹Then he summoned Hermon, who was in charge of the

---

status, not total annihilation. The translation follows L's πόρον, rather than AV's τόπον, which is printed in the text.
19. BRIBED: This seems to tie in with the statement of the Jews' evasion in 2.32. What lies back of this passage, then, is the *original* measure of the king against the Jews.
20. PAPER ... PENS ... HAD GIVEN OUT: A remarkable enough miracle, but perhaps not an absurd touch in a country whose administration involved such huge masses of paper work.
21. PROVIDENCE: An attribute of God, not a periphrasis for God.

1–51. *The king orders the execution of the Jews, but is twice thwarted.* If forgetfulness and oversleeping do not seem very impressive forms of divine intervention, our author nevertheless shows considerable dramatic skill in building up to the crescendo of the denouement, which, in keeping with the practice of the rhetorical writers of fiction, takes place in a crowded hippodrome.

ἐλεφάντων ἐπιμελείᾳ βαρείᾳ μεμεστωμένος ὀργῇ καὶ χόλῳ
κατὰ πᾶν ἀμετάθετος ²ἐκέλευσεν ὑπὸ τὴν ἐπερχομένην
ἡμέραν δαψιλέσι δράκεσι λιβανωτοῦ καὶ οἴνῳ πλείονι
ἀκράτῳ ἅπαντας τοὺς ἐλέφαντας ποτίσαι ὄντας τὸν ἀριθμὸν
πεντακοσίους καὶ ἀγριωθέντας τῇ τοῦ πόματος ἀφθόνῳ
χορηγίᾳ εἰσαγαγεῖν πρὸς συνάντησιν τοῦ μόρου τῶν Ιουδαίων.
³ὁ μὲν τάδε προστάσσων ἐτρέπετο πρὸς τὴν εὐωχίαν συναγαγὼν τοὺς μάλιστα τῶν φίλων καὶ τῆς στρατιᾶς ἀπεχθῶς
ἔχοντας πρὸς τοὺς Ιουδαίους. ⁴ὁ δὲ ἐλεφαντάρχης τὸ προσταγὲν ἀραρότως Ἕρμων συνετέλει. ⁵οἵ τε πρὸς τούτοις λειτουρ-
γοὶ κατὰ τὴν ἑσπέραν ἐξιόντες τὰς τῶν ταλαιπωρούντων
ἐδέσμευον χεῖρας τήν τε λοιπὴν ἐμηχανῶντο περὶ αὐτοὺς
ἀσφάλειαν ἔννυχον δόξαντες ὁμοῦ λήμψεσθαι τὸ φῦλον
πέρας τῆς ὀλεθρίας. ⁶οἱ δὲ πάσης σκέπης ἔρημοι δοκοῦντες
εἶναι τοῖς ἔθνεσιν Ιουδαῖοι διὰ τὴν πάντοθεν περιέχουσαν
αὐτοὺς μετὰ δεσμῶν ἀνάγκην ⁷τὸν παντοκράτορα κύριον καὶ
πάσης δυνάμεως δυναστεύοντα, ἐλεήμονα θεὸν αὐτῶν καὶ
πατέρα, δυσκαταπαύστῳ βοῇ πάντες μετὰ δακρύων ἐπεκα-
λέσαντο δεόμενοι ⁸τὴν κατ' αὐτῶν μεταστρέψαι βουλὴν
ἀνοσίαν καὶ ῥύσασθαι αὐτοὺς μετὰ μεγαλομεροῦς ἐπιφανείας
ἐκ τοῦ παρὰ πόδας ἐν ἑτοίμῳ μόρου. ⁹τούτων μὲν οὖν ἐκτενῶς
ἡ λιτανεία ἀνέβαινεν εἰς τὸν οὐρανόν.
¹⁰Ὁ δὲ Ἕρμων τοὺς ἀνηλεεῖς ἐλέφαντας ποτίσας πεπλη-
ρωμένους τῆς τοῦ οἴνου πολλῆς χορηγίας καὶ τοῦ λιβάνου
μεμεστωμένους ὄρθριος ἐπὶ τὴν αὐλὴν παρῆν περὶ τούτων
προσαγγεῖλαι τῷ βασιλεῖ. ¹¹τὸ δὲ ἀπ' αἰῶνος χρόνου κτίσμα
καλὸν ἐν νυκτὶ καὶ ἡμέρᾳ ἐπιβαλλόμενον ὑπὸ τοῦ χαριζομένου
πᾶσιν, οἷς ἂν αὐτὸς θελήσῃ, ὕπνου μέρος ἀπέστειλεν εἰς
τὸν βασιλέα, ¹²καὶ ἡδίστῳ καὶ βαθεῖ κατεσχέθη τῇ ἐνεργείᾳ

---

11 χρονου... κτισμα) A+ transpose

2. FIVE HUNDRED IN NUMBER: The number would strike an ancient reader as so fantastic (the 73 elephants Philopator had at Raphia were impressive) that he would likely adjust his reception, as the author doubtless intended he should, to the key of romance rather than history.
5. BOUND THE HANDS: This detail had already been attended to (3.25, 4.9), but perhaps the bonds had been loosened when the Jews were enclosed in the hippodrome. *Cf.* on 5.49.

elephants; filled to overflowing with passionate fury and with rage, and altogether inflexible, ²he bade him for the following day to drug all the elephants, five hundred in number, with copious handfuls of frankincense and with abundant unmixed wine, and then, after they had been made savage by the plentiful supply of drink, to bring them in to compass the fate of the Jews. ³When he had given these orders he turned to his feasting, having gathered about him those of his friends and of the army who were especially hostile to the Jews. ⁴The superintendent of the elephants attended to his bidding scrupulously. ⁵The functionaries whose charge it was went out in the evening and bound the hands of the unfortunates, and took other precautions to keep them safe through the night, supposing that the race would meet its final destruction at one blow. ⁶But the Jews, who seemed to the heathen to be destitute of any shelter because of the constraint of fetters which encompassed them on all sides, ⁷all called upon the Almighty Lord and Ruler of all power, their merciful God and Father, tearfully and with a cry that would not be silenced, beseeching Him ⁸to frustrate the impious design against them, and to deliver them with a glorious manifestation from the fate ready prepared at their feet.

⁹Their supplication, then, ascended fervently to heaven; ¹⁰but Hermon had given the pitiless elephants drink until they were surfeited with the plentiful supply of wine and sated with frankincense; and early in the morning he was present at court to report on these matters to the king. ¹¹But the portion of slumber, that fair creation from everlasting, bestowed by night or by day by Him Who doth graciously grant it to all, whomsoever He wills, He sent upon the king. ¹²And the king was overborne, by the working of the Lord,

---

11. SLUMBER: The divine gift of sleep is extolled in the Latin poets; *cf.* Seneca, *Hercules Furens* 1066 ff.; Statius, *Silvae* 5.4. "Night" preceding "day" reveals a Hebrew rather than a Greek habit of thought.

12. BY THE WORKING OF THE LORD: This minor miracle is at least in keeping with the king's traditionally somnolent character, as the paper and pens miracle was appropriate to the Egyptian bureaucracy.

τοῦ δεσπότου τῆς ἀθέσμου μὲν προθέσεως πολὺ διεσφαλμένος, τοῦ δὲ ἀμεταθέτου λογισμοῦ μεγάλως διεψευσμένος. ¹³οἵ τε Ἰουδαῖοι τὴν προσημανθεῖσαν ὥραν διαφυγόντες τὸν ἅγιον ᾔνουν θεὸν αὐτῶν καὶ πάλιν ἠξίουν τὸν εὐκατάλλακτον δεῖξαι μεγαλοσθενοῦς ἑαυτοῦ χειρὸς κράτος ἔθνεσιν ὑπερηφάνοις. ¹⁴μεσούσης δὲ ἤδη δεκάτης ὥρας σχεδὸν ὁ πρὸς ταῖς κλήσεσιν τεταγμένος ἀθρόους τοὺς κλητοὺς ἰδὼν ἔνυξεν προσελθὼν τὸν βασιλέα. ¹⁵καὶ μόλις διεγείρας ὑπέδειξε τὸν τῆς συμποσίας καιρὸν ἤδη παρατρέχοντα τὸν περὶ τούτων λόγον ποιούμενος. ¹⁶ὃν ὁ βασιλεὺς λογισάμενος καὶ τραπεὶς εἰς τὸν πότον ἐκέλευσεν τοὺς παραγεγονότας ἐπὶ τὴν συμποσίαν ἄντικρυς ἀνακλῖναι αὐτοῦ. ¹⁷οὗ καὶ γενομένου παρῄνει εἰς εὐωχίαν δόντας ἑαυτοὺς τὸ παρὸν τῆς συμποσίας ἐπὶ πολὺ γεραιρομένους εἰς εὐφροσύνην καταθέσθαι μέρος. ¹⁸ἐπὶ πλεῖον δὲ προβαινούσης τῆς ὁμιλίας τὸν Ἕρμωνα προσκαλεσάμενος ὁ βασιλεὺς μετὰ πικρᾶς ἀπειλῆς ἐπυνθάνετο, τίνος ἕνεκεν αἰτίας εἰάθησαν οἱ Ἰουδαῖοι τὴν περιοῦσαν ἡμέραν περιβεβιωκότες. ¹⁹τοῦ δὲ ὑποδείξαντος ἔτι νυκτὸς τὸ προσταγὲν ἐπὶ τέλος ἀγειοχέναι καὶ τῶν φίλων αὐτῷ προσμαρτυρησάντων ²⁰τὴν ὠμότητα χείρονα Φαλάριδος ἐσχηκὼς ἔφη τῷ τῆς σήμερον ὕπνῳ χάριν ἔχειν αὐτούς· ἀνυπερθέτως δὲ εἰς τὴν ἐπιτελοῦσαν ἡμέραν κατὰ τὸ ὅμοιον ἑτοίμασον τοὺς ἐλέφαντας ἐπὶ τὸν τῶν ἀθεμίτων Ἰουδαίων ἀφανισμόν. ²¹εἰπόντος δὲ τοῦ βασιλέως ἀσμένως πάντες μετὰ χαρᾶς οἱ παρόντες ὁμοῦ συναινέσαντες εἰς τὸν ἴδιον οἶκον ἕκαστος ἀνέλυσεν. ²²καὶ οὐχ οὕτως εἰς ὕπνον κατεχρή-

---

18 προβαινουσης) προσκοπτουσης Α+   επιουσαν L, several have επιτελλ.
19 ετι L) οτι Α, several omit   22 ως εις το) ωστε VL
20 επιτελουσαν V) υποστελλουσαν, Α+,

13. MANIFEST TO THE ARROGANT HEATHEN: The relief of the Jews at the respite is understandable, but one might have expected a more sensational intervention.
14. MIDDLE OF THE TENTH HOUR: 4:30 P.M. by Roman usage, 3:30 by Egyptian; in either case toward the end of the customary siesta, and not too early an—
15. HOUR FOR THE BANQUET: For among the ancients the elaborateness

by a sweet and deep sleep; and thus was he much balked in his lawless purpose, and greatly frustrated in his stubborn design. ¹³But the Jews, when they escaped the hour designated, praised their holy God, and again they besought Him Who is readily appeased to manifest to the arrogant heathen the might of His all-powerful hand.

¹⁴When it was nearly the middle of the tenth hour, the official in charge of invitations, seeing that the guests were assembled, approached the king and shook him. ¹⁵And when he had with difficulty awakened him, he pointed out that the hour for the banquet was already passing, and explained the circumstances. ¹⁶The king reflected on the matter, and then, turning to his drink, bade those present for the banquet to take their places opposite him. ¹⁷It was so done, and he admonished them to give themselves up to revelry, and in view of the honor done them to count the present portion of the feast in the reckoning of good cheer. ¹⁸And when the entertainment had gone on for some time, the king summoned Hermon, and asked with sharp menace why it was that the Jews had been suffered to survive that day. ¹⁹When Hermon showed that he had carried out the king's injunctions to the full during the night, and his friends had added their testimony, ²⁰the king was seized with savagery worse than Phalaris', and declared that the Jews owed thanks for that day's grace to sleep. "For the day approaching," he added, "prepare the elephants in the same manner without delay for the annihilation of the accursed Jews." ²¹When the king had thus spoken, all those present assented joyfully with one accord, and each departed to his own house. ²²But they did not em-

---

of a banquet was marked rather by an early start than by a late conclusion.
16. TURNING TO HIS DRINK: The conduct of the king in these verses is in keeping with his traditional character.
20. PHALARIS: Tyrant of Agrigentum in the 6th century, was proverbial for cruelty; he roasted people alive in his hollow brazen bull, and enjoyed their realistic bellowing. *Cf.* also 4.42.

σαντο τὸν χρόνον τῆς νυκτός, ὡς εἰς τὸ παντοίους μηχανᾶσθαι τοῖς ταλαιπώροις δοκοῦσιν ἐμπαιγμούς. ²³"Ἄρτι δὲ ἀλεκτρυὼν ἐκέκραγεν ὄρθριος, καὶ τὰ θηρία καθωπλικὼς ὁ Ἕρμων ἐν τῷ μεγάλῳ περιστύλῳ διεκίνει. ²⁴τὰ δὲ κατὰ τὴν πόλιν πλήθη συνήθροιστο πρὸς τὴν οἰκτροτάτην θεωρίαν προσδοκῶντα τὴν πρωίαν μετὰ σπουδῆς. ²⁵οἱ δὲ Ἰουδαῖοι κατὰ τὸν ἀμερῆ ψυχουλκούμενοι χρόνον πολύδακρυν ἱκετείαν ἐν μέλεσιν γοεροῖς τείνοντες τὰς χεῖρας εἰς τὸν οὐρανὸν ἐδέοντο τοῦ μεγίστου θεοῦ πάλιν αὐτοῖς βοηθῆσαι συντόμως. ²⁶οὔπω δὲ ἡλίου βολαὶ κατεσπείροντο, καὶ τοῦ βασιλέως τοὺς φίλους ἐκδεχομένου ὁ Ἕρμων παραστὰς ἐκάλει πρὸς τὴν ἔξοδον ὑποδεικνύων τὸ πρόθυμον τοῦ βασιλέως ἐν ἑτοίμῳ κεῖσθαι. ²⁷τοῦ δὲ ἀποδεξαμένου καὶ καταπλαγέντος ἐπὶ τῇ παρανόμῳ ἐξόδῳ κατὰ πᾶν ἀγνωσίᾳ κεκρατημένος ἐπυνθάνετο, τί τὸ πρᾶγμα, ἐφ' οὗ τοῦτο αὐτῷ μετὰ σπουδῆς τετέλεσται· ²⁸τοῦτο δὲ ἦν ἡ ἐνέργεια τοῦ πάντα δεσποτεύοντος θεοῦ τῶν πρὶν αὐτῷ μεμηχανημένων λήθην κατὰ διάνοιαν ἐντεθεικότος. ²⁹ὑπεδείκνυεν ὁ Ἕρμων καὶ πάντες οἱ φίλοι τὰ θηρία καὶ τὰς δυνάμεις ἠτοιμάσθαι, βασιλεῦ,

---

27 παρανομω) ανομω A+ / τι το τουτο) οτι το διασαφουμενον ετι AV
29 ητοιμασθαι) -μασται A. After 29 L add ηδη δε του βασιλεως πτολεμαιου κατα θειας προνοιας εγκεντρισμον ελεειν το εθνος των ιουδαιων εγνωκοτος και αφειναι λοιπον αυτους σπευδοντος τοις τε περι αυτον ενδοξοις συμβουλευομενου οι περι αυτον φιλοι και μεγιστανες αυτου ηγανακτουν και σφοδρα εχαλεπαινον. εις δε τις των εντιμων εν αυτοις ος και συντροφος ην του βασιλεως ερμων τουνομα τολμησας ειπεν Ουκ επι τουτοις ω βασιλευ την κατ αυτων εξ αρχης επιχειρησιν εποιησω; λαβων δε αναγνωθι τα πρωην περι αυτων υπο σου γραφεντα· υπερ γαρ του μη γενεσθαι αυτους ημιν φυσει δυσμενεις και κατα νωτου συμφωνησαντας τοις αντιπαλοις ημων καθ ημων γενεσθαι προνοουμενος ταυτα περι αυτων εδογματισας εν αρχη α νυν ουκ οιδας και ανατρεπειν επιχειρεις· μηδαμως ω βασιλευ· εκφερωμεν δε δια ταχεων την καλως επ αυτοις εξενεχθεισαν ψηφον και τους ελεφαντας επαγοντες πληρωμεν την επ αυτοις εξ αρχης υπο σου γενομενην προθεσιν

---

24. CROWDS WERE ASSEMBLED: New details for enhancing the drama are skillfully added as the story draws toward its crisis. A crowd is essential

ploy the night hours for sleep as much as in contriving every manner of indignity for those they thought doomed.

²³As soon as the cock crowed the dawn, Hermon accoutered the beasts, and began to put them in motion in the great colonnade. ²⁴Throughout the city crowds were assembled for the piteous spectacle, and they awaited the morning eagerly. ²⁵But the Jews, drawing their last brief breath in tearful supplication and with strains of lamentation, stretched their hands forth to heaven and implored God the Greatest again to succor them speedily. ²⁶The rays of the sun were not yet scattered abroad, and the king was receiving his friends, when Hermon presented himself and invited him to go forth, explaining that the king's desire was ready to be fulfilled. ²⁷When the king heard his speech he was amazed at the extraordinary invitation to go forth, because he was overwhelmed by complete oblivion; and he inquired what the matter was for which such zeal had been employed for his sake. ²⁸But this was the working of the God Who rules all things, Who had put into his mind forgetfulness of his former devices. ²⁹Hermon and all the king's friends pointed to the beasts and the troops, saying, "This has been prepared, O

---

for the denouement of an ancient romance; see Introd. 13.
26. RECEIVING HIS FRIENDS: This appears to reflect the *salutatio matutina* or early morning levee of *Roman* grandees. *Cf.* 5.46.
29. After this verse L inserts a palpable interpolation: "And now when King Ptolemy had determined, by the instigation of divine providence, to show compassion to the Jewish race and was eager to release them for the future and took counsel with the men of repute about him, his friends and grandees grew angry and took it sore amiss. And a man of distinction among them, one who had even been brought up with the king, Hermon by name, made bold to say, 'Was it not for this purpose, your majesty, that you fashioned this enterprise against them from the beginning? Take and read that which you yourself wrote concerning them previously. It was because you took thought that they should not become naturally hostile to us and, entering into agreement with our enemies behind our back, come to oppose us that you issued against them in the beginning the decree which you do not now recognize and endeavor to overturn. Not so, your majesty. Let us speedily carry out the vote passed against them, and by bringing the elephants upon them let us fulfil the purpose designed against them by you from the beginning.' "

30 κατὰ τὴν σὴν ἐκτενῆ πρόθεσιν. ³⁰ὁ δὲ ἐπὶ τοῖς ῥηθεῖσιν πληρωθεὶς βαρεῖ χόλῳ διὰ τὸ περὶ τούτων προνοίᾳ θεοῦ διεσκεδάσθαι πᾶν αὐτοῦ τὸ νόημα ἐνατενίσας μετὰ ἀπειλῆς εἶπεν ³¹"Οσοι γονεῖς παρῆσαν ἢ παίδων γόνοι, τήνδε θηρσὶν ἀγρίοις ἐσκεύασα ἂν δαψιλῆ θοῖναν ἀντὶ τῶν ἀνεγκλήτων ἐμοὶ καὶ προγόνοις ἐμοῖς ἀποδεδειγμένων ὁλοσχερῆ βεβαίαν πίστιν ἐξόχως Ἰουδαίων. ³²καίπερ εἰ μὴ διὰ τὴν τῆς συντροφίας στοργὴν καὶ τῆς χρείας, τὸ ζῆν ἀντὶ τούτων ἐστερήθης. ³³οὕτως ὁ Ἕρμων ἀπροσδόκητον ἐπικίνδυνον ὑπήνεγκεν ἀπειλὴν καὶ τῇ ὁράσει καὶ τῷ προσώπῳ συνεστάλη. ³⁴ὁ καθεὶς δὲ τῶν φίλων σκυθρωπῶς ὑπεκρέων τοὺς συνηθροισ-
35 μένους ἀπέλυσαν ἕκαστον ἐπὶ τὴν ἰδίαν ἀσχολίαν. ³⁵οἵ τε Ἰουδαῖοι τὰ παρὰ τοῦ βασιλέως ἀκούσαντες τὸν ἐπιφανῆ θεὸν κύριον βασιλέα τῶν βασιλέων ᾔνουν καὶ τῆσδε τῆς βοηθείας αὐτοῦ τετευχότες.

³⁶Κατὰ δὲ τοὺς αὐτοὺς νόμους ὁ βασιλεὺς συστησάμενος πᾶν τὸ συμπόσιον εἰς εὐφροσύνην τραπῆναι παρεκάλει. ³⁷τὸν δὲ Ἕρμωνα προσκαλεσάμενος μετὰ ἀπειλῆς εἶπεν Ποσάκις δὲ δεῖ σοι περὶ τούτων αὐτῶν προστάττειν, ἀθλιώτατε; ³⁸τοὺς ἐλέφαντας ἔτι καὶ νῦν καθόπλισον εἰς τὴν αὔριον ἐπὶ τὸν τῶν Ἰουδαίων ἀφανισμόν. ³⁹οἱ δὲ συνανακείμενοι συγγενεῖς τὴν ἀσταθῆ διάνοιαν αὐτοῦ θαυμάζοντες προ-
40 εφέροντο τάδε ⁴⁰Βασιλεῦ, μέχρι τίνος ὡς ἀλόγους ἡμᾶς διαπειράζεις προστάσσων ἤδη τρίτον αὐτοὺς ἀφανίσαι καὶ πάλιν ἐπὶ τῶν πραγμάτων ἐκ μεταβολῆς ἀναλύων τὰ σοὶ δεδογμένα; ⁴¹ὧν χάριν ἡ πόλις διὰ τὴν προσδοκίαν ὀχλεῖ καὶ πληθύουσα συστροφαῖς ἤδη καὶ κινδυνεύει πολλάκις διαρπασθῆναι. ⁴²ὅθεν ὁ κατὰ πάντα Φάλαρις βασιλεὺς ἐμπληθυνθεὶς ἀλογιστίας καὶ τὰς γινομένας πρὸς ἐπισκοπὴν τῶν

---

31 οσοι) ει σοι L / εσκευασα αν L) -ασαν 33 τη ορασει) τω θρασει VL
AV   36 τους αυτους νομους) τουτους μονους VL
32 καιπερ) διοπερ L+   40 τα σοι) τας οικιας A+

31. IF YOUR PARENTS WERE HERE, OR YOUR OFFSPRING: The Gk. forms an iambic line, and is doubtless a tag from some tragic poet.   LOYALTY: An allusion to the Jewish military and civil officials in Egypt; see on 3.21.
36. ACCORDING TO THE SAME RULES: Some such formula introduces each

30 king, according to your urgent purpose." ³⁰But the king was filled with heavy anger at these words, because by God's Providence in this matter all his reason had been dispersed; he fixed his eye upon him menacingly, and said: ³¹"If your parents were here, or your offspring, I had served them as a rich repast to these savage beasts in place of the Jews, against whom I have no complaint, and who have shown me and my ancestors full and firm loyalty in extraordinary measure. ³²Indeed, if it were not for the affection of our common upbringing and your service, you would have forfeited your life in their place." ³³Thus Hermon met with an unlooked-for and dangerous threat, and he shrank in aspect and visage. ³⁴The king's friends slunk away sullenly one by one, and dismissed the assembled folk each to his own business. ³⁵The
35 Jews, when they heard what transpired before the king, praised the Lord, the God manifest, the King of Kings, having obtained this help from Him also.

³⁶Now the king arranged the banquet anew according to the same rules, and bade the company address themselves to good cheer. ³⁷Hermon he summoned, and said to him menacingly, "How often, wretched creature, must I give you orders about the very same things? ³⁸Make the elephants ready directly for tomorrow, for the annihilation of the Jews." ³⁹But his Kinsmen, who reclined at table with him, wondered at the instability of his purpose, and remonstrated with him
40 as follows: ⁴⁰"How long, O king, will you make trial of us as though we were fools? For the third time now you are ordering this people to be destroyed; and again when the matter is in hand, you change your purpose and cancel what you have decreed. ⁴¹As a result the city is in tumult because of its expectation; it is filled with throngs of people, and frequently in peril of being ravaged."

⁴²Thereupon the king, who was in every respect a very

---

of the seven successive banquets in Aristeas.
39. KINSMEN: Like "Friends," a court title, but of higher grade.
42. PHALARIS: See on 5.20.

Ἰουδαίων ἐν αὐτῷ μεταβολὰς τῆς ψυχῆς παρ' οὐδὲν ἡγούμενος
ἀτελέστατον βεβαίως ὅρκον ὁρισάμενος τούτους μὲν ἀνυπερθέτως πέμψειν εἰς ᾅδην ἐν γόνασιν καὶ ποσὶν θηρίων ἠκισ-
μένους, ⁴³ἐπιστρατεύσαντα δὲ ἐπὶ τὴν Ἰουδαίαν ἰσόπεδον
πυρὶ καὶ δόρατι θήσεσθαι διὰ τάχους καὶ τὸν ἄβατον ἡμῖν
αὐτῶν ναὸν πυρὶ πρηνέα ἐν τάχει τῶν συντελούντων ἐκεῖ
θυσίας ἔρημον εἰς τὸν ἅπαντα χρόνον καταστήσειν. ⁴⁴τότε
περιχαρεῖς ἀναλύσαντες οἱ φίλοι καὶ συγγενεῖς μετὰ πίστεως
διέτασσον τὰς δυνάμεις ἐπὶ τοὺς εὐκαιροτάτους τόπους τῆς
45 πόλεως πρὸς τὴν τήρησιν. ⁴⁵ὁ δὲ ἐλεφαντάρχης τὰ θηρία
σχεδὸν ὡς εἰπεῖν εἰς κατάστεμα μανιῶδες ἀγειοχὼς εὐωδεστάτοις πόμασιν οἴνου λελιβανωμένου φοβερῶς κεκοσμημένα
κατασκευαῖς ⁴⁶περὶ τὴν ἕω τῆς πόλεως ἤδη πλήθεσιν ἀναριθμήτοις κατὰ τοῦ ἱπποδρόμου καταμεμεστωμένης εἰσελθὼν
εἰς τὴν αὐλὴν ἐπὶ τὸ προκείμενον ὤτρυνε τὸν βασιλέα. ⁴⁷ὁ
δὲ ὀργῇ βαρείᾳ γεμίσας δυσσεβῆ φρένα παντὶ τῷ βάρει
σὺν τοῖς θηρίοις ἐξώρμησε βουλόμενος ἀτρώτῳ καρδίᾳ καὶ
κόραις ὀφθαλμῶν θεάσασθαι τὴν ἐπίπονον καὶ ταλαίπωρον
τῶν προσεσημαμμένων καταστροφήν. ⁴⁸ὡς δὲ τῶν ἐλεφάντων
ἐξιόντων περὶ πύλην καὶ τῆς συνεπομένης ἐνόπλου δυνάμεως
τῆς τε τοῦ πλήθους πορείας κονιορτὸν ἰδόντες καὶ βαρυηχῆ
θόρυβον ἀκούσαντες οἱ Ἰουδαῖοι ⁴⁹ὑστάτην βίου ῥοπὴν αὐτοῖς
ἐκείνην δόξαντες εἶναι τὸ τέλος τῆς ἀθλιωτάτης προσδοκίας
εἰς οἶκτον καὶ γόους τραπέντες κατεφίλουν ἀλλήλους περι-
πλεκόμενοι τοῖς συγγενέσιν ἐπὶ τοὺς τραχήλους ἐπιπίπ-
τοντες, γονεῖς παισὶν καὶ μητέρες νεάνισιν, ἕτεραι δὲ νεογνὰ
πρὸς μαστοὺς ἔχουσαι βρέφη τελευταῖον ἕλκοντα γάλα.
50 ⁵⁰οὐ μὴν δὲ ἀλλὰ καὶ τὰς ἔμπροσθεν αὐτῶν γεγενημένας
ἀντιλήμψεις ἐξ οὐρανοῦ συνιδόντες πρηνεῖς ὁμοθυμαδὸν

43 πρηνεα) πρην A+, πρη(σα)ν(τα)   45 ειπειν) –πεν A+
Swete / ερημον L) A omits

43. CAMPAIGN AGAINST JUDAEA: The awkwardness of this sentence is indicated by its textual difficulties; it reads like an afterthought, the author's or another's.
45. ARMAMENT: Apparently scythes and knives attached to the beasts, as they were to war chariots.
49. EMBRACED: In so high-flown and withal moving an account it would

Phalaris, was filled with madness. The changes of spirit which had been wrought in him for the protection of the Jews he took no account of, but swore a mighty but futile oath that he would inexorably dispatch the Egyptian Jews to Hades, mangled by the knees and feet of the beasts, ⁴³and then campaign against Judaea and speedily raze it to the ground with fire and sword; he would speedily burn with fire the Temple to which he was denied admission, and for all time make it desolate of any that offered sacrifice there. ⁴⁴Then his friends and Kinsmen departed in high glee and with full assurance, and they ordered troops to convenient spots in the city to keep watch. ⁴⁵The superintendent of the elephants drove the beasts to a state, one might say, almost of madness, with fragrant draughts of wine mingled with frankincense, and accoutered them fearfully with armament. ⁴⁶About dawn, when the city was already filled full with countless multitudes streaming to the hippodrome, he entered the palace and urged the business in hand upon the king. ⁴⁷The king's impious heart was filled with fierce fury, and with great vehemence he started forth along with the beasts, wishing to gaze with heart unfeeling and with his own eyes upon the grievous and piteous catastrophe of those we have described. ⁴⁸And now, when the elephants came out at the gate, and the Jews saw the cloud of dust raised by the armed troops following them and by the progress of the crowd, and when they heard the deep resounding noise, ⁴⁹they thought that this was their very last mortal crisis and the end of their miserable suspense. They betook themselves to lamentations and groans, they kissed one another, they embraced their relatives, falling upon their necks, parents and children, mothers and daughters; some had newborn infants at their breasts, drawing their last milk. ⁵⁰Nevertheless they reflected upon their former heaven-sent deliverances, and with one

---

be ungracious to object that the victims had their hands bound (5.5).
50. REMOVED THE BABES: A realistic touch, to give verisimiltude to their flinging themselves on the ground and making supplication.

ῥίψαντες ἑαυτοὺς καὶ τὰ νήπια χωρίσαντες τῶν μαστῶν ⁵¹ἀνεβόησαν φωνῇ μεγάλῃ σφόδρα τὸν τῆς ἁπάσης δυνάμεως δυνάστην ἱκετεύοντες οἰκτῖραι μετὰ ἐπιφανείας αὐτοὺς ἤδη πρὸς πύλαις ᾅδου καθεστῶτας.

6 ¹Ελεαζαρος δέ τις ἀνὴρ ἐπίσημος τῶν ἀπὸ τῆς χώρας ἱερέων, ἐν πρεσβείῳ τὴν ἡλικίαν ἤδη λελογχὼς καὶ πάσῃ τῇ κατὰ τὸν βίον ἀρετῇ κεκοσμημένος, τοὺς περὶ αὐτὸν καταστείλας πρεσβυτέρους ἐπικαλεῖσθαι τὸν ἅγιον θεὸν προσηύξατο τάδε ²Βασιλεῦ μεγαλοκράτωρ, ὕψιστε παντοκράτωρ θεὲ τὴν πᾶσαν διακυβερνῶν ἐν οἰκτιρμοῖς κτίσιν, ³ἔπιδε ἐπὶ Αβρααμ σπέρμα, ἐπὶ ἡγιασμένου τέκνα Ιακωβ, μερίδος ἡγιασμένης σου λαὸν ἐν ξένῃ γῇ ξένον ἀδίκως ἀπολλύμενον, πάτερ. ⁴σὺ Φαραω πληθύνοντα ἅρμασιν, τὸν πρὶν Αἰγύπτου ταύτης δυνάστην, ἐπαρθέντα ἀνόμῳ θράσει καὶ γλώσσῃ μεγαλορρήμονι, σὺν τῇ ὑπερηφάνῳ στρατιᾷ ποντοβρόχους ἀπώλεσας φέγγος ἐπιφάνας ἐλέους Ισραηλ γένει. ⁵⁵σὺ τὸν ἀναριθμήτοις δυνάμεσιν γαυρωθέντα Σενναχηριμ, βαρὺν Ἀσσυρίων βασιλέα, δόρατι τὴν πᾶσαν ὑποχείριον

---

51 δυναμεως) A omits

VI

1 ιερεων) ιουδαιων A+

1–15. *The prayer of Eleazar.* The simpler language of this prayer is in marked contrast to the rhetorical embellishment of what precedes and follows. Like Simon's prayer in 2.1–20, it is plainly Jewish in form and language, and perhaps a direct translation from a Heb. original. Its Hebraisms are like those noted in Simon's prayer; and it even more plainly follows the scheme of listing historical manifestations of God on behalf of Israel, on the analogy of Ps. 105 and 106, as an introduction to a petition for present help.

1. ELEAZAR: Like "Simon," a favorite name for a hero of the spirit. One thinks (as he is doubtless meant to) of the martyr of II Maccabees, of the Eleazar of IV Maccabees, of the High Priest in Aristeas.   PRIESTS: The variant reading "Jews" is probably motivated by the incongruity of "priests" in Egypt. But "priests" seems to be the correct reading; and may refer to those of Onias' temple at Leontopolis, or the word may have come to be used (like כהן) in a broader sense; *cf.* 7.13.   TO CEASE CALLING seems as odd with "priests," from what we know of Jewish practice. Perhaps the author has in mind some customary signal used to

accord flung themselves prone; they removed the babes from their breasts, ⁵¹and cried out with an exceedingly loud cry, supplicating the Ruler of all power by a manifestation to take pity upon them that were now standing at the very gates of death.

6 ¹Now a certain Eleazar, a man of note among the priests of the country, whose years had already reached old age, and who was adorned with every virtue of life, directed the Elders who were around him to cease calling upon the Holy God, and prayed as follows: ²King great in power, Most High, Almighty God, Who governest all creation with lovingkindness, ³look upon the seed of Abraham, the children of Jacob Thy sanctified one, the people of Thy sanctified inheritance, who are unjustly perishing, strangers in a strange land. O Father, ⁴Pharaoh, the former ruler of this Egypt, with his multitude of chariots, when he was lifted high with his lawless insolence and a tongue speaking great things, Thou didst destroy with his proud host in the depths of the sea, and didst cause the light of Thy mercy to shine upon the people of Israel. ⁵Thou, when Sennacherib, the cruel king of the Assyrians, was puffed up with his countless hosts, after he

---

indicate that a public prayer was about to be pronounced by a precentor.
6.2 The opening of this prayer is very like the opening of the *'Amidah*, which includes all the attributes of God mentioned here.
3. SEED OF ABRAHAM: Αβρααμ σπέρμα is a manifest Hebraism, זרע אברהם.
4. PHARAOH: It is quite normal for any list of deliverances to begin with Pharaoh, and if our author adapted an existing prayer the parallel of history would have attracted him. THE FORMER RULER OF THIS EGYPT: Might then be a simple addition to emphasize the parallel. It is striking that in this rather complete list the deliverance of Esther is not mentioned, though the parallel is very close. It has been argued from the omission that III Maccabees was written before Esther became known in Egypt, or, as is more likely, that our author intentionally ignored it; see Introd. 24.
5. SENNACHERIB: *Cf.* 11 Kings 19.35. It is to be noted that the Scriptural passage speaks of "an angel of the Lord" smiting the Assyrians, whereas in the present passage God acts directly. This is in keeping with our author's conscious avoidance of divine intermediaries; see on 6.18.

ἤδη λαβόντα γῆν καὶ μετεωρισθέντα ἐπὶ τὴν ἁγίαν σου πόλιν, βαρέα λαλοῦντα κόμπῳ καὶ θράσει σύ, δέσποτα, ἔθραυσας ἔκδηλον δεικνὺς ἔθνεσιν πολλοῖς τὸ σὸν κράτος. ⁶σὺ τοὺς κατὰ τὴν Βαβυλωνίαν τρεῖς ἑταίρους πυρὶ τὴν ψυχὴν αὐθαιρέτως δεδωκότας εἰς τὸ μὴ λατρεῦσαι τοῖς κενοῖς διάπυρον δροσίσας κάμινον ἐρρύσω μέχρι τριχὸς ἀπημάντους φλόγα πᾶσιν ἐπιπέμψας τοῖς ὑπεναντίοις. ⁷σὺ τὸν διαβολαῖς φθόνου λέουσι κατὰ γῆς ῥιφέντα θηρσὶν βορὰν Δανιηλ εἰς φῶς ἀνήγαγες ἀσινῆ. ⁸τόν τε βυθοτρεφοῦς ἐν γαστρὶ κήτους Ιωναν τηκόμενον ἀφιδὼν ἀπήμαντον πᾶσιν οἰκείοις ἀνέδειξας, πάτερ. ⁹καὶ νῦν, μίσυβρι πολυέλεε τῶν ὅλων σκεπαστά, τὸ τάχος ἐπιφάνηθι τοῖς ἀπὸ Ισραηλ γένους ὑπὸ ἐβδελυγμένων 10 ἀνόμων ἐθνῶν ὑβριζομένοις. ¹⁰εἰ δὲ ἀσεβείαις κατὰ τὴν ἀποικίαν ὁ βίος ἡμῶν ἐνέσχηται, ῥυσάμενος ἡμᾶς ἀπὸ ἐχθρῶν χειρός, ᾧ προαιρῇ, δέσποτα, ἀπόλεσον ἡμᾶς μόρῳ. ¹¹μὴ τοῖς ματαίοις οἱ ματαιόφρονες εὐλογησάτωσαν ἐπὶ τῇ τῶν ἠγαπημένων σου ἀπωλείᾳ λέγοντες Οὐδὲ ὁ θεὸς αὐτῶν ἐρρύσατο αὐτούς. ¹²σὺ δέ, ὁ πᾶσαν ἀλκὴν καὶ δυναστείαν ἔχων ἅπασαν αἰώνιε, νῦν ἔπιδε· ἐλέησον ἡμᾶς τοὺς καθ' ὕβριν ἀνόμων ἀλόγιστον ἐκ τοῦ ζῆν μεθισταμένους ἐν ἐπιβούλων τρόπῳ. ¹³πτηξάτω δὲ ἔθνη σὴν δύναμιν ἀνίκητον σήμερον, ἔντιμε δύναμιν ἔχων ἐπὶ σωτηρίᾳ Ιακωβ γένους. ¹⁴ἱκετεύει σε τὸ πᾶν πλῆθος τῶν νηπίων καὶ οἱ τούτων γονεῖς μετὰ δακρύων. 15 ¹⁵δειχθήτω πᾶσιν ἔθνεσιν ὅτι μεθ' ἡμῶν εἶ, κύριε, καὶ οὐκ ἀπέστρεψας τὸ πρόσωπόν σου ἀφ' ἡμῶν, ἀλλὰ καθὼς εἶπας ὅτι Οὐδὲ ἐν τῇ γῇ τῶν ἐχθρῶν αὐτῶν ὄντων ὑπερεῖδον αὐτούς, οὕτως ἐπιτέλεσον, κύριε.

---

8 αφιδων A+) αφελων V+, επιδων L, A+
αφειδως several 10 ω AL) ως V
9 σκεπταστα) δικαστα A+) απο) αγιοις 13 εντιμε δυναμιν) εν τινι με δυναμει A+

6. THREE COMPANIONS IN BABYLONIA: Apparently a citation of LXX Dan. 3.50, and hence an important indication of date: see Introd. 19. UNHARMED . . . HAIR: *Cf.* Dan. 3.27: "Nor was the hair of their head singed."   AND DIDST SEND THE FLAME: *Cf.* Add. to Dan. 25.
7. DANIEL: *Cf.* Dan. 6.24.
8. RESTORE . . . TO HIS HOUSEHOLD: This restoration of Jonah is not mentioned in the Bible.

had made the whole earth subject to his spear, and was lifted up against Thy holy city, uttering grievous words of boasting and insolence, Thou, Lord, didst break him in pieces, making Thy power manifest to many peoples. ⁶Thou, when the three companions in Babylonia did freely give their life to the flames that they should not serve vain things, didst make the fiery furnace as dew and didst deliver them unharmed, even to their very hair, and didst send the flame upon all their adversaries. ⁷Thou, when by the slanders of envy Daniel was cast to lions underground as food for wild beasts, didst bring him up to the light unhurt. ⁸And when Jonah was languishing unpitied in the belly of the sea-nurtured monster, Thou didst free him, Father, and restore him uninjured to all his household. ⁹So now, Thou hater of insolence, rich in mercy, Protector of all, speedily manifest Thyself to those of the people of Israel who are being insolently entreated by the abominable and lawless heathen. ¹⁰If our life is forfeit by reason of irreverent deeds during our foreign sojourn, deliver us from the hand of the enemy, Lord, and destroy us by whatever fate Thou mayest choose. ¹¹Let not those whose thoughts are vanity bless their vanities for the destruction of those beloved of Thee, saying 'Neither did their God deliver them.' ¹²Thou that dost possess all might and all power, Thou Eternal, look now upon us; pity us who by the mad insolence of lawless men are being put to death after the manner of traitors. ¹³Let the heathen fear Thine invincible might this day, O Thou revered One, Who hast done mighty works for the salvation of the people of Jacob. ¹⁴This whole multitude of babes with their parents beseeches Thee with tears. ¹⁵Let it be shown to all the heathen that Thou art with us, Lord, and hast not turned Thy face away from us; but even as Thou hast said, 'Not even when they were in the land of their enemies have I forgotten them,' so bring it to pass, O Lord."

---

11. LET NOT THOSE: *Cf.* Wis. 2.16 ff.; Ps. 115.2.
15. NOT EVEN ... : *Cf.* Lev. 26.44.

¹⁶Τοῦ δὲ Ελεαζαρου λήγοντος ἄρτι τῆς προσευχῆς ὁ βασιλεὺς σὺν τοῖς θηρίοις καὶ παντὶ τῷ τῆς δυνάμεως φρυάγματι κατὰ τὸν ἱππόδρομον παρῆγεν. ¹⁷καὶ θεωρήσαντες οἱ Ιουδαῖοι μέγα εἰς οὐρανὸν ἀνέκραξαν ὥστε καὶ τοὺς παρακειμένους αὐλῶνας συνηχήσαντας ἀκατάσχετον πτόην ποιῆσαι παντὶ τῷ στρατοπέδῳ. ¹⁸τότε ὁ μεγαλόδοξος παντοκράτωρ καὶ ἀληθινὸς θεὸς ἐπιφάνας τὸ ἅγιον αὐτοῦ πρόσωπον ἠνέῳξεν τὰς οὐρανίους πύλας, ἐξ ὧν δεδοξασμένοι δύο φοβεροειδεῖς ἄγγελοι κατέβησαν φανεροὶ πᾶσιν πλὴν τοῖς Ιουδαίοις ¹⁹καὶ ἀντέστησαν καὶ τὴν δύναμιν τῶν ὑπεναντίων ἐπλήρωσαν ταραχῆς καὶ δειλίας καὶ ἀκινήτοις ἔδησαν πέδαις. ²⁰καὶ ὑπόφρικον καὶ τὸ τοῦ βασιλέως σῶμα ἐγενήθη, καὶ λήθη τὸ θράσος αὐτοῦ τὸ βαρύθυμον ἔλαβεν. ²¹καὶ ἀπέστρεψαν τὰ θηρία ἐπὶ τὰς συνεπομένας ἐνόπλους δυνάμεις καὶ κατεπάτουν αὐτὰς καὶ ὠλέθρευον.

²²Καὶ μετεστράφη τοῦ βασιλέως ἡ ὀργὴ εἰς οἶκτον καὶ δάκρυα ὑπὲρ τῶν ἔμπροσθεν αὐτῷ μεμηχανευμένων. ²³ἀκούσας γὰρ τῆς κραυγῆς καὶ συνιδὼν πρηνεῖς ἅπαντας εἰς τὴν ἀπώλειαν δακρύσας μετ' ὀργῆς τοῖς φίλοις διηπειλεῖτο λέγων ²⁴Παραβασιλεύετε καὶ τυράννους ὑπερβεβήκατε ὠμότητι καὶ ἐμὲ αὐτὸν τὸν ὑμῶν εὐεργέτην ἐπιχειρεῖτε τῆς ἀρχῆς ἤδη καὶ τοῦ πνεύματος μεθιστᾶν λάθρᾳ μηχανώμενοι τὰ μὴ συμφέροντα τῇ βασιλείᾳ. ²⁵τίς τοὺς κρατήσαντας ἡμῶν ἐν πίστει τὰ τῆς χώρας ὀχυρώματα τῆς οἰκίας ἀποστήσας ἕκαστον ἀλόγως ἤθροισεν ἐνθάδε; ²⁶τίς τοὺς ἐξ ἀρχῆς εὐνοίᾳ πρὸς ἡμᾶς κατὰ πάντα διαφέροντας πάντων ἐθνῶν καὶ τοὺς χειρίστους πλεονάκις ἀνθρώπων ἐπιδεδεγ-

---

17 πτοην) many have οιμωγην, V omits   25 αποστησας) αποδησας VL
18 παντοκρατωρ) A+ prefix και

16–29. *The Jews are delivered, and the king now favors them.* The dramatic change of fortune is presented with great effectiveness, which is enhanced by reason of its taking place before a great concourse.
18. ANGELS: The apparition is an integral part of the story, being mentioned in the Josephus parallel, and could not be omitted. Similar terror-inspiring apparitions are found in II Mac. 3.24 ff., 10.29; Wis. 17.3, 15, 18.17. The appearance of a divine apparition at a critical juncture on behalf of the ostensibly weaker party is familiar in pagan literature also;

¹⁶Just as Eleazar was bringing his prayer to a close, the king with the wild beasts and the entire insolent array of his army came to the hippodrome. ¹⁷When the Jews observed this, they raised a very great cry to heaven, so that the adjacent valleys resounded with it, and caused an uncontrollable trembling in all the hosts. ¹⁸Then the greatly glorious, almighty, and true God, making His countenance manifest, opened the gates of heaven, from which two glorified angels of terrible aspect descended, visible to all except the Jews, ¹⁹and they confronted the force of their adversaries, and filled them with confusion and terror, and bound them with immovable fetters. ²⁰And a great horror seized the body of the king also, and oblivion covered his vehement insolence. ²¹And the beasts turned back on the armed hosts that followed them, and began to tread them down and destroy them.

²²The king's wrath was turned to pity and tears for the things he had previously devised. ²³For when he heard the outcry and saw them all prostrate to meet their death, he wept, and angrily threatened his friends, saying, ²⁴"You usurp the kingly power, and you surpass the tyrants in cruelty; you are even endeavoring to deprive me, your benefactor, of my rule and even of my life, secretly contriving, as you do, measures disadvantageous to my kingship. ²⁵Who has driven from their homes those who faithfully kept our country's strongholds, and foolishly gathered them, every one, here? ²⁶Who has so unlawfully overwhelmed with indignities those who from the beginning have been more conspicuous than all peoples in their good will toward us, and who have frequently encountered mankind's worst dan-

---

such apparitions are mentioned in connection with the battles of Marathon and Salamis.   VISIBLE TO ALL EXCEPT THE JEWS: This seems difficult to explain except as an effort to reconcile the received story, to which the apparition was indispensable, with the author's belief (possibly asserted in refutation of a contrary opinion; see Introd. 26), which had no place for intermediary forces. *Cf.* on 6.5.
21. THE BEASTS TURNED: This detail is also found in the Josephus parallel.
25. STRONGHOLDS: See on 3.21.

μένους κινδύνους οὕτως ἀθέσμως περιέβαλεν αἰκίαις; ²⁷λύσατε ἐκλύσατε ἄδικα δεσμά· εἰς τὰ ἴδια μετ' εἰρήνης ἐξαποστείλατε τὰ προπεπραγμένα παραιτησάμενοι. ²⁸ἀπολύσατε τοὺς υἱοὺς τοῦ παντοκράτορος ἐπουρανίου θεοῦ ζῶντος, ὃς ἀφ' ἡμετέρων μέχρι τοῦ νῦν προγόνων ἀπαραπόδιστον μετὰ δόξης εὐστάθειαν παρέχει τοῖς ἡμετέροις πράγμασιν. ²⁹ὁ μὲν οὖν ταῦτα ἔλεξεν· οἱ δὲ ἐν ἀμερεῖ χρόνῳ λυθέντες τὸν ἅγιον σωτῆρα θεὸν αὐτῶν εὐλόγουν ἄρτι τὸν θάνατον ἐκπεφευγότες.

³⁰Εἶτα ὁ βασιλεὺς εἰς τὴν πόλιν ἀπαλλαγεὶς τὸν ἐπὶ τῶν προσόδων προσκαλεσάμενος ἐκέλευσεν οἴνους τε καὶ τὰ λοιπὰ πρὸς εὐωχίαν ἐπιτήδεια τοῖς Ιουδαίοις χορηγεῖν ἐπὶ ἡμέρας ἑπτὰ κρίνας αὐτοὺς ἐν ᾧ τόπῳ ἔδοξαν τὸν ὄλεθρον ἀναλαμβάνειν, ἐν τούτῳ ἐν εὐφροσύνῃ πάσῃ σωτήρια ἀγαγεῖν. ³¹τότε οἱ τὸ πρὶν ἐπονείδιστοι καὶ πλησίον τοῦ ᾅδου, μᾶλλον δὲ ἐπ' αὐτῷ βεβηκότες ἀντὶ πικροῦ καὶ δυσαιάκτου μόρου κώθωνα σωτήριον συστησάμενοι τὸν εἰς πτῶσιν αὐτοῖς καὶ τάφον ἡτοιμασμένον τόπον κλισίαις κατεμερίσαντο πλήρεις χαρμονῆς. ³²καταλήξαντες δὲ θρήνων πανόδυρτον μέλος ἀνέλαβον ᾠδὴν πάτριον τὸν σωτῆρα καὶ τερατοποιὸν αἰνοῦντες θεόν· οἰμωγήν τε πᾶσαν καὶ κωκυτὸν ἀπωσάμενοι χοροὺς συνίσταντο εὐφροσύνης εἰρηνικῆς σημεῖον. ³³ὡσαύτως δὲ καὶ ὁ βασιλεὺς περὶ τούτων συμπόσιον βαρὺ συναγαγὼν ἀδιαλείπτως εἰς οὐρανὸν ἀνθωμολογεῖτο μεγαλομερῶς ἐπὶ τῇ παραδόξῳ γενηθείσῃ αὐτῷ σωτηρίᾳ. ³⁴οἵ τε πρὶν εἰς ὄλεθρον καὶ οἰωνοβρώτους αὐτοὺς ἔσεσθαι τιθέμενοι καὶ μετὰ χαρᾶς

---

27 προπεπραγμ.) προστεταγμ. A+   32 σωτηρα) ισραηλ V+, ισραηλ ορα A+
28 παρεχει) προφερει A+   34 ακλεως) ακμαιως A+
30 απαλλαγεις) A+ omit

30–41. *The Jews celebrate their deliverance.* The intention of this passage seems to be aetiological, *i.e.*, the explanation of the origin of an established festival, apparently celebrated in Alexandria. The festival for which the *aition* is supplied in 7.19 seems to have been located at Ptolemais. The duplication may be due to awkward dovetailing of the Alexandrian elephant episode into the older tradition of Philopator, and may also reflect partisan views on the proper date and locale of a current festival; see Introd. 24.

31. THOSE WHO HAD BEEN REVILED ...: The author is specially concerned, in the manner of tragedy and romance, to emphasize the melodramatic

gers on our behalf? ²⁷Loose their unjust bonds, loose them utterly; send them back to their own in peace, when you have begged their forgiveness for what has already been done. ²⁸Set free the children of the Almighty and heavenly living God, who from the days of our ancestors until now has conferred upon our estate unimpaired stability and glory." ²⁹These things the king said; the Jews were set free in an instant, and praised the Holy God their Savior, having but just escaped death.

³⁰Then the king, returning to the city, summoned the official in charge of revenues, and bade him supply the Jews with wine and other things appropriate for a feast for seven days; judging it meet that in that place where they had expected destruction to overtake them, there they should celebrate with all gladness a festival of deliverance. ³¹Then did those who had been reviled and had been brought near Hades, nay, to its very gate, instead of a bitter and grievous fate celebrate a festival of deliverance; filled with joy, they apportioned to festive groups the space that had been made ready for their fall and their burial. ³²They put an end to the piteous strain of dirges, and raised their ancestral chant, praising God, the deliverer and worker of wonders. They put away every sort of lamentation and wailing, and formed dances in token of their peaceful good cheer. ³³The king likewise assembled a weighty banquet on account of these things, and rendered solemn thanks to heaven unceasingly for the deliverance which had so unexpectedly been vouchsafed him. ³⁴But those who had supposed that the Jews were doomed to destruction and to be a prey for birds, and had joyfully

---

reversal: black despair is suddenly converted to jubilation, gloating success to humiliation.
32. CHANT . . . DANCES: Perhaps an echo of the prescriptions for an actual festival, in which mournful Psalms or the like would be omitted and joyful ones substituted.
33-34. KING . . . BANQUET: A decision taken at a king's banquet which causes discomfiture to high-placed enemies of the Jews is strikingly like Esth. 9.

ἀπογραψάμενοι κατεστέναξαν αἰσχύνην ἐφ' ἑαυτοῖς περιβαλόμενοι καὶ τὴν πυρόπνουν τόλμαν ἀκλεῶς ἐσβεσμένοι. 35 ³⁵οἵ τε Ἰουδαῖοι, καθὼς προειρήκαμεν, συστησάμενοι τὸν προειρημένον χορὸν μετ' εὐωχίας ἐν ἐξομολογήσεσιν ἱλαραῖς καὶ ψαλμοῖς διῆγον. ³⁶καὶ κοινὸν ὁρισάμενοι περὶ τούτων θεσμὸν ἐπὶ πᾶσαν τὴν παροικίαν αὐτῶν εἰς γενεὰς τὰς προειρημένας ἡμέρας ἄγειν ἔστησαν εὐφροσύνους, οὐ πότου χάριν καὶ λιχνείας, σωτηρίας δὲ τῆς διὰ θεὸν γενομένης αὐτοῖς. ³⁷ἐνέτυχον δὲ τῷ βασιλεῖ τὴν ἀπόλυσιν αὐτῶν εἰς τὰ ἴδια αἰτούμενοι. ³⁸ἀπογράφονται δὲ αὐτοὺς ἀπὸ πέμπτης καὶ εἰκάδος τοῦ Παχων ἕως τῆς τετάρτης τοῦ Επιφι ἐπὶ ἡμέρας τεσσαράκοντα, συνίστανται δὲ αὐτῶν τὴν ἀπώλειαν ἀπὸ πέμπτης τοῦ Επιφι ἕως ἑβδόμης ἡμέραις τρισίν, ³⁹ἐν αἷς καὶ μεγαλοδόξως ἐπιφάνας τὸ ἔλεος αὐτοῦ ὁ τῶν πάντων 40 δυνάστης ἀπταίστους αὐτοὺς ἐρρύσατο ὁμοθυμαδόν. ⁴⁰εὐωχοῦντο δὲ πανθ' ὑπὸ τοῦ βασιλέως χορηγούμενοι μέχρι τῆς τεσσαρεσκαιδεκάτης, ἐν ᾗ καὶ τὴν ἐντυχίαν ἐποιήσαντο περὶ τῆς ἀπολύσεως αὐτῶν. ⁴¹συναινέσας δὲ αὐτοῖς ὁ βασιλεὺς ἔγραψεν αὐτοῖς τὴν ὑπογεγραμμένην ἐπιστολὴν πρὸς τοὺς κατὰ πόλιν στρατηγοὺς μεγαλοψύχως τὴν ἐκτενίαν ἔχουσαν.

7 ¹Βασιλεὺς Πτολεμαῖος Φιλοπάτωρ τοῖς κατ' Αἴγυπτον στρατηγοῖς καὶ πᾶσιν τοῖς τεταγμένοις ἐπὶ πραγμάτων χαίρειν καὶ ἐρρῶσθαι· ²ἐρρώμεθα δὲ καὶ αὐτοὶ καὶ τὰ τέκνα ἡμῶν κατευθύναντος ἡμῖν τοῦ μεγάλου θεοῦ τὰ πράγματα, καθὼς προαιρούμεθα. ³τῶν φίλων τινὲς κατὰ κακοήθειαν πυκνότερον ἡμῖν παρακείμενοι συνέπεισαν ἡμᾶς εἰς τὸ τοὺς

---

35 χορον) χρονον A, χρον V+   VII

2 πραγματα) προσταγματα A+

---

35. AS WE HAVE SAID ... AFOREMENTIONED: This is a particularly awkward juncture with 32, and suggests that the author found the parallel to Esther (mentioned in the previous note) so irresistible that he included it anyhow.
36. ESTABLISHED ... A FESTIVAL: This festival is not elsewhere recorded, except in the Josephus parallel; but even aside from Esther such festivals are a common feature in the literature of the period: cf. I Mac. 4.56, 6.59, 13.50; II Mac. 10.6, 15.36; (Vulgate) Jud. 16.25.

registered their names, now groaned, because they were overwhelmed with shame, and their fiery blast of insolence was ingloriously quenched. ³⁵But the Jews, as we have said, set up the aforementioned dance and passed the time in festivity, with joyful thanksgiving and psalms. ³⁶And they instituted a general law concerning these things, for all their community throughout the generations: they established that the aforementioned days should be celebrated as a festival, not for the sake of drinking and gluttony, but for the deliverance that had come to them through God. ³⁷And they procured their request of the king to be dismissed to their homes.

³⁸Their registration had continued from the 25th of Pachon to the 4th of Epiphi, forty days. Their destruction was appointed from the 5th of Epiphi to the 7th, three days. ³⁹On these days did the Ruler of all with great glory manifest His mercy and did deliver them unharmed, one and all. ⁴⁰They feasted, being supplied by the king with all things, until the 14th, on which day they made petition concerning their departure. ⁴¹The king consented to their request, and wrote on their behalf the subjoined letter to the generals in the cities, magnanimously declaring his purpose.

7 ¹"King Ptolemy Philopator to the generals in Egypt and to those in charge of administration, greetings and good health: ²We too enjoy good health, and our children also, the great God directing our estate as our desire is. ³Certain of our friends, by continually pressing it upon us in the evil of their

---

38. PACHON ... EPIPHI: Pachon, April 26 to May 25; Epiphi, June 25 to July 24. For a similar precise reckoning *cf.* Esth. 9.22.

1–9. *Philopator's letter on behalf of the Jews*. This letter, unlike the other "documents" used in this book, seems largely fictional, both because of inherent improbability and because of factual errors and unconvincing style.
1. PHILOPATOR: See on 3.12.
2. OUR CHILDREN: Philopator had only one son, born in 209/8. Our author's knowledge of Philopator's life and times is less sure here than in the first three chapters.

ὑπὸ τὴν βασιλείαν Ἰουδαίους συναθροίσαντας σύστημα κολάσασθαι ξενιζούσαις ἀποστατῶν τιμωρίαις ⁴προφερόμενοι μηδέποτε εὐσταθήσειν τὰ πράγματα ἡμῶν δι' ἣν ἔχουσιν οὗτοι πρὸς πάντα τὰ ἔθνη δυσμένειαν, μέχρι ἂν συντελεσθῇ 5 τοῦτο. ⁵οἳ καὶ δεσμίους καταγαγόντες αὐτοὺς μετὰ σκυλμῶν ὡς ἀνδράποδα, μᾶλλον δὲ ὡς ἐπιβούλους, ἄνευ πάσης ἀνακρίσεως καὶ ἐξετάσεως ἐπεχείρησαν ἀνελεῖν νόμου Σκυθῶν ἀγριωτέραν ἐμπεπορπημένοι ὠμότητα. ⁶ἡμεῖς δὲ ἐπὶ τούτοις σκληρότερον διαπειλησάμενοι καθ' ἣν ἔχομεν πρὸς ἅπαντας ἀνθρώπους ἐπιείκειαν μόγις τὸ ζῆν αὐτοῖς χαρισάμενοι καὶ τὸν ἐπουράνιον θεὸν ἐγνωκότες ἀσφαλῶς ὑπερησπικότα τῶν Ἰουδαίων ὡς πατέρα ὑπὲρ υἱῶν διὰ παντὸς συμμαχοῦντα ⁷τήν τε τοῦ φίλου ἣν ἔχουσιν βεβαίαν πρὸς ἡμᾶς καὶ τοὺς προγόνους ἡμῶν εὔνοιαν ἀναλογισάμενοι δικαίως ἀπολελύκαμεν πάσης καθ' ὁντινοῦν αἰτίας τρόπον ⁸καὶ προστετάχαμεν ἑκάστῳ πάντας εἰς τὰ ἴδια ἐπιστρέφειν ἐν παντὶ τόπῳ μηθενὸς αὐτοὺς τὸ σύνολον καταβλάπτοντος μήτε ὀνειδίζειν περὶ τῶν γεγενημένων παρὰ λόγον. ⁹γινώσκετε γὰρ ὅτι κατὰ τούτων ἐάν τι κακοτεχνήσωμεν πονηρὸν ἢ ἐπιλυπήσωμεν αὐτοὺς τὸ σύνολον, οὐκ ἄνθρωπον, ἀλλὰ τὸν πάσης δεσπόζοντα δυνάμεως θεὸν ὕψιστον ἀντικείμενον ἡμῖν ἐπ' ἐκδικήσει τῶν πραγμάτων κατὰ πᾶν ἀφεύκτως διὰ παντὸς ἕξομεν. ἔρρωσθε.

10 ¹⁰Λαβόντες δὲ τὴν ἐπιστολὴν ταύτην οὐκ ἐσπούδασαν εὐθέως γενέσθαι περὶ τὴν ἄφοδον, ἀλλὰ τὸν βασιλέα προσηξίωσαν τοὺς ἐκ τοῦ γένους τῶν Ἰουδαίων τὸν ἅγιον θεὸν αὐθαιρέτως παραβεβηκότας καὶ τοῦ θεοῦ τὸν νόμον τυχεῖν

---

4 παντα) A+ omit
5 εμπεπορπημενοι) ενπεπηρμενοι A+
7 πασης) V+ omit

8 τοπω) τροπω A+
10 γενεσθαι) A+ omit / αφοδον) ανοδ. V+, εφοδ. L / δι αυτων) δια την A+

---

5. SCYTHIANS: Proverbial for barbarism and cruelty, and so used in II Mac. 4.47, IV Mac. 10.7.
9. GOD ... AS OUR ADVERSARY: To show that the Jews were not as defenseless as they seemed, and that it was dangerous to tamper with them, is clearly one of the main objects of the book; but, like other pious expressions in this letter, the phrase is hardly credible in the mouth of a Ptolemy.

hearts, persuaded us to gather the Jews in the kingdom in a body and to inflict upon them extraordinary punishments as traitors, ⁴urging that our state would never be stable, because of the ill will the Jews bear all nations, until this should be accomplished. ⁵And so they brought them down in bonds, with harsh treatment, like slaves or rather like conspirators, and they sought to put them to death without legal inquiry or examination, outdoing the Scythians' law in their savage cruelty. ⁶We upbraided them severely for this conduct, and barely granted them their lives, in keeping with the kindliness we have for all men. And because we knew of a surety that God in heaven protects the Jews, being their ally always as a father to his children, ⁷and because we took account of the firm good will, like a friend's, which they had for us and our forebears, we have justly absolved them of all blame, on whatsoever account. ⁸And we have ordained for all of them to return, each to his own, and that no one should injure them at all in any place, nor reproach them for what had befallen them without reason. ⁹Know well that if we devise any mischief against them, or harm them in any way, we shall have not man but the Most High God, Who is master of all power, as our adversary to exact vengeance for what is done, in every way and at every time, ineluctably. Farewell."

¹⁰When they received this letter the Jews did not at once make haste for their departure; but they requested of the king that those of the Jewish people who had voluntarily transgressed against the Holy God and His Law should re-

---

10–23. *The Jews punish their renegades and return home.* This is rather a punishment for backsliders than a general exaction of vengeance, for unlike the parallel element in Esth. 8 only *Jewish* renegades are punished, and their number is only three hundred. The author's strict view of the demands of Jewish loyalty is here made plain: the world of the Gentile authorities is totally alien and generally hostile, and no compromise with it is permissible. There seems to be a conscious opposition between this view and the more latitudinarian attitude set forth in the body of Aristeas; see Introd. 24.

δι' αὐτῶν τῆς ὀφειλομένης κολάσεως ¹¹προφερόμενοι τοὺς γαστρὸς ἕνεκεν τὰ θεῖα παραβεβηκότας προστάγματα μηδέποτε εὐνοήσειν μηδὲ τοῖς τοῦ βασιλέως πράγμασιν. ¹²ὁ δὲ τἀληθὲς αὐτοὺς λέγειν παραδεξάμενος καὶ παραινέσας ἔδωκεν αὐτοῖς ἄδειαν πάντων, ὅπως τοὺς παραβεβηκότας τοῦ θεοῦ τὸν νόμον ἐξολεθρεύσωσιν κατὰ πάντα τὸν ὑπὸ τὴν βασιλείαν αὐτοῦ τόπον μετὰ παρρησίας ἄνευ πάσης βασιλικῆς ἐξουσίας καὶ ἐπισκέψεως. ¹³τότε κατευφημήσαντες αὐτόν, ὡς πρέπον ἦν, οἱ τούτων ἱερεῖς καὶ πᾶν τὸ πλῆθος ἐπιφωνήσαντες τὸ αλληλουια μετὰ χαρᾶς ἀνέλυσαν. ¹⁴οὕτως τε τὸν ἐμπεσόντα τῶν μεμιαμμένων ὁμοεθνῆ κατὰ τὴν ὁδὸν ἐκολάζοντο καὶ 15 μετὰ παραδειγματισμῶν ἀνῄρουν. ¹⁵ἐκείνῃ δὲ τῇ ἡμέρᾳ ἀνεῖλον ὑπὲρ τοὺς τριακοσίους ἄνδρας, ἣν καὶ ἤγαγον εὐφροσύνην μετὰ χαρᾶς βεβήλους χειρωσάμενοι. ¹⁶αὐτοὶ δὲ οἱ μέχρι θανάτου τὸν θεὸν ἐσχηκότες παντελῆ σωτηρίας ἀπόλαυσιν εἰληφότες ἀνέζευξαν ἐκ τῆς πόλεως παντοίοις εὐωδεστάτοις ἄνθεσιν κατεστεμμένοι μετ' εὐφροσύνης καὶ βοῆς ἐν αἴνοις καὶ παμμελέσιν ὕμνοις εὐχαριστοῦντες τῷ θεῷ τῶν πατέρων αὐτῶν αἰωνίῳ σωτῆρι τοῦ Ισραηλ.

¹⁷Παραγενηθέντες δὲ εἰς Πτολεμαΐδα τὴν ὀνομαζομένην διὰ τὴν τοῦ τόπου ἰδιότητα ῥοδοφόρον, ἐν ᾗ προσέμεινεν αὐτοὺς ὁ στόλος κατὰ κοινὴν αὐτῶν βουλὴν ἡμέρας ἑπτά, ¹⁸ἐκεῖ ἐποίησαν πότον σωτήριον τοῦ βασιλέως χορηγήσαντος αὐτοῖς εὐψύχως τὰ πρὸς τὴν ἄφιξιν πάντα ἑκάστῳ ἕως εἰς τὴν ἰδίαν οἰκίαν. ¹⁹καταχθέντες δὲ μετ' εἰρήνης ἐν ταῖς πρεπούσαις ἐξομολογήσεσιν ὡσαύτως κἀκεῖ ἔστησαν καὶ ταύτας ἄγειν τὰς ἡμέρας ἐπὶ τὸν τῆς παροικίας αὐτῶν

---

11 πραγμασιν) προσταγμ. A
14 ουτως) ουτοι AL / εκολαζοντο) απεκτεννον A+
15 ην) VL omit
16 απολαυσιν) απολυσιν A+ / ειληφοτες)

εσχηκοτες A+ / αιωνιω VL) αγιων A+, many have αγιω / σωτηρι) σοι A+, V+ omit
17 ροδοφορον) -φονον A+

---

11. NEVER BE WELL DISPOSED TO THE KING'S ESTATE EITHER: The political expediency of having religiously devout subjects was a conscious principle in Roman (see especially Poly. VI 56.9) but not in Greek political thought; but the idea had become familiar to political theorists.

ceive condign punishment at their hands; ¹¹urging that those who had transgressed the divine commandments for their belly's sake would never be well disposed to the king's estate either. ¹²The king acknowledged the truth of what they said, and praised them for it, and he gave them full immunity so that they might destroy those who had transgressed the Law of God in every place in his realm, with freedom and without any royal license or inquiry. ¹³Then they applauded his words, as was proper, their priests and all the people; and they departed with joy, shouting the Hallelujah. ¹⁴Any one of their countrymen who had been defiled [by idolatry] whom they came upon on their way they punished; they put them to death with ignominy. ¹⁵On that day they put to death more than three hundred men; and they kept that day as a joyous festival, having worsted the unclean. ¹⁶But those that held fast to God even unto death received full enjoyment of their deliverance; they departed from the city crowned with all manner of fragrant flowers, with gladness and with shouting, giving thanks to the God of their fathers, the Eternal Savior of Israel, with praises and melodious hymns.

¹⁷When they reached Ptolemais—called "rose-bearing" because of the peculiar quality of the place—the fleet waited for them, following their general wish, for seven days; ¹⁸and there they made a banquet of deliverance, the king having generously supplied all things necessary until the arrival of each one at his own house. ¹⁹And when they finished their voyage in peace with appropriate thanksgivings, there too in like manner they determined to celebrate these days also as

---

14. THEY PUT THEM TO DEATH: Goodenough, *The Jurisprudence of Jewish Courts* (New Haven, 1929) 36 takes this, somewhat rashly, as evidence for recognized lynch law among the Egyptian Jews.
17. PTOLEMAIS: "Ptolemais at the harbor" in the Arsinoite nome, not the better-known Ptolemais near Thebes in Upper Egypt. "ROSE BEARING:" not elsewhere applied to it.
19. DAYS . . . FESTIVE: This appears to be a doublet of the festival at Alexandria (6.36 *q.v.*), perhaps the reflection of a rival theory of its origin and proper date.

20 χρόνον εὐφροσύνους. ²⁰ἃς καὶ ἀνιερώσαντες ἐν στήλῃ κατὰ τὸν τῆς συμποσίας τόπον προσευχῆς καθιδρύσαντες ἀνέλυσαν ἀσινεῖς, ἐλεύθεροι, ὑπερχαρεῖς, διά τε γῆς καὶ θαλάσσης καὶ ποταμοῦ ἀνασῳζόμενοι τῇ τοῦ βασιλέως ἐπιταγῇ, ἕκαστος εἰς τὴν ἰδίαν, ²¹καὶ πλείστην ἢ ἔμπροσθεν ἐν τοῖς ἐχθροῖς ἐξουσίαν ἐσχηκότες μετὰ δόξης καὶ φόβου, τὸ σύνολον ὑπὸ μηδενὸς διασεισθέντες τῶν ὑπαρχόντων. ²²καὶ πάντα τὰ ἑαυτῶν πάντες ἐκομίσαντο ἐξ ἀπογραφῆς ὥστε τοὺς ἔχοντάς τι μετὰ φόβου μεγίστου ἀποδοῦναι αὐτοῖς, τὰ μεγαλεῖα τοῦ μεγίστου θεοῦ ποιήσαντος τελείως ἐπὶ σωτηρίᾳ αὐτῶν. ²³εὐλογητὸς ὁ ῥύστης Ισραηλ εἰς τοὺς ἀεὶ χρόνους. αμην.

20 ιδιαν (21) και πλειστην η) A+ omit   22 φοβου) φορου A+ / second μεγιστου) μεγαλου A+

---

20. PILLAR . . . HOUSE OF PRAYER: It is generally unsafe to disregard the citation of a specific monument, and it may therefore be assumed that the author had some basis, however distorted, for his report. There is in fact mention of a proseuche, "prayer-house," in the Arsinoite nome in the papyri (see Emmet, ad loc.).   SEA: may refer by hyperbole to Lake Moeris, or it may be hyperbole with no reference to a specific sea.

₂₀ festive for the duration of their community. ²⁰They inscribed them as holy on a pillar, and dedicated a house of prayer at the site of the banquet; and then they departed, unharmed, free, and rejoicing, being brought safely, by the ordinance of the king, by land, sea, and river, each to his own place. ²¹They had got greater authority than before among their enemies, along with glory and awe; and no one at all disturbed them in their possessions. ²²All their property they recovered, according to the registration; and those who had any of it returned it with great fear, God the Greatest having perfectly wrought great things for their deliverance. ²³Blessed be the Deliverer of Israel for ever and ever! Amen.

22. ALL THEIR PROPERTY THEY RECOVERED: No confiscation has been specifically mentioned, though one might be assumed in the general punishment. On the other hand, this may may well be an indication of the conflation of accounts of disparate persecutions.

23. The closing blessing may indicate that the entire book was in fact a kind of *megillah* to be read as part of the liturgy on the festival whose origin it purports to explain. On the other hand, such closing formulae occur at the end of other religious writings—IV Maccabees, Sirach, Tobit, and of course Psalms.

THE FOURTH BOOK OF MACCABEES

CONTENTS

	Introduction	91
I.	Summary	91
II.	Sources	92
III.	Date	95
IV.	Historicity	99
V.	Form	100
VI.	Occasion	103
VII.	Place	109
VIII.	Author and Title	113
IX.	Philosophy	115
X.	Religion	118
XI.	Influence	123
XII.	The Story in Rabbinic Literature	127
XIII.	Texts, Versions, Editions	135
	Text, Translation, Commentary, and Critical Notes	143

INTRODUCTION

The little book, commonly called IV Maccabees, but more accurately entitled "On the Sovereignty of Reason," is of capital importance for understanding a significant stage in the spiritual history of Europe. In it a writer of high intellectual and artistic competence interweaves noble strands of Jewish and pagan thought to produce a work of edification, as thoughtful as it is devout, which both by its form and by the attitudes it promulgates has exercised a profound influence on subsequent religious expression. As a work of devotion the book speaks for itself; but a closer examination of its form and content, and its historical and intellectual background and affinities, may enhance appreciation of its worth. Here we shall first present a summary of the contents of the book; next endeavor to determine its sources, the occasion for which it was composed and the place of its composition; then analyze the sources and character of the doctrine it presents; and finally deal with its influence in religious development.

I

SUMMARY

The book is in the form of a discourse, delivered by a speaker who uses the first person. In the opening verses (1.1–6) he declares that his theme is the sovereignty of pious reason over the passions, and he reiterates this statement at appropriate junctures (1.7, 9, 13, 19, 30; 2.6, 24; 6.31; 7.16; 13.1; 16.1; 18.2). The theme may best be illustrated, he continues (1.7–12), by the martyrdom of Eleazar and of the seven brethren and their mother; and in fact the panegyric of the martyrs occupies the major portion of the work. The next section (1.13–3.18) sets forth the relationship between reason and the passions, with examples drawn from Scripture. To provide background for the story of the martyrdoms, short sections recount the attempt of Apollonius on the Temple treasures (3.19–4.14), and Antiochus Epiphanes' attitude toward the Jews (4.15–26). The martyrdom of Eleazar, including speeches by both Eleazar and Antiochus, a description of the tortures, and reflections upon the event, occupies chs. 5–7. The story of the seven brethren is introduced by the admonition of the king to the young men, and their response (8.1–9.9). The martyrdom of the brothers, from the eldest down, is then described (9.10–12.20); and the magnitude of their achievement and its witness to the power of pious reason is celebrated (13.1–14.10). Next we are told of the heroism of the mother, who mastered her natural feelings, and preferred the anguish of seeing her sons tortured to death to encouraging them to transgress the Law (14.11–16.24); her own death is related in a lyric apostrophe to her virtue (17.1–6). The heroism of the martyrs is eulogized, and the practical benefits it brought to their people recorded (17.7–18.6). A concluding section recalls the mother's exhortation to her children, and her appeal to the teachings of their father (18.7–19); and closes with an assurance of blessedness and a doxology (18.20–24).

II

Sources

So closely do the stories of the martyrdoms and their historical preamble parallel similar material in II Maccabees that a literary relationship between the two is obvious. Closer examination makes it equally certain that the fuller and more ornate account in IV Maccabees is an elaboration of that in II Maccabees,[1] and indeed that the author of IV Maccabees used no other source for the substance of his story. The doctrinal

[1] H. Willrich, *Judaica* 166 f., seems to be alone in holding the odd opinion that II Maccabees drew from IV Maccabees.

elements are another matter; and, as we shall see, point to later conditions and needs. But even in the factual account there are, to be sure, divergences in scale and detail; and certain scholars have endeavored to explain them by the hypothesis that our author made direct use of the five books of Jason of Cyrene, which the author of II Maccabees acknowledges as his source.[2] But all divergences can be adequately explained by the different purpose of the author of IV Maccabees and the different historical circumstances in which he wrote.

The most striking discrepancy is in scale. II Maccabees has a much fuller account of the historical background (3-7), and the martyrdoms of Eleazar and the brethren are presented almost incidentally, as a specially edifying instance of resistance to persecution, in just two chapters (6.18-7.41); whereas in IV Maccabees the martyrdoms occupy 14 chapters (5-18) and the historical preamble is correspondingly brief. But the author of II Maccabees is a historian, and hence quite properly enlarges on history; he includes the martyrdoms only, as it were, as an appropriate footnote. Our author is interested in the martyrdoms for their own sake, as a subject for an edifying discourse; he therefore reduces the historical preamble to the barest essentials, and expands where his interest lies. In II Maccabees the martyrdom of Eleazar and those of the brethren are separate incidents; in IV Maccabees (8.1) the martyrdom of Eleazar serves as the opening of the common trial, and all are regarded as a single incident. In II Maccabees (7.41) the death of the mother is merely mentioned; in IV Maccabees (17.1) we are told that she committed suicide so that her body might not be tainted by the soldiers' touch. These details are quite clearly intended to enhance the effectiveness of the story for the specific purpose of inculcating appropriate attitudes. This purpose is even more obvious in the elaboration of the brief state-

---

[2] The arguments in favor of our author's use of Jason are presented most fully by Freudenthal, 72-90. His views are accepted by, among others, Deissmann, 156. For works cited by name of author alone, full bibliographical data will be found at 139, below.

ments attributed to the martyrs in II Maccabees into formal speeches characterized by pronounced Stoic coloring and ornate rhetorical devices. The sufferings of the martyrs are presented as vicarious expiation for the sins of their people, and requital in a future state is promised. Our author is not only a devout teacher but an accomplished rhetorician, and antiquity freely granted the rhetorician certain liberties in the interest of enhancing the effectiveness of his art. Neither our author nor his audience would take exception to the liberty taken with even Scriptural matter, as in the reference to David's thirst (3.6–16; cf. II Sam. 3.13–17 or I Chron. 11.15–19); surely, then, for so worthy a purpose as promoting religious loyalty it would be regarded as entirely legitimate to deal freely with details in II Maccabees which are not essential to the purpose, and to embroider the torments and the speeches of the martyrs which are essential to it.

One or two factual discrepancies might be more disturbing, but are not difficult to explain. In II Maccabees 2.1–3 the Syrian king under whom the incident which precipitated the persecutions took place is named Seleucus, *i.e.*, Seleucus IV Philopator, who began his rule in 187 BCE and was succeeded by Antiochus Epiphanes in 175. Our text (3.20) calls him Seleucus Nicanor, who was actually a general of Alexander the Great and the founder of the Seleucid dynasty; Seleucus IV Philopator was his sixth successor. So blatant an error must have been due to our author's carelessness or ignorance of early history; he can hardly have drawn it from any respectable source. Apparently more serious is the discrepancy in the name and title of the minister whom Seleucus despatched to confiscate the treasures at Jerusalem. II Mac. 3.17 names him Heliodorus; in IV Mac. 4.9 he is Apollonius. Here the explanation of the error is doubtless our author's mistaken identification of the antecedents of pronouns in the II Maccabees account. Nor is Apollonius' title the same in the two versions. In II Mac. 3.5 he is described as governor (*strategos*) of Coele Syria and Phoe-

INTRODUCTION 95

nicia; in the IV Maccabees passage he is called *strategos* of Syria, Phoenicia, and Cilicia. But this divergence, as we shall see in the section following, actually testifies to our author's good faith, and supplies our best foothold for fixing his date.

III

DATE

The widest possible limits for the composition of our book cover the period from *ca*. 168 BCE, when the events it describes took place, to the reign of Hadrian, to which Talmudic accounts assign some of those events.[3] Internal evidence permits us to bring these limits much closer together. At 5.7 and 13 the word for religion is *threskeia*; that word is never so used in the Hellenistic age, but is common from Augustus onward.[4] At 5.4 Eleazar is described as *nomikos* ("expert in the law"): that word came to be used for legal experts only in the Roman period, and in II Mac. 6.18 Eleazar is in fact called by the older word *grammateus*. These considerations bring the *terminus post quem* down to Augustus. At the other end, besides questions of doctrine and form which we will discuss presently, we note that the Temple and its service are apparently conceived of as still existing,[5] which naturally excludes any date after 70 CE. But the clincher is the title assigned to Apollonius in 4.9: "governor of Syria, Phoenicia, and Cilicia." It is natural for a writer to use titles appropriate in his own day, as can be shown by many examples; and, as Professor Bickermann has demonstrated,[6] there was only a single short period in the early Roman Empire when Cilicia was associated with Syria for administrative pur-

[3] The fullest passage is Gittin 57b; see below, 127, for a discussion of the rabbinic versions. A date under Trajan or Hadrian is accepted by many earlier scholars and by DuP-S, who summarizes earlier opinions.
[4] See L. Robert, in *Études Épigraphiques et Philologiques*, 1938, 234.
[5] *Cf.* 4.20, 14.9; and see Heinemann in PWK, 14.802.
[6] Bickermann, "The Date of IV Maccabees," in *Louis Ginzberg Jubilee Volume* (New York, 1945), 105–112.

poses, and that was the period of 20–54 CE. If we date IV Maccabees in the middle of that span we hit upon the reign of Caligula (37–41 CE).

That period is exactly suitable as providing a historical conjuncture which would evoke such a consideration of religious persecution as is contained in our book. Two years after he became emperor Caligula decreed the erection of a statue to himself in the Temple at Jerusalem.[7] The decree was transmitted to Petronius, with orders to march to Judaea; and in order to avoid conflict, Petronius summoned a meeting of important Jewish personages—doubtless at the governor's residence in Antioch—to counsel submission.[8] It was the Jews of Antioch, then, who first heard of the intended desecration of the Temple; and from the reception which the Jewish leaders gave the news we may surmise that there were mass meetings of protest. Josephus tells us that Petronius encountered such at Ptolemais and Tiberias while en route to execute the order,[9] and there must surely have been similar manifestations at Antioch. When in 41 CE Claudius countermanded Caligula's edict, issued a proclamation ordering the cessation of pogroms in Egypt, and in the same document guaranteed the continuance of the privileges granted to the Jews there, a copy of this document was sent to Antioch at the special request of King Agrippa.[10] The end of Caligula's reign, therefore, or about 40 CE, appears to be the most likely date for the composition of our book.

Determination of date is after all useful mainly for fuller appreciation of intellectual premises and historical background, and these do in fact become more meaningful if we place our book in the reign of Caligula, as comparison with the parallel accounts makes clear.[11] In II Maccabees, which was written

[7] Philo, *Ad Gaium* 185–190; the date is fixed in, *e.g.*, Schürer, 1.501, n. 1.74.
[8] Philo, *ibid.*, 207, 222–224.
[9] *Ant.* 18. 262–272.
[10] *Ibid.*, 19.279.
[11] For the substance of this comparison I am indebted to Gutman, 27–35.

probably a century earlier, there is real doubt of Jewish survival in the face of the novel phenomenon of religious persecution. Antiochus is reproved as being guilty of *theomachia*, or fighting against deity; the crime looms large in Greek tragedy,[12] and it is quite probable that the author had in mind and meant to suggest Euripides' *Bacchae*, which was a favorite in the East, and in which the petulant King Pentheus comes to grief for not yielding to a divinity previously unrecognized by him. The mere fact that a deity had suffered persecutions to take place would indicate, in the ancient view, that the victims had indeed been forsaken by their God; and II Maccabees accordingly takes pains to assure its readers that the martyrs were receiving, in the immediate present, merited chastisement which would visit the persecutor in far greater measure in the future.

In the Talmudic accounts, which reflect the Hadrianic persecutions about a century after our book, succumbing to idolatry is no longer an issue. What the Romans demanded and the Jews refused was recognition of the divinity of the Emperor. There was no question of Judaism compromising with paganism, and no ambiguity concerning future retribution. The persecutors were considered as an impersonal force, a rod of chastisement for disciplining the Jews. In both II Maccabees and the Talmud, then, the Jews are a group apart, facing (and despising) an opposition which belonged to another world.

In IV Maccabees the Jews are *members* of a single world. Their Hellenization is not external, but integral to and even central in their lives and thoughts. Their special responsibility as Jews serves the larger interest of the world of which they are members, though the ruling powers may sometimes be unaware of this service. Awareness of this service, and freedom to contribute to it, is all they desire; they do not wish to destroy the king or utterly discredit his philosophy, but only to enlighten him, just as they wish not to extirpate emotions but only to

[12] See W. C. Greene, *Moira* (Cambridge, 1944), 211 ff.

control them. The possibility of persecution must naturally have been present to the author's mind; yet one does not sense an inflamed urgency which the determined ruthlessness of the Hadrianic persecutions would surely have aroused, but rather such an examination of issues as the rumor of Caligula's mad designs may have occasioned. Antiochus is capable of showing genuine sympathy and admiration for his opponents, whom he can only regard as unreasonable; and in the end he can be convinced by their perseverance and ready to profit by their example. There is no presumption of continual hostility between the Jews and their politically dominant environment, as there is in Hadrian's day or in III Maccabees, but a reasonable *modus vivendi* with the prospect of even fuller understanding in the future, as there is in Aristeas.[13] From what we know of intellectual movements and historical backgrounds, then, our book gains in meaning if it is dated in the reign of Caligula and placed (as we shall endeavor presently to place it) in Antioch.

Stylistic considerations are of little service in fixing a date for a book like this; we need only note that nothing in the style militates against the date proposed. The form of the book and its affinities in Greek literature we shall examine in a subsequent section. Of the style proper, all that can be said is that it is a first-rate example of the rhetorician's art, and that its opulence and proclivity to novel compounds are characteristic of the so-called Asianic style. Eduard Norden, who is our greatest authority in such matters, pronounced IV Maccabees an excellent example of that style;[14] its very freedom from aberrations makes it difficult to place the work at any specific point during the currency of the Asianic style; though, if we date it early, an origin in Asia Minor (and Antioch was a great center for rhetoric) is likely; unlike Egyptian Hellenism, Asiatic was unaffected by the Attic reaction. Scholars have seen in our book affinities with the style, as well as outlook, of Dio Chrysos-

[13] See my Aristeas 63 ff.
[14] Eduard Norden, *Die Antike Kunstprosa* (Leipzig, 1923), 1.[4] 416–418.

INTRODUCTION 99

tom[15] and the Second Sophistic, but the Asianic style, as well as popular applications of Stoicism, flourished in the days of Cicero.

IV
HISTORICITY

The emotional warmth of our book, and the rhetorical elaboration of mere hints in his source, are obviously our author's own; but it is equally obvious that he himself believed in the fact of the martyrdoms. Ancient literary theory prescribed that, except for chronicles and the like, a historical narrative might be embellished out of the writer's imagination, provided that he did no violence to the essence of the historical facts, that his additions possessed verisimilitude, and that the whole was edifying.[16] Was our author correct in assuming an actual historical basis for his story? Is not the fact that I Maccabees makes no mention of the martyrdoms significant? But I Maccabees deals with broader political and military movements, and no inferences are to be drawn from an omission of stories concerning individuals. II Maccabees does include the story, as appropriate illustration; and perhaps the best evidence for its historicity is that the author of II Maccabees, who is a conscientious and competent historian, accepted it without question. But perhaps that author was gullible, and put excessive trust in his source Jason; and we know that Jason was of the "pathetic" school of historians, who went to all lengths to arouse their readers' emotions.[17] Nevertheless, though in his

[15] The analogy to Dio Chrysostom is suggested, but by no means convincingly, by DuP-S, 76 f. For a characterization of Dio and of the Second Sophistic, see my *History of Greek Literature* (New York, 1950), 247 ff. and 275 ff.

[16] I have dealt with this more fully in *Aristeas to Philocrates* 57 ff.

[17] On Jason see F. Jacoby in PWK 9.778–781. The "pathetic" school of historians is characterized in Polybius' "pragmatic" strictures on Timaeus (25b.5): "He does not set down the words spoken, but having made up his mind as to what ought to have been said he recounts all these speeches and all else that follows upon events like a man in a school of rhetoric attempting to speak on a given subject, and shows off his oratorical power, but gives no report of what was actually spoken."

efforts to play upon his readers' heartstrings the "pathetic" historian might intensify the emotional aspect of events or introduce an emotional aspect where none was present, he was not free to invent an entire episode out of whole cloth. On the basis of regular practice, then—to which Jason must have adhered—there is great probability that the story of the martyrdoms is essentially true. Furthermore, physical relics of the martyrs were preserved and venerated by Christians in Antioch in the 4th century; and, as we shall see in the section on Antioch, there is every reason to believe that the Jews from whom the site was taken over had maintained a continuous tradition with regard to it from a period near the events which it commemorated. The probability, then, is that this discourse, composed and delivered about 40 CE, commemorated a series of martyrdoms which actually took place in the reign of Antiochus Epiphanes, about 167 BCE.

V

Form

IV Maccabees is profoundly concerned with religious edification, but in form and manner has no analogue in contemporary Hebrew literature. Its atmosphere is one of thorough Hellenization. Eleazar, who is the scholar of the piece, is described even by the pagan tyrant as a philosopher, and proves his claim to the title. Plainest of all, when the martyrs wish to communicate with one another privately they are said to employ Hebrew (16.15), which proves that their ordinary speech was Greek. Not only the words but the imagery also is Greek, and the artistic and systematic structure is unlike anything in rabbinic literature. Its alternations of philosophic exposition, "pathetic" description, and fervid exhortation, with skillful transitions between the sections, are carefully designed to build and reinforce the conviction and attitude the author wishes to communicate. Before his mind is the concept of Greek tragedy with its chorus. At several points he actually calls the brethren a chorus; and like a chorus he has them speak with a single voice, and at a point of stress break into separate ejaculations and join again in a triumphant finale (13.11 ff.). When he wishes to speak of a retributive curse pursuing a wrongdoer he uses *alastor* (9.24, 11.23, 18.22), which must evoke the atmosphere of tragedy. When he wishes to underscore the innocence of the martyrs and the injustice of the persecutor, he copies the Euripidean device of constructing a damning epitaph (17.9–10). Like a good Greek tragedy, and unlike melodrama, our discourse avoids making its tyrant a capricious monster, brought to his knees, crushed and grovelling, in the last act. The tyrant is a reasonably good man, and all the cast—and vicariously the audience—learn by suffering.

If the influence of tragedy is evident in concept and vocabulary, the influence of Plato is even more palpable. Eleazar is like Socrates at too many points for the resemblance to be accidental; and it has been argued with considerable plausibility that Socrates' conversation with Callicles in Plato's *Gorgias* is specifically in our author's mind.[18] Both men confront the problem of what a man with moral convictions is to do in the face of an obdurate opponent who relies upon force; and both emerge with the assurance that the man of convictions must proudly go his way and that the man of force will yield and profit.

But in form IV Maccabees is no more a Platonic dialogue than a tragedy; and a Greek rhetorician was strictly bound by the doctrine of literary forms. Probably our book would be classified as a diatribe—a term applied to edifying or monitory philosophic essays or discourses. The use of the first person by our author, the direct addresses to the audience in the second person, and the tone of the whole certainly suggest a real discourse; on the other hand, as Norden points out, philosophic diatribes intended for private reading regularly

[18] Gutman (see note 7), 33 ff. Specific instances will be discussed at 116.

employed the form of a fictive discourse with direct addresses.[19] The question of whether the discourse form of IV Maccabees is merely a literary convention, as in the pamphlets of an Isocrates, or whether the discourse was intended for delivery, is of some moment. It may be argued that despite its strong philosophic coloring our book is rather a panegyric or encomium than a diatribe; but even so Norden's position is hard to refute except by the subjective feeling of sympathetic readers. In a verse like 14.9—"Even now we, when we hear of the agonies of those young men, must shudder"—the author might as easily have written "when we read." The doxologies at 1.12 and 18.24, and the use of the expression "on this occasion" at 1.10 and 3.19, reinforce the impression that our work was intended for oral presentation.

Whether diatribe or panegyric, IV Maccabees is patently the work of a learned and thoughtful and devout man but also of a notably skillful craftsman. He writes, as Professor Torrey has said,[20] "with dignity and with an evident consciousness of mastery." Today we are inclined to associate rhetoric with empty turgidity; but the effective use of language has always been a powerful instrument, and at certain periods (of which our author's was one) it has been regarded as a high art. From staccato exposition of philosophic doctrine he rises to a diapason of tropes—similes of stormy seas and jutting crags and besieged cities, artistically set out with antitheses, paradoxes, climaxes, apostrophes, anacolutha, and all the other resources of the trained rhetorician. If his colors are anywhere too intense for modern readers, it is in the detailed description of the tortures. But here we have to do with a change of taste. Not only

[19] *Antike Kunstprosa* 1.4.416. Norden cites a telling example of the use of the discourse form for an ordinary essay from Cicero's *Paradoxa*. At 1.6 Cicero speaks of "this speech," using the first person himself and addressing his audience in the second; but in the preceding paragraph (Preface, 5) he tells us that he wrote the essay late at night and chose the discourse form as being most effective.

[20] C. C. Torrey, *The Apocryphal Literature* (New Haven, 1945), 105. Torrey has a judicious appreciation of our book, 103–106. S. Zeitlin, *JQR*, 1947, pp. 231–239.

the roughly contemporary tragedies of Seneca and epic of Lucan, but early Christian literature and even the Elizabethan tragedy of blood are (to use a word derived from Maccabees) no less macabre.

VI

Occasion

If a discourse, under what circumstances was it delivered? Some admirers have characterized it as a magnificent and even unique specimen of Jewish sermonizing.[21] Others, who agree as to its quality, insist that as a sermon it is by no means unique— or that it is not a sermon. A sermon, it is argued, posits a canonical Scriptural text, not a philosophical tenet[22] or a text from an Apocryphal book.[23] The slight evidence we possess does indicate that homiletic usage, in Alexandria as well as Palestine, involved Midrashic elaboration of a Scriptual text or texts; yet it would be rash to insist upon the use of a Scriptural text as an irrefragable rule in all homiletic discourses. Townshend[24] does in fact compromise by granting that the rule applied to all *sermons*, and suggesting that our book is not a sermon but rather a "lecture." If we assume that the discourse was actually spoken, then its warm monitory and hortatory tone, and its frequent use of the word "God," are wholly unbecoming to an academic exercise, and can be suitable only to a gathering assembled for some devotional purpose. Hence Heinemann,[25]

[21] H. Ewald, *Geschichte des Volkes Israel* (Göttingen, 1864) 4.³ 634. Freudenthal, 4, agrees that it is excellent, and shows how it influenced Christian sermonizers, but insists that it is not unique.

[22] Schürer. 3.³ 393.

[23] Grimm, 286 f. But, as DuP-S points out (21 f.) II Maccabees is not used as a "text"; furthermore, such a usage as "in the Scripture" to designate a noncanonical book (II Mac. 2.4) shows that distinctions were not yet fixed.

[24] 653.

[25] PWK, 14.801 f. *Cf.* B. W. Bacon, "The Festival of Lives Given for the Nation," *Hibbert Journal*, XV (1917) 256–278. Bacon holds that both Hanukkah and the commemoration of the Maccabean martyrs are aspects of a pre-existing Feast of Renewal, to which each was assimilated.

largely on the basis of "this occasion" in 1.10 and 3.19, suggests that the discourse was intended for some special occasion, and specifically the celebration of Hanukkah. That the "occasion" is not defined in the text is an argument in favor of actual delivery: the audience (unlike the reader) would not need to be told what the occasion was.

That the discourse was intended for actual delivery on a solemn occasion of religious significance seems highly probable; but that the occasion was Hanukkah is doubtful. Surely in a piece intended for Hanukkah we should expect some specific allusion (as in the familiar *al ha-nisim*) to the events and heroes which that festival celebrates. The persecutions which led to our martyrdoms are indeed connected with the uprising under the Maccabees; and that circumstance is doubtless responsible for the present title of the book (which can hardly have been its original designation) and its position with other books of "Maccabees." But even if the current title is genuine, the connection with the Hasmonaean heroes is not sufficiently explicit —unless we see in Hanukkah a general and more ancient festival to which various historical or legendary episodes could properly be attached.[26] But the hypothesis that our book was intended for a solemn occasion does not depend upon our identifying that occasion as Hanukkah. Upon the analogy of long established usage in the Hellenistic world the occasion may well have been an annual commemoration of the martyrs celebrated *at the site*, actual or supposed, of their burial.[27]

The objection at once arises that such a practice would be repugnant to established tradition, which specifically forbade anything like a cult of the dead. Any contact with the dead is prohibited in the Law;[28] and in Is. 65.4 we read a condemnation of—among other followers of strange rites—them "That sit

[26] As Bacon maintained (see preceding note).
[27] Cardinal Rampolla de Tindaro, "Martyre et Sépulture des Machabées," in *Revue de l'Art Chrétien*, 1899, 295 ff., proposed this view with great learning and acumen, and has been followed by a number of scholars, e.g., DuP-S, 67 ff.
[28] Lev. 21.1–5, 10–11; Num. 6.6–9, 19.11–13; Deut. 18.9–12, 26.14.

among the graves and lodge in the vaults." The rabbis particularly disclaimed any association between a place of worship and a tomb.[29] If our book actually reflects the establishment of religious commemoration at the site of a tomb, we should have a case of a usage adopted by a Hellenized community from their environment and then transmitted to the general spiritual store.

In Greek life at all periods the annual commemoration of heroes (in the precise sense of the word) was a familiar phenomenon. Beginning with the heroes of saga and continuing through the historical period, men of stature who had achieved or suffered greatly, and whose careers were therefore meaningful to their fellow men, received as it were official beatification as heroes and became the objects of a cult. Offerings were made to them annually on a significant anniversary, and they were invoked for assistance or inspiration in their particular spheres of activity.[30] For our purposes it is important to notice that the cult offered heroes differed markedly from that offered to the Olympians. The hour and the manner of the offerings, the nature of the victim and the character of the ritual, were calculated to make it obvious that the object of veneration was essentially different from the usual recipients of worship. If we are careful to avoid anachronistic implications of the word we might say that the cult of heroes tended to be rather a secular observance. Secularization becomes more patent in the Hellenistic age, when heroization is reduced to little more than recognition or flattery of outstanding political figures. Ultimately even the deification of kings and emperors was quite emptied of religious significance in our sense and became a purely political act, though Jews and Christians continued to eschew participation in the cult aspect. But the widespread practice of commemorating figures who had served their people well must

[29] Meg. 26b, Ber. 17b, and elsewhere.
[30] For the theory and practice of the cult of heroes, see M. P. Nilsson, *Geschichte der griechisch. Religion* (Munich, 1950) 2.128 ff.; L. R. Farnell, *Greek Hero Cults* (Oxford, 1921); W. J. Ferguson and A. D. Nock, in *Harvard Theological Review*, XXXVII (1944).

have been peculiarly attractive to leaders of Hellenized communities who wished to strengthen national pride and cement religious loyalties. It was easy enough, in the case of an essentially secular usage, to eliminate objectionable pagan aspects, and make proper adaptation to the requirements of Judaism. Even where certain doctrinal implications were involved, it has been argued, the Hasmonaeans adapted certain Greek usages with reference to the annual celebration of Hanukkah itself.[31] In so thoroughly Hellenized an environment as that which must have produced and received IV Maccabees it is as probable that a practice so widespread, so edifying, and so serviceable should be adapted to Jewish use as it was for the philosophic ideas and rhetorical form of IV Maccabees to be adopted.

Even in the classical period stories of human sacrifice which can originally have had no such implications were transformed into martyrdoms for the national well-being. Thus Euripides makes Iphigenia say before her immolation at Aulis (1374 ff.):[32]

> Hear, mother, the thought that occurred to me as I pondered the thing. I am resolved to die. And I will do it gloriously. I have put all mean thoughts out of my heart. Come, see it with me, mother, see how right I am. The whole might of Hellas depends on me. Upon me depends the passage of the ships over the sea, and the overthrow of the Phrygians. With me it rests to prevent the barbarians from carrying our women off from happy Hellas in the future, should they attempt such a thing. All these things I shall achieve by my death, and my name, as the liberator of Hellas, shall be blessed.

[31] See Bickermann, *The Maccabees* (trans. M. Hadas, New York, 1947) 85 ff. *Cf.* Bacon (note 25). Bickermann's theory, it must be noted, is completely rejected by Zeitlin.

[32] Trans. M. Hadas and J. H. McLean, *The Plays of Euripides* (New York, 1936) 483 f.

And Iphigenia, we know, was the object of a cult.[33] When Hellenized Jews began to seek parallels in their own literature for impressive and accepted items in Greek tradition, the examples of Isaac, of Daniel, and of the Three Hebrew Children (all of which are invoked in our book) naturally claimed attention. Most effective of all, for those seeking to inculcate and preserve national and religious loyalty in an environment where a rival culture was politically dominant, would be such a martyrdom as is recounted in our book which celebrated resistance to the initial stages of the opposition still encountered.

Nor is the annual commemoration of a national hero unknown in Jewish tradition. The violent death of Gedaliah (II Kings 25.25), who was governor of Palestine under Nebuchadnezzar, and who saved Jeremiah's life, was early commemorated by an annual fast. In the Talmud (Ned. 12a) the commemoration of the death day of a father or teacher is spoken of as being similar to that for Gedaliah. Something of the nature of the commemoration is suggested by Rashi (in Yeb. 122a), who tells us that it was customary for the disciples and the general public to sit around the grave of a great man and otherwise honor him on the anniversary of his death.

The martyrdoms most familiar to rabbinic tradition and most instructive in the present context are those of the ten teachers of the Law who are said to have perished in the Hadrianic persecutions. There are a number of allusions to these martyrdoms in rabbinic literature,[34] but the details are consolidated in a systematic and richly embellished account in the Midrash *Asarah Haruge Malkhut*, otherwise called *Eleh Ezkerah*. A *seliha* embodying this Midrash is included in the liturgy for the Day of Atonement. The martyrdoms of the Ten have generally been accepted as substantially true. There can of course be no doubt that the Romans persecuted Jews for religion's sake, or even that individuals named in the Midrash

[33] Farnell, 55 ff.
[34] Abodah Zarah 17b; Ber. 61b; San. 14a; Lam. R 2.2; Prov. R 1.6.

suffered martyrdom. But the individuals mentioned were not in fact contemporaries, the various rosters of names do not coincide, and the number ten is not mentioned in the Talmudic sources.

On the basis of these discrepancies Professor Zeitlin[35] has argued that the Midrash in its present form is fictional, though based, to be sure, on actual persecutions. Professor Zeitlin then connects the account of the martyrdom of the Ten with ideas contained in the Book of Jubilees, to which he assigns a pre-Hellenistic date. Jubilees tells the story of the crime committed by the sons of Jacob against their brother Joseph, and then proceeds (34.18–19):

> For this reason it is ordained for the children of Israel that they should afflict themselves on the tenth of the seventh month—on the day that the news which made him weep for Joseph came to Jacob his father—that they should make atonement for themselves thereon with a young goat on the tenth of the seventh month, once a year, for their sins; for they had grieved the affection of their father regarding Joseph his son.

The principle of atonement was a characteristic belief of the Apocalyptic circle from which Jubilees emanated, and was rejected by the teachers who represented the main stream of rabbinic development; but in the permutations which the story and the doctrine it embodied underwent before it reached the rabbinic writers who were unsympathetic to it the number ten was retained, as was also the connection with the Day of Atonement. Of the bearing of this material on the doctrine of vicarious expiation we shall have more to say below (121); for our present purpose we need only note that the recitation of *Eleh Ezkerah* on the Day of Atonement is in effect a commemoration of a martyrdom on a suitable annual occasion.

[35] S. Zeitlin, "The Legend of the Ten Martyrs and its Apocalyptic Origin," *JQR* 1945, 1–16.

INTRODUCTION 109

Similarly commemorative is the reading of *Arze ha-Lebanon* (which also deals with the Hadrianic martyrs) on the ninth of Ab—and indeed the reading of various medieval martyrologies on that day. The story of delivery from imminent martyrdom told in III Maccabees culminates with the appointing of a commemorative festival (7.19). This occasion was of course not sombre but festive, and analogous to Purim. For festival addresses there is of course abundant evidence; the *Pesikta* (which is our oldest Midrashic work) contains elements of 32 such discourses for Sabbaths and festival days. Reverent allusions to the memorials of national heroes, ancient and recent, recur in the Talmud.[36] For eyewitness evidence of places of worship connected with tombs we must wait for Benjamin of Tudela,[37] but some of the sepulcher synagogues he mentions must surely go back to early centuries. Among others Benjamin speaks of synagogues in connection with the tombs of Burak, King Jeconiah, Nahum, Ezekiel, Ezra, Meir, Isaac Nappaha Rav, and Samuel; frequently he says, "X is buried near [*samukh*] or before [*liphneh*] the synagogue."

It is true that Jewish tradition offers no direct evidence of a commemoration of the martyrs of IV Maccabees; but it is natural to assume that the Christian commemoration of these martyrs was a continuation of a Jewish institution. It was, in all probability, for an observance of this annual Jewish commemoration that IV Maccabees was composed.

VII

Place

If we can accept it as fact that our discourse was composed for delivery at a commemoration of the martyrdoms which it describes, we have a basis for determining the place of its composition. Palestine may be excluded from consideration, for

[36] Semahot, *passim;* Moed Katan 19b ff.
[37] See M. N. Adler, *The Itinerary of Benjamin of Tudela* (London, 1907), 28, 34 ff., 48 f. *al.*

though we now know that Palestinian Jews were familiar with the Greek language and Greek usages,[38] they could hardly have been so far Hellenized as to produce or receive a work so markedly Greek in style and approach. In the one passage, moreover, where the author alludes to the topography of Jerusalem he betrays his ignorance. At 4.20 the gymnasium is located "upon the very citadel" at Jerusalem; II Mac. 4.12 correctly places it "under the citadel."

Because so much of our Jewish-Hellenistic literature (including III Maccabees) demonstrably derives from Alexandria, where we know that the Jewish population was numerous and reached a high degree of Hellenization, there has been a tendency to place the origin of IV Maccabees in Alexandria also.[39] But neither the contents nor the religious outlook of our book seem appropriate to Alexandria at any probable date of its composition. Freudenthal marshals cogent arguments against Alexandrian (as against Palestinian) authorship, but does not attempt to fix a precise locality elsewhere in the Diaspora.[40] The greatest metropolis after Alexandria in the Hellenistic world was Antioch; and general probability, supported by later tradition, points, as Cardinal Rampolla and others have shown, to Antioch as the scene of the martyrdom and of the composition and publication of our book.[41]

In the book itself there is no unequivocal indication of locality. All we are told of the scene is that Antiochus was

[38] See S. Lieberman, *Greek in Jewish Palestine* (New York, 1942), and *Hellenism in Jewish Palestine* (New York, 1950). Langen, *Das Judenthum in Palästina* (Freiburg, 1866) 76, thought our book was written in Palestine, but only because he could not believe that it was written in Alexandria.

[39] So A. Gfrörer, *Philo und die alexandrinische Theosophie* (Stuttgart, 1831) 2.175; Grimm, 293; M. J. Lagrange, *Le Judaisme avant J. C.* (Paris, 1931) 517; H. Lietzmann, *The Beginnings of the Christian Church* (New York, 1922), 107.

[40] 112. Ewald, 4.³ 633, says that the book was written by "a thorough Hellenist living in Egypt or elsewhere outside of Palestine." Norden, 14.419, thinks Alexandrian authorship improbable, and prefers "some coastal city of Asia Minor."

[41] See note 27.

(5.1) "sitting with his counsellors upon a lofty place." Because the persecutions mentioned in the section immediately preceding belong to Jerusalem, it might be supposed that this scene also belongs to the same setting. But the preceding section is in the nature of a general historical introduction, and it is in fact easier to suppose that the scene of the martyrdoms was Antiochus' own capital; indeed, if he were actually present in person no site other than Antioch is possible. Moreover, in view of the special position of the Jewish community in Antioch, no other city is as probable a site both for the martyrdoms and for a Jewish commemoration of them according to Hellenistic usage.[42] Antioch was the third city in the Roman Empire (after Rome and Alexandria), and the seat of administration for Palestine as well. It was a thoroughly Hellenized city, Greek in architecture, education, and way of life, and a great center of commerce and industry. Josephus tells us that it included a large Jewish population from its foundation (*Jewish War* 7.3.3), that the Jews received from Seleucus Nicanor full civic rights which were inscribed upon bronze tablets (*Ant.* 12.3.1), and that Syrian kings succeeding Antiochus Epiphanes presented many votive offerings to the synagogue of the Jews (*Ant.* 13.5.3). Mark Antony ordered the Antiochenes to restore to the Antiochene Jews the property they had taken from them (*Ant.* 14.12.6). Herod the Great presented the city of Antioch with a marble avenue 20 stades in length (*Jewish War* 1.21.11).

The Jews of Antioch[43] made many converts, and thus facilitated the early and rapid spread of Christianity there; indeed it was in Antioch that the term "Christians" was first applied to the followers of the new sect (Acts 11.26)—perhaps in derision—and that Christianity first entered the stream of

[42] Obermann, 253 ff., argues on the basis of the Arabic *Farag-Book* (see 134 below) that the synagogue connected with our story was built in Jerusalem, and after the destruction of the Temple.

[43] E. G. Kraeling, "The Jewish Community at Antioch," *Journal of Biblical Literature*, LI (1932), 130–160, is a convenient summary of information on the subject, ancient and modern. See also S. Krauss, "Antioche," in *Revue des Études Juives*, XLV (1902) 27–49.

Mediterranean civilization.[44] Dissensions with the established Jewish community concerning the observance of dietary regulations (Acts 15), and rivalry between the increasingly divergent groups, were inevitable. Not only is a series of Christian leaders, beginning with Paul, reported to have taught there, but we know from rabbinic literature of a number of teachers who lived or visited in Antioch. Among these are Isaac Nappaha, R. Aha, R. Tanhuma; the latter is reported to have had a discussion on religion at Antioch, probably with Christians (Genesis R. 19.4).[45] In Gittin 44b the Antiochenes are named as the type of non-Palestinians. As late as the 4th century Jewish observances were still attractive to Christians; and the first canon of the first synod in Antioch declared that Easter should not be celebrated at the same time as Passover.[46] From the sermons of John Chrysostom, before he became patriarch of Constantinople, we infer that Christians, especially women, visited the synagogue rather than the church on Sabbaths and holidays. From Chrysostom we know that the Christians believed that the tomb of the Maccabean martyrs was situated in the quarter of Kerateion, near the synagogue.[47] The Christians took both over, and made them places of pilgrimage and commemoration.[48] The fact that distinguished Christian teachers questioned the propriety of adopting martyrs who suffered not for Christianity but for Judaism, and the fact that many found it permissible to do so,[49] shows that the synagogue and the relics of the martyrs had enjoyed high repute among non-

[44] On the beginnings of Christianity at Antioch, see K. Bauer, *Antiochia in der ältesten Kirchengeschichte* (Tübingen, 1919).
[45] For references see Kraeling, 132 ff., or *Jewish Encyclopedia* s.v.
[46] See Kraeling, 156 ff., for documentation.
[47] *PG* 50.617, 63.523–4; see H. Delehaye, *Les Origines du Culte des Martyres* (Brussels, 1933) 201 f.
[48] See Max Maas, "Die Maccabäer als Christliche Heilige," *Monatsschrift für Geschichte und Wissenschaft des Judentums*, XLIV (1900) 145–156.
[49] Augustine, *Sermons* 300.5 (Augustine also mentions our martyrs in *City of God* 18.36); Gregory of Nazianz, *PG* 35.912; John Chrysostom, *PG* 63.525.

Christians. Two first class contemporary witnesses state factually that a sepulcher of the martyred brothers and their mother existed in Antioch in the 4th century; one is the authentic manuscript of a Syriac calendar of Edessa of 412 CE,[50] and the other is an Arabic version of an equally ancient topographical description of Antioch.[51] If the Christians were not the first to attach sanctity to the site in Kerateion, it is clear that their predecessors had done so; and where the traditions of the Jewish community were so strong and continuous it is unlikely that the location or its significance should have been invented.[52] The essential truth of our story and its association with Antioch are, then, as probable as such things can well be.

Corroboration of Antiochene provenance is afforded by the regular use of "Hebrew" in our book, where an Alexandrian work like III Maccabees regularly uses "Jew". Elaboration of this point will be found in Professor Zeitlin's Introduction to II Maccabees in the present series.

VIII

AUTHOR AND TITLE

We have reasonable surmises, then, concerning our author's place and date; we can sense that he had an easy familiarity with Greek philosophy and poetry and with Jewish Scripture and traditions; we see that he was master of a good Greek style. We know too that he was concerned to raise Judaism to the highest level his intellect was capable of, and devoted to the cause of perpetuating loyalty to that faith. Knowing so much—really more than we do of the authors of many anonymous works—we can bear not to know his precise name. That knowledge would be useful, after all, only for connecting him

---

[50] Published by W. Wright in *The Journal of Sacred Literature*, 8 N.S. 45 ff., and trans. 423 ff.
[51] Vatican MS No. 286, described by Rampolla, 390. Obermann (265) confirms the evidence of this MS.
[52] See Gutman, 37.

with other works. It is not likely that he is mentioned in any work that we have; and though it is quite probable that he wrote other works (*cf.* "as is my custom," 1.12) it is quite certain that none survive; there are none extant that could have come from his hand. All that remains to be said of our author's personality is that he was surely not Josephus, to whom our earliest authorities assign the work and among whose writings it has been included. Considerations of style and of religious outlook put Josephus completely out of the question, though most of our manuscripts bear his name in the title.

Our earliest authorities not only attribute the authorship of our book to Josephus—which is certainly wrong—but they give it a different title, which is probably right—or at least a more accurate description of its contents than "Maccabees." The first to mention our book is Eusebius (*ca.* 260-340), who says (*Eccles. Hist.* 3.10.6): "Another quite distinguished work was produced by this man [Josephus], *On the Sovereignty of Reason*, which some style *A Book of Maccabees*, by reason of its inclusion of the heroic deeds of the Hebrews in the cause of piety to the divine which are included also in the books called Maccabees." Eusebius was a good scholar, where his prejudices were not engaged; and despite his wrong attribution of authorship, the title he prefers, as well as his explanation of the alternative title, seem correct. Jerome, writing in 412, has much the same; speaking of Josephus in *De viris illustribus*, 13, he says: "Another book of his, entitled *On the Sovereignty of Reason*, is an extremely polished work; it also deals with the martyrdoms of the Maccabees." In *Contra Pelagianos* 2.6 he implies that "Maccabees" was actually an alternative title: "Josephus, the writer of the History of the Maccabees, says that emotions can be mastered and controlled, not eradicated." Later authors who speak of the book or its author have no independent authority, but merely adapt what they found in Eusebius or Jerome. Surely, of the choices before us, *On the Sovereignty of Reason* is preferable as being a statement of the professed thesis of the book. But the alternative *Maccabees* is not as remote as it is in the case of III Maccabees; for though the Maccabees and their uprising are not mentioned in the book, the episode it deals with is connected with the same series of events, and its heroes came to be called Maccabean martyrs. Hence, though "Maccabees" can hardly have been the original title—and certainly not "Fourth Maccabees"— that title probably came to be applied to the book rather early. Of all the books of Maccabees the Fourth would be most attractive to the Christians, who alone preserved them; and it is not impossible that the other three were saved because their title connected them with our book. St. Augustine wrote[53] that the *books* of the Maccabees were preserved by the Church because of the martyrdoms they contain—which points primarily to our book.

IX

Philosophy

Under whatever title, IV Maccabees was written, we assume, by an unknown author about 40 CE for delivery to a congregation of Hellenized Jews assembled at Antioch near the site of the martyrdoms on a day of commemoration. What is the shape of our author's thought, and what attitudes on religion and ethics does he wish to communicate? As we have seen from the comparison of our author's treatment of his story with those of II Maccabees and of the rabbis, the atmosphere is that of a Hellenized group, living with little strain in a Hellenized environment, adopting some of its manners even in religious observances, endeavoring to promote the general culture, and at odds with it only when it conflicted with their own religious views, which they believed were of service to the general welfare. As his familiarity with Scripture and his accurate knowledge of the requirements of the Law show, our author is at home in the Jewish tradition to which he

[53] *City of God* 18.36.

so warmly urges loyalty; but the philosophic structure of his thought is Greek. Plato is not merely an armory of adventitious arguments to confute the pagans with their own weapons, but a way of thought espoused by our author and presumably by his audience. From Plato comes such specific doctrine as the four cardinal virtues, the two parts of the soul, the destiny of human beings after death, the question of the animality of the stars. These things, it is clear, our author drew directly from Plato and not from secondary sources, just as he was quite obviously at home with the tragic poets.

If we look for a single Platonic treatise which might have been in his mind as a model, we should choose the *Gorgias*.[54] Here Socrates refutes the Sophist Callicles, who maintains the justice of capricious tyranny on the grounds that justice is the power of the strong, employing the argument that the laws of morality are only convention (*nomos* means both "law" and "convention"), whereas the true criterion of morality is "nature" (*physis*), which is notoriously red in tooth and claw. The position of Eleazar—and of our author—generally is very like that of Socrates, as a few excerpts from the *Gorgias* will show.[55] Socrates presents two paradoxes: "If it is necessary either to do or to suffer wrong, it is better to suffer than to do it" (469c); and "The wrong-doer is worse off if he is not punished than if he is (472e)." Callicles objects that the tyrant can nevertheless subject his victim to torture; but Socrates insists that "any wrong whatsoever done me or mine is worse and more shameful to the wrong-doer than to me the wronged" (508e). There is an "art of providing so that we suffer no wrong" (510a), and that is by "avoiding any unjust word or deed in regard to either men or gods" (522cd). The important thing is for a man to persevere in his own true values, and retain his control despite the assaults of immediate fear and interest. "The temperate man, being just and brave and pious,

[54] Gutman, 35 f., is convinced that the *Gorgias* was actually the model.
[55] The translations which follow are adapted from W. R. M. Lamb, in the Loeb Classical Library.

INTRODUCTION 117

is the perfection of the good man, and a good man fares well however he fares and is blessed and happy, while the wicked man or evil-doer is wretched" (507b). True judgment will take place in the future when men are stripped of their bodies, which confuse judgment in this life, and their bare souls can be examined (523). This must be kept in mind in shaping our conduct. "No man fears the mere act of dying, except he be utterly irrational and unmanly; doing wrong is what one fears: for to arrive in the nether world bearing one's soul fraught with a heap of misdeeds is the uttermost of all evils" (522e). And here is Socrates' conclusion: "Let us therefore take as our guide the doctrine now disclosed, which indicates to us that this way of life is best—to live and die in the practice alike of justice and of all other virtue. This then let us follow, and to this invite everyone else; not that to which you trust yourself and invite me, for it is nothing worth, Callicles" (527e).

Against the background of Socrates' attitude and moral position in the *Gorgias* much that is in our book falls into focus, not only with regard to the similar posture of Eleazar confronting an actual tyrant but also in individual details.[56] There can be no doubt that our author was a consistent Platonist. He knew Stoicism, of course, and at many points uses Stoic language and echoes Stoic views;[57] but the general opinion that he is himself predominantly Stoic is quite mistaken. The most obvious Stoic points, it must be noted, are put in the mouth of the king, who apparently assumes that Eleazar must be a Stoic, and then proceeds to chide him for deviations from Stoic orthodoxy. Eleazar's replies are then tantamount to a refutation of Stoicism, usually with reliance on the more congenial Platonism, reinforced with Jewish doctrine. The Stoics defined wisdom as "the knowledge of things human and divine and their causes"; for Eleazar this knowledge is what is prescribed

[56] See, *e.g.*, on 5.11, 5.30, 9.31.
[57] See, *e.g.*, on 1.1, 1.6, 1.16 f., 1.33, 2.7, 2.14, 3.11 f., 5.7 ff., 5.19 f., 5.22, 5.25, 5.38, 12.13, 13.19, 14.2, 15.4.

in the Law. The Stoics insisted that the sage must extirpate his emotions; Eleazar (following Jewish tradition and Aristotle) says that they must not be extirpated but controlled and directed. The Stoics allowed no gradations in sin—a miss, in their sight, being as bad as a mile. Eleazar follows the opponents of Stoicism (and Jewish tradition) in distinguishing between grave and light transgression.

In this connection it is interesting to observe that these identical objections to Stoicism appear (and naturally with greater fullness) in Philo, who is roughly contemporary with our author.[58] There are other respects in which our author stands with Philo, as against pagan philosophers or against Palestinian Judaism. Like Philo and like rabbinic Judaism,[59] our author believes in an individual Providence; Plato's Providence is not concerned with the individual—certainly not to the extent of disturbing nature on his behalf—and for the Stoics Providence is merely another name for the immutable laws of nature, which override care for the individual. Like Philo, again, our author believes in immortality, in the sense of the persistence of the individual soul as a distinct entity;[60] he markedly avoids speaking of bodily resurrection, which is stressed in II Maccabees.[61] Parallels between the two are of little significance in establishing priority; but they are of considerable significance in demonstrating that at Antioch as well as at Alexandria learned Jews accommodating Jewish tradition to Greek molds arrived at similar views of religion and ethics.

X

Religion

A cursory reader can see that Eleazar and the others died in witness to their faith; but a cynical one might wonder whether

[58] See Wolfson, 2.271 f., and notes on 1.16 f., 3.11 f., 5.7 ff., 5.19 f.
[59] Wolfson, 2.293.
[60] *Quaest. in Genes.* 3.11; see Wolfson, 1.396 f.
[61] *Cf.* San. 91b, M. San. 10.1–4; II Mac. 7.9, 23, 14.46.

the king was not right in calling him stubborn and foolish for refusing to take a mouthful of forbidden food when his life depended on it, and wonder too whether (as the hypothetical argument which the young men might have used but did not puts it) he was only indulging in vainglory and braggadocio. It is therefore important to realize that Eleazar's conduct was strictly in accordance with the laws—and laws which, granting the premises of Judaism, were necessary and reasonable. In the first place, the swine's flesh which Eleazar was required to eat was a portion of sacrificial meat (5.2), and hence partaking of it involved service to a pagan cult and therefore came under the head of idolatry. Idolatry was the one sin which might under no circumstance be committed; when the rabbis came to codify conduct under threat of martyrdom, they ordained that under threat of death any prohibition might be disregarded except, first, idolatry, and then adultery and murder.[62]

In the second place, a great distinction in gravity is made between sins committed in private and in public (*b'parhesia*).[63] Sins that might be venial if committed in private take on a much more serious character if committed in public; and more especially if public issue is being made of the transgression. Even permissible acts which might *seem* like sins to an onlooker are prohibited *mi-pne mar'it ayin*, "for the sake of appearance." When an issue *is* made, then even a slight transgression involves *hillul ha-Shem*, "profanation of the divine name," avoidance of which is the highest obligation.[64] The regular expression for martyrdom is the opposite of *hillul ha-Shem*, to wit *kiddush ha-Shem*, or "sanctification of the divine name," and the regular expression for martyrs is "those that succumbed for the sanctification of the divine name." Hence it is no mere point of personal pride when Eleazar objects that he will be laughed at for violating his principles, no bolstering of pride when he refers to his reputation, and no bravado

[62] Pes. 25a and parallels.
[63] Sifre Deut. 76 and parallels.
[64] Kid. 40a; Yoma 86a.

when he expresses indignation at the proffered ruse by which he would only *appear* to be transgressing. At all points Eleazar is behaving precisely as later codification—and doubtless current usage—demanded.

In the case of the brethren these matters remain in the background, though they are several times specifically implied; and always the example of Eleazar (who had made the case clear) is invoked. In the case of the mother the motivation is different. Her contribution is the supreme manifestation of the sovereignty of religious reason over the strongest of emotions— maternal love; and she is given the highest praise of all. Her voluntary death is attributed to her unwillingness to have her body touched by alien hands; this, it must be noted, would come under the head of the second of the cardinal sins to which martyrdom was to be preferred, for any violation of chastity was classed as adultery. For murder, which is the third, our story offered no occasion; nor was it necessary to stress a point on which general enlightened opinion would be in agreement. But if our discourse is in fact directed to a fashionable metropolitan congregation, one can surmise that the extended exhortation to loyalty to the cause of religion and even to chastity by the example of the mother was in fact a necessary *argumentum ad feminas*.[65]

Eleazar, we see, consistently followed a well-reasoned line of conduct, which, whether it had yet been crystallized into a code, was pragmatically the only road to survival for a communion confronted by liability to persecution; its codification is evidence of its practicality in this respect. But was survival of the communion important enough to induce men to take the hard road? Here our author has no slightest doubt. The divine origin of the Law is axiomatic; and wisdom itself is only culture acquired under the Law (1.16). This conviction carries with it obligation to all the responsibilities demanded by the Law; and hence no more need be said of our author's religion than

[65] For "some examples of Maccabean Halaka" see L. Finkelstein's paper with that title in *Journal of Biblical Literature*, XLIX (1930) 20–42.

that he conformed to the Judaism of his day. What he learned from the Greeks he put to the service of Judaism—not the other way. Perhaps, if we had more from his hand, we should find him as ready as Philo to allegorize uncomfortable passages of Scripture; where he does deal with Scriptural stories homiletically (David, Dathan and Abiram) his treatment is doctrinally unexceptionable. On Providence, as we have seen, and on rewards and punishments he stands with the rabbis. The only disagreement in this connection is that he apparently avoids the question of resurrection, and speaks only of immortality.

Doctrinally the most interesting of our author's teachings is his belief that the suffering of the righteous martyr is an expiation for the sins of the community (1.11, 17.19–23, 18.24). In early strata of thought the notion that group pollution can be expiated mechanically by blood is commonplace; among the Greeks it is exemplified by the function of the Erinyes, and among the Hebrews by the ritual for the expiation of an unapprehended murder (Deut. 21.1–9). "It is the blood," we read in Lev. 17.11, "that maketh atonement." In the Temple sacrifices, or the annual atonement ritual (Lev. 16.7–22) which involved expiation for the whole people, the mechanical notion of the atoning power of blood is spiritualized; but the notion of group responsibility persists. Jer. 31.29 and Ezek. 18.2 cite as a time-honored proverb, "The fathers have eaten sour grapes, and the children's teeth are set on edge." Each prophet proceeds to correct the ancient belief, and to assert the doctrine of individual responsibility. Jeremiah says (31.30), "But everyone shall die for his own iniquity; every man that eateth the sour grapes, his teeth shall be set on edge"; and Ezekiel (18.4), "the soul that sinneth, it shall die." It is interesting to observe that Aeschylus (*Agamemnon* 756 ff.) similarly declares that he "holds a mind apart from other men" in rejecting the notion of hereditary guilt.

The doctrine of individual responsibility stressed by the prophets remained normative in rabbinic Judaism; and the notion that the guilt of an ancestor had to be expiated by his descendants could come only from the Apocalyptic sect, which held heterodox views on the matter. From this group emanated the concept that death was introduced for Adam's transgression;[66] and also the notion that the original sin will be redeemed by a blameless figure who "shall be delivered up for the lawless man, and the sinless one shall die for ungodly men."[67] Formulation so specific is not part of the rabbinic tradition, and after the advent of Christianity would surely have been sharply rejected. The later rabbis do speak of the sufferings or death of the righteous as an atonement for the whole community;[68] but of such ideas it may be said that they crept in by the back door. In the intertestamentary period such notions were in the air, among the Apocalyptic group if not in the main stream of Jewish tradition; and the notion that the martyrs of his account would serve as an expiation for the whole community is a perfectly natural one for our author to have and express, and would not be regarded by his hearers as an innovation.

If it was indeed written under Caligula, our book antedates the books of the New Testament; but whether it is earlier or later there is no need to assume a literary dependence, in either direction, between it and the New Testament. Not only the striking parallel of vicarious expiation, but other similarities are due to the fact that these works derive from a common religious (and linguistic) climate. "Abraham, Isaac, and Jacob will receive us" (13.17) and "Abraham's bosom" in Luke 16.23; or "stand before the throne of God" (17.18) and the same expression in Rev. 7.15, prove no more than that the notions represented by these words were in the air. No more significance can attach to them than to the occurrence of an image involving spectators and an athletic contest at both 17.14 and Heb. 12.1. There is no more necessity to assume interdependence for religious terminology than for such a secular image; and certainly no need to assume that expressions like

[66] II Baruch 23.4; see Zeitlin (as in note 35), 7 ff.
[67] Testament of Benjamin 3.8.
[68] M. Tanhuma, *Vayakhel* 9; Ex. R. 35.4; Lev. R. 2; *cf.* Moore, 1.546 ff.

those in the New Testament are interpolations when they occur in IV Maccabees.

If our author is an innovator, it is in his attempt to acclimate Judaism to a Hellenized Diaspora, and thus prepare the way for making of it, and of its daughter religion, a universal faith. It was at Antioch, as we observed, that Christianity entered the general stream of Mediterranean culture. The main motive in our author's discourse, then, is not the exposition of a novel theology, but rather the exploitation of novel methods for the traditional tasks of exhortation and admonition. Because he is an intelligent man addressing intelligent men, he provides philosophical framework, which was part of his thought; but the framework is essentially mere scaffolding for a spiritual message which has retained its relevance through the centuries. What he urges upon his readers is loyalty to a high standard of rectitude, based upon divine revelation; and what he promises is that steadfast resistance to temptation and oppression is rewarded by the serenity which comes from consciousness of rectitude, and by full spiritual justification in another existence.

XI

INFLUENCE

Great as the substantive worth of IV Maccabees may be, its importance as providing precept and example for significant expressions of religion in Europe is far greater. From the point of view of influence, the opinion may be ventured that IV Maccabees is the most important of the literary works with which it is commonly associated. Among Jews, apparently, the book did not survive the Hellenized milieu out of which it rose; versions of the martyrdoms in later rabbinic literature probably derived, as we shall see, from an independent historical tradition. But among Christians the book enjoyed a great vogue, as allusions to it in the golden age of patristic oratory, in Gregory of Nazianz and John Chrysostom, in Ambrose and Augustine[69] prove.

[69] On the use of IV Maccabees by Church orators see Freudenthal, 29 ff.

Gregory's discourse "To the Maccabean"[70] uses our book generally, for matter and form, and warmly recommends its reading. John Chrysostom wrote four homilies on the Maccabean martyrs,[71] and his use of our book is very evident. It is important to note that these men, who became the acknowledged models for structure and style in religious discourses, borrowed from the manner as well as the matter of our book. They had both been students of the masters of the Second Sophistic,[72] but Libanius and the others did not teach the application of rhetoric to religious themes. Ambrose, who was the only Latin Father to make large use of the Greek—and so the principal channel through which Greek influence reached the West— makes patent use of IV Maccabees in two treatises: *De officiis minoribus*[73] and *De Jacob et vita beata*;[74] the latter is virtually a transcript of our book.

The use of IV Maccabees by these eminent and influential Christian orators suggests one aspect of its importance in the spiritual history of Europe. A more tangible contribution is the impulse and direction it gave to the concept and literary treatment of martyrdoms, which occupied so important a place in the Christianity of the early centuries. It has been demonstrated —most recently by Surkau[75]—that Christian views on the subject of martyrdoms and their literary expression were an outgrowth of antecedent Jewish ideas and literary formulations; and of these IV Maccabees was the best example, as it was the most accessible. The share of our book in shaping a significant aspect of Christianity is therefore very considerable. Of the whole episode of the Maccabean uprising, the new and important aspect—and the aspect most meaningful for posterity—is

[70] *PG* 35.911–934; *cf.* Freudenthal, 29.
[71] *PG* 50.617–628, 64.523–550; *cf.* Freudenthal, 32.
[72] See my *History of Greek Literature* 271 f., 281 f.
[73] *PL* 14.627 ff.
[74] *PL* 14.662 f.; *cf.* Freudenthal, 32 f.
[75] H. W. Surkau, *Martyrien in jüdischer und frühchristlicher Zeit* (Göttingen, 1938). Surkau effectively disposes of the arguments of von Campenhausen, whose *Die Idee des Martyriums in der alten Kirche* (Göttingen, 1936) denied Jewish influence.

that it was a life and death struggle on behalf of a religion against an oppressor determined to annihilate it;[76] for later ages, at least, the nationalist aspects of the struggle were only incidental. Posterity was not interested in the political exchanges and military campaigns, but in the religious struggle; and this IV Maccabees dramatizes and crystallizes by embodying the issues in personal protagonists. The essence of all that was meaningful in the history of the Maccabees is therefore subsumed in our book; and when the Christian community came to be persecuted by Rome only the story of the Maccabees could serve as example and inspiration for resistance. Augustine (*City of God*, 18.36) says specifically that the Books of the Maccabees were received and preserved by the Church "on account of the extreme and wonderful suffering of the martyrs told therein." The discourse of Gregory of Nazianz, mentioned above, had actually used the word "protomartyr" in speaking of Eleazar.

Our earliest official evidence of Rome's attitude toward the Christians is contained in the famous inquiry on procedures addressed by Pliny from Bithynia to the Emperor Trajan, and Trajan's rescript on the subject (Pliny, 10.96-97). Here are Trajan's words:[77]

> It is not possible to lay down any general rule which can be applied as the fixed standard in all cases of this nature. No search should be made for these people; when they are denounced and found guilty they must be punished; with the restriction, however, that when the party denies himself to be a Christian, and shall give proof that he is not (that is, by adoring our Gods) he shall be pardoned on the ground of repentance, even though he may have formerly incurred suspicion.

This remained the official attitude during the persecutions of the succeeding centuries, until the edict of Constantine made

---
[76] See Zeitlin, Introd. to I Maccabees in present series, 1.
[77] Trans. Melmoth-Hutchinson, in Loeb Classical Library.

Christianity the religion of the state. Like Eleazar before Antiochus, any Christian might save himself by publicly recanting his Christianity; and it was Eleazar that Christian teachers had in mind when they held the Maccabeans up as models of fortitude and perseverance. The earliest literary account of a martyrdom we have is that of Polycarp, dated in the 2d century. (Polycarp, it is worth noting, was also a nonagenarian.) The description of the constancy of the martyrs in the *Martyrdom of Polycarp* (ch. 2), and especially of the reasoning which gave them courage, is remarkably reminiscent of IV Maccabees.[78]

> All the martyrdoms, then, were blessed and noble which took place according to the will of God. For it becomes us who profess greater piety than others, to ascribe the authority over all things to God. And truly, who can fail to admire their nobleness of mind, and their patience, with that love towards their Lord which they displayed?—who, when they were so torn with scourges, that the frame of their bodies, even to the very inward veins and arteries, was laid open, still patiently endured, while even those that stood by pitied and bewailed them. But they reached such a pitch of magnanimity, that not one of them let a sigh or a groan escape them; thus proving to us all that those holy martyrs of Christ, at the very time when they suffered such torments, were absent from the body, or rather, that the Lord then stood by them, and communed with them. And, looking to the grace of Christ, they despised all the torments of this world, redeeming themselves from eternal punishment by a single hour. For this reason the fire of their savage executioners appeared cool to them. For they kept before their view escape from that fire which is eternal and never shall be quenched, and looked forward

---

[78] Trans. A. Roberts and J. Donaldson, in *Ante-Nicene Christian Library* 1.84.

with the eyes of their heart to those good things which are laid up for such as endure.

This martyrdom set the tone for subsequent works of the same nature; if IV Maccabees influenced one it influenced all. The *Passio SS. Machabaeorum*, which is a free adaptation of IV Maccabees, was probably composed in the 4th century, and continued to be read until Erasmus paraphrased it.[79] "At the close of the fourth century," a competent authority writes,[80] "we find all the great orators of the Church both in the East and the West preaching panegyrics of the holy martyrs before vast audiences assembled to pay respects to these champions of the faith on their festivals." Such a martyrdom as that of Felicitas and her Seven Sons (though the case may have been historical) is obviously influenced by the story of our book. Even the author of *Barlaam and Joasaph* can say (23), in quoting from IV Maccabees, that the martyrs of that book are "the crown and model of martyrdom." Relics of the Maccabean martyrs were shown not only in Antioch but also in Constantinople, Rome, and even Cologne.[81]

XII

The Story in Rabbinic Literature

The rabbis in Palestine also developed artistic homiletic discourses, and appreciated the religious implications of martyr-

[79] See 136, and note 69.

[80] H. Thurston, in *Encyclopedia of Religion and Ethics* (New York, 1921) 11.55.

[81] See Cardinal Rampolla, 259 ff. Erasmus, who dedicates his version to Elias Maraeus, president of the "most honorable college of Maccabees at Cologne," says that the Maccabean relics were highly revered at Cologne in his day. Helen (mother of Constantine) was said to have conveyed them from Antioch to Byzantium, when Eustorgius brought them to Milan, whence Reginald, Bishop of Cologne, brought them to that city.

doms;[82] but, as far as we can see, in neither respect were they influenced by our book, and there is no evidence that they were aware of its existence. They did know of a mother whose seven sons were martyred, and their account of the martyrdom bears a certain resemblance to that in IV Maccabees; but the discrepancies make any dependence on our book dubious, and rather argue for the historicity of the martyrdoms by showing that knowledge of them survived in an independent tradition. For one thing, the story is transposed to the reign of Hadrian, where any indication of time is given;[83] which would show that the tradition was oral, and not dependent upon a written source. For another thing, Eleazar is entirely omitted from the account, which he could hardly have been if IV Maccabees were the source, but which is entirely likely in an independent tradition; for, as we have seen,[84] the association of Eleazar with the story of the brethren is our author's own invention.

An interesting aspect of the rabbinic passages is that the principal ones (Lam. R 1.50, Gittin 57b, Seder Eliyahu R 29) occur in contexts dealing with the ninth Ab; and it would on general grounds seem likely that the commemoration of our martyrs would be assimilated to, if it were not originally fixed, on that day. The liturgy for the ninth Ab shows reminiscences of the Maccabean martyrdoms which may represent a continuing tradition.[85] Professor Obermann, who believes that IV Maccabees was in fact connected with the ninth Ab, finds support in the circumstance that the Christian commemoration of the

---

[82] See the remarks on the *Asarah Haruge Malkhut* or *Eleh Ezkerah*, 107-8 above.

[83] Seder Eliyahu R. 30 (28) says specifically, "Hadrian came and seized upon a widow." Pesikta R. 43 (180b) says "In the days of the *shemad*,"—i.e., the Hadrianic persecutions.

[84] See 93.

[85] *Cf.* Zunz, *Die gottesdienstliche Vorträge der Juden*, 2.131; Steinschneider, *Die arabische Literatur der Juden* 287, lists a *kinah* on Hannah and her Seven Sons, probably for the ninth Ab. The *Arze ha-Lebanon* in our ritual may be a replacement for a piece dealing with the martyrs of IV Maccabees.

INTRODUCTION 129

seven martyrs, which was probably adopted from the Jewish, fell on the first of August.[86] The character of the rabbinic tradition may best be appreciated from a specimen. The fullest (though naturally not the oldest) rabbinic parallel to our book is that in Lam. R 1.50 (on Lam. 1.16, "For these things I weep"); and it may conveniently be reproduced here:[87]

It is related of Miriam, the daughter of Tanhum, that she was taken captive with her seven sons. The emperor took and placed them in the innermost of seven rooms. He had the eldest brought and said to him, Prostrate yourself before the image. He answered, God forbid! I will not prostrate myself before an image." "Why?" asked the king. "Because it is thus written in our Torah, *I am the Lord thy God*" (Ex. 20.2). He immediately had him taken out and slain. He had the second brought and said to him, "Prostrate yourself before the image." He answered, "God forbid! My brother did not prostrate himself and I will not." "Why?" the king asked. He replied, "Because it is thus written in our Torah, *Thou shalt have no other gods before Me*" (*ibid.* 3). He immediately ordered him to be slain. He had the third brought and said to him, "Prostrate yourself before the image." He answered, "I will not prostrate myself." "Why?" the king asked. "Because it is written in the Torah, *For thou shalt bow down to no other god*" (*ibid.* 34.14). He immediately ordered him to be slain. He had the fourth brought, who quoted, *He that sacrificeth unto the gods, save unto the Lord only, shall be utterly destroyed* (*ibid.* 22.19), and he was ordered to be slain. He had the fifth

---

[86] J. Obermann, "The Sepulchre of the Maccabean Martyrs," in *Journal of Biblical Literature*, L (1931) 250–265. For his date Obermann cites Nilles, *Kalendarium Manuale*, 2.1.230, and recalls that Taanit 4.6 prescribes the period of mourning as from the first of Ab—*mishenikhnas Ab*.

[87] Trans. A. Cohen in the Soncino series: *Midrash Rabbah: Lamentations* (London, 1937).

brought, who also quoted, *Hear, O Israel, the Lord our God, the Lord is one* (Deut. 6.4), and he was immediately ordered to be slain. He had the sixth brought, who likewise quoted, *For the Lord thy God is in the midst of thee, a God great and awful* (*ibid.* 7.21), and he was ordered to be slain. He had the seventh brought, who was the youngest of them all, and the king said, "My son, prostrate yourself before the image." He answered, "God forbid!" "Why?" asked the King. "Because it is thus written in our Torah, *Know this day, and lay it to thy heart, that the Lord, he is God in heaven above and upon the earth beneath; there is none else* (*ibid.* 4.39). Not only that, but we have sworn to our God that we will not exchange Him for any other god; as it is said, *Thou hast avouched the Lord this day to be thy God* (*ibid.* 26.17). And as we swore to Him, so He swore to us not to exchange us for another people; as it is said, *And the Lord hath avouched thee this day to be His own treasure*" (*ibid.* 18). The emperor said to him, "Your brothers had had their fill of years and of life and had experienced happiness; but you are young, you have had no fill of years and life, and have not yet experienced happiness. Prostrate yourself before the image, and I will bestow favours upon you." He replied, "It is written in our Torah, *The Lord shall reign for ever and ever* (Ex. 15.18), and it is said, *The Lord is King for ever; the nations are perished out of His land* (Ps. 10.16). You are of no account and so are His enemies. A human being lives to-day and is dead to-morrow, rich to-day and poor to-morrow; but the Holy One, blessed be He, lives and endures for all eternity." The emperor said to him, "See, your brothers are slain before you. Behold, I will throw my ring to the ground in front of the image; pick it up so that all may know that you have obeyed my command." He answered, "Woe unto you, O emperor! If you are afraid of human beings, who are the same as yourself, shall I not fear the supreme King of Kings, the Holy One, blessed be He, the God of the universe!" He asked him, "Has, then, the universe a God?" He replied, "Shame on you, O emperor! Do you, then, behold a world without a Master?" He asked, "Has your God a mouth?" He answered, "In connection with your gods it is written, *They have mouths, but they speak not* (*ibid.* 15.5); in connection with our God it is written, *By the word of the Lord were the heavens made*" (*ibid.* 33.6). "Has your God eyes?" He answered, "In connection with your gods it is written, *Eyes have they, but they see not* (*ibid.* 115.5); in connection with our God it is written, *The eyes of the Lord, that run to and fro through the whole earth*" (Zech. 4.10). "Has your God ears?" He answered, "In connection with your gods it is written, *They have ears, but they hear not* (Ps. 115.6); in connection with our God it is written, *And the Lord hearkened, and heard*" (Mal. 3.16). "Has your God a nose?" He answered, "In connection with your gods it is written, *Noses have they, but they smell not* (Ps. *loc. cit.*); in connection with our God it is written, *And the Lord smelled the sweet savour*" (Gen. 8.21). "Has your God hands?" He answered, "In connection with your gods it is written, *They have hands, but they handle not* (Ps. 115.7); in connection with our God it is written, *Yea, My hand hath laid the foundation of the earth*" (Is. 48.13). "Has your God feet?" He answered, "In connection with your gods it is written, *Feet have they, but they walk not* (Ps. *loc. cit.*); in connection with our God it is written, *And his feet shall stand in that day upon the Mount of Olives*" (Zech. 14.4). "Has your God a throat?" He answered, "In connection with your gods it is written, *Neither speak they with their throat* (Ps. *loc. cit.*); in connection with our God it is written, *And sound goeth out of His mouth*" (Job 37.2). The king asked, "If there are all these attributes in your God, why does He not deliver you out of my hand in the same manner that He rescued Hananiah, Mishael, and Azariah from the hands of Nebuchadnezzar?" He answered, "Hananiah,

Mishael, and Azariah were worthy men, and king Nebuchadnezzar was deserving that a miracle should be performed through him. You, however, are undeserving; and as for ourselves, our lives are forfeit to heaven. If you do not slay us, the Omnipresent has numerous executioners. There are many bears, wolves, serpents, leopards, and scorpions to attack and kill us; but in the end the Holy One, blessed be He, will avenge our blood on you." The king immediately ordered him to be put to death.

The child's mother said to him, "By the life of your head, O emperor, give me my son that I may embrace and kiss him." They gave him to her, and she bared her breasts and suckled him. She said to the king, "By the life of your head, O emperor, put me to death first and then slay him." He answered her, "I cannot agree to that, because it is written in your Torah, *And whether it be cow or ewe, ye shall not kill it and its young both in one day*" (Lev. 22.28). She retorted, "You unutterable fool! Have you already fulfilled all the commandments save only this one?" He immediately ordered him to be slain. The mother threw herself upon her child and embraced and kissed him. She said to him, "My son, go to the patriarch Abraham and tell him, 'Thus said my mother, "Do not preen yourself (on your righteousness), saying I built an altar and offered up my son, Isaac." Behold, our mother built seven altars and offered up seven sons in one day. Yours was only a test, but mine was in earnest.' " While she was embracing and kissing him, the king gave an order and they killed him in her arms. When he had been slain, the Sages calculated the age of that child, and found that he was two years, six months, and six and a half hours old. At that time all the peoples of the world cried out, "What does their God do for them that they are all the time slain for His sake!" And concerning them it is written, *Nay, but for Thy sake are we killed all the day* (Ps. 44.23). After a few days the woman became demented and fell from a roof and died,[88] to fulfil what is said, *She that hath borne seven languisheth* (Jer. 15.9). A *Bath Kol* issued forth and proclaimed, "*A joyful mother of children*" (Ps. 113.9); and the Holy Spirit cried out, "For these things I weep."

The divergences of this account (which effectively summarizes the main points of the rabbinic tradition[89]) from that in our book are plain, and such as one should expect in a version so transmitted. The less obvious implications are of greater interest, and set the premises of IV Maccabees in sharper relief.[90] Here there is no real effort to make a place for Judaism in a conflict of religions, as there is in the Greek story. The assurance of the martyrs is as absolute as their contempt for the authority which persecutes them; even a babe in arms knows that paganism is negligible. There is no attempt at philosophic refutation, no implication that yielding is conceivable. The dialogue with the king is no real exchange of ideas, to furnish guidance to readers perplexed by real alternatives, but merely a device for glorifying God. The audience does not need or desire help to confound the heathen. It is for this reason too that the details of the torture are omitted. Experience of Roman persecutions had made it all too plain that perseverance inevitably brought real torture, as surely as rain brought moisture; and certainty was so absolute that no conjured-up tortures could weigh in the balance of decision. Actually, there is not even a question of the real acceptance of paganism (which in the Maccabees story is the implication of sharing in food offered to idols), but only of bowing down to the imperial image, which we may imagine the Maccabeans might recognize as a patriotic rather than a religious gesture, and so yield. IV Maccabees,

---

[88] Gittin 57b says nothing of her being demented: the later version apparently seeks to avoid the imputation of suicide.

[89] The relevant passages are: Gittin 57b; Seder Eliyahu R. 30 (28); Pesikta R. 43 (p. 180b); Lam. R. 1.50. Of the Josippon version (4.18-19) something will be said below.

[90] Gutman, 25-28.

then, reflects a conflict of ideologies in one world of which they and their opponents are both members; in their separate world the rabbis were not concerned with the motivation of their persecutions, but only with the effects upon themselves.

In the rabbinic versions there is no effort to fit the story into a historical framework, other than by allusions to the Hadrianic persecutions. Josippon[91]—which was the main channel by which the contents of the Books of the Maccabees reached Jewish readers before modern times—is careful to preserve the historical nexus; it even makes an impossible connection with Aristeas, by identifying our Eleazar with the High Priest in that book; and explains how Antiochus could have happened to be in Jerusalem when the martyrdoms took place. Josippon's account is manifestly a conflation of the Greek books with the rabbinic material, and so of value only as reflecting the interests of its own day. To begin with, Eleazar is on extremely friendly terms with Antiochus' ministers, who plead with him in secret to make only a show of yielding. The bearing of the sons, on the other hand, is like that in the rabbinic accounts. The notions of future retribution and of expiation (the word *kapparah* is used) are made prominent. A fine prayer is ascribed to Eleazar, and two beautiful lyrical utterances to the mother. She is called Hannah, and her prayers are reminiscences of the meditation of her Biblical namesake in I Sam. 2.

Another interesting conflation, based primarily on the familiar rabbinic material but containing one or two additional points, is the Arabic *Farag-Book* of Nissim Ibn Shahin of Kairowan.[92] Two ambiguous clauses have been interpreted by Professor Obermann to say that (a) the name of the mother in whose honor the synagogue was built was Hashmonith, and (b) that the synagogue was the first to be built after the destruction

[91] Ed. Guenzburg, 124 ff.; 4.18–19 in the ordinary editions. The so-called *Chronicles of Jerahmeel* (ed. Gaster, 263) adds nothing significant.

[92] For the relevance of this book to our subject see the paper of J. Obermann (its first editor) note 86. The paragraph that follows is based on Obermann's article, *q.v.* for documentation.

of the Temple. The name is of course the feminine of "Hasmonaean"; and if it derives—as the rest of the account does—from rabbinic sources, would supply evidence (of which there is no trace in our rabbinic writings) that the story of the martyrdoms was connected with the Hasmonaeans in the rabbinic as well as in the Greek tradition. Obermann notes that in the Syrian Church the Maccabean memorial day was known as the Festival of Shamuni and her Sons, and suggests that the Christians adopted the heroine's name along with the festival. To confront the inevitable objection that the name Hashmonith may have entered Nissim's account from a Christian source, Obermann adduces his second point, that the synagogue was the first to be built after the destruction of the Temple; Christians would not date the building of the martyrs' sanctuary by the Temple, and would not call it *Bayit sheni* ("the second house"), as Jews regularly did. Professor Obermann's interpretations of the difficult clauses are not wholly convincing; and they involve the further difficulty that the site of the Hashmonith synagogue would then have to be placed in Jerusalem. The evidence that the site of the martyrdom and sanctuary was at Antioch seems too strong to be disturbed by a passage so dubious and so late.

XIII

Texts, Versions, Editions

The text of IV Maccabees is contained in the two great manuscripts of the Greek Bible, the Sinaiticus of the 4th century ("S"), and the Alexandrinus of the 5th ("A"); in both the title is "Fourth Book of the Maccabees." None of the books of the Maccabees is included in the third of the great uncials, the Vaticanus. The place of the Vaticanus is supplied for us by Venetus Graecus, ("V"), of the 8th or 9th century; the section from 5.11 to 12.1 is wanting in V, but it is of great importance in establishing the text of the remainder. Aside from the lesser cursive manuscripts—concerning which information will be found in the editions presently to be mentioned—our book is included also in most of our Josephus manuscripts; these are, however, of less value in establishing a text.

There is a Syr. version in the Peshitto,[93] under the title *Fourth Book of the Maccabees and Their Mother*. In general the Syr. supports S as against A. IV Maccabees does not appear in the Vulgate, and (unlike I and II Maccabees) is not canonical in the Roman Catholic Church, nor properly part of the Apocrypha in the Protestant canon. There is, however, a Latin paraphrase under the title *Passio SS. Machabaeorum*,[94] of which the some 30 MSS. extant go back to an archetype of the 8th century, which they generally abridge. The original appears to have been composed about the 4th century. In general the *Passio* follows the Greek text closely, but there are omissions and expansions, especially in the apostrophes eulogizing the martyrs. There is also an Old Slavic version of our book.[95]

IV Maccabees first appeared in print in Vol. III of the Strasbourg Septuagint in 1526. This edition, based on a single poor MS. and filled with printer's errors, was the basis of the numerous 16th century editions. In 1590 Lloyd published an edition at Oxford, based on the Strasbourg text and "a New College MS." This superior text was included in the numerous editions of Josephus which appeared in the 18th and 19th centuries. During

---

[93] Facsimile in Ceriani, *Translatio Syra Pescitto V.T. ex codice Ambrosiano saec. fere VI photolithographice edita* (Milan, 1876–1883), II. A translation of the Syr. with introduction is available in Bensly-Barnes (see bibliographical list). This ed. compares the Gk. and Syr. in some 200 passages. Swete, 32 (1899) 900–902, presents a list of variants on the basis of the Syr.

[94] The text is presented for the first time by H. Dörrie, *Passio SS. Machabaeorum, die antike lateinische Uebersetzung des IV Makkabäerbuches*, in *Abhandlungen der Gesellschaft der Wissenschaften zu Göttingen, Philologisch-Historische Klasse*, Series 3, No. 22 (Göttingen, 1938). This was prepared with a view to the requirements of the Septuagint ed. of Göttingen.

[95] Bonwetsch, in Harnack, *Geschichte der altchristlichen Litteratur* 1.917, mentions two MSS of this, but says nothing of the merits of this version or of its date.

the same period two editions of the LXX (Grabe, Oxford, 1719, and Breitinger, Zurich, 1731) and one of the Apocrypha (Apel, Leipzig, 1837) all included IV Maccabees on the basis of the Alexandrinus. The first critical text, based on a number of MSS., was that of O. F. Fritzsche, *Libri Apocryphi Veteris Testamenti Graeci* (Leipzig, 1871). The text of H. B. Swete in Vol. III of his *The Old Testament in Greek*² (Cambridge, 1899) simply reproduces the Alexandrinus, and records the variants in Sinaiticus and Venetus Graecus. The Sinaiticus as well as the Alexandrinus (but only these) are the basis of the text in Rahlfs' Septuagint (Stuttgart, 1935). It is this text which is reproduced in the present volume. The meager critical apparatus, supplied by the present editor, on the basis of Rahlfs' fuller apparatus and of other editions, aims only to record such variants as might affect the translation significantly.

The list of modern translations begins with a 14th century version by Petrarch's friend Lapo da Castiglionchio, which, however, was never printed. Popular knowledge of our martyrdoms in the 16th century was provided by the frequently reprinted paraphrase of Erasmus, first published at Cologne in 1524, and dedicated to his friend Elias Maraeus, president of "the most honorable College of Maccabees" at Cologne.[96] Scholars have abused Erasmus' version as inexcusably unfaithful to the Greek original, as indeed it is. But Erasmus never saw the Greek text (which was first printed after his own work was published); and, as the editor of the *Passio SS. Machabaeorum* points out,[97] it was from that text that Erasmus worked. This not only explains many of Erasmus' divergences from the Greek, but excuses the rest, and justifies him completely by the flowing and elegant style he bestowed upon the work. Of the Latin versions which accompanied the 16th century editions of the Greek text, that of Lloyd is most highly praised by Freudenthal,[98] who

[96] For remarks on the Erasmus version see Townshend, 660.
[97] Dörrie (see note 94).
[98] Freudenthal, 136.

thinks it even superior to that published in 1672 by the Dominican Combefis in Part 1 of the *Bibliotheca Graecorum patrum* (1672).

The first modern commentary on IV Maccabees is that of C. L. W. Grimm (1857).[99] The translations which appear in the large English and German collections of so-called Apocrypha and Pseudepigrapha, that of R. B. Townshend in Charles' collection (1913) and that of A. Deissmann in Kautzsch's (1900), each has introduction and notes; Deissmann's translation is based on his own construction of the text, of which he prints only significant notes. The most recent and most complete work on the subject is André DuPont-Sommer's *Le Quatrième Livre des Machabées* (1939), which has an accurate translation based on an independently considered text, useful notes, a full introduction, and such subsidia as an extremely helpful *Index Graecitatis*. Perhaps the most stimulating single study remains that of J. Freudenthal (1869), which first suggested directions of interest which the book possesses for modern readers.

A word may be said of other modern translations of more popular design. In French we find mention only of a 17th century version by Arnauld d'Ardilly and an 18th century by Calmet. In German there are translations of IV Maccabees in the *Bibliothek der griechischen und römischen Schriftsteller über Judentum und Juden* (Leipzig, 1867), and in *Altjüdisches Schriftum ausserhalb des Bibel* (Berlin, 1928). In English the ineffable Roger L'Estrange produced a paraphrase in his usual florid style in the 17th century. Other translations are to be found in Colton, *The Five Books of Maccabees in English* (1832); Bagster, *Apocrypha, Greek and English* (1882); and Churton, *Uncanonical and Apocryphal Scripture* (1884). The latest English version is that of C. W. Emmet (listed below). There is a translation into modern Hebrew in *Hasephorim Hahizonim.* by T. H. Gaster.

[99] For bibliographical data on the works listed below, additional information will be found, where necessary, in the subjoined list of books.

INTRODUCTION 139

Subjoined is a short list of works frequently referred to in the present edition, with abbreviations where such are used:

B. W. Bacon, "The Festival of Lives Given for the Nation," *Hibbert Journal*, XV (1917), 256–278.

Elias J. Bickermann, "The Date of IV Maccabees," in *Louis Ginzberg Jubilee Volume* (New York, 1945), 105–112.

R. L. Bensly, *The Fourth Book of Maccabees and Kindred Documents in Syriac, First Edited on manuscript authority . . . with an introduction and translations* by W. E. Barnes (Cambridge, 1895).

A. Deissmann, *Das vierte Makkabäerbuch*, in L. Kautzsch's *Die Apokryphen und Pseudepigraphen des alten Testaments* (Tübingen, 1900) 2.149–177. Abbreviated "Deissmann."

H. Dörrie, *Passio SS. Machabaeorum, die antike lateinische Uebersetzung des IV Makkabäerbuches*, in *Abhandlungen der Gesellschaft der Wissenschaften zu Göttingen, Philologishch Historische Klasse*, Series 3, No. 22 (Göttingen, 1938).

A. DuPont-Sommer, *Le Quatriéme Livre des Machabées* (Bibliothèque de l'École des Hautes Études, fasc. 274, Paris, 1939). Abbreviated "DuP-S."

C. W. Emmet, *The Fourth Book of Maccabees* (Society for Promoting Christian Knowledge, London, 1918).

H. Ewald, *Geschichte des Volkes Israel*, 4³, (Göttingen, 1864).

J. Freudenthal, *Die Flavius Josephus beigelegte Schrift ueber Herrschaft der Vernunft (IV Makkabäerbuch), eine Predigt aus dem ersten nachchristlichen Jahrhundert* (Breslau, 1869). Abbreviated "Freudenthal."

O. F. Fritzsche, *Libri Apocryphi Veteris Testamenti Graeci* (Leipzig, 1871).

L. Ginzberg, *Legends of the Jews*, 7 vols. (Philadelphia, 1909–1946). Abbreviated "Ginzberg."

C. L. W. Grimm, *Viertes Buch der Maccabäer*, in *Kurzgefasstes exegetisches Handbuch zu den Apokryphen des alten Testaments* (Leipzig, 1857). Abbreviated "Grimm."

J. Gutman, "Ha-em v'Shivat Baneha b'Aggada u'b'Sifre Hashmonaim II v'IV," in *Commentationes Iudaico-Hellenisticae in Memoriam Iohannis Lewy*, ed. M. Schwabe and I. Gutman (Jerusalem, 1949), 25–37. Abbreviated "Gutman."

M. Hadas, *Aristeas to Philocrates* (New York, 1951). Abbreviated "Aristeas."

E. G. Kraeling, "The Jewish Community at Antioch," in *Journal of Biblical Literature*, LI (1932), 130–160.

S. Krauss, "Antioche," in *Revue des Études Juives*, XLV (1902), 27–49.

Max Maas, "Die Maccabäer als Christliche Heilige," *Monatsschrift für Geschichte und Wissenschaft des Judentums*, XLIV (1900), 145–156.

G. F. Moore, *Judaism in the First Centuries of the Christian Era*, 3 vols. (Cambridge, 1927).

E. Norden, *Die antike Kunstprosa vom VI. Jahrhundert v. Chr. bis in die Zeit der Renaissance*, 14 (Leipzig, 1923).

J. Obermann, "The Sepulchre of the Maccabean Martyrs," in *Journal of Biblical Literature*, L (1931), 250–265.

Patrologia Graeca, ed. Migne. Abbreviated *PG*.

Patrologia Latina, ed. Migne. Abbreviated *PL*.

Pualy-Wissowa-Kroll, *Encyklopädie der classischen Altertumswissenschaft*. Abbreviated PWK.

A. Rahlfs, *Septuaginta* (Stuttgart, 1935).

Rampolla de Tindaro (Cardinal), "Martyre et Sépulture des Machabées," in *Revue de l'Art Chrétien*, 1899, 295 ff.

E. Schürer, *Geschichte des jüdischen Volkes im Zeitalter Jesu Christi*, 3[3] (Leipzig, 1898).

H. W. Surkau, *Martyrien in jüdischer und frühchristlicher Zeit (Forschungen zur Religion und Literatur des alten und neuen Testaments, N. F. 36*, Göttingen, 1938).

H. B. Swete, *The Old Testament in Greek*, 3[3] (Cambridge, 1899).

C. C. Torrey, *The Apocryphal Literature* (New Haven, 1945).

R. B. Townshend, *The Fourth Book of Maccabees*, in R. H. Charles, *The Apocrypha and Pseudepigrapha of the Old Testament* (Oxford, 1913), II 653–685. Abbreviated "Townshend."

H. A. Wolfson, *Philo*, 2 vols. (Cambridge, 1947). Abbreviated "Wolfson."

S. Zeitlin, "The Legend of the Ten Martyrs and its Apocalyptic Origin," *Jewish Quarterly Review*, 1945, 1–16.

TEXT, TRANSLATION, COMMENTARY, AND CRITICAL NOTES

ΜΑΚΚΑΒΑΙΩΝ Δ'

1 ¹Φιλοσοφώτατον λόγον ἐπιδείκνυσθαι μέλλων, εἰ αὐτοδέσποτός ἐστιν τῶν παθῶν ὁ εὐσεβὴς λογισμός, συμβουλεύσαιμ' ἂν ὑμῖν ὀρθῶς ὅπως προσέχητε προθύμως τῇ φιλοσοφίᾳ. ²καὶ γὰρ ἀναγκαῖος εἰς ἐπιστήμην παντὶ ὁ λόγος καὶ ἄλλως τῆς μεγίστης ἀρετῆς, λέγω δὴ φρονήσεως, περιέχει ἔπαινον. ³εἰ ἄρα τῶν σωφροσύνης κωλυτικῶν παθῶν ὁ λογισμὸς φαίνεται ἐπικρατεῖν, γαστριμαργίας τε καὶ ἐπιθυμίας, ⁴ἀλλὰ καὶ τῶν τῆς δικαιοσύνης ἐμποδιστικῶν παθῶν κυριεύειν

3 ει αρα] see commentary

1–12. *Exordium.* An opening statement of a proposition, which is then to be demonstrated by proofs drawn from logic and from history, is characteristic of the philosophical diatribe.
1. THOROUGHLY PHILOSOPHICAL: at once sets the tone our author professes; the superlative is striking, but occurs in Plato (*Republic*, 6.498a). TO DISCUSS: in the sense of "demonstrate," is also Platonic. WHETHER: A modest understatement instead of the expected "that" (*ei* for *hoti*). RELIGIOUS: The most generally suitable translation of *eusebes* in this work; Townshend uses "inspired," and Emmet "God-directed." The meaning is wider, as appears from the frequent application of the word to Hasidim in Jewish writings. Its use to qualify "reason," which is central in our author's thought, is a logical solecism only if we equate "reason" with "rationalism." In the Stoic view it is nearer tautology, for all reason is God-directed. REASON: *Logismos* (not *logos*), following regular Stoic usage. SOVEREIGN: Here and at 1.30 and 13.1 *autodespotos*, which is almost unexampled; the usual word for the same idea (5 occurrences in our author) is *autokrator*, which is regularly applied to the Roman emperor. EMOTIONS: The common (and technically correct) translation of *pathe* is "passions," but our ordinary usage gives that word a wrong connotation. All ethical philosophies urged that reason must prevail over the emotions; but the form in which the proposition is here stated is Stoic, though, as 1.6 (end) shows, our author diverges from Stoicism in the kind of sovereignty which reason must use. I ... ADVISE YOU TO ATTEND: Not necessarily proof that the discourse was spoken, for essays were frequently couched in the form of a spoken address.
2. ESSENTIAL ... IN ADDITION: The author justifies the importance of his

✥ THE FOURTH BOOK OF MACCABEES ✥

1 ¹Thoroughly philosophical is the subject I propose to discuss, namely, whether religious reason is sovereign over the emotions; and I may properly advise you to attend earnestly to my philosophical exposition. ²The theme is essential to everyone as a branch of knowledge, but in addition it embraces a eulogy of the highest virtue—I mean, of course, prudence. ³If it is demonstrated that reason is sovereign over the emotions which hamper temperance, to wit, gluttony and concupiscence, ⁴it is also demonstrated that it rules over the

subject by pointing up its theoretical ("branch of knowledge") as well as practical ("prudence") aspects. The expression *anagkaios eis epistemen* suggests Philo's *anagkaion eis ktesin aretes* (*Quod omnis probus liber* 80). EULOGY: Actually not of prudence, but of those who died in a good cause. Eulogy (panegyric, encomium) was a favorite department of rhetoric; perhaps our book is rather a panegyric than a diatribe. "Prudence" here, and "temperance," "justice," and "courage" in 3–4, are the four Platonic cardinal virtues, adopted by the Stoics. They occur also in Wis. 8.7, and frequently in Philo; see Wolfson, 2.208 ff.
3. IF: Strictly speaking, the Gk. *ei ara* should imply that the hypothesis is doubtful (which is inappropriate here); or, as in the LXX, introduce a question. The reading is in fact uncertain; and indeed the entire passage, through v. 6, presents serious difficulties. Freudenthal (148 f.) believed that the first page of the MS. was mutilated, and that some copyist (before the Syr. version, which presents the text as we have it) arbitrarily filled the lacunae with words and ideas derived from other parts of the book. "Gluttony," for example, is really a species of the genus "concupiscence," and it is odd to find the two equally opposed to "temperance." "Malice" is a general emotion (as in 1.25, 2.16), and not the appropriate counter to "justice." "Anger" (*thumos*) is opposed to "courage," whereas Plato and Aristotle make it of the same nature as courage. We can surmise the sources of some of the copyist's contributions: "emotions which hamper temperance" echoes 1.30, and "emotions which impede justice" echoes 2.6. So the various emotions are recalled, but in confused order, from later parts of the book: *cf.* 1.23, 26, 31; 2.4, 7, 16; 3.4.

ἀναφαίνεται, οἷον κακοηθείας, καὶ τῶν τῆς ἀνδρείας ἐμποδιστι-
5 κῶν παθῶν, θυμοῦ τε καὶ φόβου καὶ πόνου. ⁵πῶς οὖν, ἴσως
εἴποιεν ἄν τινες, εἰ τῶν παθῶν ὁ λογισμὸς κρατεῖ, λήθης
καὶ ἀγνοίας οὐ δεσπόζει; γελοῖον ἐπιχειροῦντες λέγειν.
⁶οὐ γὰρ τῶν αὐτοῦ παθῶν ὁ λογισμὸς κρατεῖ, ἀλλὰ τῶν
τῆς δικαιοσύνης καὶ ἀνδρείας καὶ σωφροσύνης ἐναντίων, καὶ
τούτων οὐχ ὥστε αὐτὰ καταλῦσαι, ἀλλ' ὥστε αὐτοῖς μὴ
εἶξαι. ⁷πολλαχόθεν μὲν οὖν καὶ ἀλλαχόθεν ἔχοιμ' ἂν
ὑμῖν ἐπιδεῖξαι ὅτι αὐτοκράτωρ ἐστὶν τῶν παθῶν ὁ λογισμός,
⁸πολὺ δὲ πλέον τοῦτο ἀποδείξαιμι ἀπὸ τῆς ἀνδραγαθίας
τῶν ὑπὲρ ἀρετῆς ἀποθανόντων, Ελεαζαρου τε καὶ τῶν ἑπτὰ
ἀδελφῶν καὶ τῆς τούτων μητρός. ⁹ἅπαντες γὰρ οὗτοι τοὺς
ἕως θανάτου πόνους ὑπεριδόντες ἐπεδείξαντο ὅτι περικρατεῖ
10 τῶν παθῶν ὁ λογισμός. ¹⁰τῶν μὲν οὖν ἀρετῶν ἔπεστί μοι
ἐπαινεῖν τοὺς κατὰ τοῦτον τὸν καιρὸν ὑπὲρ τῆς καλοκἀγαθίας
ἀποθανόντας μετὰ τῆς μητρὸς ἄνδρας, τῶν δὲ τιμῶν μακα-
ρίσαιμ' ἄν. ¹¹θαυμασθέντες γὰρ οὐ μόνον ὑπὸ πάντων
ἀνθρώπων ἐπὶ τῇ ἀνδρείᾳ καὶ ὑπομονῇ, ἀλλὰ καὶ ὑπὸ τῶν
αἰκισαμένων, αἴτιοι κατέστησαν τοῦ καταλυθῆναι τὴν κατὰ
τοῦ ἔθνους τυραννίδα νικήσαντες τὸν τύραννον τῇ ὑπομονῇ

6 A adds και φρονησεως after σωφροσυνης / τουτων] των τοιουτων
7 A prefixes ευσεβης to λογισμος
8 ανδραγαθειας] καλοκαγαθιας S /

αρετης] αρετην A / AS omit last των
9 τους ... πονους] των ... πονων A
10 επεστι] επεστη Deissmann

5–6. These verses are an almost identical doublet of 2.24 and 3.1, where they fit better, for, as Freudenthal points out (150), a supposed objection is premature before the argument has been presented. Editors like Deissmann and Townshend are not troubled by the repetition, because (a) our author is frequently repetitious; and (b), whereas in the present passage the Stoic view is mocked by the Sceptics, in the later occurrence the Sceptics are mocked by the author. But (b) is not convincing, and our author's repetitiousness is really confined to repeated asseverations of his main thesis that reason rules the passions. NOT WITH THE DESIGN OF DESTROYING THEM: A significant departure from the hard perfectionism and absolute insistence of the Stoics on *apatheia*, based on the more naturalist and relativist Aristotelian view and on Jewish tradition, which, unlike Stoicism, held (a) that emotions should be controlled, not extirpated, and (b) that there are degrees in sin; cf. on 1.34–35 and 3.1–2; and see Wolfson, 2.271 f.

emotions which impede justice, such as malice, and over those
⁵ which impede courage, to wit, anger and pain and fear. ⁵How,
some might ask, if reason is sovereign over the emotions, does
it not rule over forgetfulness and ignorance? Their attempt
at argument is laughable. ⁶It is not over its own emotions
that reason is sovereign, but over those that are opposed to
justice and courage and temperance; and over these it rules
not with the design of destroying them but of not yielding to
them. ⁷Many and diverse sources would enable me to demonstrate to you that reason is sovereign over emotions, ⁸but I
could far best prove it from the heroism of those who died for
virtue's sake—Eleazar, and the seven brothers, and their
mother. ⁹All these despised suffering even unto death, and so
¹⁰ proved that reason is sovereign over emotions. ¹⁰For their virtues I might indeed eulogize those stalwarts who at this season died with their mother in the cause of what is noble; but
I would rather felicitate them for their eminent distinction.
¹¹By their courage and perseverance they won the admiration
not only of all mankind but even of their very torturers, and
they became responsible for the dissolution of the tyranny
which oppressed our nation; the tyrant they overcame by
their perseverance, so that through them the fatherland was

---

7. MANY AND DIVERSE: But actually all that are cited are Scriptural.
8. HEROISM (*andragathia*): Common in the classics, but in the LXX only in Esth. 10.2, I Mac. 5.56, II Mac. 14.18.   ELEAZAR: Indicating that his martyrdom is an integral part of a single incident; in II Maccabees it is a separate episode. The name is common, and no argument for historicity or the reverse can be based upon it. Yosippon 4.18, identifies him with the Eleazar of Aristeas, who supplied the translators to Ptolemy. The mother is variously called Hannah, or Miriam daughter of Tanhum (or Nahtum), in the rabbinic stories.
10. AT THIS SEASON: This expression (repeated in 3.19) is the best proof that our book was composed for delivery on a day of commemoration. NOBLE (*kalokagathias*): A classical word and notion (properly "gentlemanliness"); it is common in Philo, occurs once in Aristeas, 5 times in our book, and nowhere else in the Gk. Bible.
11. THE TYRANNY: A general reference to the Maccabean uprising, and the nearest justification for the common title of our book.   NATION (*ethnos*): in the N.T. this word comes to mean "Gentile."   PURGED: *Cf.* 6.29, 17.21.

ὥστε καθαρισθῆναι δι' αὐτῶν τὴν πατρίδα. ¹²ἀλλὰ καὶ περὶ τούτου νῦν αὐτίκα δὴ λέγειν ἐξέσται ἀρξαμένῳ τῆς ὑποθέσεως, ὅπερ εἴωθα ποιεῖν, καὶ οὕτως εἰς τὸν περὶ αὐτῶν τρέψομαι λόγον δόξαν διδοὺς τῷ πανσόφῳ θεῷ. ¹³Ζητοῦμεν δὴ τοίνυν εἰ αὐτοκράτωρ ἐστὶν τῶν παθῶν ὁ λογισμός. ¹⁴διακρίνομεν τί ποτέ ἐστιν λογισμὸς καὶ τί πάθος, καὶ πόσαι παθῶν ἰδέαι, καὶ εἰ πάντων ἐπικρατεῖ τούτων ὁ λογισμός. ¹⁵λογισμὸς μὲν δὴ τοίνυν ἐστὶν νοῦς μετὰ ὀρθοῦ λόγου προτιμῶν τὸν σοφίας βίον. ¹⁶σοφία δὴ τοίνυν ἐστὶν γνῶσις θείων καὶ ἀνθρωπίνων πραγμάτων καὶ τῶν τούτων αἰτιῶν. ¹⁷αὕτη δὴ τοίνυν ἐστὶν ἡ τοῦ νόμου παιδεία, δι' ἧς τὰ θεῖα σεμνῶς καὶ τὰ ἀνθρώπινα συμφερόντως μανθάνομεν. ¹⁸τῆς δὲ σοφίας ἰδέαι καθεστήκασιν φρόνησις καὶ δικαιοσύνη καὶ ἀνδρεία καὶ σωφροσύνη· ¹⁹κυριωτάτη δὲ πάντων ἡ φρόνησις, ἐξ ἧς δὴ τῶν παθῶν ὁ λογισμὸς ἐπικρατεῖ. ²⁰παθῶν δὲ φύσεις εἰσὶν αἱ περιεκτικώταται δύο ἡδονή τε καὶ πόνος· τούτων δὲ ἑκάτερον καὶ περὶ τὸ σῶμα καὶ περὶ τὴν ψυχὴν πέφυκεν. ²¹πολλαὶ δὲ καὶ περὶ τὴν ἡδονὴν καὶ τὸν πόνον παθῶν εἰσιν ἀκολουθίαι. ²²πρὸ μὲν οὖν τῆς ἡδονῆς ἐστιν ἐπιθυμία, μετὰ δὲ τὴν ἡδονὴν χαρά. ²³πρὸ δὲ τοῦ

---

12 αρξαμενω] -μενων A   20 και περι το σωμα not in AS
15 λογου ... βιον] βιου ... λογον A

---

12. AS IS MY CUSTOM: An apparent indication that our author habitually delivered such discourses. RENDERING GLORY: This doxology at the close of the exordium, like that at the close of the book (18.24), gives the impression that the discourse was actually spoken. It is the only manifest Hebraism in our book, and was doubtless drawn from the LXX.

13–3.18. *Reason and the emotions.* This section is in a dry, pedagogical style, with short and simple sentences, suitable for establishing the philosophic basis as axiomatic. When our author comes to the hortatory part of his work his rhetoric grows lavish. Vv. 13–16 might have been written by a Greek philosopher; and 16 is in fact very closely paralleled in a number of pagan authors. The specifically Jewish and religious content is taken up with the mention of the Law in 17.

14. WHAT EMOTION IS: This is not in fact defined, perhaps because of the difficulty of definition; but types of emotion are dealt with.

15. Vv. 15–17 each open with *de toinun*, equivalent, in this inventory of definitions, to "I say that."

purged. ¹²But of these things there will be occasion to speak presently; I shall commence, as is my custom, by presenting my general thesis, and then I may address myself to their history, rendering glory to God the All-wise.

¹³Our inquiry, then, is whether reason is sovereign over the emotions. ¹⁴We must determine what reason is, and what emotion is, how many types of emotion there are, and whether reason holds the mastery over all of them. ¹⁵Reason, then, is the intellect choosing with correct judgment the life of wisdom; ¹⁶and wisdom is knowledge of things human and divine and of their cause. ¹⁷Such wisdom is education in the Law, through which we learn things divine reverently and things human advantageously. ¹⁸The types comprised in wisdom are prudence, justice, courage, and temperance. ¹⁹Of these, prudence has the greatest authority of all, for it is through it that reason rules over the emotions. ²⁰Of the emotions, the two most comprehensive classes are pleasure and pain, and of these each involves both the body and the soul. ²¹A numerous suite of emotions attends upon both pleasure and pain: ²²desire precedes pleasure, and joy follows after pleasure;

---

16. KNOWLEDGE OF THINGS HUMAN AND DIVINE: Precisely equivalent to the Stoic definition in Cicero, *Tusculan Disputations* 4.25.57: *rerum divinarum et humanarum scientiam cognitionemque quae cuiusque rei causa sit*; and to Philo's definition in *De congr. erud. gratia* 79. Virtually the same words are employed in Cicero, *De officiis* 2.2.5; Seneca, *Epist.* 89; and Plutarch, *Placit. philos.* 1.2. See DuP-S 34 f., and Wolfson 1.22.

17. WISDOM IS EDUCATION IN THE LAW: The equation of "wisdom" and "the Law," like the qualification of "reason" by "religious," is the keynote of our author's thought; but the antemundane existence of this wisdom is not emphasized as it is in Philo and Palestinian Judaism; see Wolfson, 1.20 ff. As the quotations in the note on v. 16 show, pagans too, in the century in which our book was written, acknowledged the insufficiency of mere reason.

18. TYPES . . . : The exposition of the virtues and their relationships are philosophical commonplaces; only 33-34 make a specific (and easy) application to Jewish practice, and form a natural transition to what follows. The division of virtue into four classes goes back to Plato, and is found in Aristotle and the Stoics, and also in Wis. 8.7 and Philo, *Leg. allegor.* 1.71.

πόνου ἐστὶν φόβος, μετὰ δὲ τὸν πόνον λύπη. ²⁴θυμὸς δὲ κοινὸν πάθος ἐστὶν ἡδονῆς καὶ πόνου, ἐὰν ἐννοηθῇ τις ὅτι 25 αὐτῷ περιέπεσεν. ²⁵ἐν τῇ ἡδονῇ δὲ ἔνεστιν καὶ ἡ κακοήθης διάθεσις, πολυτροπωτάτη πάντων οὖσα τῶν παθῶν, ²⁶καὶ τὰ μὲν ψυχῆς ἀλαζονεία καὶ φιλαργυρία καὶ φιλοδοξία καὶ φιλονεικία καὶ βασκανία, ²⁷κατὰ δὲ τὸ σῶμα παντοφαγία καὶ λαιμαργία καὶ μονοφαγία. ²⁸καθάπερ οὖν δυεῖν τοῦ σώματος καὶ τῆς ψυχῆς φυτῶν ὄντων ἡδονῆς τε καὶ πόνου πολλαὶ τούτων τῶν φυτῶν εἰσιν παραφυάδες, ²⁹ὧν ἑκάστην ὁ παγγέωργος λογισμὸς περικαθαίρων καὶ ἀποκνίζων καὶ περιπλέκων καὶ ἐπάρδων καὶ πάντα τρόπον μεταχέων 30 ἐξημεροῖ τὰς τῶν ἠθῶν καὶ παθῶν ὕλας. ³⁰ὁ γὰρ λογισμὸς τῶν μὲν ἀρετῶν ἐστιν ἡγεμών, τῶν δὲ παθῶν αὐτοκράτωρ.

Ἐπιθεωρεῖτε τοίνυν πρῶτον διὰ τῶν κωλυτικῶν τῆς σωφροσύνης ἔργων ὅτι αὐτοδέσποτός ἐστιν τῶν παθῶν ὁ λογισμός. ³¹σωφροσύνη δὴ τοίνυν ἐστὶν ἐπικράτεια τῶν ἐπιθυμιῶν, ³²τῶν δὲ ˙ἐπιθυμιῶν αἱ μέν εἰσιν ψυχικαί, αἱ δὲ σωματικαί, καὶ τούτων ἀμφοτέρων ἐπικρατεῖν ὁ λογισμὸς φαίνεται. ³³ἐπεὶ πόθεν κινούμενοι πρὸς τὰς ἀπειρημένας τροφὰς ἀποστρεφόμεθα τὰς ἐξ ˙αὐτῶν ἡδονάς; οὐχ ὅτι δύναται τῶν ὀρέξεων ἐπικρατεῖν ὁ λογισμός; ἐγὼ μὲν οἶμαι. ³⁴τοιγαροῦν ἐνύδρων ἐπιθυμοῦντες καὶ ὀρνέων καὶ τετραπόδων καὶ παντοίων βρωμάτων τῶν ἀπηγορευμένων

24 οτι] οτε A; Freudenthal adds αισχυνη
26 ψυχης] ψυχην Deissmann
28 For the second φυτων AV have παθων (so translated)
29 εκαστην] εκαστος A / μεταχεων] μεταχοτευων Deissmann
30 επιθεωρειτε Fritzsche, -ρει γε AV, -ρει δε S, -ρειται inferior MSS

24. IF ONE CONSIDERS: The entire close of this verse is surely defective, and neither of the readings editors have chosen really gives good sense.
27. INDISCRIMINATE: Prepares the way for the story to come. SECRET GOURMANDIZING: Cf. Job 31.17.
28. BURGEONING . . . OFFSHOOTS: This metaphor, replacing that of the "suite" in 21, is burgeoning in 29 and occasionally alluded to in the sequel, e.g., in 2.21. Such elaborate metaphors are characteristic of our author; cf. 7.1, 13.6, 15.25, 31, 17.3.
29. IRRIGATES: *Metakheon* should properly mean "pouring from one vessel to another." TAMES: As in rabbinic teaching (see on 33) evil inclina-

²³fear precedes pain, and sorrow follows after pain. ²⁴Anger is an emotion common to both pleasure and pain, if one considers how it affects him. ²⁵Under pleasure too is included malicious temper, which presents the most varied aspects of all the emotions: ²⁶those of the soul are braggadocio and avarice and publicity seeking and quarrelsomeness and backbiting; ²⁷those of the body are indiscriminate voracity and gluttony and secret gourmandizing. ²⁸Pleasure and pain thus being as it were two branches burgeoning from body and soul, there are many offshoots of these emotions. ²⁹Each of these reason, the universal gardener, purges and prunes and binds up and waters and irrigates by diverse devices; and so tames the wild growth of inclinations and emotions. ³⁰For reason is the guide of virtues, and of emotions the sovereign.

Observe in the first place how, in the case of deeds which hamper temperance, reason is sovereign over the emotions. ³¹Temperance is in fact mastery over desires, ³²of which some pertain to the soul and others to the body; over both of these reason manifestly exercises mastery. ³³How is it that when we are drawn to forbidden foods we turn away from the pleasures they afford? Is it not because reason possesses the power to master the appetites? I think it is. ³⁴When we crave sea food or fowl or quadrupeds or any sort of food which is forbidden

---

tions must be controlled—not extirpated, as the Stoics held.
30. REASON . . . THE SOVEREIGN: Following the rhetoricians' usage, the metaphor of 28–29 is concluded in a formula, which is made the "text" for a long exhortation, ending at 3.18. TEMPERANCE: is made the prime virtue; it is the expression of intellect and reason. The phrase "temperate mind" recurs at 1.35, 2.16, 18, 3.17, and 3.19.
33. FORBIDDEN FOODS: *Cf.* Lev. 11.1–31, Deut. 14.1–10, Acts 10.10 f. Note again the turn from general philosophic principles to actual usages, which in turn form a natural transition to what follows. TURN AWAY . . . MASTER THE APPETITES: Not, as in Stoicism, extirpate them. *Cf.* Sifra, Kedoshim 11.93d: "A man should not say 'I have no desire to eat swine's flesh' . . . Nay, he should say, 'I have a desire for it, but may not do so, for my Father who is in heaven has forbidden me.'" So Abot 4.1 defines the moral hero not as one who has destroyed his evil inclination, but rather as one who has brought it under control. *Cf.* also Yoma 69b; and see Wolfson, 2.270 f.

ἡμῖν κατὰ τὸν νόμον ἀπεχόμεθα διὰ τὴν τοῦ λογισμοῦ
35 ἐπικράτειαν. ³⁵ἀνέχεται γὰρ τὰ τῶν ὀρέξεων πάθη ὑπὸ
τοῦ σώφρονος νοὸς ἀνακοπτόμενα, καὶ φιμοῦται πάντα τὰ
τοῦ σώματος κινήματα ὑπὸ τοῦ λογισμοῦ.

2 ¹Καὶ τί θαυμαστόν, εἰ αἱ τῆς ψυχῆς ἐπιθυμίαι πρὸς τὴν
τοῦ κάλλους μετουσίαν ἀκυροῦνται; ²ταύτῃ γοῦν ὁ σώφρων
Ιωσηφ ἐπαινεῖται, ὅτι διανοίᾳ περιεκράτησεν τῆς ἡδυπαθείας.
³νέος γὰρ ὢν καὶ ἀκμάζων πρὸς συνουσιασμὸν ἠκύρωσε τῷ
λογισμῷ τὸν τῶν παθῶν οἶστρον. ⁴καὶ οὐ μόνον δὲ τὴν
τῆς ἡδυπαθείας οἰστρηλασίαν ὁ λογισμὸς ἐπικρατεῖν φαίνεται,
5 ἀλλὰ καὶ πάσης ἐπιθυμίας. ⁵λέγει γοῦν ὁ νόμος Οὐκ ἐπιθυ-
μήσεις τὴν γυναῖκα τοῦ πλησίον σου οὐδὲ ὅσα τῷ πλησίον
σού ἐστιν. ⁶καίτοι ὅτε μὴ ἐπιθυμεῖν εἴρηκεν ἡμᾶς ὁ νόμος,
πολὺ πλέον πείσαιμ' ἂν ὑμᾶς ὅτι τῶν ἐπιθυμιῶν κρατεῖν
δύναται ὁ λογισμός.
Ὥσπερ καὶ τῶν κωλυτικῶν τῆς δικαιοσύνης παθῶν· ⁷ἐπεὶ
τίνα τις τρόπον μονοφάγος ὢν τὸ ἦθος καὶ γαστρίμαργος
ἢ καὶ μέθυσος μεταπαιδεύεται, εἰ μὴ δῆλον ὅτι κύριός ἐστιν
τῶν παθῶν ὁ λογισμός; ⁸αὐτίκα γοῦν τῷ νόμῳ πολιτευόμενος,
κἂν φιλάργυρός τις ᾖ, βιάζεται τὸν αὐτοῦ τρόπον τοῖς
δεομένοις δανείζων χωρὶς τόκων καὶ τὸ δάνειον τῶν ἑβδο-

---

35 ανακοπτομεθα] ανακαμπτομεθα A / II
φιμουται] φιλοτιμουνται A   2 διανοια A prefixes τω λογισμω

35. A neat parallelism to conclude a section. The genitive *noos* (for *nou*) is common in Hellenistic Gk. and the N.T.

1. FOR UNION WITH BEAUTY: Proper Gk. word order, elsewhere strictly observed by our author, would require these words to be placed between "the" and "desires" of the phrase preceding. This displacement, and that of "of sexual appetite" after "prime" in v. 3, has led DuP-S to believe that both expressions crept into the text from glosses of a reader eager to emphasize that the reference was to sex. The phrase itself is an echo of Plato, *Symposium* 206e.

2. JOSEPH: The recognized type of sexual temperance, which is equated (1.30) with self-control.   VIRTUOUS: Here represents *ha-saddik*, the regular rabbinic epithet for Joseph; see Ginzberg, 5.24.

to us according to the Law, it is due to the mastery of reason
35 that we abstain. ³⁵For the emotions of the appetites are reduced and checked by the temperate intellect, and all the motions of the body are muzzled by reason.

2 ¹What wonder, then, if the desires of the soul for union with beauty lose their force? ²It is for this reason that the praise of the temperate Joseph is merited: rationality gave him the upper hand over voluptuousness; ³though a young man and at the prime of sexual appetite, he frustrated the goad of passion by the force of reason. ⁴And not only over the goadings of voluptuousness is reason seen to possess
5 mastery, but over all desire; ⁵for the Law says, "Thou shalt not covet they neighbor's wife nor anything that is his." ⁶Well, then, if the Law has bidden us not to covet, it becomes easier for me to persuade you that reason is able to exercise rule over the desires.

And so it does over the emotions which hamper justice; ⁷for how could a man whose character is that of a secret gourmandizer or a glutton, or even a drunkard, be reformed by education, unless it were evident that reason is lord over the emotions? ⁸As soon as a man subjects his conduct to the Law, then even if he be covetous he constrains his own inclination and lends to the needy without interest, cancelling

---

5. THOU SHALT NOT COVET . . . : Ex. 20.17, abbreviated.   WIFE: Of course represents voluptuousness in v. 4, and "nor anything" represents "all desire."
7. GOURMANDIZER . . . : Notice that applications to religious Law alternate with general principles which are applicable to all men, in keeping with Stoic notions of universal brotherhood.
8. LENDS . . . WITHOUT INTEREST: Since Ex. 22.24, Lev. 25.36 f., and Deut. 23.20 permit exaction of interest from Gentiles, this conduct, like that in v. 9, applies specifically to Jews.   SEVEN-YEAR PERIOD: The reading and translation of this clause (is the entire debt, or only the interest, to be cancelled?) are doubtful, but the allusion is clearly to years of release (Deut. 15.1 ff). From I Mac. 6.53 we know that a Sabbatical year was observed 164–3 BCE; see 254 ff. of Zeitlin's ed. of I Maccabees in the present series.

μάδων ἐνστασῶν χρεοκοπούμενος· ⁹κἂν φειδωλός τις ᾖ, ὑπὸ τοῦ νόμου κρατεῖται διὰ τὸν λογισμὸν μήτε ἐπικαρπολογούμενος τοὺς ἀμητοὺς μήτε ἐπιρρωγολογούμενος τοὺς ἀμπελῶνας. Καὶ ἐπὶ τῶν ἑτέρων δὲ ἔστιν ἐπιγνῶναι τοῦτο, ὅτι τῶν 10 παθῶν ἐστιν ὁ λογισμὸς κρατῶν· ¹⁰ὁ γὰρ νόμος καὶ τῆς πρὸς γονεῖς εὐνοίας κρατεῖ μὴ καταπροδιδοὺς τὴν ἀρετὴν δι' αὐτοὺς ¹¹καὶ τῆς πρὸς γαμετὴν φιλίας ἐπικρατεῖ διὰ τὴν παρανομίαν αὐτὴν ἀπελέγχων ¹²καὶ τῆς τέκνων φιλίας κυριεύει διὰ κακίαν αὐτὰ κολάζων ¹³καὶ τῆς φίλων συνηθείας δεσπόζει διὰ πονηρίαν αὐτοὺς ἐξελέγχων. ¹⁴καὶ μὴ νομίσητε παράδοξον εἶναι, ὅπου καὶ ἔχθρας ἐπικρατεῖν ὁ λογισμὸς δύναται διὰ τὸν νόμον μήτε δενδροτομῶν τὰ ἥμερα τῶν πολεμίων φυτά, τὰ δὲ τῶν ἐχθρῶν τοῖς ἀπολέσασι διασώζων καὶ τὰ πεπτωκότα συνεγείρων.

15 ¹⁵Καὶ τῶν βιαιοτέρων δὲ παθῶν κρατεῖν ὁ λογισμὸς φαίνεται, φιλαρχίας καὶ κενοδοξίας καὶ ἀλαζονείας καὶ μεγαλαυχίας καὶ βασκανίας· ¹⁶πάντα γὰρ ταῦτα τὰ κακοήθη πάθη ὁ σώφρων νοῦς ἀπωθεῖται, ὥσπερ καὶ τὸν θυμόν· καὶ γὰρ τούτου δεσπόζει. ¹⁷θυμούμενός γέ τοι Μωυσῆς κατὰ Δαθαν καὶ Αβιρων οὐ θυμῷ τι κατ' αὐτῶν ἐποίησεν, ἀλλὰ λογισμῷ τὸν θυμὸν διῄτησεν. ¹⁸δυνατὸς γὰρ ὁ σώφρων νοῦς, ὡς ἔφην, κατὰ τῶν παθῶν ἀριστεῦσαι καὶ τὰ μὲν

---

9. GLEAN... GARNER: Lev. 19.9 f., 23.22; Deut. 24.19 ff.
10. LAW: Which in previous verses operated through reason is now silently equated with reason. See on 1.17.
14. FRUIT TREES OF THE ENEMY: Deut. 20.19. CATTLE: Not expressed in the Gk., which is so elliptical as to be unintelligible; but the allusion is plainly to Ex. 23.4–5: "If thou meet thine enemy's ox or his ass going astray, thou shalt surely bring it back to him again. If thou see the ass of him that hateth thee lying under its burden, thou shalt forbear to pass by him; thou shalt surely release it with him." The assumption that such an allusion would be recognized tells us something of the author and his audience. The specific precepts of the previous verses are broadened into general humanitarian principles, congenial to Stoicism and fully shared by Philo. See Wolfson, 2.218 ff.; and *cf.* E. Bréhier, *Les idées philosophiques et religieuses de Philon d'Alexandrie*² (Paris, 1925) 253: "*Chez lui se trouve textuellement le précepte non seulement de ne pas nuire à ses ennemis, mais tâcher de leur être utile. Il n'accepte pas sans réserves les dispositions de la*

the debt at the approach of the seven-year period. [9]And if a man be niggardly, he rules himself through reason to obey the Law, and neither to glean over his harvested fields nor to garner the last grapes on his vines.

And so in other instances also we are enabled to perceive [10]that reason holds mastery over the emotions. [10]For the Law prevails even over benevolence to parents, and will not for their sake betray virtue; [11]it maintains the upper hand over love for a wife, and chides her for transgression; [12]it takes precedence over love for children, and punishes their wickedness; [13]and it bears sway over the attachment of friends, and rebukes them for evil. [14]Nor must you regard it as a paradox that reason is able to bear rule even over enmity: the fruit trees of the enemy must not be cut down; one must save cattle of a personal enemy, and help raise up his beast if it has fallen.

[15]Reason manifestly holds mastery also over the more violent emotions—love of authority, vain self-esteem, braggadocio, arrogance, backbiting; [16]all these malicious emotions the temperate intellect thrusts out, as it does anger—for over anger too it holds sway. [17]Moses was indeed angry at Dathan and Abiram, yet he took no measure against them in anger, but regulated his anger by reason. [18]For the temperate intellect, as I have said, is able to triumph over the emotions, and

---

Loi qui distinguent entre juif et étranger; il est d'une vertu supérieure de détruire cette distinction." Cf. also Jos., *Against Apion* 2.211 f.: "We must ... show consideration even to declared enemies. He does not allow us to burn up their country or to cut down their fruit trees, and forbids us even the spoiling of fallen combatants; he has taken measures to prevent outrage to prisoners of war, especially women."

17. MOSES: The accepted type of the "meek" man.   DATHAN AND ABIRAM: See Num. 16; and *cf.* Ps. 106.17 and Sir. 45.18.   REGULATED HIS ANGER: Nothing is said of this in Scripture, though "neither have I hurt one of them" (Num. 16.15) may afford ground for such an interpretation, as may certain Midrashic treatments (see refs. in Ginzberg, *Legends of the Jews* 6.102). Our author was surely acquainted with ancient treatises on anger, like the extant (later) essays of Seneca and Plutarch.

αὐτῶν μεταθεῖναι, τὰ δὲ καὶ ἀκυρῶσαι. [19]ἐπεὶ διὰ τί ὁ πάνσοφος ἡμῶν πατὴρ Ιακωβ τοὺς περὶ Συμεων καὶ Λευιν αἰτιᾶται μὴ λογισμῷ τοὺς Σικιμίτας ἐθνηδὸν ἀποσφάξαντας [20]λέγων Ἐπικατάρατος ὁ θυμὸς αὐτῶν; [20]εἰ μὴ γὰρ ἐδύνατο τοῦ θυμοῦ ὁ λογισμὸς κρατεῖν, οὐκ ἂν εἶπεν οὕτως. [21]ὁπηνίκα γὰρ ὁ θεὸς τὸν ἄνθρωπον κατεσκεύασεν, τὰ πάθη αὐτοῦ καὶ τὰ ἤθη περιεφύτευσεν· [22]ἡνίκα δὲ ἐπὶ πάντων τὸν ἱερὸν ἡγεμόνα νοῦν διὰ τῶν αἰσθητηρίων ἐνεθρόνισεν, [23]καὶ τούτῳ νόμον ἔδωκεν, καθ' ὃν πολιτευόμενος βασιλεύσει βασιλείαν σώφρονά τε καὶ δικαίαν καὶ ἀγαθὴν καὶ ἀνδρείαν.

[24]Πῶς οὖν, εἴποι τις ἄν, εἰ τῶν παθῶν δεσπότης ἐστὶν ὁ

3 λογισμός, λήθης καὶ ἀγνοίας οὐ κρατεῖ; [1]ἔστιν δὲ κομιδῇ γελοῖος ὁ λόγος· οὐ γὰρ τῶν ἑαυτοῦ παθῶν ὁ λογισμὸς

III

1 αλλα των σωματικων Freudenthal, Deissmann, DuP-S find this reading inadmissible (cf. commentary for reasons), and suggest instead, on the basis of the doublet in 1.5–6, the

following, which the present translation accepts: αλλα των της δικαιοσυνης και ανδρειας και σωφροσυνης και φρονησεως εναντιων, και τουτων ουχ ωστε αυτα καταλυσαι αλλ ωστε αυτοις μη ειξαι

---

19. EMINENTLY WISE: the same epithet (*pansophos*) is applied to Jacob in Philo, *De Sacrif. Abel et Caini* 48, and also to Abraham, Isaac, and Moses. INCULPATE . . . : Gen. 34.30. CURSED: Gen. 49.7, verbatim from the LXX. In Jud. 9.2, Job 30, Test. Levi 5 and 6 the conduct of Simeon and Levi is approved.

21. HE IMPLANTED IN HIM EMOTIONS AND INCLINATIONS: Note that, as in the rabbis and Philo (cf. Wolfson, 2.225 ff.), the evil inclinations as well as the good are God-given; hence they are to be controlled rather than destroyed.

22. HE ENTHRONED INTELLECT: Intellect or reason (in Philo equated with "good inclination"; Wolfson, 2.288) is opposed to emotions. DuP-S cites an apposite passage of the Pythagorean Crito from Stobaeus, 2.7.24: "God so contrived man . . . He implanted in him such substance in him as embraces both capacity and choice . . . and thereby made him look upwards towards the heavens and perception of the stars, and implanted in him a vision of such sort, styled intellect, that he may perceive God. . . . Of this vision God is not the giver, but it is the essence of creation and the choice of the soul itself." THROUGH THE AGENCY OF THE SENSES: The connection of this phrase with its sentence is awkward, and may be a gloss of a scholarly reader who knew the Stoic doctrine that nothing reaches the intellect except through the senses; cf. Diogenes

to transform some of them and render others impotent. [19]Why else did our eminently wise father Jacob inculpate Simeon and Levi and their friends for massacring, without employing reason, the whole tribe of Shechemites, and exclaim "Cursed be their anger"? [20]Unless reason were able to master anger, he would not have so spoken. [21]When God fashioned man He implanted in him emotions and inclinations; [22]but at the same time He enthroned intellect, through the agency of the senses, as the sacred guide over all. [23]To the intellect He gave the Law; and he who lives subject to it shall reign over a realm of temperance, and justice, and goodness, and courage.

[24]How is it, then, someone may object, if reason is lord of the emotions, that it has no mastery over forgetfulness and ignorance?

3 [1]Such logic is altogether laughable, for reason is manifestly master not of its own emotions but of those [contrary to

---

Laertius, 7.52: "The Stoics apply the term sense to the current passing from the directing soul to the senses . . . and to the apparatus of the sense organs."

23. SHALL REIGN OVER A REALM: The kingship of the sage is a Stoic commonplace, and occurs in Philo, *e.g., De migr. Abrah.* 197: "We call wisdom kingship for we call the sage a king." *Cf.* also Wis. 6.20. The future tense does not here imply retribution in a future existence. GOODNESS: Here takes the place of prudence.

24. The supposed objection fits much better in the present context than does its doublet in 1.5-6. The argument runs as follows: Reason is sovereign over the emotions, but does not destroy them; it cannot master its own emotions of forgetfulness or ignorance; the emotions do not (as the Stoics held) affect the intellect. On man's inability to master forgetfulness, *cf.* Philo, *De migr. Abr.* 206: "Forgetfulness is not a voluntary emotion but one of those attached to us from without." Philo frequently mentions forgetfulness and ignorance together, *e.g., De spec. leg.*, 1.223, 4.70. By Plato's theory of learning as remembering the two are one.

1. See critical note for the text here translated. The MS reading, which yields "but of those of the body," seems impossible, for the passions enumerated—desire, anger, malice—belong to the intellect rather than the body. The supplement, transferred by Freudenthal, Deissmann, and DuP-S from 1.5-6, incidentally affords a better connection to what follows. *Cf.* on 1.3.

ἐπικρατεῖν φαίνεται, ἀλλὰ τῶν σωματικῶν. ²οἷον ἐπιθυμίαν τις οὐ δύναται ἐκκόψαι ἡμῶν, ἀλλὰ μὴ δουλωθῆναι τῇ ἐπιθυμίᾳ δύναται ὁ λογισμὸς παρασχέσθαι. ³θυμόν τις οὐ δύναται ἐκκόψαι ὑμῶν τῆς ψυχῆς, ἀλλὰ τῷ θυμῷ δυνατὸν τὸν λογισμὸν βοηθῆσαι. ⁴κακοήθειάν τις ἡμῶν οὐ δύναται ἐκκόψαι, ἀλλὰ τὸ μὴ καμφθῆναι τῇ κακοηθείᾳ δύναιτ᾿ ἂν ὁ λογισμὸς συμ- 5 μαχῆσαι· ⁵οὐ γὰρ ἐκριζωτὴς τῶν παθῶν ὁ λογισμός ἐστιν, ἀλλὰ ἀνταγωνιστής. ⁶Ἔστιν γοῦν τοῦτο διὰ τῆς Δαυιδ τοῦ βασιλέως δίψης σαφέστερον ἐπιλογίσασθαι. ⁷ἐπεὶ γὰρ δι᾿ ὅλης ἡμέρας προσβαλὼν τοῖς ἀλλοφύλοις ὁ Δαυιδ πολλοὺς αὐτῶν ἀπέκτεινεν μετὰ τῶν τοῦ ἔθνους στρατιωτῶν, ⁸τότε δὴ γενομένης ἑσπέρας ἱδρῶν καὶ σφόδρα κεκμηκὼς ἐπὶ τὴν βασίλειον σκηνὴν ἦλθεν, περὶ ἣν ὁ πᾶς τῶν προγόνων στρατὸς ἐστρατοπεδεύκει. ⁹οἱ μὲν οὖν ἄλλοι πάντες ἐπὶ τὸ δεῖπνον ἦσαν, 10 ¹⁰ὁ δὲ βασιλεὺς ὡς μάλιστα διψῶν, καίπερ ἀφθόνους ἔχων πηγάς, οὐκ ἠδύνατο δι᾿ αὐτῶν ἰάσασθαι τὴν δίψαν, ¹¹ἀλλά τις αὐτὸν ἀλόγιστος ἐπιθυμία τοῦ παρὰ τοῖς πολεμίοις ὕδατος ἐπιτείνουσα συνέφρυγεν καὶ λύουσα κατέφλεγεν. ¹²ὅθεν τῶν ὑπασπιστῶν ἐπὶ τῇ τοῦ βασιλέως ἐπιθυμίᾳ σχετλιαζόντων δύο νεανίσκοι στρατιῶται καρτεροὶ καταιδεσθέντες τὴν τοῦ βασιλέως ἐπιθυμίαν τὰς παντευχίας

---

3 λογισμον omitted in A, supplied by SV and Syriac

4 δυναιτ αν] δυνατον A, -αται inferior

8 ιδρων] S prefixes εσπευδεν

---

2. YOU: The direct address, repeated at intervals, reinforces the impression that our discourse was actually spoken. REASON CAN SECURE: The reiterated asseveration of the power of reason over various emotions in vv. 2–4 properly emphasizes the main philosophical thesis of the book; and also indicates its divergence from ordinary Stoicism, in that reason only controls but does not extirpate the emotions.

5. REASON IS NOT THE UPROOTER: The essence of our author's position (see on 1.33); placed, according to his regular practice, at the conclusion of a logical demonstration, to serve as an introduction to edifying examples.

6. The story of King David's thirst affords a perfect example of a passion mastered by a virtue. The present account differs from that in Scripture (II Sam. 23.13–17, I Chron. 11.15–19; cf. Jos., Ant. 7.12.3) in details. The volunteers are two young soldiers, not three chieftains; the spring is

justice, courage, temperance, and prudence; and of these it is master not in order to destroy them, but in order not to yield to them]. ²None of you, for example, can extirpate desire; but reason can secure that you be not enslaved to desire. ³Anger none of you can extirpate from his soul; but reason is able to assuage anger. ⁴Malice none of you can extirpate; but reason may be your ally in not submitting to malice. ⁵For reason is not the uprooter of emotions, but their antagonist.

⁶This can be explained quite clearly by the story of King David's thirst. ⁷David had been fighting against the Philistines for a whole day, and with the soldiers of his own people had slain many of them; ⁸and then when evening fell he went to the royal pavilion, around which the entire army of our forebears was bivouacked. ⁹All the others addressed themselves to their supper; ¹⁰but the king, intensely parched as he was, though he had abundant springs of water, was not able to allay his thirst from them. ¹¹An irrational desire for the water which was in the enemy's sector tensed the king and inflamed him, loosed and consumed him. ¹²When his guards chafed at the king's desire, two stout young warriors who reverenced it attired themselves in full panoply, and carrying

---

in the enemy camp, not at Bethlehem; and the Bible says nothing of the army at supper nor of the chafing of the guards. Probably our author drew from current Midrashic embellishments; though, as his language shows, he clearly used the LXX. The expression *epethumesen Daueid* in LXX II Sam. 23.15 furnishes both the word and idea for the discussion of *epithumia* (11, 12 *bis*, 16), which is the main point of the story.

7. PHILISTINES: *Allophuloi* ("of other race"), the regular LXX word for Philistines.

8. ROYAL PAVILION (*skene*): II Sam. 23 says nothing of a royal pavilion nor of an army encamped about it. David was in his "stronghold" at the cave of Adullam, and had only a small force. Our author idealizes the scene, as is shown by "the entire army of our forebears."

10. ABUNDANT SPRINGS: A poetic cliché; *cf*. III Mac. 5.2.

11. AN IRRATIONAL DESIRE: The description of the king's psychology employs current Stoic concepts and terminology. His desire is "irrational," and he is "tensed" and "loosed," tension and relaxation being, for the Stoics and for Philo, the bases for the explanation of matter; "inflamed" describes the effect of desire when it is tense, and "consumed" when it is loosed.

καθωπλίσαντο καὶ κάλπην λαβόντες ὑπερέβησαν τοὺς τῶν πολεμίων χάρακας ¹³καὶ λαθόντες τοὺς τῶν πυλῶν ἀκροφύλακας διεξῆεσαν ἀνερευνώμενοι κατὰ πᾶν τὸ τῶν πολεμίων στρατόπεδον ¹⁴καὶ ἀνευράμενοι τὴν πηγὴν ἐξ αὐτῆς θαρραλέως ἐκόμισαν τῷ βασιλεῖ τὸ ποτόν· ¹⁵ὁ δὲ καίπερ τῇ δίψῃ διαπυρούμενος ἐλογίσατο πάνδεινον εἶναι κίνδυνον ψυχῇ λογισθὲν ἰσοδύναμον ποτὸν αἵματι, ¹⁶ὅθεν ἀντιθεὶς τῇ ἐπιθυμίᾳ τὸν λογισμὸν ἔσπεισεν τὸ πόμα τῷ θεῷ. ¹⁷δυνατὸς γὰρ ὁ σώφρων νοῦς νικῆσαι τὰς τῶν παθῶν ἀνάγκας καὶ σβέσαι τὰς τῶν οἴστρων φλεγμονὰς ¹⁸καὶ τὰς τῶν σωμάτων ἀλγηδόνας καθ' ὑπερβολὴν οὔσας καταπαλαῖσαι καὶ τῇ καλοκἀγαθίᾳ τοῦ λογισμοῦ ἀποπτύσαι πάσας τὰς τῶν παθῶν ἐπικρατείας.
¹⁹"Ηδη δὲ καὶ ὁ καιρὸς ἡμᾶς καλεῖ ἐπὶ τὴν ἀπόδειξιν τῆς ἱστορίας τοῦ σώφρονος λογισμοῦ.
²⁰Ἐπειδὴ γὰρ βαθεῖαν εἰρήνην διὰ τὴν εὐνομίαν οἱ πατέρες ἡμῶν εἶχον καὶ ἔπραττον καλῶς ὥστε καὶ τὸν τῆς Ἀσίας βασιλέα Σέλευκον τὸν Νικάνορα καὶ χρήματα εἰς τὴν ἱερουργίαν αὐτοῖς ἀφορίσαι καὶ τὴν πολιτείαν αὐτῶν ἀποδέχεσθαι, ²¹τότε δή τινες πρὸς τὴν κοινὴν νεωτερίσαντες ὁμόνοιαν πολυτρόποις ἐχρήσαντο συμφοραῖς.

4 ¹Σίμων γάρ τις πρὸς Ονιαν ἀντιπολιτευόμενος τόν ποτε τὴν ἀρχιερωσύνην ἔχοντα διὰ βίου, καλὸν καὶ ἀγαθὸν ἄνδρα,

15 καιπερ τη διψη] καιπερ την διψαν S, και περι την διψαν A / ψυχη] A prefixes τη	IV 1 ποτε] τοτε Deissmann / εχοντα κτλ] οντα δια βιου καλον κτλ Freudenthal

15. DRINK RECKONED OF LIKE VALUE WITH BLOOD: A mitigation of the Scriptural "Shall I drink the blood . . . ?"
17. THE TEMPERATE INTELLECT IS ABLE TO VANQUISH: The aptness of the story to illustrate the main thesis is pointed up, and in terms—
18. TO SURMOUNT THE SUFFERINGS OF THE BODY: Which make the perfect transition to the story of the martyrdoms, which constitutes the chief part of the book (3.19–end) and the real center of our author's interest.
19–4.26. *Historical preamble*. This is an abbreviation of the fuller account in II Maccabees, and aims merely to provide necessary historical background for the martyrdoms. The first portion (3.19–4.14) recounts the

a pitcher, scaled the enemy's ramparts. ¹³They eluded the sentries at the gates, and in their search traversed the entire encampment of the enemy; ¹⁴and when they discovered the spring, they boldly drew from it and conveyed the drink to the king. ¹⁵But he, though feverish with thirst, reasoned that a drink reckoned of like value with blood was a very terrible danger to his soul; ¹⁶and so, setting reason against desire, he made libation of the drink to God. ¹⁷For the temperate intellect is able to vanquish the compulsion of the emotions and quench their flaming goads; ¹⁸to surmount the sufferings of the body, however extreme; and through the nobility of reason to scorn and reject the tyranny of the emotions.

¹⁹But the season now summons us to the demonstration of the theme of temperate reason. ²⁰When our fathers were enjoying profound peace because of their observance of the Law, and were prospering to the degree that even the King of Asia, Seleucus Nicanor, furnished them moneys for the Temple service and recognized their polity, ²¹at that very time certain persons acting subversively against the communal harmony occasioned manifold disasters.

4 ¹A certain Simon was at feud with Onias, who currently held the high priesthood with life tenure and was a man of the

---

attempt on the Temple treasures.

19. THE SEASON: Probably an allusion to the occasion of the commemoration, like the same word (*kairos*) in 1.10; but possibly here merely an announcement that the proem is finished and the exposition proper about to begin.

20. THE KING . . . FURNISHED THEM MONEYS: An abbreviation of II Mac. 2.1–3. That text names the king Seleucus, *i.e.*, Seleucus IV Philopator, who began his rule in 187 BCE and was succeeded by Antiochus Epiphanes in 175. Our text is therefore grossly in error in naming the king Seleucus Nicanor, who was a general of Alexander the Great and the founder of the Seleucid dynasty; Seleucus IV Philopator was his sixth successor.

21. SUBVERSIVELY: Lit. "introducing innovations," a regular expression for revolutionary activity.

1. SIMON . . . ONIAS: For the rivalry between the two see II Mac. 3.4 and commentary.   LIFE TENURE: A regular part of the high priestly title,

ἐπειδὴ πάντα τρόπον διαβάλλων ὑπὲρ τοῦ ἔθνους οὐκ ἴσχυσεν κακῶσαι, φυγὰς ᾤχετο τὴν πατρίδα προδώσων. ²ὅθεν ἥκων πρὸς Ἀπολλώνιον τὸν Συρίας τε καὶ Φοινίκης καὶ Κιλικίας στρατηγὸν ἔλεγεν ³Εὔνους ὢν τοῖς τοῦ βασιλέως πράγμασιν ἥκω μηνύων πολλὰς ἰδιωτικῶν χρημάτων μυριάδας ἐν τοῖς Ἱεροσολύμων γαζοφυλακίοις τεθησαυρίσθαι τοῖς ἱεροῖς μὴ ἐπικοινωνούσας, καὶ προσήκειν ταῦτα Σελεύκῳ τῷ βασιλεῖ. ⁴τούτων ἕκαστα γνοὺς ὁ Ἀπολλώνιος τὸν μὲν Σίμωνα τῆς εἰς τὸν βασιλέα κηδεμονίας ἐπαινεῖ, πρὸς δὲ τὸν Σέλευκον 5 ἀναβὰς κατεμήνυσε τὸν τῶν χρημάτων θησαυρόν. ⁵καὶ λαβὼν τὴν περὶ αὐτῶν ἐξουσίαν ταχὺ εἰς τὴν πατρίδα ἡμῶν μετὰ τοῦ καταράτου Σίμωνος καὶ βαρυτάτου στρατοῦ ⁶προσελθὼν ταῖς τοῦ βασιλέως ἐντολαῖς ἥκειν ἔλεγεν ὅπως τὰ ἰδιωτικὰ τοῦ γαζοφυλακίου λάβοι χρήματα. ⁷καὶ τοῦ ἔθνους πρὸς τὸν λόγον σχετλιάζοντος ἀντιλέγοντός τε, πάνδεινον εἶναι νομίσαντες εἰ οἱ τὰς παρακαταθήκας πιστεύσαντες τῷ ἱερῷ θησαυρῷ στερηθήσονται, ὡς οἷόν τε ἦν ἐκώλυον. ⁸μετὰ

---

added by our author, and of no particular significance. The deposition of Onias (4.16) to the contrary notwithstanding, the high priesthood was a hereditary office, held for life, though the sanction of the suzerain power—Persian, Ptolemaic, or Seleucid—was required. Only in the time of Antiochus Epiphanes did the office come to depend on Syrian appointment; see on I Mac. 10.20. Later the High Priests were appointed by the Roman procurators (Jos., *Ant.* 18.2.2, 20.10).   HIGHEST MERIT: *Kalon kai agathon*, Gk. for "thorough gentlemen." This praise of Onias is based on II Mac. 3.1: ". . . the laws were kept very well because of the godliness of Onias the high priest and his hatred of wickedness. . . ."

2. APOLLONIUS, GOVERNOR OF SYRIA, PHOENICIA, AND CILICIA: II Mac. 3.5 makes Apollonius governor of Coele Syria and Phoenicia, which correctly represents the administrative situation in Seleucid times. Cilicia was united with Syria and Phoenicia for administrative purposes only in Roman times, and only during the period 20–54 CE. Since it is natural for a writer to use the governmental titles appropriate in his own day, this circumstance provides our best foothold for dating our book, which should accordingly be placed at *ca.* 40 CE. See Introd. 95.

3. BECAUSE I AM ZEALOUS: This preamble and Apollonius' thanks in v. 4 do not occur in II Mac. 3, but are additions of our author to enliven his story.

5. OBTAINED FULL AUTHORITY: In II Mac. 3.7 ff. Seleucus' commander on this expedition was not Apollonius but his master Heliodorus. This is the most serious discrepancy in the two accounts, and has been taken by some

highest merit; and when despite every sort of calumny he was unable to injure Onias in the eyes of the people, he exiled himself for the purpose of betraying his country. ²He made his way to Apollonius, governor of Syria, Phoenicia, and Cilicia, and said: ³"Because I am zealous for the interests of the king, I have come to give information that many thousands in private funds are deposited in the treasury at Jerusalem; the Temple possesses no share in these funds, and they therefore belong to King Seleucus." ⁴Apollonius informed himself of the details of this matter, thanked Simon for his care of the king's interests, and went up to Seleucus and informed him concerning those large sums. ⁵He obtained full authority to deal with the matter, and proceeded quickly to our country with the accursed Simon and a powerful army; ⁶upon his arrival he declared that he had come by the king's command in order to receive the private funds deposited in the treasury. ⁷At this speech our people voiced indignant complaints, and protested, maintaining that it would be a scandalous thing if those who had entrusted their deposits to the sacred treasury should be deprived of their property; and they did what they could to prevent him. ⁸Apollonius, how-

---

scholars as proof that our author did not use II Maccabees, and that both II and IV Maccabees drew independently from Jason of Cyrene. But our author is little concerned with history as such, and would not hesitate to simplify and tighten his story by reducing its cast and making one personage take the roles of two. Livy does precisely the same thing with Roman legends, as we can see from the fuller parallels in Dionysius of Halicarnassus. The preliminaries to the violation of the Temple which occupy II Mac. 3.7–23 are here condensed to five verses (5–9). For Apollonius' repulse, similarly, our 4.10–14 corresponds to II Mac. 3.24–39.

6. PRIVATE FUNDS: An important distinction; to these the crown could urge a claim, as appears in v. 7.

7. OUR PEOPLE: Simply *ethnos*, as in 1.11 and elsewhere.   MAINTAINING: Strictly speaking, only property in which a sanctuary had some interest enjoyed the sacrosanctity of *anathemata*, and in pagan sanctuaries an interest in deposits was usually made over to the deity, if only by some legal fiction. Property under sacred protection was universally respected, and the severest indictment in the vocabulary of abuse was "temple-robber." For private deposits in the Temple at Jerusalem see Jos. *Jewish War* 1.13.9, 6.5.2.

164   ΜΑΚΚΑΒΑΙΩΝ Δ'   4 9-15

ἀπειλῶν δὲ ὁ Ἀπολλώνιος ἀπῄει εἰς τὸ ἱερόν. ⁹τῶν δὲ ἱερέων μετὰ γυναικῶν καὶ παιδίων ἐν τῷ ἱερῷ ἱκετευσάντων τὸν θεὸν ὑπερασπίσαι τοῦ ἱεροῦ καταφρονουμένου τόπου 10 ¹⁰ἀνιόντος τε μετὰ καθωπλισμένης τῆς στρατιᾶς τοῦ Ἀπολλωνίου πρὸς τὴν τῶν χρημάτων ἁρπαγὴν οὐρανόθεν ἔφιπποι προυφάνησαν ἄγγελοι περιαστράπτοντες τοῖς ὅπλοις καὶ πολὺν αὐτοῖς φόβον τε καὶ τρόμον ἐνιέντες. ¹¹καταπεσών γέ τοι ἡμιθανὴς ὁ Ἀπολλώνιος ἐπὶ τὸν πάμφυλον τοῦ ἱεροῦ περίβολον τὰς χεῖρας ἐξέτεινεν εἰς τὸν οὐρανὸν καὶ μετὰ δακρύων τοὺς Εβραίους παρεκάλει ὅπως περὶ αὐτοῦ προσευξάμενοι τὸν οὐράνιον ἐξευμενίσωνται στρατόν. ¹²ἔλεγεν γὰρ ἡμαρτηκὼς ὥστε καὶ ἀποθανεῖν ἄξιος ὑπάρχειν πᾶσίν τε ἀνθρώποις ὑμνήσειν σωθεὶς τὴν τοῦ ἱεροῦ τόπου μακαριότητα. ¹³τούτοις ὑπαχθεὶς τοῖς λόγοις Ονιας ὁ ἀρχιερεύς, καίπερ ἄλλως εὐλαβηθείς, μήποτε νομίσειεν ὁ βασιλεὺς Σέλευκος ἐξ ἀνθρωπίνης ἐπιβουλῆς καὶ μὴ θείας δίκης ἀνῃρῆσθαι τὸν Ἀπολλώνιον ηὔξατο περὶ αὐτοῦ. ¹⁴καὶ ὁ μὲν παραδόξως διασωθεὶς ᾤχετο δηλώσων τῷ βασιλεῖ τὰ συμβάντα αὐτῷ.
15 ¹⁵Τελευτήσαντος δὲ Σελεύκου τοῦ βασιλέως διαδέχεται τὴν ἀρχὴν ὁ υἱὸς αὐτοῦ Ἀντίοχος ὁ Ἐπιφανής, ἀνὴρ ὑπερήφανος

12 Freudenthal suggests ωμολογει γαρ ημαρτηκεναι ωστε και αποθανειν αξιος υπαρχειν, πασι τε ανθρωποις υμνησειν σωθεις την του ιερου τοπου αρετην

13 καιπερ] Freudenthal followed by DuP-S substitutes και; this reading is here followed for reasons set forth in the commentary

9. PLACE: Frequently used alone (like the Heb. *maqom*) to designate the Temple.
10. ARMY: Another embellishment; II Mac. 3.24 speaks only of guards. ANGELS: In II Mac. 3.25–26 the instruments of divine intervention are a horseman splendidly mounted and armed in gold, and two beautifully dressed youths. Here there is an unspecified number of angels to cope with the enlarged "army." In III Mac. 2.21–24 Philopator is divinely repulsed from the Temple upon the supplication of the populace, but the divine agents are not specified. On the other hand, in III Mac. 6.18 the deliverance is effected by two glorious and terrible angels, who were visible to all except the Jews.
11. FALL HALF DEAD: II Mac. 4.27–30 gives a fuller account of Heliodorus' collapse, and adds moral reflections; *cf.* Wis. 18.15–18.   COURT OF THE GENTILES: According to Jos., *Jewish War* 5.184–227, and M. Middot, 2,

ever, made his way toward the Temple with menaces. ⁹The priest and the women and children in the Temple supplicated God to defend the sacred place which was being desecrated; ¹⁰and when Apollonius with his army under arms advanced to seize the money, there appeared from heaven angels, with flashing armor, mounted on horses, who filled them with dread and terror. ¹¹Then did Apollonius fall half dead in the Court of the Gentiles; and he stretched his hands to heaven, and with tears besought the Hebrews to pray for him and propitiate the heavenly host. ¹²He had so sinned, he said, as to deserve death; but promised, if he were saved, to hymn the blessedness of the Holy Place before all men. ¹³Swayed by these words, and by a special anxiety lest King Seleucus think that Apollonius had been overthrown by a human plot and not by divine justice, the High Priest Onias interceded for him. ¹⁴And when he was thus miraculously saved, he departed to inform the king what had befallen him.

¹⁵When King Seleucus died his son Antiochus Epiphanes succeeded to the rule. He was an arrogant and terrible man;

---

there was no Court so designated. There were Courts which Gentiles might not enter, and some where no Israelites but only priests could enter. BESOUGHT THE HEBREWS: In II Mac. 3.31 ff. Heliodorus's companions, and not himself, ask the High Priest's prayers, and the angels inform Heliodorus that the Lord had hearkened to Onias' intercessions.
12. TO HYMN: In II Mac. 3.34 it is the two young men who enjoin the intruder to proclaim the greatness and power of God.
13. AND BY A SPECIAL ANXIETY: Reading *kai* for the concessive *kaiper*. The ordinary reading yields "moved by these words, though otherwise scrupulous"—apparently in not offering prayer for a heathen; but this thought is rather subtle, and the emended reading makes easier Gk. In II Mac. 3.32 Onias is moved only by the political consideration; nothing is said of the effect of the intruder's prayer. There too both Onias (3.32) and Heliodorus (3.35) offer sacrifice as well. DIVINE JUSTICE: A central doctrine in our book, and frequently emphasized.
14. TO INFORM THE KING: Much briefer than the II Maccabees parallel, which reports Heliodorus' statement to the king. On the other hand, IV Mac. 4.1–6 is not found in II Maccabees.
15–26. *Antiochus Epiphanes and the Jews.*
15. ANTIOCHUS EPIPHANES: Of course not the son of "Seleucus," nor even of Seleucus IV Philopator, but the latter's brother.

καὶ δεινός, ¹⁶ὃς καταλύσας τὸν Ονιαν τῆς ἀρχιερωσύνης Ιασονα τὸν ἀδελφὸν αὐτοῦ κατέστησεν ἀρχιερέα ¹⁷συνθέμενον δώσειν, εἰ ἐπιτρέψειεν αὐτῷ τὴν ἀρχήν, κατ' ἐνιαυτὸν τρισχίλια ἑξακόσια ἑξήκοντα τάλαντα. ¹⁸ὁ δὲ ἐπέτρεψεν αὐτῷ καὶ ἀρχιερᾶσθαι καὶ τοῦ ἔθνους ἀφηγεῖσθαι· ¹⁹καὶ ἐξεδιήτησεν τὸ ἔθνος καὶ ἐξεπολίτευσεν ἐπὶ πᾶσαν παρανομίαν 20 ²⁰ὥστε μὴ μόνον ἐπ' αὐτῇ τῇ ἄκρᾳ τῆς πατρίδος ἡμῶν γυμνάσιον κατασκευάσαι, ἀλλὰ καὶ καταλῦσαι τὴν τοῦ ἱεροῦ κηδεμονίαν. ²¹ἐφ' οἷς ἀγανακτήσασα ἡ θεία δίκη αὐτὸν αὐτοῖς τὸν Ἀντίοχον ἐπολέμωσεν. ²²ἐπειδὴ γὰρ πολεμῶν ἦν κατ' Αἴγυπτον Πτολεμαίῳ ἤκουσέν τε ὅτι φήμης διαδοθείσης περὶ τοῦ τεθνάναι αὐτὸν ὡς ἔνι μάλιστα χαίροιεν οἱ Ιεροσολυμῖται, ταχέως ἐπ' αὐτοὺς ἀνέζευξεν, ²³καὶ ὡς ἐπόρθησεν αὐτούς, δόγμα ἔθετο ὅπως, εἴ τινες αὐτῶν φάνοιεν τῷ πατρίῳ πολιτευόμενοι νόμῳ, θάνοιεν. ²⁴καὶ ἐπεὶ κατὰ μηδένα τρόπον ἴσχυεν καταλῦσαι διὰ τῶν δογμάτων τὴν τοῦ ἔθνους εὐνομίαν, ἀλλὰ πάσας τὰς ἑαυτοῦ ἀπειλὰς καὶ 25 τιμωρίας ἑώρα καταλυομένας ²⁵ὥστε καὶ γυναῖκας, ὅτι περιέτεμον τὰ παιδία, μετὰ τῶν βρεφῶν κατακρημνισθῆναι προειδυίας ὅτι τοῦτο πείσονται· ²⁶ἐπεὶ οὖν τὰ δόγματα αὐτοῦ κατεφρονεῖτο ὑπὸ τοῦ λαοῦ, αὐτὸς διὰ βασάνων ἕνα ἕκαστον τοῦ ἔθνους ἠνάγκαζεν μιαρῶν ἀπογευομένους τροφῶν ἐξόμνυσθαι τὸν Ιουδαϊσμόν.

19 εξεδιητησεν] εξεζητ. A   24 ευνομιαν] ευνοιαν A

16. For "Onias" and "Jason" see II Mac. 4.7–10.
17. 3,660 TALENTS: In II Maccabees the total payment is 590 talents; the larger figure, hardly credible, is an index to our author's tendency to exaggerate and glorify.
19. JASON CHANGED THE NATION'S MANNER OF LIFE: Again a sharp condensation of II Maccabees, mentioning only the two items in v. 20.
20. GYMNASIUM UPON THE VERY CITADEL: Betrays our author's ignorance of the topography of Jerusalem, and hence a proof that he belonged to the Diaspora; II Mac. 4.12 correctly has "under the citadel."   EVEN SUPPRESSED THE SERVICE OF THE TEMPLE: The implication is that the Temple and its service were in existence at the time of writing; this would fix the date of our book as before 70 CE.
21. DIVINE JUSTICE: A highly significant and characteristic alteration; in II Mac. 4.16–17 Antiochus' hostility is attributed simply to the people's errors.

¹⁶he deposed Onias from the high priesthood, and appointed as High Priest his brother Jason, ¹⁷who had agreed to pay him three thousand, six hundred and sixty talents annually if he would bestow the office upon him. ¹⁸And so Antiochus appointed Jason to serve as High Priest and to rule over the nation. ¹⁹Jason changed the nation's manner of life and altered its polity, in complete defiance of the Law; ²⁰not only did he construct a gymnasium upon the very citadel of our country, but he even suppressed the service of the Temple. ²¹At these things divine justice was angered, and brought Antiochus himself to war against them. ²²For while he was waging war against Ptolemy in Egypt he heard that upon a rumor of his death being spread abroad the people of Jerusalem had exhibited the very greatest delight, and so he speedily marched against them; ²³and when he had ravaged them he issued a decree to the effect that any who were found living according to the Law of their fathers must die. ²⁴And when he could in no wise avail to suppress the nation's fidelity to its Law through his decrees, but perceived that all his threats and penalties were utterly disregarded, ²⁵to the degree that even women who knew this would be their fate were flung headlong from the walls with their babes for having circumcised them—²⁶when, as I say, his decrees were utterly despised by the people, he himself endeavored to compel each individual of the nation to taste of unclean food through tortures, and to abjure Judaism.

---

22. WHILE HE WAS WAGING . . . : Vv. 22–26 are clearly a condensation of II Mac. 4.18–6.17 (*q.v.*), to provide the barest essentials for an introduction to the eulogy of the martyrs, which is our author's principal object, in form and purpose. When he arrives at the matter which is his chief concern, he reverses the proportions and enlarges freely on mere hints in II Maccabees.

26. TASTE OF UNCLEAN FOOD . . . ABJURE JUDAISM: As the second verb indicates, the tasting of unclean food was not merely a seduction to indulgence, but an overt acknowledgment of a pagan cult, whose service required participation in cult meals. Even if service to a pagan cult were not involved, the overtness of the act made an important issue of the trial, both for the persecutor, whose authority was thus publicly chal-

ΜΑΚΚΑΒΑΙΩΝ Δ' 5 1-6

5 ¹Προκαθίσας γέ τοι μετὰ τῶν συνέδρων ὁ τύραννος Ἀντίοχος ἐπί τινος ὑψηλοῦ τόπου καὶ τῶν στρατευμάτων αὐτῷ παρεστηκότων κυκλόθεν ἐνόπλων ²παρεκέλευεν τοῖς δορυφόροις ἕνα ἕκαστον Εβραῖον ἐπισπᾶσθαι καὶ κρεῶν ὑείων καὶ εἰδωλοθύτων ἀναγκάζειν ἀπογεύεσθαι· ³εἰ δέ τινες μὴ θέλοιεν μιαροφαγῆσαι, τούτους τροχισθέντας ἀναιρεθῆναι. ⁴πολλῶν δὲ συναρπασθέντων εἷς πρῶτος ἐκ τῆς ἀγέλης ὀνόματι Ελεαζαρος, τὸ γένος ἱερεύς, τὴν ἐπιστήμην νομικὸς καὶ τὴν ἡλικίαν προήκων καὶ πολλοῖς τῶν περὶ τὸν τύραννον διὰ τὴν ἡλικίαν γνώριμος, παρήχθη πλησίον αὐτοῦ.

5 ⁵Καὶ αὐτὸν ἰδὼν ὁ Ἀντίοχος ἔφη ⁶Ἐγὼ πρὶν ἄρξασθαι τῶν κατὰ σοῦ βασάνων, ὦ πρεσβῦτα, συμβουλεύσαιμ' ἄν

V
4 αγελης] A adds εβραιος / for the second ηλικιαν V and other MSS have φιλοσοφιαν which is almost certainly right, ηλικιαν being a dittography: see commentary

---

lenged, and for the victims, who might justify enforced violation of a prohibition other than idolatry in private, but might not transgress even a lesser prohibition publicly (b' parhesia); for that involved kiddush ha-Shem, and would be tantamount to public profanation. In the rabbinic versions of the martyrdom the issue is no longer one of participating in a pagan cult, but merely of proskynesis to the Roman emperor, in keeping with altered historical circumstances. See Introd. 133.

Chs. 5–7. *Martyrdom of Eleazar*. In II Maccabees this is a separate episode; here it is made to serve as a sort of dramatic prologue to the even more pathetic martyrdoms that follow. Rhetorical usage—followed, significantly, by the writers of romances (see III Mac., Introd. 14)—regularly made such demonstrations theatrical by creating a solemn setting in a public place before a large concourse of spectators.

1. ANTIOCHUS, SITTING: Sets the stage and introduces the dramatic note; in II Maccabees the king is present only at the martyrdom of the brothers. UPON A LOFTY PLACE: A vague location, but adequate to the purpose of the rhetorician. Neither II nor IV Maccabees tells us whether the scene was Jerusalem or Antioch. The latter seems more probable, and virtually certain if the king himself was actually present. See Introd. 109.

3. EAT OF SWINE'S FLESH AND . . . CONSECRATED TO IDOLS: Two major transgressions are involved: (a) idolatry, which is one of the three sins that must be avoided even at the cost of martyrdom; and (b) profanation

5 ¹And so the tyrant Antiochus, sitting with his counsellors upon a lofty place and surrounded by his soldiers under arms, ²ordered his guards to hale the Hebrews one by one, and force them to eat of swine's flesh and of meat consecrated to idols; ³and those who refused to eat of the contamination he ordered to be broken on the wheel and killed. ⁴Many were seized and corralled; and the first of the herd to be haled before the tyrant was a man called Eleazar, a priest by family and an expert in the Law, advanced in age, and known to many of the king's court because of his philosophy. ⁵When Antiochus saw him, he said: ⁶"Before I commence inflicting torture upon you, graybeard, I would give you this counsel: eat of the

---

of the divine name, which arises when even a lesser sin is committed overtly as a public act (*b'parhesia*) (see Introd. 119). The compound verb *mierophagesai* occurs only in this book, but here nine times.
4. CORRALLED ... HERD: The use of words appropriate to cattle heightens the pathos.   ELEAZAR: Some MSS add "a Hebrew." The name may have become traditional for heroes of edifying tales. III Maccabees also has an aged and heroic priest so named; and a high priest named Eleazar (whom Josippon identifies with our Eleazar) provides Ptolemy with the translators of the LXX in Aristeas. The Lazarus of John 11 is of course an Eleazar; and Bacon (*Hibbert Journal* XI [1917], 260), maintains that all are separate expressions of a single myth. In any case the name is so common that no argument concerning the historicity of our book can be drawn from its use. In II Mac. 6.18 Eleazar is described as a leading scribe (*grammateus*), an old man (6.24 says he was ninety), and very handsome, but nothing is said of his being either a priest or philosopher; his transformation into a philosopher is characteristic of our author. Actually, the usual reading here is "old age" instead of "philosopher"; but Eleazar's age had already been mentioned, and it is an integral part of our story that Eleazar be a philosopher.   EXPERT IN THE LAW: The use of *nomikos* where II Mac. 6.18 uses *grammateus* is an indication of Roman date, when *nomikos* came into use for "legal expert." Neither Philo nor Josephus uses *grammateus* for Jewish sages. *Cf.* J. Jeremias in G. Kittel's *Theolog. Woerterbuch* 1.740.
5. ANTIOCHUS ... SAID: Neither the king's speech (5–13) nor Eleazar's response (14–38) occur in II Maccabees. For our author the speeches are the main means of conveying doctrine. The practice of using invented speeches for such a purpose was regarded as perfectly legitimate, and had been employed by serious writers from Thucydides onward.
6. SAVE YOURSELF: The king's formal courtesy (he insists on his own benevolence in v. 12) makes the encounter more dramatic.

σοι ταῦτα, ὅπως ἀπογευσάμενος τῶν ὑείων σώζοιο· ⁷αἰδοῦμαι γάρ σου τὴν ἡλικίαν καὶ τὴν πολιάν, ἣν μετὰ τοσοῦτον ἔχων χρόνον οὔ μοι δοκεῖς φιλοσοφεῖν τῇ Ἰουδαίων χρώμενος θρησκείᾳ. ⁸διὰ τί γὰρ τῆς φύσεως κεχαρισμένης καλλίστην τὴν τοῦδε τοῦ ζῴου σαρκοφαγίαν βδελύττῃ; ⁹καὶ γὰρ ἀνόητον τοῦτο, τὸ μὴ ἀπολαύειν τῶν χωρὶς ὀνείδους ἡδέων, καὶ ἄδικον ἀποστρέφεσθαι τὰς τῆς φύσεως χάριτας. ¹⁰σὺ δέ μοι καὶ ἀνοητότερον ποιήσειν δοκεῖς, εἰ κενοδοξῶν περὶ τὸ ἀληθὲς ἔτι κἀμοῦ καταφρονήσεις ἐπὶ τῇ ἰδίᾳ τιμωρίᾳ. ¹¹οὐκ ἐξυπνώσεις ἀπὸ τῆς φλυάρου φιλοσοφίας ὑμῶν καὶ ἀποσκεδάσεις τῶν λογισμῶν σου τὸν λῆρον καὶ ἄξιον τῆς ἡλικίας ἀναλαβὼν νοῦν φιλοσοφήσεις τὴν τοῦ συμφέροντος ἀλήθειαν ¹²καὶ προσκυνήσας μου τὴν φιλάνθρωπον παρηγορίαν οἰκτιρήσεις τὸ σεαυτοῦ γῆρας; ¹³καὶ γὰρ ἐνθυμήθητι ὡς, εἰ καί τίς ἐστιν τῆσδε τῆς θρησκείας ὑμῶν ἐποπτικὴ δύναμις, συγγνωμονήσειεν ἄν σοι ἐπὶ πάσῃ δι᾽ ἀνάγκην παρανομίᾳ γινομένῃ.

¹⁴Τοῦτον τὸν τρόπον ἐπὶ τὴν ἔκθεσμον σαρκοφαγίαν ἐποτρύνοντος τοῦ τυράννου λόγον ᾔτησεν ὁ Ελεαζαρος ¹⁵καὶ λαβὼν τοῦ λέγειν ἐξουσίαν ἤρξατο δημηγορεῖν οὕτως ¹⁶Ἡμεῖς, Ἀντίοχε, θείῳ πεπεισμένοι νόμῳ πολιτεύεσθαι

---

11 των λογισμων] τον λογισμον A;
Deissmann condemns as gloss

---

7. PHILOSOPHER . . . STILL CLING: The king argues on the basis of the Stoic philosophy which he assumes Eleazar follows; Jewish particularism, he implies, is incompatible with Stoic universalism.
8. ABOMINATE . . . EXCELLENT MEAT: Ridicule of Jewish abstinence from pork becomes a commonplace; cf. Juvenal, 14.96 ff.   NATURE: Another Stoic touch; one must live according to nature (homologoumenos te physei zen; secundum naturam vivere), and to reject nature's bounty is therefore impiety. On rejecting the bounties of nature, the rabbis too held an analogous opinion: the Nazarite was said to have committed sin in avoiding the moderate use of wine (Taanit 11b).
9. FOLLY: Stoicism recognized no intervening grades between a sage and a fool, and hence conduct unbecoming a sage is folly.   FREE OF REPROACH: A Stoic qualification, to counter Epicureanism which made pleasure a principle, qualified only by the calculus of hedonism.   UNRIGHTEOUS: A religious argument is characteristically added: recalcitrance is not merely folly but actual transgression, in that Providence (equated with

swine's flesh and save yourself. ⁷I respect your age and your hoary head; but I cannot think you a philosopher when you have so long been an old man and still cling to the religion of the Jews. ⁸Why do you abominate eating the excellent meat of this animal which nature has freely bestowed upon us? ⁹It is folly not to enjoy pleasures which are free of reproach, and unrighteous to reject the bounties of nature. ¹⁰To me your conduct will seem even greater folly, if by reason of your empty opinions in regard to truth you despise even me, at the cost of your own punishment. ¹¹Will you not awaken from your crazy philosophy? Will you not disperse the vaporings of that reasoning of yours, adopt a frame of mind suitable to your years, and adhere to the true philosophy of the advantageous? ¹²Will you not yield to my humane benevolence, and show mercy to your own gray hairs? ¹³Bethink you, that even if there is some power that watches over that religion of yours, it would pardon you for a transgression arising out of extreme compulsion."

¹⁴When the tyrant had in this fashion sought to urge him on to the eating of forbidden flesh, Eleazar begged leave to speak; ¹⁵and when he had received permission to do so, he began his discourse as follows: ¹⁶"We, Antiochus, who out of

---

nature in Stoicism) is despised.
10. DESPISE EVEN ME . . . PUNISHMENT: As is to be expected, the tyrant confronting the man of spirit moves at once to ridicule and bluster.
12. HUMANE BENEVOLENCE: Another expected turn: the tyrant salts his threats with protestations of charity. *Cf.* 8.5.
13. POWER THAT WATCHES OVER (*epoptike dynamis*): The expression is chosen for its philosophic associations; *cf.* Plato, *Timaeus;* Epictetus, 2.11.6. It is frequent in Jewish writers; *cf.* II Mac. 7.35, 9.5; III Mac. 2.21; Philo, *In Flaccum* 121, *De aetern. mundi* 83. *Cf.* Wolfson, 2.292 ff. PARDON . . . TRANSGRESSION . . . COMPULSION: The argument is a cogent one, and must have weighed heavily with our author's audience, who had somehow to adjust themselves to the demands of their environment. It is repeated under similar circumstances in 8.14 and 8.25. On the legal principles involved, see Introd., 118. Our author closes the tyrant's speech with the argument that would be most disturbing to the Jews, as the proper point of departure for Eleazar's reply.
16. CONVICTION . . . DIVINE LAW: Eleazar begins his defense with a statement of belief in the divine authority of the Law, and then—

ΜΑΚΚΑΒΑΙΩΝ Δ' 5 17-24

οὐδεμίαν ἀνάγκην βιαιοτέραν εἶναι νομίζομεν τῆς πρὸς τὸν νόμον ἡμῶν εὐπειθείας· ¹⁷διὸ δὴ κατ' οὐδένα τρόπον παρανομεῖν ἀξιοῦμεν. ¹⁸καίτοι εἰ κατὰ ἀλήθειαν μὴ ἦν ὁ νόμος ἡμῶν, ὡς ὑπολαμβάνεις, θεῖος, ἄλλως δὲ ἐνομίζομεν αὐτὸν εἶναι θεῖον, οὐδὲ οὕτως ἐξὸν ἦν ἡμῖν τὴν ἐπὶ τῇ εὐσεβείᾳ δόξαν ἀκυρῶσαι. ¹⁹μὴ μικρὰν οὖν εἶναι νομίσῃς ταύτην, εἰ 20 μιαροφαγήσαιμεν, ἁμαρτίαν· ²⁰τὸ γὰρ ἐπὶ μικροῖς καὶ μεγάλοις παρανομεῖν ἰσοδύναμόν ἐστιν, ²¹δι' ἑκατέρου γὰρ ὡς ὁμοίως ὁ νόμος ὑπερηφανεῖται. ²²χλευάζεις δὲ ἡμῶν τὴν φιλοσοφίαν ὥσπερ οὐ μετὰ εὐλογιστίας ἐν αὐτῇ βιούντων· ²³σωφροσύνην τε γὰρ ἡμᾶς ἐκδιδάσκει ὥστε πασῶν τῶν ἡδονῶν καὶ ἐπιθυμιῶν κρατεῖν καὶ ἀνδρείαν ἐξασκεῖ ὥστε πάντα πόνον ἑκουσίως ὑπομένειν ²⁴καὶ δικαιοσύνην παιδεύει ὥστε διὰ πάντων τῶν ἠθῶν ἰσονομεῖν καὶ εὐσέβειαν

---

17. UNDER NO CIRCUMSTANCE: Counters Antiochus' argument of v. 13 by insisting that no *force majeure* could absolve a Jew from observing it.
18. EVEN IF: Not merely countering casuistry with casuistry, for "to invalidate our reputation for piety" involves a great deal more than a point of personal honor. The consideration of appearance (*ma'arit ayin*) is important. Not only does a minor offense whose commission in private might be venial become serious if committed flagrantly in public, but even the mere appearance of an offense, when no offense is actually committed, is forbidden because of *mar'it ayin*. Where the offense, real or apparent, is committed in the presence of Gentiles, the sin is more serious; for it involves desecration of the divine name, or *hillul ha-Shem*; Kid. 40a. The question of *hillul ha-Shem* is discussed in Yoma 86a, where instances are given, and the appropriate Scriptural basis is cited from Ezek. 36.20: "And when they came unto the nations, whither they came, they profaned My holy name; in that men said of them: These are the people of the Lord, and are gone forth out of His land."
19. SMALL OFFENSE . . . : 20. TRANSGRESSION IS OF EQUAL WEIGHT . . . :
21. THE LAW IS EQUALLY DESPISED: On the surface this appears to be in keeping with the Stoic concept of making no gradations in error, and commentators (*e.g.*, Townshend) have so taken it; but in this important connection, as in the question of controlling rather than extirpating emotions, our author significantly diverges from Stoicism. Stoic perfectionism, which made a miss as bad as a mile, was ridiculed by such practical teachers as Cicero and Plutarch; and the later Stoa did in fact retreat from the uncompromising position ascribed to Chrysippus (Diogenes Laertius 7.120). That position is echoed in Jas. 2.10: "For whosoever shall keep the whole law, and yet offend in one point, he is guilty of all." But Jewish tradition did make a distinction, suggested by gradations in

conviction lead our lives in accordance with the divine Law, believe no constraint more compelling than our own willing obedience to the Law; ¹⁷and therefore under no circumstance do we deem it right to transgress the Law. ¹⁸Nay, even if our Law were in good truth, as you suppose, not divine, and we merely believed it to be divine, even so it would not be possible for us to invalidate our reputation for piety. ¹⁹And do not regard the eating of unclean flesh a small offense; ²⁰transgression is of equal weight in small matters as in large, ²¹for in either case the Law is equally despised. ²²You mock at our philosophy, and say our living according to it is contrary to reason. ²³Yet it teaches us temperance, so that we rule over all pleasures and desires; and it inures us to courage, so that we willingly endure any difficulty; ²⁴and it educates us in justice, so that we keep an even balance whatever our tem-

---

penalties and expiatory sacrifices in Scripture itself, between "light" and "heavy" transgressions (Abot 2.1, Kid. 1.7, 61b). Yet, though not all sins (and virtues) are equal, all must be observed with equal scrupulousness. That is the position of our present passage (as it is Philo's; cf. Wolfson, 2.271 f.); for as much emphasis is laid on differences in grades of prescriptions as on the need of observing all equally.

21. THE LAW IS EQUALLY DESPISED: This assignment of cause corroborates what has been said in the previous note. The transgression Eleazar is concerned with is not the act itself, which might be "light," but the sin of *hillul ha-Shem* or desecration of the divine name; see on v. 18.

22. CONTRARY TO REASON: A Stoic locution (*ou meta eulogistias*); the king had attributed to Eleazar a Stoic position, and from that point of view had charged him with inconsistency.

23. YET IT TEACHES US: *I.e.*, though it is a different and better thing than Stoicism, it produces the same beneficial effects in ethical conduct. Vv. 23–24 certainly seem a refutation of the charge made in 22; but the particles *te gar* in 23 would seem to indicate that 23–24 are part of the imagined charge. In that case "it teaches us temperance" would be ironic.

24. KEEP AN EVEN BALANCE: The active form of this verb (*isonomein*) is not elsewhere used; it would mean "give each his due." The middle (*isonomeisthai*) means "to enjoy equal rights." Our translation is therefore tentative.   PIETY: After temperance, courage, and justice we expect the fourth of the cardinal virtues, prudence, which in 1.19 is declared to be the greatest of all. Philo similarly makes prudence the first of the virtues (*Leg. allegor.* 1.71); yet sometimes substitutes piety for the first place (*De spec. leg.* 4.147, *De decal.* 119). In Xenophon's *Memorabilia* 4.6, Socrates lists the cardinal virtues as piety, justice, courage, wisdom.

ἐκδιδάσκει ὥστε μόνον τὸν ὄντα θεὸν σέβειν μεγαλοπρεπῶς. 25 ²⁵διὸ οὐ μιαροφαγοῦμεν· πιστεύοντες γὰρ θεοῦ καθεστάναι τὸν νόμον οἴδαμεν ὅτι κατὰ φύσιν ἡμῖν συμπαθεῖ νομοθετῶν ὁ τοῦ κόσμου κτίστης· ²⁶τὰ μὲν οἰκειωθησόμενα ἡμῶν ταῖς ψυχαῖς ἐπέτρεψεν ἐσθίειν, τὰ δὲ ἐναντιωθησόμενα ἐκώλυσεν σαρκοφαγεῖν. ²⁷τυραννικὸν δὲ οὐ μόνον ἀναγκάζειν ἡμᾶς παρανομεῖν, ἀλλὰ καὶ ἐσθίειν, ὅπως τῇ ἐχθίστῃ ἡμῶν μιαροφαγίᾳ ταύτῃ ἐπεγγελάσῃς. ²⁸ἀλλ' οὐ γελάσεις κατ' ἐμοῦ τοῦτον τὸν γέλωτα, ²⁹οὔτε τοὺς ἱεροὺς τῶν προγόνων 30 περὶ τοῦ φυλάξαι τὸν νόμον ὅρκους οὐ παρήσω, ³⁰οὐδ' ἂν ἐκκόψειάς μου τὰ ὄμματα καὶ τὰ σπλάγχνα μου τήξειας. ³¹οὐχ οὕτως εἰμὶ γέρων ἐγὼ καὶ ἄνανδρος ὥστε μοι διὰ τὴν εὐσέβειαν μὴ νεάζειν τὸν λογισμόν. ³²πρὸς ταῦτα τροχοὺς εὐτρέπιζε καὶ τὸ πῦρ ἐκφύσα σφοδρότερον. ³³οὐχ οὕτως οἰκτίρομαι τὸ ἐμαυτοῦ γῆρας ὥστε δι' ἐμαυτοῦ τὸν πάτριον καταλῦσαι νόμον. ³⁴οὐ ψεύσομαί σε, παιδευτὰ νόμε, οὐδὲ 35 ἐξομοῦμαί σε, φίλη ἐγκράτεια, ³⁵οὐδὲ καταισχυνῶ σε, φιλόσοφε λόγε, οὐδὲ ἐξαρνήσομαί σε, ἱερωσύνη τιμία καὶ νομοθεσίας ἐπιστήμη· ³⁶οὐδὲ μιανεῖς μου τὸ σεμνὸν γήρως

---

27 παρανομειν αλλα και εσθιειν] μιερο-
φαγειν αλλα και παρανομειν S

---

25. THEREFORE DO WE NOT EAT: The implication of the context is that the dietary observances serve as discipline and symbol for general ethical conduct, as in Philo and Aristeas.   ESTABLISHED THE LAW . . . CONFORMED IT TO OUR NATURE: This is not, as it has been taken to be, a mechanical synthesis of Judaism and Stoicism, but rather an affirmation of the one (the Law as divinely ordained) and a refutation of the other. Man is not to bring himself into harmony with an impersonal natural law; rather has the Law itself been designed to conform to and serve the nature of man, who is paramount, as the dietary regulations prove.
26. APPROPRIATE . . . CONTRARY: Foods are prescribed or forbidden in accordance with the true interests of man; the prescriptions are not necessarily in accord with the Stoic principle of living according to nature, and the Stoic principle can therefore not be invoked as an argument to disregard the dietary prescriptions of the Law.
27. NOT ONLY TO TRANSGRESS . . . BUT ALSO TO EAT, SO THAT YOU MAY THEN LAUGH: A plain enough indication that Eleazar (and our author) considered the offense of eating less serious than the ridicule the act would bring on the upholders of the Law and hence on the Law. Eleazar is

pers; and it instructs us in piety, so that we reverence the sole living God with due magnificence. ²⁵Therefore do we not eat unclean foods. We believe that God has established the Law, and we know that the Creator of the world, in giving us the Law, has conformed it to our nature. ²⁶That which will be appropriate to our souls He has bidden us eat, and that food which is contrary He has prevented us from eating. ²⁷A tyrant's way it is, to force us not only to transgress the Law but also to eat, so that you may then laugh at us for eating the unclean food we abominate. ²⁸But in my case you shall have no such joke to laugh at: ²⁹I shall not violate the sacred oaths of my ancestors in regard to keeping the Law, ³⁰not even if you cut my eyes out and burn my entrails. ³¹I am neither so decrepit, nor so ignoble, that my reason should lose the vigor of youth in the cause of religion. ³²So make ready your torturer's wheel, fan your fires to a fiercer heat. ³³I am not so tender of my old age as to annul by my own act the Law of my fathers. ³⁴Never, O Law, my teacher, will I be false to you, never will I abjure you, beloved self-control; ³⁵never will I shame you, philosophic reason; never will I deny you, honored priesthood and knowledge of the Law. ³⁶You shall not defile the sacred lips of my old age, nor the hoariness of a

---

willing to undergo martyrdom *al kiddush ha-Shem*, to sanctify the divine name, for which it is of the highest importance to avoid *hillul ha-Shem*.
28-38. This part of Eleazar's speech is an eloquent exhortation to and defense of martyrdom *al kiddush ha-Shem*. It shows the author's competence not only in effective rhetoric, but in building up the reader's suspense, and preparing him psychologically for the horrors to come.
34. O LAW: The personification is in keeping with the rhetorical manner; cf. such familiar personifications of the laws and the state as Plato, *Crito* 50, or Cicero, *I Catiline* 7. Somewhat more strained are the apostrophes to "beloved self-control," "philosophic reason," and "priesthood and knowledge of the Law." MY TEACHER (*paideuta*): Not merely as imparting instruction in a given subject, for *paideia* in Gk. usage is the entire complex of culture that sets a Greek apart from a barbarian, a gentleman from a boor. *Paidagogos*, as used of the Law by Paul in Gal. 3.24, is more limited in sense.
35. PHILOSOPHIC REASON: "Philosophic" is applied to reason (*nous*) in Philo, *De mutatione nominum* 209.

στόμα οὐδὲ νομίμου βίου ἡλικίαν. ³⁷ἁγνόν με οἱ πατέρες εἰσδέξονται μὴ φοβηθέντα σου τὰς μέχρι θανάτου ἀνάγκας. ³⁸ἀσεβῶν μὲν γὰρ τυραννήσεις, τῶν δὲ ἐμῶν ὑπὲρ τῆς εὐσεβείας λογισμῶν οὔτε λόγοις δεσπόσεις οὔτε δι' ἔργων.

6 ¹Τοῦτον τὸν τρόπον ἀντιρρητορεύσαντα ταῖς τοῦ τυράννου παρηγορίαις παραστάντες οἱ δορυφόροι πικρῶς ἔσυραν ἐπὶ τὰ βασανιστήρια τὸν Ελεαζαρον. ²καὶ πρῶτον μὲν περιέδυσαν τὸν γεραιὸν ἐγκοσμούμενον τῇ περὶ τὴν εὐσέβειαν εὐσχημοσύνῃ· ³ἔπειτα περιαγκωνίσαντες ἑκατέρωθεν μάστιξιν κατήκιζον, ⁴Πείσθητι ταῖς τοῦ βασιλέως ἐντολαῖς, ἑτέρωθεν 5 κήρυκος ἐπιβοῶντος. ⁵ὁ δὲ μεγαλόφρων καὶ εὐγενὴς ὡς ἀληθῶς Ελεαζαρος ὥσπερ ἐν ὀνείρῳ βασανιζόμενος κατ' οὐδένα τρόπον μετετρέπετο, ⁶ἀλλὰ ὑψηλοὺς ἀνατείνας εἰς οὐρανὸν τοὺς ὀφθαλμοὺς ἀπεξαίνετο ταῖς μάστιξιν τὰς σάρκας ὁ γέρων καὶ κατερρεῖτο τῷ αἵματι καὶ τὰ πλευρὰ κατετιτρώσκετο. ⁷καὶ πίπτων εἰς τὸ ἔδαφος ἀπὸ τοῦ μὴ φέρειν τὸ σῶμα τὰς ἀλγηδόνας ὀρθὸν εἶχεν καὶ ἀκλινῆ τὸν λογισμόν. ⁸λάξ γέ τοι τῶν πικρῶν τις δορυφόρων εἰς τοὺς

---

37. MY FATHERS WELCOME ME: The first of several references to future retribution; see Introd. 119.
38. NEITHER ... SHALL YOU LORD IT OVER MY REASON: Eleazar concludes his discourse with a solemn proclamation of the absolute freedom of conscience. This corresponds to the Stoic principle of the freedom of the sage; cf. Cicero, Paradoxa, 5.1.34: soli igitur hoc contingit sapienti ut nihil faciat invitus, nihil dolens, nihil coactus, "To the sage alone does it pertain that he does nothing against his will, nothing in grief, nothing under constraint." Admirable formulations of the same principle are found in Epictetus, 1.12.9, 4.1.1, 4.1.128, and in other authors. Philo, Quod omnis probus, Liber 60, has: "The good man ... alone is free. One who cannot be compelled to do anything or prevented from doing anything cannot be a slave. But the good man cannot be compelled or prevented; the good man, therefore, cannot be a slave." Apposite (as being from a non-Greek) is the reply of the Indian philosopher Calanus to Alexander's invitation to join him, cited by Philo, ibid., 96: "Bodies you will transport from place to place, but souls you will not compel to do what they will not do, any more than force bricks or sticks to talk. Fire causes the greatest trouble and ruin to living bodies: we are superior to this: we burn ourselves alive. There is no kind, no ruler, who will compel us to do what we do not freely wish to do. We are not like those philosophers of the Greeks, who

life spent in the service of the Law. ³⁷Unsullied shall my fathers welcome me; unafraid of your compulsion even unto death. ³⁸Tyrannize if you will over the ungodly; neither by word nor by deed shall you lord it over my reason, where religion is at stake."

6 ¹Such was Eleazar's eloquent response to the exhortations of the tyrant; and then the guards who stood by brutally dragged him to the instruments of torture. ²First, they stripped the garb of the old man, who was yet attired in the comeliness of his piety; ³and then they bound his arms on either side, and scourged him with whips, ⁴while a herald who faced him cried out, "Obey the bidding of the king!" ⁵But the great-spirited and noble man, an Eleazar in very truth, was in no way moved, as though it were in a dream he was tortured. ⁶With his eyes raised high to heaven the old man suffered his flesh to be torn by the scourges; he was flowing with blood, and his sides were lacerated. ⁷He fell to the ground, when his body was no longer able to endure the torment; but his reason he kept erect and unbent. ⁸With his foot one of the

---

practice words for a festal assembly. With us deeds accord with words and words with deeds. Deeds pass swiftly and words have short-lived power: virtues secure to us blessedness and freedom." Philo adds (97): "Protestations and judgments like these may well bring to our lips the saying of Zeno: 'Sooner will you sink an inflated bladder than compel any virtuous man to do against his will anything he does not wish.' For never will that soul surrender or suffer defeat which right reason has braced with principles firmly held" (trans. F. H. Colson, in Loeb Classical Library).

1. TORTURE: The details of torture here and elsewhere in our book are much fuller than in II Maccabees, in keeping with the author's aim to engage his hearers' sympathies.
5. ELEAZAR IN VERY TRUTH: Perhaps an allusion to the Heb. meaning of the name ("God will help" or "seed of God") or to some other popular etymology.
6. EYES RAISED HIGH: The classic attitude of the martyr; cf. 6.26, and Acts 7 55 (martyrdom of Stephen).
7. BODY . . . REASON: The contrast emphasizes the author's main thesis. "Reason . . . erect" (*orthon . . . logismon*) is something of a play on words, *orthos* being usually applied to *logos* in the sense of right (not physically erect) reason.

κενεῶνας ἐναλλόμενος ἔτυπτεν, ὅπως ἐξανίσταιτο πίπτων. ⁹ὁ δὲ ὑπέμενε τοὺς πόνους καὶ περιεφρόνει τῆς ἀνάγκης καὶ διεκαρτέρει τοὺς αἰκισμούς, ¹⁰καὶ καθάπερ γενναῖος ἀθλητὴς τυπτόμενος ἐνίκα τοὺς βασανίζοντας ὁ γέρων· ¹¹ἱδρῶν γέ τοι τὸ πρόσωπον καὶ ἐπασθμαίνων σφοδρῶς καὶ ὑπ' αὐτῶν τῶν βασανιζόντων ἐθαυμάζετο ἐπὶ τῇ εὐψυχίᾳ.

¹²Ὅθεν τὰ μὲν ἐλεῶντες τὰ τοῦ γήρως αὐτοῦ, ¹³τὰ δὲ ἐν συμπαθείᾳ τῆς συνηθείας ὄντες, τὰ δὲ ἐν θαυμασμῷ τῆς καρτερίας προσιόντες αὐτῷ τινες τοῦ βασιλέως ἔλεγον ¹⁴Τί τοῖς κακοῖς τούτοις σεαυτὸν ἀλογίστως ἀπόλλεις, Ελεαζαρ; ¹⁵ἡμεῖς μέν τοι τῶν ἡψημένων βρωμάτων παραθήσομεν, σὺ δὲ ὑποκρινόμενος τῶν ὑείων ἀπογεύεσθαι σώθητι.

¹⁶Καὶ ὁ Ελεαζαρος ὥσπερ πικρότερον διὰ τῆς συμβουλίας αἰκισθεὶς ἀνεβόησεν ¹⁷Μὴ οὕτως κακῶς φρονήσαιμεν οἱ Αβρααμ παῖδες ὥστε μαλακοψυχήσαντας ἀπρεπὲς ἡμῖν δρᾶμα ὑποκρίνασθαι. ¹⁸καὶ γὰρ ἀλόγιστον εἰ πρὸς ἀλήθειαν ζήσαντες τὸν μέχρι γήρως βίον καὶ τὴν ἐπ' αὐτῷ δόξαν νομίμως φυλάσσοντες νῦν μεταβαλοίμεθα ¹⁹καὶ αὐτοὶ μὲν ἡμεῖς γενοίμεθα τοῖς νέοις ἀσεβείας τύπος, ἵνα παράδειγμα γενώμεθα τῆς μιαροφαγίας. ²⁰αἰσχρὸν δὲ εἰ ἐπιβιώσομεν

13 θαυμασμω] θαυμαστω A   15 ηψημενων] Freudenthal suggests καθαρων

---

10. LIKE A NOBLE ATHLETE: The simile recurs in 17.12–16, and was a favorite with Stoic moralizers—especially Epictetus. Philo several times (e.g., *De sobriebate* 65) speaks of Jacob as an "athlete of virtue." For the persistence of such figures see J. A. Sawhill, *The Use of Athletic Metaphors in the Biblical Homilies of St. John Chrysostom* (Princeton, 1928).

12–15. The suggestion that Eleazar save himself by dissembling, is taken, with variations to make the scene more dramatic, from II Mac. 6.21–22.

13. PERSEVERANCE (*hypomone*): a Stoic term.

15. COOKED: Freudenthal and Deissmann would add "clean"—in which case "pretend" could refer only to the false impression given the bystanders that the meat was in fact pork. Without "clean" the fact that the meat was dressed might permit those who wished to do so to believe that the meat was not in fact pork.

16. CRIED OUT: His speech is an expansion of II Mac. 6.24–28.

17. CHILDREN OF ABRAHAM: Adds a solemn note of responsibility; cf. 6.22, 9.21, 13.12, 17.6, 18.1, 23.   ENACT A COMEDY: Eleazar is indignant, not only because of the dishonesty of the ruse, but because his main concern

savage guards struck his flanks to make him rise up when he fell; ⁹but he endured the pain, despised the compulsion, prevailed over the torments, ¹⁰and like a noble athlete under blows outstripped his torturers, old man as he was. ¹¹With his face bathed in sweat and his panting breath coming hard, his stoutness of heart won the admiration even of his torturers.

¹²Thereupon, partly out of pity for his old age, ¹³partly in sympathy because of their earlier intimacy, partly in admiration for his perseverance, some of the king's courtiers approached him and said: ¹⁴"Why, Eleazar, will you so unreasonably destroy yourself with these evils? ¹⁵We will put before you some of the cooked food; do you pretend to taste of the swine's flesh and be saved."

¹⁶But Eleazar cried out, as if his torments had been rendered only the more cruel by this counsel: ¹⁷"Never may we children of Abraham be so misguided in our thoughts, that out of weakness of spirit we should enact a comedy which becomes us so ill. ¹⁸Contrary to reason indeed would it be, if having lived our lives in accordance with truth, and having, in keeping with the Law, guarded our reputation for so doing, we should now change ¹⁹and ourselves prove to be a model of impiety to the young by setting an example for the eating of forbidden food. ²⁰Shameful indeed would it be, if, having but

and his main compulsion to martyrdom was not so much the act (which he might avoid) but the public nature of even an apparent transgression, which involved *hillul ha-Shem.*
18. CONTRARY TO REASON: Answering the courtiers' "unreasonably" in v. 14.   GUARDED OUR REPUTATION: Cf. 5.18 and note; in such a public trial, appearance and "reputation" are of the essence, for it would be a dereliction of responsibility to—
19. PROVE TO BE A MODEL OF IMPIETY: Such stressing of individual responsibility for shaping patterns must have been especially appropriate to the Hellenizing audience our discourse envisages.   BY SETTING AN EXAMPLE: In the Gk. this is a result clause introduced by *hina*. It is somewhat awkward to consider the clause a definition of "model," and it may possibly be, as DuP-S regards it, a gloss.
20. SHORT SHRIFT: Not necessarily because Eleazar was old (though the audience was surely expected to recall Socrates' similar argument in the *Crito*), but because any human span is insignificant as compared with eternal salvation; *cf.* 15.2, 8.27.

ὀλίγον χρόνον καὶ τοῦτον καταγελώμενοι πρὸς ἁπάντων ἐπὶ δειλίᾳ ²¹καὶ ὑπὸ μὲν τοῦ τυράννου καταφρονηθῶμεν ὡς ἄνανδροι, τὸν δὲ θεῖον ἡμῶν νόμον μέχρι θανάτου μὴ προασπίσαιμεν. ²²πρὸς ταῦτα ὑμεῖς μέν, ὦ Αβρααμ παῖδες, εὐγενῶς ὑπὲρ τῆς εὐσεβείας τελευτᾶτε. ²³οἱ δὲ τοῦ τυράννου δορυφόροι, τί μέλλετε; ²⁴Πρὸς τὰς ἀνάγκας οὕτως μεγαλοφρονοῦντα αὐτὸν ἰδόντες καὶ μηδὲ πρὸς τὸν οἰκτιρμὸν αὐτῶν μεταβαλλόμενον ἐπὶ τὸ πῦρ αὐτὸν ἀνῆγον· ²⁵ἔνθα διὰ κακοτέχνων ὀργάνων καταφλέγοντες αὐτὸν ὑπερρίπτοσαν, καὶ δυσώδεις χυλοὺς εἰς τοὺς μυκτῆρας αὐτοῦ κατέχεον. ²⁶ὁ δὲ μέχρι τῶν ὀστέων ἤδη κατακεκαυμένος καὶ μέλλων λιποθυμεῖν ἀνέτεινε τὰ ὄμματα πρὸς τὸν θεὸν καὶ εἶπεν ²⁷Σὺ οἶσθα, θεέ, παρόν μοι σῴζεσθαι βασάνοις καυστικαῖς ἀποθνῄσκω διὰ τὸν νόμον. ²⁸ἵλεως γενοῦ τῷ ἔθνει σου ἀρκεσθεὶς τῇ ἡμετέρᾳ ὑπὲρ αὐτῶν δίκῃ. ²⁹καθάρσιον αὐτῶν ποίησον τὸ ἐμὸν αἷμα καὶ ἀντίψυχον αὐτῶν λαβὲ τὴν ἐμὴν ψυχήν. ³⁰καὶ ταῦτα εἰπὼν ὁ ἱερὸς ἀνὴρ εὐγενῶς ταῖς βασάνοις ἐναπέθανεν καὶ μέχρι τῶν τοῦ θανάτου βασάνων ἀντέστη τῷ λογισμῷ διὰ τὸν νόμον. ³¹Ὁμολογουμένως οὖν δεσπότης τῶν παθῶν ἐστιν ὁ εὐσεβὴς λογισμός. ³²εἰ γὰρ τὰ πάθη τοῦ λογισμοῦ κεκρατήκει, τούτοις ἂν ἀπέδομεν τὴν τῆς ἐπικρατείας μαρτυρίαν· ³³νυνὶ δὲ τοῦ λογισμοῦ τὰ πάθη νικήσαντος αὐτῷ προσηκόντως τὴν τῆς ἡγεμονίας προσνέμομεν ἐξουσίαν. ³⁴καὶ δίκαιόν ἐστιν ὁμολογεῖν ἡμᾶς τὸ κράτος εἶναι τοῦ λογισμοῦ, ὅπου γε καὶ τῶν ἔξωθεν ἀλγηδόνων ἐπικρατεῖ, ἐπεὶ καὶ γελοῖον.

34 επει και γελοιον] Freudenthal deletes; Deissmann suggests επιγελοιων, omitting punctuation after επικρατει

23. WHY DO YOU DELAY?: Similar gallant impatience is expressed in 9.1 and in II Mac. 7.30. So Socrates in the *Phaedo* reproves his friends who seek to postpone the inevitable.

26. SKELETON . . . SAID: Such exaggerations (*cf.* 9.14, 9.28, 10.9, and especially 10.18, where the young man speaks after his tongue has been cut out) are disturbing only to literal-minded readers, who do not realize that hyperbole is the natural idiom of rhetoric, and as such effective. Dozens of parallels, equally exaggerated, and ghoulish merely for the sake of

a short shrift of life remaining, we should become ludicrous in the eyes of all for our cowardice, ²¹and earn the tyrant's contempt as ignoble by failing to protect our divine Law unto death. ²²Therefore do you, children of Abraham, die nobly for piety's sake; ²³and you, guards of the tyrant, why do you delay?"

²⁴When they saw him so lofty of spirit in the face of hard constraint, and wholly unmoved by their own pity, they brought him to the fire, ²⁵and there they burned him with evilly devised instruments, and flung him under the fire; and into his nostrils they poured a noisome brew. ²⁶And when he was now consumed to his very skeleton, and on the point of perishing, he raised his eyes to God, and said: "²⁷Thou knowest, God, that though I might have saved myself, I die in fiery torment for the sake of the Law. ²⁸Be merciful to Thy people, and let my punishment be sufficient for their sake. ²⁹Make my blood an expiation for them, and take my life as a ransom for theirs." ³⁰Uttering these words, the holy man nobly succumbed to his torments; even in the tortures of death he resisted, by virtue of reason, for the Law's sake.

³¹Confessedly, then, religious reason is master over the emotions. ³²For if the emotions dominated over reason, to them should I have rendered the testimony of their domination. ³³But now that reason has conquered the emotions, fittingly may we attribute to it the authority of leadership. ³⁴We must needs, then, confess that the sovereignty is rea-

---

ghoulishness, could be collected from the nearly contemporary tragedies of Seneca and the epic of his nephew Lucan.

27. THOU KNOWEST: This speech follows II Mac. 6.30 rather closely, but makes the highly significant addition—

29. MY BLOOD AN EXPIATION ... MY LIFE AS A RANSOM: This is perhaps the strongest of several statements of the doctrine of *kapparah* or vicarious expiation. *Cf.* 1.11, 6.28 ff., 9.24, 12.18, 17.20 ff., 18.4, and Introd. 121.

31–35 returns to the main thesis of the sovereignty of reason, and again (as in 1.13 ff.) presents curt and simple statements of principles. It is unnecessary to assume that the occurrence of these dry sentences between passages of rhetorical opulence indicates a fault in the text; the alternation is in keeping with our author's manner.

35 ³⁵καὶ οὐ μόνον τῶν ἀλγηδόνων ἐπιδείκνυμι κεκρατηκέναι τὸν λογισμόν, ἀλλὰ καὶ τῶν ἡδονῶν κρατεῖν καὶ μηδὲν αὐταῖς ὑπείκειν.

7 ¹"Ωσπερ γὰρ ἄριστος κυβερνήτης ὁ τοῦ πατρὸς ἡμῶν Ελεαζαρου λογισμὸς πηδαλιουχῶν τὴν τῆς εὐσεβείας ναῦν ἐν τῷ τῶν παθῶν πελάγει ²καὶ καταικιζόμενος ταῖς τοῦ τυράννου ἀπειλαῖς καὶ καταντλούμενος ταῖς τῶν βασάνων τρικυμίαις ³κατ' οὐδένα τρόπον ἔτρεψε τοὺς τῆς εὐσεβείας οἴακας, ἕως οὗ ἔπλευσεν ἐπὶ τὸν τῆς ἀθανάτου νίκης λιμένα. ⁴οὐχ οὕτως πόλις πολλοῖς καὶ ποικίλοις μηχανήμασιν ἀντέσχε ποτὲ πολιορκουμένη, ὡς ὁ πανάγιος ἐκεῖνος. τὴν ἱερὰν ψυχὴν αἰκισμοῖς τε καὶ στρέβλαις πυρπολούμενος ἐνίκησεν τοὺς πολιορκοῦντας διὰ τὸν ὑπερασπίζοντα τῆς 5 εὐσεβείας λογισμόν. ⁵ὥσπερ γὰρ πρόκρημνον ἄκραν τὴν ἑαυτοῦ διάνοιαν ὁ πατὴρ Ελεαζαρ ἐκτείνας περιέκλασεν τοὺς ἐπιμαινομένους τῶν παθῶν κλύδωνας. ⁶ὦ ἄξιε τῆς ἱερωσύνης ἱερεῦ, οὐκ ἐμίανας τοὺς ἱεροὺς ὀδόντας οὐδὲ τὴν θεοσέβειαν καὶ καθαρισμὸν χωρήσασαν γαστέρα ἐκοίνωσας μιαροφαγίᾳ. ⁷ὦ σύμφωνε νόμου καὶ φιλόσοφε θείου βίου. ⁸τοιούτους δεῖ

VII

2 καταικιζομενος] καταιγιζομενος suggested by Grimm al. as more appropriate to winds; καταικ. would be a natural error here, the word being used at 6.3, 9.15, 11.1, 12.13, 13.27

3 αθανατου] omitted in A; Deissmann suggests θανατου was a gloss on an original τον της νικης λιμενα, which was corrected to αθανατον. But αθανατου is the reading of V and fits the author's thought and style

4 ενικησεν] S, edd.; A has the colorless εκινησεν

6 εκοινωσας] εκοινωνησας A

8 δημιουργουντας Grimm, followed by DuP-S conjectures ιερεργουντας; see commentary

35. RIDICULOUS THING: Various solutions have been suggested for these puzzling words. Townshend and Emmet, on the basis of the Syr., render "for it were ridiculous to deny it." Instead of epei kai geloion Freudenthal reads epigeloion, which he regards as merely a dittography of algedonon above. Deissmann also reads epigeloion, but makes it in apposition to exothen algedonon: "external torments as ridiculous things." None of these solutions seems satisfactory; perhaps additional words have fallen

₃₅son's, for it rules over external torments. ³⁵A ridiculous thing it is ... ³⁶And it is not only over torments that I prove the reason sovereign; it rules also over pleasures, and yields to them no whit.

7 ¹Like an excellent pilot, indeed, the reason of our father Eleazar, steering the bark of religion in the sea of emotion, ²though he was buffeted by the threats of the tyrant and submerged by the triple wave of torture, ³in no way swerved the rudder of religion until he had entered the harborage of deathless victory. ⁴No city besieged with numerous and ingenious works has offered such resistance as did that perfect saint. When his holy soul was set aflame with rack and torture, he overcame his besiegers through the bulwark of his religion—
₅reason. ⁵Making his mind taut like a jutting crag, our father Eleazar shattered the frenzied surge of the emotions. ⁶Ah, priest worthy of the priesthood, never did you sully your sacred teeth, never, by eating of abomination, did you defile those entrails which harbored piety and purity. ⁷Ah, thou harmonious music of the Law, thou philosopher of the divine life! ⁸Such is it fitting for functionaries to be—so to defend

out, and it is best to leave a lacuna.
36. PROVE (*deiknusthai*): See on 1.1.
1–3. PILOT . . . SEA . . . BUFFETED . . . TRIPLE WAVE . . . RUDDER . . . HARBORAGE: Common Gk. figures, frequent in tragedy and favored by the rhetors. Philo frequently speaks of reason as a pilot, *e.g.*, *De spec. leg.* 4.95, *Leg. alleg.* 3.118, 223b. In *De sacrif. Abel et Caini* 90, he speaks of the religious man entering the harborage of deathlessness.
4–5. CITY BESIEGED . . . JUTTING CRAG: Rhetorical commonplaces for determined resistance.
6. SULLY . . . DEFILE: The power of unclean food to defile is regarded as very real, and (as in the power of bacilli to infect) the fact that the victim is unwilling is irrelevant. So, in II Mac. 6.20, the old man spits out the food forcibly introduced into his mouth. But, as vv. 8–9 show, Eleazar is more concerned with, and praised for, avoiding public profanation.
7. HARMONIOUS MUSIC: A more peculiarly Gk. figure than those in vv. 1–5. PHILOSOPHER OF THE DIVINE LIFE: Perhaps (with Grimm) "philosopher who has dedicated himself to divine life." Philo, *De ebrietate* 100, also uses *bion theion*, "divine life."
8. FUNCTIONARIES: A straddle between the here awkward *demiourgountas*

εἶναι τοὺς δημιουργοῦντας τὸν νόμον ἰδίῳ αἵματι καὶ γενναίῳ ἱδρῶτι τοῖς μέχρι θανάτου πάθεσιν ὑπερασπίζοντας. [9]σύ, πάτερ, τὴν εὐνομίαν ἡμῶν διὰ τῶν ὑπομονῶν εἰς δόξαν ἐκύρωσας καὶ τὴν ἁγιαστίαν σεμνολογήσας οὐ κατέλυσας καὶ διὰ τῶν ἔργων ἐπιστοποίησας τοὺς τῆς θείας φιλοσοφίας 10 σου λόγους, [10]ὦ βασάνων βιαιότερε γέρων καὶ πυρὸς εὐτονώτερε πρεσβῦτα καὶ παθῶν μέγιστε βασιλεῦ Ἐλεαζαρ. [11]ὥσπερ γὰρ ὁ πατὴρ Ααρων τῷ θυμιατηρίῳ καθωπλισμένος διὰ τοῦ ἐθνοπλήθους ἐπιτρέχων τὸν ἐμπυριστὴν ἐνίκησεν ἄγγελον, [12]οὕτως ὁ Ααρωνίδης Ἐλεαζαρ διὰ τοῦ πυρὸς ὑπερτηκόμενος οὐ μετετράπη τὸν λογισμόν. [13]καίτοι τὸ θαυμασιώτατον, γέρων ὢν λελυμένων μὲν ἤδη τῶν τοῦ σώματος τόνων, περικεχαλασμένων δὲ τῶν σαρκῶν, κεκμηκότων δὲ καὶ τῶν νεύρων ἀνενέασεν [14]τῷ πνεύματι διὰ τοῦ λογισμοῦ καὶ τῷ Ἰσακίῳ λογισμῷ τὴν πολυκέφαλον στρέβλαν 15 ἠκύρωσεν. [15]ὦ μακαρίου γήρως καὶ σεμνῆς πολιᾶς καὶ βίου νομίμου, ὃν πιστὴ θανάτου σφραγὶς ἐτελείωσεν.

[16]Εἰ δὴ τοίνυν γέρων ἀνὴρ τῶν μέχρι θανάτου βασάνων περιεφρόνει δι᾽ εὐσέβειαν, ὁμολογουμένως ἡγεμών ἐστιν τῶν

---

9 αγιαστιαν] απασπαν S. Grimm, Deissmann, DuP-S read αγιστιαν for the hapax	14 δια του λογισμου] DuP-S deletes as spoiling the balance and influenced by τω Ισακιω λογισμω following.
13 τονων] πονων A	A omits the δια

(which Deissmann and Townshend render "whose office is to serve the Law") and the conjectural *hierergountas* (see critical note) which is appropriate to a *hiereus* or priest.

9. IN THE PUBLIC GAZE: *Eis doxan*, usually rendered "unto glory," which is the normal meaning and certainly involved here. But *doxa* also means "public repute"; and the point here seems to be not that Eleazar won glory for himself but that his steadfastness was more meaningful and necessary because of the public nature of the trial, *i.e.*, he did not commit *hillul ha-Shem*.

10. THOU ELEAZAR: His achievements have made his bare name the epitome of glory: *gadol mikulam sh'mo*.

11. AARON: The allusion is to Num. 17.1–15, where, however, there is no "angel of fire." The later development of angelology appears in a parallel allusion in Wis. of Sol. 18.20–25, which speaks of "the chastiser" (*ton kolazonta*), "the destroyer" (*ho olethreuon*), and perhaps (if we accept the

the Law with their own blood, and with their noble sweat in the face of sufferings unto death. ⁹You, father, by your perserverance in the public gaze, have made strong our adherence to the Law; your lofty speech on holiness you did not render vain; by your deeds you gave credit to your words concerning divine philosophy—¹⁰thou aged hero, mightier than torture; thou stalwart Elder, fiercer than flame; thou king, supreme over suffering; thou Eleazar! ¹¹Even as our father Aaron, armed with the censer, ran through the multitude of his people and overcame the angel of fire, ¹²so did Aaron's scion Eleazar not swerve in his reason, though consumed in the flame. ¹³But—most marvellous of all—though he was an old man, and the tautness of his body was already unstrung and his muscles relaxed and his sinews enfeebled, he renewed youth ¹⁴in his spirit by means of reason, and by reason like Isaac's he prevailed over many-headed torture. ¹⁵Ah, blessed old age, hoary head revered, life loyal to the Law, and consummated by the faithful seal of death!

¹⁶If, then, an aged man despised tortures unto death, we must acknowledge that religious reason is leader over the

---

suggested reading *ton angelon* for *ton okhlon*) of Aaron conquering the angel. Grimm objects that the point of comparison seems feeble, the common denominator being merely the heroic action of a high priest in which fire is involved. But the real point of comparison is that both heroic actions were public manifestations calculated to protect and assert true religion.

14. IN HIS SPIRIT: *I.e.*, in his moral sense; *cf.* II Cor. 4.16. Freudenthal (163–4) takes it in a physical sense, *Lebensgeist, Kraft.*   LIKE ISAAC'S: Isaac (on the basis of Gen. 22) is employed as the type of piety and courage also in 13.12, 16.20, and 18.11. On Isaac as a "type" for religious reason, see E. R. Goodenough, *By Light Light*, 268; and for Philo's use, *idem*, 153 ff. Deissmann takes "like Isaac's" to mean "youthful."   MANY-HEADED TORTURE: Probably merely a rhetorical figure; hence Townshend translates "hydra-headed." But Grimm thinks the reference is to a special implement so called; and Deissmann offers "cat o' nine tails" as a parallel.

16–23. The panegyric is again interrupted for direct philosophical reflection, which draws the moral of the martyrdom of Eleazar and makes the transition to the martyrdoms to come; but here the style is not as dry and magisterial as in 6.31–35.

παθῶν ὁ εὐσεβὴς λογισμός. ¹⁷ἴσως δ' ἂν εἴποιέν τινες Τῶν παθῶν οὐ πάντες περικρατοῦσιν, ὅτι οὐδὲ πάντες φρόνιμον ἔχουσιν τὸν λογισμόν. ¹⁸ἀλλ' ὅσοι τῆς εὐσεβείας προνοοῦσιν ἐξ ὅλης καρδίας, οὗτοι μόνοι δύνανται κρατεῖν τῶν τῆς σαρκὸς παθῶν ¹⁹πιστεύοντες ὅτι θεῷ οὐκ ἀποθνῄσκουσιν, ὥσπερ οὐδὲ οἱ πατριάρχαι ἡμῶν Αβρααμ καὶ Ισαακ καὶ Ιακωβ, ἀλλὰ 20 ζῶσιν τῷ θεῷ. ²⁰οὐδὲν οὖν ἐναντιοῦται τὸ φαίνεσθαί τινας παθοκρατεῖσθαι διὰ τὸν ἀσθενῆ λογισμόν· ²¹ἐπεὶ τίς πρὸς ὅλον τὸν τῆς φιλοσοφίας κανόνα φιλοσοφῶν καὶ πεπιστευκὼς θεῷ ²²καὶ εἰδὼς ὅτι διὰ τὴν ἀρετὴν πάντα πόνον ὑπομένειν μακάριόν ἐστιν, οὐκ ἂν περικρατήσειεν τῶν παθῶν διὰ τὴν θεοσέβειαν; ²³μόνος γὰρ ὁ σοφὸς καὶ ἀνδρεῖός ἐστιν τῶν παθῶν κύριος.

8 ¹Διὰ τοῦτό γέ τοι καὶ μειρακίσκοι τῷ τῆς εὐσεβείας λογισμῷ φιλοσοφοῦντες χαλεπωτέρων βασανιστηρίων ἐπεκράτησαν. ²ἐπειδὴ γὰρ κατὰ τὴν πρώτην πεῖραν ἐνικήθη περιφανῶς ὁ τύραννος μὴ δυνηθεὶς ἀναγκάσαι γέροντα μιαροφαγῆσαι, τότε δὴ σφόδρα περιπαθῶς ἐκέλευσεν ἄλλους ἐκ τῆς λείας τῶν Εβραίων ἀγαγεῖν, καὶ εἰ μὲν μιαροφαγήσαιεν, ἀπολύειν φαγόντας, εἰ δ' ἀντιλέγοιεν, πικρότερον βασανίζειν.

---

23 σοφος A adds και σοφρων which was probably intended as a substitute for ανδρειας

VIII

2 περιφανως] περιφανης A

---

17. SOME MAY SAY: The identical expression is used in 1.5, and in the singular in 2.24. But in these passages the objection is cited only to be refuted; the difficulty here, emphasized by the optative "may say," is that the objection is confirmed, as appears in—
18. THEY ALONE: Only the true believers (like the true Stoic sages) can dominate emotion by reason.
19. BELIEVING . . . : Grimm regards this verse as an interpolation, drawn from 16.25, which is very similar, and suggested by the similarity of *pisteuontes* here to *pepisteukos theo* in v. 21. The expression "living to" (or in) "God" is frequent in the N.T.; *cf.* Rom. 6.10, 14.8; Gal. 2.19. On the continued life of the patriarchs, *cf.* Mark 12.26, Matt. 22.32, Luke 20.37-38 (where the same expression, *theo zosin*, is used); *Berakhot* 19ab; *cf.* Ginzberg, 6.56.

THE FOURTH BOOK OF MACCABEES

emotions. ¹⁷But some may say that not all men are in control of their emotions, because not all men possess prudent reason. ¹⁸Those who take thought for religion with their whole heart, they alone are able to dominate the passions of the flesh, ¹⁹believing that to God they die not, as neither did our patri-
20 archs Abraham, Isaac, and Jacob, but live to God. ²⁰No contradiction is then involved in the fact that certain persons seem to be dominated by their emotions because of the weakness of their reason. ²¹Could anyone who lives as a philosopher according to the full rule of philosophy, and believes in God, ²²and knows that it is blessed to endure any pain for virtue's sake, fail to control his emotions for the cause of religion? ²³Only the wise man and the courageous is master of his emotions.

8   ¹Yes, and even young lads have achieved philosophy by religious reason, and so have prevailed over torments yet more cruel. ²When the tyrant had been so manifestly worsted in his first trial, having proved powerless to compel the old man to eat forbidden food, then with vehement passion he bade others of the Hebrew captives to be brought, to try whether they would eat of the forbidden food: if they would eat, he would release them; but if they refused he would

20. DOMINATED BY THEIR EMOTIONS: *Pathokrateisthai* is an *hapax legomenon*. The noun *pathokratia* occurs in 13.5, 16, but in the active sense—"dominance over emotions."
21. RULE: *Kanon*. Philo has "sound rule of truth" in *Leg. allegor.* 3.233, *Quod det. potiori insid. soleat*, 125.
23. AND THE COURAGEOUS: The summary adds this word, which introduces an idea prominent in the following account, which deals with—

1. YOUNG LADS: This ingenious transition has no counterpart in II Maccabees, where the stories are distinct, and the second is introduced by "It also came to pass." In older texts 8.1 is numbered 7.24; it is more appropriate as the introduction to a new episode.
1–9.9. *Antiochus and the seven brothers*.
2. MANIFESTLY: *I.e.*, in a public exhibition, not merely plainly. Note the alliteration in *proten peiran periphanos*, and the paronomasia of the latter with *peripathos*.

³ταῦτα διαταξαμένου τοῦ τυράννου, παρῆσαν ἀγόμενοι μετὰ γεραιᾶς μητρὸς ἑπτὰ ἀδελφοὶ καλοί τε καὶ αἰδήμονες καὶ γενναῖοι καὶ ἐν παντὶ χαρίεντες. ⁴οὒς ἰδὼν ὁ τύραννος καθάπερ ἐν χορῷ μέσην τὴν μητέρα περιέχοντας ἤσθετο ἐπ' αὐτοῖς καὶ τῆς εὐπρεπείας ἐκπλαγεὶς καὶ τῆς εὐγενείας 3 προσεμειδίασεν αὐτοῖς καὶ πλησίον καλέσας ἔφη ⁵"Ὦ νεανίαι, φιλοφρόνως ἐγὼ καθ' ἑνὸς ἑκάστου ὑμῶν θαυμάζω, τὸ κάλλος καὶ τὸ πλῆθος τοσούτων ἀδελφῶν ὑπερτιμῶν οὐ μόνον συμβουλεύω μὴ μανῆναι τὴν αὐτὴν τῷ προβασανισθέντι γέροντι μανίαν, ἀλλὰ καὶ παρακαλῶ συνείξαντάς μοι τῆς ἐμῆς ἀπολαύειν φιλίας· ⁶δυναίμην δ' ἂν ὥσπερ κολάζειν τοὺς ἀπειθοῦντάς μου τοῖς ἐπιτάγμασιν, οὕτω καὶ εὐεργετεῖν τοὺς εὐπειθοῦντάς μοι. ⁷πιστεύσατε οὖν καὶ ἀρχὰς ἐπὶ τῶν ἐμῶν πραγμάτων ἡγεμονικὰς λήμψεσθε ἀρνησάμενοι τὸν πάτριον ὑμῶν τῆς πολιτείας θεσμόν· ⁸καὶ μεταλαβόντες Ἑλληνικοῦ βίου καὶ μεταδιαιτηθέντες ἐντρυφήσατε ταῖς νεότησιν ὑμῶν· ⁹ἐπεί, ἐὰν ὀργίλως με διάθησθε διὰ τῆς ἀπειθείας, ἀναγκάσετέ με ἐπὶ δειναῖς κολάσεσιν ἕνα ἕκαστον 10 ὑμῶν διὰ τῶν βασάνων ἀπολέσαι. ¹⁰κατελεήσατε οὖν ἑαυτούς, οὒς καὶ ὁ πολέμιος ἔγωγε καὶ τῆς ἡλικίας καὶ τῆς εὐμορφίας οἰκτίρομαι. ¹¹οὐ διαλογιεῖσθε τοῦτο, ὅτι οὐδὲν ὑμῖν ἀπειθήσασιν πλὴν τοῦ μετὰ στρεβλῶν ἀποθανεῖν ἀπόκειται;

¹²Ταῦτα δὲ λέγων ἐκέλευσεν εἰς τὸ ἔμπροσθεν τιθέναι τὰ βασανιστήρια, ὅπως καὶ διὰ τοῦ φόβου πείσειεν αὐτοὺς μιαροφαγῆσαι. ¹³ὡς δὲ τροχούς τε καὶ ἀρθρέμβολα, στρεβ-

---

3. HANDSOME . . . : The moral and physical excellence of the heroes is praised (cf. 4, 5, 10, and 15.9–10); a fall from a height is of course more pitiful.
4. CHORUS: This thoroughly Hellenistic image is absent from II Maccabees, but recurs here in 13.8 and 14.8. TOOK PLEASURE . . . SMITTEN: This, Antiochus' address to the young men (5–11), the display of the instruments of torture (12–14), the account of the attitude of the young men (15–29), and their collective response to the tyrant (9.1–9), are oratorical embellishments invented by our author.
5. FRIENDSHIP: Implying official preferment as "Friends" of the king, a regular title of honor; cf. v. 7.
8. SHARE . . . TAKE PLEASURE: In addition to flattery, promises, and threats, the king also appeals to what he genuinely believes is for the young men's best interest. We have, then, a real dramatic conflict between

punish them yet more severely. ³When the tyrant had so bidden, there were brought into his presence seven brothers, along with their aged mother—handsome and modest and well-born and in every way charming ⁴Upon seeing them, posed about their mother in the center like a chorus, the tyrant took pleasure, being smitten by their comeliness and nobility; he smiled upon them, and called them near, and said: "⁵Young men, with right good will do I admire you, each and every one; and because I pay high honor to such beauty and such a numerous band of brothers, I not only counsel you against raging with the same madness as that old man who has just been tortured, but I urge you further to yield to me and enjoy my friendship. ⁶Just as I am able to punish those who disobey my orders, so am I also able to benefit those who show me obedience. ⁷Repose your trust in me; you shall receive executive positions over my domains, if you renounce the ancestral Law of your citizenship. ⁸Share in the Greek way; change your mode of life; take pleasure in your youth. ⁹If by your intransigence you rouse my anger, you will force me to have recourse to terrible punishments, and to destroy you with torture. ¹⁰Take pity upon yourselves: even I your foe have compassion for your youth and your beauty. ¹¹Will you not reflect that if you disobey nothing except death upon the rack awaits you?"

¹²When he had said this, he ordered that the instruments of torture be brought forward, so that terror might sway them to eat of the forbidden food. ¹³The guards brought forward

---

two sincerely held points of view, which is much more meaningful than a melodramatic picture of a jet-black villain capriciously persecuting a snow-white hero.

11. NOTHING EXCEPT DEATH: The king effectively closes his appeal with the starkest alternative.

13. THE GUARDS BROUGHT FORWARD . . . : The instruments here enumerated figure, specifically or otherwise, in the actual tortures to be described: the inventory sets the requisite tone of horror. The identification of some of the items is uncertain. "Instruments for dislocating joints" (*arthrembola*), whose function is defined in 10.5, and "racks" (*strebloteria*), whose function is similarly indicated in 9.17, would seem to serve the same

λωτήριά τε καὶ τροχαντῆρας καὶ καταπέλτας καὶ λέβητας, τήγανά τε καὶ δακτυλήθρας καὶ χεῖρας σιδηρᾶς καὶ σφῆνας καὶ τὰ ζώπυρα τοῦ πυρὸς οἱ δορυφόροι προέθεσαν, ὑπολαβὼν ὁ τύραννος ἔφη [14]Μειράκια, φοβήθητε, καὶ ἣν σέβεσθε δίκην, ἵλεως ὑμῖν ἔσται δι' ἀνάγκην παρανομήσασιν.

15 [15]Οἱ δὲ ἀκούσαντες ἐπαγωγὰ καὶ ὁρῶντες δεινὰ οὐ μόνον οὐκ ἐφοβήθησαν, ἀλλὰ καὶ ἀντεφιλοσόφησαν τῷ τυράννῳ καὶ διὰ τῆς εὐλογιστίας τὴν τυραννίδα αὐτοῦ κατέλυσαν. [16]καίτοι λογισώμεθα, εἰ δειλόψυχοί τινες ἦσαν ἐν αὐτοῖς καὶ ἄνανδροι, ποίοις ἂν ἐχρήσαντο λόγοις; οὐχὶ τούτοις; [17]ͺΩ τάλανες ἡμεῖς καὶ λίαν ἀνόητοι· βασιλέως ἡμᾶς καλοῦντος καὶ ἐπὶ εὐεργεσίᾳ παρακαλοῦντος, εἰ πεισθείημεν αὐτῷ, [18]τί βουλήμασιν κενοῖς ἑαυτοὺς εὐφραίνομεν καὶ θανατηφόρον ἀπείθειαν τολμῶμεν; [19]οὐ φοβηθησόμεθα, ἄνδρες ἀδελφοί, τὰ βασανιστήρια καὶ λογιούμεθα τὰς τῶν βασάνων ἀπειλὰς καὶ φευξόμεθα τὴν κενοδοξίαν ταύτην καὶ ὀλεθροφόρον ἀλα-
20 ζονείαν; [20]ἐλεήσωμεν τὰς ἑαυτῶν ἡλικίας καὶ κατοικτίρωμεν τὸ τῆς μητρὸς γῆρας [21]καὶ ἐνθυμηθῶμεν ὅτι ἀπειθοῦντες

---

purpose. WOODEN HORSES (DuP-S's suggestion for *trokhanteras*): In Galen the word means "one of the two processes at the head of the thighbone." The present is its only use for an instrument of torture; how it operated is not clear. CATAPULTS: Not artillery, but (according to Hesychius) an instrument of torture which employed a similar mechanism, again for dislocating joints; it is mentioned in 9.26, 11.9, 26, 18.20. The use of "caldrons" (*lebetas*) and "braziers" (*tegana*) is indicated in 12.1, 10, 20, 18.20; these are mentioned also in II Mac. 7.3. "Thumbscrews" (*daktylethras*) are mentioned in IV Maccabees only here. The use of "iron grips" (*kheiras sideras*) is mentioned in 9.26, and of "wedges" (*sphenas*) in 11.10. "Bellows" (*zopyra pyros*) are not mentioned, but in 9.19 the fire is said to have been intensified—presumably by bellows. Some of the tortures may be elaborations of those suggested in the *Gorgias*, 473a; castration and crucifixion, mentioned in Plato, are significantly omitted here.
14. THE JUSTICE . . . UNDER DURESS: At the conclusion of Antiochus's speech to Eleazar (5.13) God is similarly designated by a philosophical circumlocution (*cf.* vv. 22, 25), and the veniality of transgression under duress is emphasized. Again, the fair appearance put on yielding sharpens the effect of the resolute refusal which immediately follows.
15. BY THEIR RIGHT REASONING NULLIFIED HIS TYRANNY: Another asseve-

wheels and instruments for dislocating joints, racks and wooden horses, and catapults, and caldrons and braziers and thumbscrews and iron grips and wedges and bellows; and the tyrant then resumed, and said: [14]"Lads, be afraid; the justice which you revere will be indulgent to transgression under duress."
[15]But they, though they heard his cajoling words and looked upon the frightful implements, not only were not affrighted, but confronted the tyrant with their own philosophy, and by their right reasoning nullified his tyranny. [16]Yet let us now reflect: if some among them had been faint-spirited and cowardly, what arguments might they have used? Surely something like this: [17]"Wretched and exceedingly senseless that we are, when the king invites us and urges our well-being, should we not hearken to him? [18]Why do we entertain ourselves with these vain resolutions, and make foolhardy venture of fatal disobedience? [19]Shall we not, dear brothers, be afraid of these instruments of torture? Shall we not ponder the threats of torment? Shall we not eschew this vainglory and this death-bringing braggadocio? [20]Let us take pity upon our own youth; let us show compassion to our mother's hoary head. [21]Let us lay it upon our hearts that if we disobey

ration of the freedom of the sage, and like that in 5.38 the ultimate defense. *Cf.*, for the same expression, 1.11, 11.24.

16. WHAT ARGUMENTS MIGHT THEY HAVE USED?: The dramatic recital of the mitigating arguments they might have used but did not (16-26) lends pathos to the plight of the young men, and makes the arguments of nature and piety vivid. The same device is employed in the case of the mother in 16.5-11.

19. VAINGLORY . . . BRAGGADOCIO: We have seen that "reputation" was in fact a prime and valid motivation to martyrdom (5.18, 6.19, and notes). It might therefore well be argued that according to Aristotle's ethical doctrine of the mean, such costly insistence on reputation constituted an undesirable extreme—"vainglory" instead of proper *doxa*. This is the only argument among those which might have been adduced by the young men which is their own and not merely an echo of those urged by the king, such as—

20. LET US TAKE PITY UPON OUR OWN YOUTH: But the subjoined "compassion to our mother's hoary head" would be their own.

τεθνηξόμεθα. ²²συγγνώσεται δὲ ἡμῖν καὶ ἡ θεία δίκη δι' ἀνάγκην τὸν βασιλέα φοβηθεῖσιν. ²³τί ἐξάγομεν ἑαυτοὺς τοῦ ἡδίστου βίου καὶ ἀποστεροῦμεν ἑαυτοὺς τοῦ γλυκέος κόσμου; ²⁴μὴ βιαζώμεθα τὴν ἀνάγκην μηδὲ κενοδοξήσωμεν 25 ἐπὶ τῇ ἑαυτῶν στρέβλῃ. ²⁵οὐδ' αὐτὸς ὁ νόμος ἑκουσίως ἡμᾶς θανατοῖ φοβηθέντας τὰ βασανιστήρια. ²⁶πόθεν ἡμῖν ἡ τοσαύτη ἐντέτηκε φιλονεικία καὶ ἡ θανατηφόρος ἀρέσκει καρτερία, παρὸν μετὰ ἀταραξίας ζῆν τῷ βασιλεῖ πεισθέντας; ²⁷ἀλλὰ τούτων οὐδὲν εἶπον οἱ νεανίαι βασανίζεσθαι μέλλοντες οὐδὲ ἐνεθυμήθησαν. ²⁸ἦσαν γὰρ περίφρονες τῶν παθῶν καὶ αὐτοκράτορες τῶν ἀλγηδόνων, ²⁹ὥστε ἅμα τῷ παύσασθαι τὸν τύραννον συμβουλεύοντα αὐτοῖς μιαροφαγῆσαι, πάντες διὰ μιᾶς φωνῆς ὁμοῦ ὥσπερ ἀπὸ τῆς αὐτῆς ψυχῆς εἶπον

9 ¹Τί μέλλεις, ὦ τύραννε; ἕτοιμοι γάρ ἐσμεν ἀποθνήσκειν ἢ παραβαίνειν τὰς πατρίους ἡμῶν ἐντολάς· ²αἰσχυνόμεθα γὰρ τοὺς προγόνους ἡμῶν εἰκότως, εἰ μὴ τῇ τοῦ νόμου εὐπειθείᾳ καὶ συμβούλῳ Μωυσεῖ χρησαίμεθα. ³σύμβουλε τύραννε παρανομίας, μὴ ἡμᾶς μισῶν ὑπὲρ αὐτοὺς ἡμᾶς ἐλέα. ⁴χαλεπώτερον γὰρ αὐτοῦ τοῦ θανάτου νομίζομεν εἶναί σου τὸν 5 ἐπὶ τῇ παρανόμῳ σωτηρίᾳ ἡμῶν ἔλεον. ⁵ἐκφοβεῖς δὲ ἡμᾶς τὸν διὰ τῶν βασάνων θάνατον ὑμῖν ἀπειλῶν ὥσπερ οὐχὶ πρὸ βραχέως παρ' Ελεαζαρου μαθών. ⁶εἰ δ' οἱ γέροντες

IX

25 εκουσιως] ακουσιους Deissmann   2 Μωυσει edd., γνωσει A
                                     6 ευσεβησαν] απεθανον A

22. WE SHALL BE PARDONED . . . DURESS: But the plea of duress did not in fact apply to the sin of idolatry; and—
25. NOT EVEN THE LAW ITSELF WOULD WILLINGLY CONDEMN US: Or, accepting Deissmann's conjecture (see critical note), "Not even the Law itself would condemn us to death for being, against our will, affrighted by torture." Note that in either case the author is careful not to state that the Law would not condemn for idolatry, but only that it would not condemn for showing fear.
29. ONE VOICE . . . A SINGLE SPIRIT: II Mac. 7.2 says simply that the eldest spoke for the group. The improbable exaggeration here may lend an element of the miraculous, or may simply be in keeping with our author's concept of a chorus (see 8.4 and note), a figure natural to him and his

we die. ²²We shall be pardoned, even by divine justice, for showing fear of the king under duress. Why do we banish ourselves out of life, that is so sweet; why do we deprive ourselves of the charms of the world? ²⁴Let us not violate necessity; let us not indulge vainglory at the price of our own torture. ²⁵Not even the Law itself would willingly condemn us to death for being affrighted by torture. ²⁶Why does such love of contention inflame us, why does such fatal obduracy attract us, when it is possible for us to lead an untroubled life if we obey the king?"

²⁷But none of these arguments did the young men use, though they were on the point of being tortured; none did they lay to heart. ²⁸For the emotions they despised, and they were sovereign over pain; ²⁹and so, when the tyrant had ceased counseling them to eat forbidden food, all together with one voice, as from a single spirit, said:

9 ¹"Why, tyrant, do you delay? Ready are we to die, rather than transgress our forefathers' commandments. ²Our forebears we should verily shame if we did not show obedience to the Law, and take Moses as our counselor. ³Tyrant counselor of transgression, do not in your hatred of us pity us more than we pity ourselves. ⁴Worse than death itself do we regard that pity of yours, which leads to safety through transgression of the Law. ⁵You seek to terrify us by threatening us with death through torture, as if you had learned nothing from Eleazar a short while ago. ⁶But if old men of the

---

Hellenized audience, who knew perfectly well that a Greek chorus spoke with one voice and a single spirit.

1. READY ARE WE: So the eldest begins his speech in II Mac. 7.2; here it is expanded to nine verses.
2. MOSES AS OUR COUNSELOR: An intentional contrast with—
3. TYRANT COUNSELOR.
5. LEARNED NOTHING FROM ELEAZAR: A justification for Eleazar's unwillingness to set a bad example.
6. MORE FITTING THAT WE WHO ARE YOUNG SHOULD DIE: The paradox may be a conscious reminiscence of the poem of Tyrtaeus (6), where the young

τῶν Ἑβραίων διὰ τὴν εὐσέβειαν καὶ βασανισμοὺς ὑπομείναντες εὐσέβησαν, ἀποθάνοιμεν ἂν δικαιότερον ἡμεῖς οἱ νέοι τὰς βασάνους τῶν σῶν ἀναγκῶν ὑπεριδόντες, ἃς καὶ ὁ παιδευτὴς ἡμῶν γέρων ἐνίκησεν. ⁷πείραζε τοιγαροῦν, τύραννε· καὶ τὰς ἡμῶν ψυχὰς εἰ θανατώσεις διὰ τὴν εὐσέβειαν, μὴ νομίσῃς ἡμᾶς βλάπτειν βασανίζων. ⁸ἡμεῖς μὲν γὰρ διὰ τῆσδε τῆς κακοπαθείας καὶ ὑπομονῆς τὰ τῆς ἀρετῆς ἆθλα ἕξομεν καὶ ἐσόμεθα παρὰ θεῷ, δι' ὃν καὶ πάσχομεν· ⁹σὺ δὲ διὰ τὴν ἡμῶν μιαιφονίαν αὐτάρκη καρτερήσεις ὑπὸ τῆς θείας δίκης αἰώνιον βάσανον διὰ πυρός. ¹⁰Ταῦτα αὐτῶν εἰπόντων οὐ μόνον ὡς κατὰ ἀπειθούντων ἐχαλέπαινεν ὁ τύραννος, ἀλλὰ καὶ ὡς κατὰ ἀχαρίστων ὠργίσθη. ¹¹ὅθεν τὸν πρεσβύτατον αὐτῶν κελευσθέντες παρῆγον οἱ ὑπασπισταὶ καὶ διαρρήξαντες τὸν χιτῶνα διέδησαν τὰς χεῖρας αὐτοῦ καὶ τοὺς βραχίονας ἱμᾶσιν ἑκατέρωθεν. ¹²ὡς δὲ τύπτοντες ταῖς μάστιξιν ἐκοπίασαν μηδὲν ἀνύοντες, ἀνέβαλον αὐτὸν ἐπὶ τὸν τροχόν· ¹³περὶ ὃν κατατεινόμενος ὁ εὐγενὴς νεανίας ἔξαρθρος ἐγίνετο. ¹⁴καὶ κατὰ πᾶν μέλος κλώμενος ἐκακηγόρει λέγων ¹⁵Τύραννε μιαρώτατε καὶ τῆς οὐρανίου δίκης ἐχθρὲ καὶ ὠμόφρων, οὐκ ἀνδροφονήσαντά με

---

8 εξομεν] A has οισομεν and omits the remainder of the verse   9 δια πυρος] omitted in S

---

are urged to die, on the ground that they make handsomer corpses than the old.   OUR AGED TEACHER: Eleazar is nowhere described as a teacher, but he is "expert in the Law" (5.4) and a "chief scribe" (II Mac. 6.18), and therefore may well have been an actual teacher, as he certainly was by his example.

7. DO NOT THINK THAT YOU ARE INJURING US: So Epictetus asserted that the master who broke his leg did not injure him, for the leg is part of the whole which Providence governs, and nothing that is beneficial to the whole can be bad for a part. Cruelty is injurious only to its perpetrator; cf. Plato, Gorgias, 472e (also in reference to a king's power to torture): "It is better to suffer wrong than to do it"—even from the tyrant's viewpoint.

8. THE PRIZE: Figures from athletic contests are recurrent; cf., e.g., 9.23, 11.20, 17.15, 16, Wis. 10.12. I Cor. 9.24, similarly addressed to a Hellenized audience, reads: "Know ye not that they which run in a race run all, but one receiveth the prize?"   The Greek figure is characteristically combined with a religious note, WE SHALL BE WITH GOD: This is found only in S, but is doubtless genuine. On the concept of retribution. see

Hebrews have died for religion's sake, and persevering through torture have abided in their religion, it is even more fitting that we who are young should die, despising the torments of your compulsion, over which our aged teacher triumphed. ⁷Proceed, then, with your trial, tyrant; and if you take our lives and inflict upon us a death for religion's sake, do not think that you are injuring us by your torments. ⁸We, by our suffering and endurance, shall obtain the prize of virtue; and we shall be with God, on Whose account we suffer; ⁹but you, for our foul murder, will endure at the hand of divine justice the condign punishment of eternal torment by fire."

10 ¹⁰When they had said these things, the tyrant was not only indignant, as at men disobedient, but also infuriated, as at men who proved ingrate. ¹¹At his orders, then, the guards brought up the eldest of the brothers, and ripped off his tunic, and bound his hands and arms on this side and that with thongs. ¹²And when they had flogged him with scourges until they were weary and had gained nothing, they cast him upon the wheel. ¹³Here the noble youth was racked until his limbs were out of joint. ¹⁴But, though he was maimed in every 15 limb, he broke into denunciations, and said: ¹⁵"Foul tyrant, enemy of heaven's justice, savage of heart, it is not as a

---

Introd. 121.
9. BY FIRE: Possibly a gloss, inspired by 12.12.
9.10–25. *Martyrdom of the eldest.* Here the victim is scourged, broken on the wheel, burned; in II Mac. 7.4–5 his tongue is cut out, he is scalped, his extremities are amputated, and he is thrown into a caldron. In IV Maccabees the amputation of the tongue and extremities is assigned to the fourth brother, scalping to the third, boiling to the seventh. Our author retains the details, but distributes them according to his own judgment of literary effectiveness. The three speeches he assigns to the eldest brother—to the tyrant, to the guards, and to the remaining brothers—are wholly his own invention, and have no basis in II Maccabees.
10. INGRATE: Our author is careful to give the king credible and even creditable motivation, so as to make his story real drama, and not a melodramatic tableau of a first capriciously cruel and then abjectly grovelling villain.
11. RIPPED OFF HIS TUNIC: The enumeration of the preparations heightens both pathos and suspense.

τοῦτον καταικίζεις τὸν τρόπον οὐδὲ ἀσεβήσαντα ἀλλὰ θείου νόμου προασπίζοντα. [16]καὶ τῶν δορυφόρων λεγόντων Ὁμολόγησον φαγεῖν, ὅπως ἀπαλλαγῇς τῶν βασάνων, [17]ὁ δὲ εἶπεν Οὐχ οὕτως ἰσχυρὸς ὑμῶν ἐστιν ὁ τροχός, ὦ μιαροὶ διάκονοι, ὥστε μου τὸν λογισμὸν ἄγξαι· τέμνετέ μου τὰ μέλη καὶ πυροῦτέ μου τὰς σάρκας καὶ στρεβλοῦτε τὰ ἄρθρα. [18]διὰ πασῶν γὰρ ὑμᾶς πείσω τῶν βασάνων ὅτι μόνοι παῖδες Ἑβραίων ὑπὲρ ἀρετῆς εἰσιν ἀνίκητοι. [19]ταῦτα λέγοντι ὑπέστρωσαν πῦρ καὶ τὸ διερεθίζον τὸν τροχὸν προσεπικατέτεινον· [20]ἐμολύνετο δὲ πάντοθεν αἵματι ὁ τροχός, καὶ ὁ σωρὸς τῆς ἀνθρακιᾶς τοῖς τῶν ἰχώρων ἐσβέννυτο σταλαγμοῖς, καὶ περὶ τοὺς ἄξονας τοῦ ὀργάνου περιέρρεον αἱ σάρκες. [21]καὶ περιτετμημένον ἤδη ἔχων τὸ τῶν ὀστέων πῆγμα ὁ μεγαλόφρων καὶ Ἀβραμιαῖος νεανίας οὐκ ἐστέναξεν, [22]ἀλλ' ὥσπερ ἐν πυρὶ μετασχηματιζόμενος εἰς ἀφθαρσίαν ὑπέμεινεν εὐγενῶς τὰς στρέβλας [23]Μιμήσασθέ με, ἀδελφοί, λέγων, μή μου τὸν ἀγῶνα λειποτακτήσητε μηδὲ ἐξομόσησθέ μου τὴν τῆς εὐψυχίας ἀδελφότητα. [24]ἱερὰν καὶ εὐγενῆ στρατείαν στρατεύσασθε περὶ τῆς εὐσεβείας, δι' ἧς ἵλεως ἡ δικαία καὶ πάτριος ἡμῶν πρόνοια τῷ ἔθνει γενηθεῖσα τιμωρήσειεν τὸν ἀλάστορα τύραννον. [25]καὶ ταῦτα εἰπὼν ὁ ἱεροπρεπὴς νεανίας ἀπέρρηξεν τὴν ψυχήν.

[26]Θαυμασάντων δὲ πάντων τὴν καρτεροψυχίαν αὐτοῦ ἦγον οἱ δορυφόροι τὸν καθ' ἡλικίαν τοῦ προτέρου δεύτερον

---

17 τροχος] τροπος A   23 αγωνα] αιωνα SA

17. STRANGLE: Grimm remarks that the image is inappropriate, because the effect of the wheel is to stretch, not to compress the body. The notion that physical tortures cannot affect the reason is of course central, and recurs in similar forms in 6.7 and 10.19. In 11.21 the invincibility of reason is stated as a general truth.

19. THE CHILDREN OF THE HEBREWS ALONE ARE INVINCIBLE: Because they possess true philosophy and true religion.

22. TRANSFORMED INTO INCORRUPTION (*aphtharsian*): In Philo the rational soul is corruptible (*phtharte*; *Leg. allegor.* 1.12.32), and mortal (*Fug.* 13.69); whereas the irrational soul or mind is incorruptible (*aphthartos*; *Immut.* 10.46), and immortal (*athanatos*: *Probus* 7.46); *Congr.* 18.97; *Spec.* 1.16.81). In this Philo reflects Platonic doctrine, especially as set forth in the *Phaedrus*; see Wolfson, 1.395 f. Elsewhere Philo speaks of the

murderer that you so torture me, nor as an impious wretch, but as a defender of the divine Law." ¹⁶The guards said to him, "Consent to eat, and save yourself from the torments." ¹⁷But he said to them: "Your wheel is not so strong, you base minions, as to strangle my reason. ¹⁸Slice my members, burn my flesh, twist my joints: through all these torments I will convince you that the children of the Hebrews alone are invincible in virtue's cause." ¹⁹When he said this they strewed fire under him and heaped it with coals, and they made the wheel yet more taut. ²⁰Besmeared with blood on all sides was the wheel, and the heap of live coals was quenched by the droppings of the fluid, and gouts of flesh whirled around on the axles of the machine. ²¹Even when the frame of his body was already dissevered, that great-spirited youth, a true son of Abraham, uttered no groan. ²²As though he were being transformed into incorruption by the fire, he nobly endured the torments, ²³and he said: "Imitate me, my brothers; do not desert your post in my trial, do not abjure our brotherhood in nobility. ²⁴Fight the sacred and noble fight for religion's sake. Through it may the just Providence which watched over our fathers also become merciful to our people, and exact punishment from the accursed tyrant." ²⁵Uttering these words, the saintly young man broke off his life.

²⁶All marvelled at his firm constancy; and the guards brought up the one next to the eldest in age, and when they

---

Logos as incorruptible (*aphthartos; Conf.* 11.41). Our passage and the Philonic parallels provide a background for such a verse as II Cor. 15.53: "For the corruptible [*to phtharton*] must put on incorruption [*aphtharsian*] and the mortal must put on immortality."
23. DO NOT ABJURE OUR BROTHERHOOD: The third brother (10.3) and the fourth (10.15) make a specific response to this exhortation.
24. FIGHT THE SACRED AND NOBLE FIGHT: See on 8.8; and *cf.* II Tim. 4.7: "I have fought a good fight, I have finished my course, I have kept the faith." ACCURSED: *Alastor*, from the vocabulary and carrying the atmosphere of tragedy. It is used again in 18.22; and in II Mac. 7.9 it is applied to the tyrant by the second brother.
26–31. *The second brother*. The torture by flaying is like that in II Mac. 7.7, but with more horrible detail. The victim speaks of future retribution, but, unlike II Mac. 7.9, says nothing of resurrection.

καὶ σιδηρᾶς ἐναρμοσάμενοι χεῖρας ὀξέσι τοῖς ὄνυξιν ὀργάνῳ καὶ καταπέλτῃ προσέδησαν αὐτόν. ²⁷ὡς δ' εἰ φαγεῖν βούλοιτο πρὶν βασανίζεσθαι πυνθανόμενοι τὴν εὐγενῆ γνώμην ἤκουσαν, ²⁸ἀπὸ τῶν τενόντων ταῖς σιδηραῖς χερσὶν ἐπισπασάμενοι μέχρι τῶν γενείων τὴν σάρκα πᾶσαν καὶ τὴν τῆς κεφαλῆς δορὰν οἱ παρδάλεοι θῆρες ἀπέσυρον. ὁ δὲ ταύτην βαρέως τὴν ἀλγηδόνα καρτερῶν ἔλεγεν ²⁹‛Ὡς ἡδὺς πᾶς θανάτου τρόπος διὰ τὴν πάτριον ἡμῶν εὐσέβειαν. ἔφη τε 30 πρὸς τὸν τύραννον ³⁰Οὐ δοκεῖς, πάντων ὠμότατε τύραννε, πλέον ἐμοῦ σε βασανίζεσθαι ὁρῶν σου νικώμενον τὸν τῆς τυραννίδος ὑπερήφανον λογισμὸν ὑπὸ τῆς διὰ τὴν εὐσέβειαν ἡμῶν ὑπομονῆς; ³¹ἐγὼ μὲν γὰρ ταῖς διὰ τὴν ἀρετὴν ἡδοναῖς τὸν πόνον ἐπικουφίζομαι, ³²σὺ δὲ ἐν ταῖς τῆς ἀσεβείας ἀπειλαῖς βασανίζῃ. οὐκ ἐκφεύξῃ δέ, μιαρώτατε τύραννε, τὰς τῆς θείας ὀργῆς δίκας.

10 ¹Καὶ τούτου τὸν ἀοίδιμον θάνατον καρτερήσαντος ὁ τρίτος ἤγετο παρακαλούμενος πολλὰ ὑπὸ πολλῶν ὅπως ἀπογευσάμενος σῴζοιτο. ²ὁ δὲ ἀναβοήσας ἔφη 'Ἀγνοεῖτε ὅτι αὐτός με τοῖς ἀποθανοῦσιν ἔσπειρεν πατήρ, καὶ ἡ αὐτὴ μήτηρ ἐγέννησεν, καὶ ἐπὶ τοῖς αὐτοῖς ἀνετράφην δόγμασιν; ³οὐκ 5 ἐξόμνυμαι τὴν εὐγενῆ τῆς ἀδελφότητος συγγένειαν. ⁵οἱ δὲ πικρῶς ἐνέγκαντες τὴν παρρησίαν τοῦ ἀνδρὸς ἀρθρεμβόλοις ὀργάνοις τὰς χεῖρας αὐτοῦ καὶ τοὺς πόδας ἐξήρθρουν

X

4 Our text omits this verse: προς ταυτα
ει τι εχετε κολαστηριον προσαγαγατε
τω σωματι μου· της γαρ ψυχης μου

ουδ αν ει θελητε αψασθαι δυνασθε.
It does not occur in A and may well
be an interpolation

---

29. HOW SWEET: In II Mac. 6.30 Eleazar speaks of suffering as "sweet."
ANCESTRAL RELIGION: Jos., Ant. 13.8.2, has the same expression.
30. YOU ARE BEING TORMENTED MORE THAN I: In the present, because the king's arrogant reasoning is being defeated, while the martyr's endurance is victorious. Cf. also Gorgias 572e.
31. I LIGHTEN MY PAIN: The martyr has the upper hand not only by reason of the present victory, but also absolutely, by the principle of retribution, the contemplation of which gives him satisfaction even in the present.

had adjusted their iron "hands" with sharp claws, they bound him to the instrument of torture and the catapult. [27]Before torturing him they inquired whether he were willing to eat; and when they heard his noble resolve, [28]they tore out his sinews with their iron hands, and they flayed all his flesh up to his chin and also the skin of his head, like savage leopards. The agony he endured with fortitude, and he said: [29]"How sweet is every form of death for the sake of our ancestral religion." And to the tyrant he said: [30]"Do you not perceive, tyrant most cruel of all, that you are being tormented more than I, when you see that your arrogant reasoning of tyranny is vanquished by our endurance in the cause of religion? [31]In my case, I lighten my pain by the joys which virtue brings; but you are tortured by the threats implicit in wickedness. You cannot, vile tyrant, escape the judgments of divine wrath."

10 [1]When he too had gloriously endured death, the third was brought forward—amid many exhortations urged by many people that he taste of the food and save himself. [2]But he cried out, and said, "Do you not know that the same father who begot my brothers who have died begot me, and the same mother bore me, and that I was nurtured in the same doctrines? [3]I do not abjure the noble kinship of our brotherhood. [4]Therefore, if you have any means of torture, apply it to my body; my soul you cannot touch, even if you would." [5]The man's free speaking irked them sharply, and with their dislocating instruments they dislocated his hands and his feet, and they pried his members asunder from their joints

---

1–11. *The third brother*. This section also is generally similar to the parallel in II Mac. 7.10–12, but again more sensational.

4. THEREFORE, . . . : This verse does not occur in A, and is therefore omitted in our text and relegated to the apparatus; it may well be an interpolation. In II Mac. 6.30 Eleazar contrasts the body, which is susceptible to martyrdom, with the soul, which is not. *Cf.* Matt. 10.28: "Fear not them which kill the body but are not able to kill the soul."

καὶ ἐξ ἁρμῶν ἀναμοχλεύοντες ἐξεμέλιζον, ⁶τοὺς δακτύλους καὶ τοὺς βραχίονας καὶ τὰ σκέλη καὶ τοὺς ἀγκῶνας περιέκλων. ⁷καὶ κατὰ μηδένα τρόπον ἰσχύοντες αὐτὸν ἄγξαι περιλύσαντες τὰ ὄργανα σὺν ἄκραις ταῖς τῶν δακτύλων κορυφαῖς ἀπεσκύθιζον. ⁸καὶ εὐθέως ἦγον ἐπὶ τὸν τροχόν, περὶ ὃν ἐκ σπονδύλων ἐκμελιζόμενος ἑώρα τὰς ἑαυτοῦ σάρκας περιλακιζομένας καὶ κατὰ σπλάγχνων σταγόνας αἵματος ἀπορρεούσας. ⁹μέλλων δὲ ἀποθνῄσκειν ἔφη ¹⁰‘Ἡμεῖς μέν, ὦ μιαρώτατε τύραννε, διὰ παιδείαν καὶ ἀρετὴν θεοῦ ταῦτα πάσχομεν· ¹¹σὺ δὲ διὰ τὴν ἀσέβειαν καὶ μιαιφονίαν ἀκαταλύτους καρτερήσεις βασάνους.

¹²Καὶ τούτου θανόντος ἀδελφοπρεπῶς τὸν τέταρτον ἐπεσπῶντο λέγοντες ¹³Μὴ μανῇς καὶ σὺ τοῖς ἀδελφοῖς σου τὴν αὐτὴν μανίαν, ἀλλὰ πεισθεὶς τῷ βασιλεῖ σῷζε σεαυτόν. ¹⁴ὁ δὲ αὐτοῖς ἔφη Οὐχ οὕτως καυστικώτερον ἔχετε κατ' ἐμοῦ τὸ πῦρ ὥστε με δειλανδρῆσαι. ¹⁵μὰ τὸν μακάριον τῶν ἀδελφῶν μου θάνατον καὶ τὸν αἰώνιον τοῦ τυράννου ὄλεθρον καὶ τὸν ἀΐδιον τῶν εὐσεβῶν βίον, οὐκ ἀρνήσομαι τὴν εὐγενῆ ἀδελφότητα. ¹⁶ἐπινόει, τύραννε, βασάνους, ἵνα καὶ δι' αὐτῶν μάθῃς ὅτι ἀδελφός εἰμι ˙ τῶν προβασανισθέντων. ¹⁷ταῦτα ἀκούσας ὁ αἱμοβόρος καὶ φονώδης καὶ παμμιαρώτατος Ἀντίοχος ἐκέλευσεν τὴν γλῶτταν αὐτοῦ ἐκτεμεῖν. ¹⁸ὁ δὲ ἔφη Κἂν ἀφέλῃς τὸ τῆς φωνῆς ὄργανον, καὶ σιωπώντων

---

6 περιεκλων] περιελκων A   7 περιλυσαντες τα οργανα] περισυραντες το δερμα AS

7. WITH THE TIPS OF THEIR FINGERS: The variant (see critical note) yields, "they flayed off his skin with the tips of his fingers and stripped off his scalp as the Scythians do." In either case "stripped off his scalp as the Scythians do" is a rendition of the single word *apeskythizon*. For the Scythian practice of scalping see Herodotus 4.64, Pliny, *N.H.* 7.11.
10. WE, TYRANT . . . : The final speech of the third brother recalls that of the second (9.31–32). Again there is no mention of resurrection, on which the third brother lays special emphasis in II Mac. 7.11.
12–21. *The fourth brother.* II Mac. 7.13 says only that this brother suffered the same torments as his predecessors; here we are told that his tongue was cut out, a detail which II Maccabees assigns to the first and third brothers.

with levers; ⁶his fingers and arms and legs and elbows they shattered. ⁷And when they could in no way prevail to strangle [his spirit], they abandoned their instruments, and with the tips of their fingers scalped him as the Scythians do. ⁸Straightway then they brought him to the wheel, and when his vertebrae were being disjointed upon it he saw his own flesh hanging in shreds, and gouts of blood dropping from his entrails. ⁹When he was on the point of death, he said, ¹⁰"We, tyrant most abominable, undergo these sufferings for our teaching and divine virtue; ¹¹but you will endure torments interminable for your impiety and your cruelty."

¹²And when he had died in a manner worthy of his brothers, they dragged forward the fourth brother, and said: ¹³"Do not you too act the madman with that same madness your brothers have shown, but obey the king and save yourself." ¹⁴But he said to them, "No fire you can bring against me is so burning hot as to make a coward of me. ¹⁵By the blessed death of my brothers, by the everlasting destruction of the tyrant, by the glorious life of the pious, I will not deny our noble brotherhood. ¹⁶Contrive [novel] tortures, tyrant, so that they may teach you further proof that I am brother to those who have already been tortured." ¹⁷Upon hearing this, the bloodthirsty and murderous and utterly abominable Antiochus ordered his tongue to be cut out. ¹⁸But he said, "Even if you take away my organ of speech, yet doth God hear

---

14. HE SAID . . . : In II Mac. 7.8 the second brother replies to a similar invitation to apostasy with the word "No" uttered in Heb.; here the single word is expanded into a fiery speech.
16. CONTRIVE: In 18.20 the king's cruelty is emphasized by attributing the means of torture to him personally.
17. BLOODTHIRSTY . . . : This appears to be the earliest instance of what became a stock characterization of a persecuting tyrant. *Cf.* H. von Campenhausen, *Die Idee des Martyriums in der alten Kirche* (Göttingen, 1936) 153, 157; H. W. Surkau, *Martyrien in jüdischer u. frühchristl. Zeit* (Göttingen, 1938).
18. YET DOTH GOD HEAR: Jos. *Jewish War* 5.413, has a similar expression, with *sigomenon* instead of *sioponton*.

ἀκούει ὁ θεός· ¹⁹ἰδοὺ προκεχάλασται ἡ γλῶσσα, τέμνε, οὐ γὰρ παρὰ τοῦτο τὸν λογισμὸν ἡμῶν γλωττοτομήσεις. ²⁰ἡδέως ὑπὲρ τοῦ θεοῦ τὰ τοῦ σώματος μέλη ἀκρωτηριαζόμεθα. ²¹σὲ δὲ ταχέως μετελεύσεται ὁ θεός, τὴν γὰρ τῶν θείων ὕμνων μελῳδὸν γλῶτταν ἐκτέμνεις.

11 ¹Ὡς δὲ καὶ οὗτος ταῖς βασάνοις καταικισθεὶς ἐναπέθανεν, ὁ πέμπτος παρεπήδησεν λέγων ²Οὐ μέλλω, τύραννε, πρὸς τὸν ὑπὲρ τῆς ἀρετῆς βασανισμὸν παραιτεῖσθαι, ³αὐτὸς δ' ἀπ' ἐμαυτοῦ παρῆλθον, ὅπως κἀμὲ κατακτείνας περὶ πλειόνων ἀδικημάτων ὀφειλήσῃς τῇ οὐρανίῳ δίκῃ τιμωρίαν. ⁴ὦ μισάρετε καὶ μισάνθρωπε, τί δράσαντας ἡμᾶς τοῦτον 5 πορθεῖς τὸν τρόπον; ⁵ὅτι τὸν πάντων κτίστην εὐσεβοῦμεν καὶ κατὰ τὸν ἐνάρετον αὐτοῦ ζῶμεν νόμον; ⁶ἀλλὰ ταῦτα τιμῶν, οὐ βασάνων ἐστὶν ἄξια. ⁹τοιαῦτα δὲ λέγοντα οἱ δορυφόροι δήσαντες αὐτὸν εἷλκον ἐπὶ τὸν καταπέλτην, 10 ¹⁰ἐφ' ὃν δήσαντες αὐτὸν ἐπὶ τὰ γόνατα καὶ ταῦτα ποδάγραις σιδηραῖς ἐφαρμόσαντες τὴν ὀσφὺν αὐτοῦ περὶ τροχιαῖον σφῆνα κατέκαμψαν, περὶ ὃν ὅλος περὶ τὸν τροχὸν σκορπίου τρόπον ἀνακλώμενος ἐξεμελίζετο. ¹¹κατὰ τοῦτον τὸν τρόπον καὶ τὸ πνεῦμα στενοχωρούμενος καὶ τὸ σῶμα ἀγχόμενος ¹²Καλάς, ἔλεγεν, ἄκων, ὦ τύραννε, χάριτας ἡμῖν χαρίζῃ

XI	πολεμεις τους ευσεβουντας εις τον θεον
7–8 These vv. are found in A but not in S: 7 ειπερ ησθανου ανθρωπου (s) ποθων και ελπιδα ειχες παρα θεω σωτηριου 8 νυνι δε αλλοτριος ων θεου	10 περι τροχιαιον A, επι τρ. S / τροχον A, τραχηλον S; DuP-S regards τροχον as a gloss for the difficult περι τροχιαιον

19. TONGUE HANGS OUT: An effective heightening of II Mac. 7.10, where the martyr puts his tongue out at the tyrant's order; readers who find it ludicrous for a tongue in such a condition to speak at all do not understand the idioms of rhetoric.
20. GLADLY . . . : Cf. 9.29 and II Mac. 6.30.
21. GOD WILL . . . OVERTAKE: See Introd. 121.

1–12. The fifth brother. II Mac. 7.15 merely states that the fifth brother was taken to the torture, without describing details as given in our passage. The speeches reported in the two documents are also entirely

them that are silent. ¹⁹Look, my tongue hangs out; cut it off, for by so doing you will not mutilate my reason to speechlessness. ²⁰Gladly, for the sake of God, do we suffer our body's members to be amputated. ²¹But you God will speedily overtake, for you are cutting out the tongue which hymned the praises divine."

11 ¹Cruelly racked by the torments, he too died; and then the fifth son leapt forward, saying, ²"I shall not, tyrant, beg off torment for the cause of virtue, ³but of my own accord have I come forward, so that by killing me also you may be liable to heavenly justice for punishment on account of misdeeds even more numerous. ⁴Ah, enemy of virtue and enemy of mankind, for what action on our part do you destroy us in this manner? ⁵Is it because we revere the Creator of all, and live in accordance with His virtuous Law? ⁶But such conduct is worthy of honors, not of torments." ⁹As he was uttering such words, the guards bound him and dragged him to the catapult. ¹⁰Upon it they fastened him by the knees, and fixed them with iron cramps; and they twisted his loins back upon the circular wedge; thus he was wholly broken upon the wheel like a scorpion, and all his members were disjointed. ¹¹In this position, struggling for breath and racked in body, ¹²"A kindly favor," said he, "have you granted us, you tyrant, though all unwilling, for by these noble suffer-

---

different.
1. LEAPT FORWARD: The action and the spirited utterance of vv. 2–3 give a moving effect of spontaneity and enthusiasm lacking in II Maccabees.
3. PUNISHMENT . . . MORE NUMEROUS: All the brothers threaten the tyrant with divine punishment, but only this brother welcomes his torture in order to multiply that punishment.
7–8. These verses, which do not occur in S, are: 7. ". . . if you but understood the desires of mankind and hopes of salvation from God. 8. But now, being estranged from God, you make war upon those who revere him."
10. TWISTED . . . CIRCULAR WEDGE: The meaning is not perfectly clear. DuP-S regards the *trokhon* ("wheel") following as a gloss.

διὰ γενναιοτέρων πόνων ἐπιδείξασθαι παρέχων τὴν εἰς τὸν νόμον ἡμῶν καρτερίαν. ¹³Τελευτήσαντος δὲ καὶ τούτου ὁ ἕκτος ἤγετο μειρακίσκος, ὃς πυνθανομένου τοῦ πυράννου εἰ βούλοιτο φαγὼν ἀπολύεσθαι, ὁ δὲ ἔφη ¹⁴'Εγὼ τῇ μὲν ἡλικίᾳ τῶν ἀδελφῶν μού εἰμι νεώτερος, τῇ δὲ διανοίᾳ ἡλικιώτης· ¹⁵εἰς ταὐτὰ γὰρ γεννηθέντες καὶ ἀνατραφέντες ὑπὲρ τῶν αὐτῶν καὶ ἀποθνήσκειν ὀφείλομεν ὁμοίως· ¹⁶ὥστε εἴ σοι δοκεῖ βασανίζειν μὴ μιαροφαγοῦντα, βασάνιζε. ¹⁷ταῦτα αὐτὸν εἰπόντα παρῆγον ἐπὶ τὸν τροχόν, ¹⁸ἐφ' οὗ κατατεινόμενος ἐπιμελῶς καὶ ἐκσπονδυλιζόμενος ὑπεκαίετο. ¹⁹καὶ ὀβελίσκους ὀξεῖς πυρώσαντες τοῖς νώτοις προσέφερον καὶ τὰ πλευρὰ διαπείραντες αὐτοῦ τὰ σπλάγχνα διέκαιον. ²⁰ὁ δὲ βασανιζόμενος *Ὦ ἱεροπρεποῦς ἀγῶνος, ἔλεγεν, ἐφ' ὃν διὰ τὴν εὐσέβειαν εἰς γυμνασίαν πόνων ἀδελφοὶ τοσοῦτοι κληθέντες οὐκ ἐνικήθημεν. ²¹ἀνίκητος γάρ ἐστιν, ὦ τύραννε, ἡ εὐσεβὴς ἐπιστήμη. ²²καλοκἀγαθίᾳ καθωπλισμένος τεθνήξομαι κἀγὼ μετὰ τῶν ἀδελφῶν μου ²³μέγαν σοὶ καὶ αὐτὸς προσβάλλων ἀλάστορα, καινουργὲ τῶν βασάνων καὶ πολέμιε τῶν ἀληθῶς εὐσεβούντων. ²⁴ἓξ μειράκια καταλελύκαμέν σου τὴν τυραννίδα· ²⁵τὸ γὰρ μὴ δυνηθῆναί σε μεταπεῖσαι τὸν λογισμὸν ἡμῶν μήτε βιάσασθαι πρὸς τὴν μιαροφαγίαν οὐ κατάλυσίς ἐστίν σου; ²⁶τὸ πῦρ σου ψυχρὸν ἡμῖν, καὶ ἄπονοι οἱ καταπέλται, καὶ ἀδύνατος ἡ βία σου. ²⁷οὐ γὰρ τυράννου, ἀλλὰ θείου νόμου προεστήκασιν ἡμῶν οἱ δορυφόροι· διὰ τοῦτο ἀνίκητον ἔχομεν τὸν λογισμόν.

---

18 επιμελως] ευμελως ("harmoniously")   20 αγωνος] αιωνος A / ενικηθημεν] A   ενικημεν S

---

11. BREATH: *Pneuma* here has merely the physical meaning of breath (not "spirit").
12. A KINDLY FAVOR: These words are equivalent to an expression of thanks, and are of course somewhat ironical.
13–27. *The sixth brother*. II Mac. 7.18–19 has none of the details of torture here given, and the speech attributed to the victim is altogether different.
13. A MERE LAD: The crescendo of pathos had reached something of a

ings you enable us to show forth our constancy toward the Law." ¹³And when he too was dead, the sixth was led forward—a mere lad. When the tyrant asked him whether he were willing to eat and so be released, he declared: ¹⁴"In years, indeed, I am younger than my brethren, but in reason I am their agefellow. ¹⁵For the same design were we born and brought up, and we are similarly obliged to die also for the same cause. ¹⁶Hence if you are minded to torture one who does not eat of pollution, torture away." ¹⁷When he said this, they brought him to the wheel. ¹⁸They stretched him out upon it with care, and disjointed his vertebrae, and roasted him with a slow fire. ¹⁹They heated sharp spits in the flame and applied them to his back; they pierced his sides, and burned away his entrails. ²⁰But in the midst of his tortures he said, "Holy and seemly is the passion to which we brethren so many have been summoned, a contest of suffering for religion's sake; and we have not been vanquished. ²¹For, tyrant, religious knowledge is invincible. ²²Armed with nobility cap-a-pie, I too shall die along with my brethren; ²³and I too shall inflict upon you an additional retribution, you deviser of novel tortures, you enemy of the truly pious. ²⁴Only six lads, and we have dissolved your tyranny! ²⁵For when you are not able to sway our reason, nor compel us to eat unclean food, is that not your dissolution? ²⁶Your fire is to us cold, your catapults painless, your violence impotent. ²⁷Not a tyrant's guards, but those of the divine Law have been our protectors, and therefore do we retain our reason unvanquished."

---

climax in the intensity of torture and gallantry of spirit of the fifth brother. For the remaining two, pathos is added by mention of their youthfulness, which in the case of the seventh wins even the king's compassion.
21. RELIGIOUS KNOWLEDGE: In the philosophical and religious sense which *episteme* frequently carries in Philo, and virtually equivalent to *gnosis* (which occurs in IV Maccabees only in 1.16).

12 ¹Ὡς δὲ καὶ οὗτος μακαρίως ἀπέθανεν καταβληθεὶς εἰς λέβητα, ὁ ἕβδομος παρεγίνετο πάντων νεώτερος. ²ὃν κατοικτίρας ὁ τύραννος, καίπερ δεινῶς ὑπὸ τῶν ἀδελφῶν αὐτοῦ κακισθείς, ὁρῶν ἤδη τὰ δεσμὰ περικείμενα πλησιέστερον αὐτὸν μετεπέμψατο καὶ παρηγορεῖν ἐπειρᾶτο λέγων ³Τῆς μὲν τῶν ἀδελφῶν σου ἀπονοίας τὸ τέλος ὁρᾷς· διὰ γὰρ ἀπείθειαν στρεβλωθέντες τεθνᾶσιν. ⁴σὺ δὲ εἰ μὲν μὴ πεισθείης, τάλας βασανισθεὶς καὶ αὐτὸς τεθνήξῃ πρὸ ὥρας, 5 ⁵πεισθεὶς δὲ φίλος ἔσῃ καὶ τῶν ἐπὶ τῆς βασιλείας ἀγήσῃφη πραγμάτων. ⁶καὶ ταῦτα παρακαλῶν τὴν μητέρα τοῦ παιδὸς μετεπέμψατο, ὅπως αὐτὴν ἐλεήσας τοσούτων υἱῶν στερηθεῖσαν παρορμήσειεν ἐπὶ τὴν σωτήριον εὐπείθειαν τὸν περιλειπόμενον. ⁷ὁ δὲ τῆς μητρὸς τῇ Ἑβραΐδι φωνῇ προτρεψαμένης αὐτόν, ὡς ἐροῦμεν μετὰ μικρὸν ὕστερον, ⁸Λύσατέ με φησιν, εἴπω τῷ βασιλεῖ καὶ τοῖς σὺν αὐτῷ φίλοις πᾶσιν. ⁹καὶ ἐπιχαρέντες μάλιστα ἐπὶ τῇ ἐπαγγελίᾳ τοῦ παιδὸς 10 ταχέως ἔλυσαν αὐτόν.. ¹⁰καὶ δραμὼν ἐπὶ πλησίον τῶν τηγάνων ¹¹Ἀνόσιέ, φησιν, καὶ πάντων πονηρῶν ἀσεβέστατε τύραννε, οὐκ ᾐδέσθης παρὰ τοῦ θεοῦ λαβὼν τὰ ἀγαθὰ καὶ τὴν βασιλείαν τοὺς θεράποντας αὐτοῦ κατακτεῖναι καὶ τοὺς

XII υιων στερηθεισαν: see commentary
6 S has οπως εαυτην ελεησασα τοσουτων

1–19. *The seventh brother.* In II Maccabees the account of the death of the youngest brother is preceded by the mother's exhortation (7.22–23); our author is aware of this, and at the appropriate place (v. 7) promises that he will report her encouragement "presently" (*i.e.*, in 16.12–24). Here the desired climactic effect is obtained by the stress laid on the victim's extreme youth, and by the momentary flash of relief and hope before the catastrophe (vv. 8–9).
2. PITIED ... TRIED TO PERSUADE: This not only heightens the pathos, but shows that the tyrant possesses human feelings, and so makes the conflict dramatic.
3. YOU SEE ...: This speech is closely paralleled in II Mac. 7.24.
5. MY FRIEND: A court title, as the conclusion of the verse shows.
6. The text is difficult, and many editors prefer the readings of S (see critical note), which gives: "We summoned the boy's mother so that in sorrow for her loss of so many sons she might urge him that was left to obey and so save himself."
7. HEBREW: The II Maccabees passage, like ours, implies that she used

12 ¹And when he too had died a blessed death, having been cast into a caldron, the seventh came up, the youngest of all. ²Him the tyrant pitied, though he had been vehemently abused by his brothers. When he saw the fetters already laid upon him, he summoned him to approach nearer, and tried to persuade him, saying: ³"You see how your brothers' folly has ended; for their disobedience they have been tortured, and are dead. ⁴Now you too, if you do not obey, you will be tortured miserably, and you will die before your time; ⁵but if you do obey, you will be my Friend, and have charge over the affairs of my realm." ⁶When he had thus advised him, he summoned the boy's mother, so that in pity of her who had been bereft of so many sons he might urge obedience as salvation for him that was left. ⁷But when his mother had encouraged him in the Hebrew tongue, as we shall presently recount, ⁸"Loose me," he said, "let me speak to the king and to all his Friends that are with him." ⁹They were greatly rejoiced at the lad's promise, and speedily loosed him. ¹⁰Then he ran to the nearest of the braziers, ¹¹and said: "Sacrilegious man, tyrant most impious of all that are wicked, are you not ashamed, when you have received all good things, including your kingdom, from God, to slay His servants, and to torture

---

her native language so that the king might not understand; but it also suggests a devotion to the sacred tongue. In any case, the special mention of the use of Heb. for appropriate purposes proves that all the martyrs (and our author's audience) habitually spoke Gk., and illustrates the Hellenizing background of the story as well as our account of it. AS WE SHALL ... RECOUNT: In 16.12-24 (cf. II Mac. 7.27-29), where the mother's exhortation is included with her address to all her sons.

8. LET ME SPEAK TO THE KING: The introduction of an unexpected prospect of a reversal before the final catastrophe is a regular technique in tragedy, and occurs, e.g., in all the plays of Sophocles. In II Maccabees it is the mother who pretends willingness to urge the son to apostasy. We can here see how our author (properly) takes liberties with his source for the purpose of heightening dramatic effect. FRIENDS: An ironic echo of 12.5.
10. THEN HE RAN: Thus making the reversal sharper.
11. SACRILEGIOUS MAN: A marked verbal echo of II Mac. 7.34. THOSE WHO CULTIVATE RELIGION: Parallels for *asketas* in this sense occur in Eusebius and Philo.

τῆς εὐσεβείας ἀσκητὰς στρεβλῶσαι; [12]ἀνθ' ὧν ταμιεύσεταί σε ἡ δίκη πυκνοτέρῳ καὶ αἰωνίῳ πυρὶ καὶ βασάνοις, αἳ εἰς ὅλον τὸν αἰῶνα οὐκ ἀνήσουσίν σε. [13]οὐκ ᾐδέσθης ἄνθρωπος ὤν, θηριωδέστατε, τοὺς ὁμοιοπαθεῖς καὶ ἐκ τῶν αὐτῶν γεγονότας στοιχείων γλωττοτομῆσαι καὶ τοῦτον καταικίσας τὸν τρόπον βασανίσαι. [14]ἀλλ' οἱ μὲν εὐγενῶς ἀποθανόντες ἐπλήρωσαν τὴν εἰς τὸν θεὸν εὐσέβειαν, σὺ δὲ κακῶς οἰμώξεις
15 τοὺς τῆς ἀρετῆς ἀγωνιστὰς ἀναιτίως ἀποκτείνας. [15]ὅθεν καὶ αὐτὸς ἀποθνῄσκειν μέλλων ἔφη [16]Οὐκ ἀπαυτομολῶ τῆς τῶν ἀδελφῶν μου ἀριστείας· [17]ἐπικαλοῦμαι δὲ τὸν πατρῷον θεὸν ὅπως ἵλεως γένηται τῷ ἔθνει ἡμῶν. [18]σὲ δὲ καὶ ἐν τῷ νῦν βίῳ καὶ θανόντα τιμωρήσεται. [19]καὶ ταῦτα κατευξάμενος ἑαυτὸν ἔρριψε κατὰ τῶν τηγάνων, καὶ οὕτως ἀπέδωκεν.

13 [1]Εἰ δὲ τοίνυν τῶν μέχρι θανάτου πόνων ὑπερεφρόνησαν οἱ ἑπτὰ ἀδελφοί συνομολογεῖται πανταχόθεν ὅτι αὐτοδέσποτός

16 αριστειας] μαρτυριας A   and others την ψυχην
19 After απεδωκεν S adds το πνευμα

12. IN RECOMPENSE... THROUGHOUT TIME: See Introd. 121.
13. WHO HAVE LIKE FEELINGS: A Stoic commonplace, to illustrate the essential brotherhood of man. Shakespeare's familiar lines in *The Merchant of Venice* (III, i) clearly echo similar Stoic doctrine in Seneca: "Hath not a Jew eyes? hath not a Jew hands, organs, dimensions, senses, affections, passions? ... If you prick us, do we not bleed? if you tickle us, do we not laugh? if you poison us do we not die?" The same notion occurs in Wis. 7.1–16. *Cf.* also Acts 14.15; Jas. 5.9; Ignatius, *Ad Trall.* 10.
14. YOU WILL GROAN: *Cf.*, *e.g.*, Wis. 5.3–13 for the lamentations of the damned who regret having persecuted the pious.   CHAMPIONS OF VIRTUE: *Agonistas*, like *asketas* in v. 11. Philo, *De somniis* 1.59, speaks of *agonistae* and *athletai* of reason.
16. HEROISM: A's reading gives "martyrdom." If that reading is sound, the use marks the first occurrence of the word in the sense of witnessing to faith by blood. In this sense the word does not occur in the N.T., but is first found in the *Martyrium Polycarpi* (1.1, 13.2, 17.1), which bears marked resemblances to our book.
17. MERCIFUL TO OUR NATION: The notion that the martyrdom of the brothers is in a sense an expiation for the nation is suggested also in the speech of Eleazar (6.28–29) and at the end of the panegyric (17.22). In II Maccabees the youngest of the brothers also expresses the idea that he

those who cultivate religion? ¹²In recompense for this, justice will keep you in store for intense and eternal fire and torment; and these shall never release you throughout time. ¹³Are you not ashamed, being but a man, you most savage of beasts, to cut out the tongues of men who have like feelings with you, and are begotten of the same elements, and to torment and torture them in this vile manner? ¹⁴They, indeed, have died nobly, and so fulfilled their piety to God; but you will groan lamentably for having slain the blameless champions of virtue." ¹⁵Thereupon, when he too was on the point of death, he declared, ¹⁶"'I shall not prove renegade to the heroism of my brothers. ¹⁷I call upon the God of my fathers to prove merciful to our nation. ¹⁸You He will punish, both in the present life and when you are dead." ¹⁹When he had uttered these imprecations he flung himself into the braziers, and so gave up his life.

13 ¹Now, therefore, if the seven brothers despised sufferings even unto death, it must be universally agreed that devout

and his brethren have suffered for the sins of their people (7.32–33, 37–38; *cf.* 16.18). See Introd. 121.

19. FLUNG HIMSELF: Not in II Maccabees, which merely says (7.39) that the king treated him more cruelly than the others. Similarly in the case of the mother, II Mac. 7.41 merely reports her death, whereas our author (17.1) has her also leap into the flames. Freudenthal thought both suicides were in the common source, and were suppressed in II Maccabees; it is more likely that they are the invention of our author, who wished to exhibit the young man's ardor (as in Ignatius, *Ad. Rom.* 5.2) and the mother's modesty ("that no one should touch her body"). It must be remembered that Stoicism approved of suicide under certain conditions. GAVE UP HIS LIFE: The Gk. has only "gave up." Some MSS. have "his breath" or "his life" after "gave up" (see critical note); but these are doubtless glosses, for the verb alone implies its object.

1–14.10. *The martyrdoms as evidence of the sovereignty of reason.* After the emotionally charged account of the martyrs we turn to apply their lesson, in a dryer style, to our main philosophic thesis—that religious reason is sovereign over the emotions. The substance of this passage, as well as its redundant and pedantic style, show an affinity with 6.31–35; and if we accept the theory (maintained by DuP-S) that they are interpolations,

ἐστιν τῶν παθῶν ὁ εὐσεβὴς λογισμός. ²εἰ γὰρ τοῖς πάθεσι δουλωθέντες ἐμιαροφάγησαν, ἐλέγομεν ἂν τούτοις αὐτοὺς νενικῆσθαι· ³νυνὶ δὲ οὐχ οὕτως, ἀλλὰ τῷ ἐπαινουμένῳ παρὰ θεῷ λογισμῷ περιεγένοντο τῶν παθῶν, ⁴ὧν οὐκ ἔστιν παριδεῖν τὴν ἡγεμονίαν τῆς διανοίας, ἐπεκράτησαν γὰρ καὶ 5 πάθους καὶ πόνων. ⁵πῶς οὖν οὐκ ἔστιν τούτοις τὴν τῆς εὐλογιστίας παθοκράτειαν ὁμολογεῖν, οἳ τῶν μὲν διὰ πυρὸς ἀλγηδόνων οὐκ ἐπεστράφησαν; ⁶καθάπερ γὰρ προβλῆτες λιμένων πύργοι τὰς τῶν κυμάτων ἀπειλὰς ἀνακόπτοντες γαληνὸν παρέχουσι τοῖς εἰσπλέουσι τὸν ὅρμον, ⁷οὕτως ἡ ἑπτάπυργος τῶν νεανίσκων εὐλογιστία τὸν τῆς εὐσεβείας ὀχυρώσασα λιμένα τὴν τῶν παθῶν ἐνίκησεν ἀκολασίαν. ⁸ἱερὸν γὰρ εὐσεβείας στήσαντες χορὸν παρεθάρσυνον ἀλλήλους λέγοντες ⁹Ἀδελφικῶς ἀποθάνωμεν, ἀδελφοί, περὶ τοῦ νόμου· μιμησώμεθα τοὺς τρεῖς τοὺς ἐπὶ τῆς Ἀσσυρίας νεανίσκους, 10 οἳ τῆς ἰσοπολίτιδος καμίνου κατεφρόνησαν. ¹⁰μὴ δειλανδρήσωμεν πρὸς τὴν τῆς εὐσεβείας ἐπίδειξιν. ¹¹καὶ ὁ μέν Θάρρει, ἀδελφέ ἔλεγεν, ὁ δέ Εὐγενῶς καρτέρησον, ¹²ὁ δὲ καταμνησθεὶς ἔλεγεν Μνήσθητε πόθεν ἐστέ, ἢ τίνος πατρὸς χειρὶ

XIII

2 ει γαρ] ωσπερ γαρ A, ωσπερ γαρ ει
τοις ... ελεγομεν αν Deissmann
3 παρα θεω λογισμω V, λογισμω παρα θεου S, θεω A

4 ων ουκ] ων και A
7 ακολασιαν] κολασιν S
9 καμινου] S adds καιομενης
12 καταμνησθεις] A omits / μνησθητε] S omits

they would come from the same hand. In 1–5 here the faulty state of the text would support the theory of interpolation. V. 13.6, where the oratorical style is resumed, might well follow 12.19.
2. FOR IF: Well-supported variants (see critical note) would yield "In a similar manner if . . ."
5. THEY DID NOT SHRINK: The Gk. has a *men* without its expected correlative *de*. Hence DuP-S surmises a mutilation of the text, and suggests (on the basis of 14.1) something like "they prevailed not only over the anguish of the fire but also over brotherly affection."
6. EVEN AS: A return to the oratorical style. The image is like that of 7.5, and is similarly placed—after a description of torment and death, and a brief reflection in the scholastic style.
8. GAVE ONE ANOTHER COURAGE: This eloquent passage (through v. 18) is an elaboration of the bare statement in II Mac. 7.5–6 that the brothers encouraged one another.

reason is sovereign over the emotions. ²For if they had been enslaved to the emotions, and had eaten unclean food, we should have said that they had been vanquished by them. ³But this was not the case; by the reason which is commended by God they got the better of emotions, ⁴over which the superiority of reason is thus made evident; for they overcame both emotion and suffering. ⁵How is it then possible not to admit, considering these men, right reason's sovereignty over emotion, when they did not shrink from the agonies of fire? ⁶Even as towers constructed at the mouths of harbors break the threatening waves, and render the anchorage calm for those that sail into it, ⁷so the seven-turreted right reason of these young men fortified the harbor of religion, and overcame the unruliness of the emotions. ⁸A holy choice of religion did they establish; and they gave one another courage, saying, ⁹"In a brotherly fashion, brothers, let us die on behalf of the Law. Let us emulate the Three Youths of Assyria who despised a similar ordeal of the furnace. ¹⁰Let us not show cowardice in the demonstration of religion." ¹¹"Courage, brother!" said one; and another, "Bear up nobly!" ¹²Another, recalling the past, said, "Remember whence ye come, and at the hand of what father Isaac endured immolation for reli-

9. THE THREE: The allusion is to Hananiah, Mishael, and Azariah (Shadrach, Meshach, and Abed-nego) in Dan. 3. The example of Daniel and the "Three Children," who withstood great trials for religion's sake, is a natural one for our author to invoke, and he does so again at 15.21. The composition of the Book of Daniel is generally attributed to the same series of events that brought about the martyrdoms that are the heart of our book.
11. SAID ONE; AND ANOTHER: The breaking up of the "chorus" into short and lively expressions by its individual members lends vividness and heightens tension. The same technique is employed, at similarly critical junctures, in tragedy; cf. Aeschylus, *Agamemnon* 1346 ff.
12. REMEMBER WHENCE YE CAME: Cf. Isa. 51.1 f.: "Look unto the rock whence ye were hewn, and to the hole of the pit whence ye were digged. Look unto Abraham your father." ISAAC: If Daniel and his companions offer the closest parallel to our martyrs, especially in the use of fire, Isaac as a patriarch remains the primal pattern of the willing martyr. Elsewhere the narrative of Gen. 22 is used to illustrate the faith and obedience of Abraham, *e.g.*, 15.28, 17.6; Wis. 10.5.

σφαγιασθῆναι διὰ τὴν εὐσέβειαν ὑπέμεινεν Ισαακ. ¹³εἶς δὲ ἕκαστος ἀλλήλους ὁμοῦ πάντες ἐφορῶντες φαιδροὶ καὶ μάλα θαρραλέοι 'Εαυτούς, ἔλεγον, τῷ θεῷ ἀφιερώσωμεν ἐξ ὅλης τῆς καρδίας τῷ δόντι τὰς ψυχὰς καὶ χρήσωμεν τῇ περὶ τὸν νόμον φυλακῇ τὰ σώματα. ¹⁴μὴ φοβηθῶμεν τὸν δοκοῦντα 15 ἀποκτέννειν· ¹⁵μέγας γὰρ ψυχῆς ἀγὼν καὶ κίνδυνος ἐν αἰωνίῳ βασάνῳ κείμενος τοῖς παραβᾶσι τὴν ἐντολὴν τοῦ θεοῦ. ¹⁶καθοπλισώμεθα τοιγαροῦν τὴν τοῦ θείου λογισμοῦ παθοκρατείαν. ¹⁷οὕτω γὰρ θανόντας ἡμᾶς Αβρααμ καὶ Ισαακ καὶ Ιακωβ ὑποδέξονται καὶ πάντες οἱ πατέρες ἐπαινέσουσιν. ¹⁸καὶ ἑνὶ ἑκάστῳ τῶν ἀποσπωμένων αὐτῶν ἀδελφῶν ἔλεγον οἱ περιλειπόμενοι Μὴ καταισχύνῃς ἡμᾶς, ἀδελφέ, μηδὲ ψεύσῃ τοὺς προαποθανόντας ἡμῶν ἀδελφούς. ¹⁹οὐκ ἀγνοεῖτε δὲ τὰ τῆς ἀδελφότητος φίλτρα, ἅπερ ἡ θεία καὶ πάνσοφος πρόνοια διὰ πατέρων τοῖς γεννωμένοις ἐμέρισεν 20 καὶ διὰ τῆς μητρῴας φυτεύσασα γαστρός, ²⁰ἐν ᾗ τὸν ἴσον ἀδελφοὶ κατοικήσαντες χρόνον καὶ ἐν τῷ αὐτῷ χρόνῳ πλασθέντες καὶ ἀπὸ τοῦ αὐτοῦ αἵματος αὐξηθέντες καὶ διὰ τῆς αὐτῆς ψυχῆς τελεσφορηθέντες ²¹καὶ διὰ τῶν ἴσων ἀποτεχθέντες χρόνων καὶ ἀπὸ τῶν αὐτῶν γαλακτοποτοῦντες πηγῶν, ἀφ' ὧν συντρέφονται ἐναγκαλισμάτων φιλάδελφοι ψυχαί· ²²καὶ αὔξονται σφοδρότερον διὰ συντροφίας καὶ τῆς καθ' ἡμέραν συνηθείας καὶ τῆς ἄλλης παιδείας καὶ τῆς ἡμετέρας

19 αδελφοτητος] ανθρωποτητος A

13. SEVERALLY AND ALL TOGETHER: After their individual expressions (see on v. 11) the members of the "chorus" unite, as in tragedy, for the triumphant closing lines. SOULS: which are not subject to corruptibility (9.22); the body is expendable.
14. LET US NOT FEAR: *Cf.* Matt. 10.28: "And fear not them which kill the body but are not able to kill the soul," and Luke 12.4.
17. WILL RECEIVE US: *Cf.* 5.37; and see Introd. 118.
19-22. The encomium of brotherly love is matched by another on maternal love in the panegyric to the mother (14.13-19). Both are commonplaces of the rhetorical schools, but presented by our author with uncommon virtuosity.
19. CHARM: The word (*philtra*) denotes any means of producing love, and in particular philtre. It recurs in v. 27 and 15.13, and is used similarly in

gion's sake." ¹³Each severally and all together, looking upon one another with faces shining and filled with courage, said, "With all our hearts let us consecrate ourselves to God, Who gave us our souls; and let us use our bodies for the guardianship of the Law. ¹⁴Let us not fear him who thinks that he kills. ¹⁵Great is the trial of soul, and the danger laid up in eternal tribulation, for those who transgress the commandment of God. ¹⁶Let us then arm ourselves with that mastery over suffering which comes from divine reason. ¹⁷When we have died in such fashion, Abraham and Isaac and Jacob will receive us, and all the patriarchs will praise us." ¹⁸And to each one of the brothers, as they were dragged away, those that remained said, "Do not shame us, brother; do not deceive those of our brothers who have died before."

¹⁹You cannot be ignorant of the charm of brotherhood, which divine and all-wise Providence has imparted through fathers upon those begotten of them—implanting it, indeed, even in their mother's womb. ²⁰There do brothers abide for a similar period; and are molded through the same span, and nurtured by the same blood, and brought to maturity through the same vitality. ²¹After equal gestation are they brought to birth, and from the same fountains do they imbibe milk; from these embracings are fraternal spirits nourished; ²²and they grow more robust by reason of their shared nurture and daily companionship and their training, both in other re-

---

Philo. DIVINE AND ALL-WISE PROVIDENCE: This Stoic concept recurs at 9.24 and 17.22. Note the precise exposition of the manner in which Providence produces fraternal love, with the instrumentality of the father and the mother made explicit. A striking parallel in Xenophon, *Cyropedia* 8.7.14, may well have been our author's model: "Those who are sprung from the same seed, nursed by the same mother, reared in the same home, loved by the same parents . . . how are they not the closest of all?"

21. FROM THE SAME FOUNTAINS: Poetic euphemism.
22. AND IN OUR DISCIPLINE: The commonplace is neatly closed with a fresh turn, which makes the transition to the case in hand.

ἐν νόμῳ θεοῦ ἀσκήσεως. ²³οὕτως δὴ τοίνυν καθεστηκυίης συμπαθοῦς τῆς φιλαδελφίας οἱ ἑπτὰ ἀδελφοὶ συμπαθέστερον ἔσχον πρὸς ἀλλήλους. ²⁴νόμῳ γὰρ τῷ αὐτῷ παιδευθέντες καὶ τὰς αὐτὰς ἐξασκήσαντες ἀρετὰς καὶ τῷ δικαίῳ συντραφέντες βίῳ μᾶλλον ἑαυτοὺς ἠγάπων. ²⁵ἡ γὰρ ὁμοζηλία τῆς καλοκἀγαθίας ἐπέτεινεν αὐτῶν τὴν πρὸς ἀλλήλους εὔνοιαν καὶ ὁμόνοιαν· ²⁶σὺν γὰρ τῇ εὐσεβείᾳ ποθεινοτέραν αὐτοῖς κατεσκεύαζον τὴν φιλαδελφίαν. ²⁷ἀλλ' ὅμως καίπερ τῆς φύσεως καὶ τῆς συνηθείας καὶ τῶν τῆς ἀρετῆς ἠθῶν τὰ τῆς ἀδελφότητος αὐτοῖς φίλτρα συναυξόντων ἀνέσχοντο διὰ τὴν εὐσέβειαν τοὺς ἀδελφοὺς οἱ ὑπολειπόμενοι, τοὺς καταικι-

14ζομένους ὁρῶντες μέχρι θανάτου βασανιζομένους, ¹προσέτι καὶ ἐπὶ τὸν αἰκισμὸν ἐποτρύνοντες, ὡς μὴ μόνον τῶν ἀλγηδόνων περιφρονῆσαι αὐτούς, ἀλλὰ καὶ τῶν τῆς φιλαδελφίας παθῶν κρατῆσαι. ²Ὦ βασιλέων λογισμοὶ βασιλικώτεροι καὶ ἐλευθέρων ἐλευθερώτεροι. ³ὦ ἱερᾶς καὶ εὐαρμόστου περὶ τῆς εὐσεβείας τῶν ἑπτὰ ἀδελφῶν συμφωνίας. ⁴οὐδεὶς ἐκ τῶν ἑπτὰ μειρακίων ἐδειλίασεν οὐδὲ πρὸς τὸν θάνατον ὤκνησεν, ⁵ἀλλὰ πάντες ὥσπερ ἐπ' ἀθανασίας ὁδὸν τρέχοντες ἐπὶ τὸν διὰ τῶν βασάνων θάνατον ἔσπευδον. ⁶καθάπερ αἱ χεῖρες καὶ οἱ πόδες συμ-

---

23 προς αλληλους] την π. α. ομονοιαν A, probably added from v. 25
24 εαυτους ηγαπων] επ αυτους ηγαγον A
25 αυτων] αυτω S / ευνοιαν και] A omits
26 συν ... ευσεβεια] Deissmann adds ο λογισμος

XIV
1 των της φ. π. Rahlfs, της των αδελφων φιλαδελφιας παθων AS; DuP-S suggests των φιλαδελφων παθων and explains the alteration by the incorporation of glosses

---

23. BUT THESE SEVEN BROTHERS POSSESSED: A bond beyond that envisaged in the commonplace, that of common loyalty to a "life of righteousness." The implication, as always, is that loyalty to religion imposes even greater responsibility than the ethic of Stoicism.
27. NEVERTHELESS: The conclusion of the argument. Though brotherhood makes for great mutual affection, and brotherhood in the Law for even greater, these young men had the fortitude to look on and—

1. EVEN URGED THEM ON TO THE TORMENTS: An illustration of the capacity of religious reason to master the profound and even praiseworthy emotion

spects and in our discipline in the Law of God. ²³The bond of fraternal affection and sympathy is, we see, firmly fixed; but these seven brothers possessed an even closer bond of sympathy with one another; ²⁴for having been trained in the same Law, and having cultivated the same virtues, and having been brought up together in a life of righteousness, they ²⁵had even greater love for one another. ²⁵Their rivalry in all excellence strengthened their affection for one another, and their concord; ²⁶and the bond of religion made their brotherly love more fervent. ²⁷Nevertheless, though in their case nature and companionship and the practices of virtue augmented the charms of brotherhood, yet for religion's sake those that survived had the fortitude to look on while their brothers were being outrageously misused and tortured to death.

14 ¹Nay, they even urged them on to the torments; and so not only despised physical anguish, but also prevailed over the emotion of brotherly love.

²O Reason, more kingly than kings, more free than freemen! ³O sacred and harmonious concord of the seven brothers for religion's sake! ⁴Not one of the seven lads turned coward, ⁵none shrank in the face of death; ⁵but all, as if running the course to deathlessness, sped onward to death by torture. ⁶Just as hands and feet move in harmony with the prompt-

---

of brotherly love.
2. O REASON: After the account of the martyrdoms, and the exposition of their significance for the main proposition, the author apostrophizes reason; and briefly eulogizes the martyrs as a transition to the even more trying martyrdom of the mother. MORE KINGLY: An echo of the Stoic principle that the sage is the true king; *cf.* Diogenes Laertius 7.122: "Not only are the wise free, they are also kings; kingship being irresponsible rule which none but the wise can maintain."
3. HARMONIOUS CONCORD: A merging of the image of the chorus (used at 13.8 and 14.8) with the Stoic expression "harmony," as in "living in harmony with nature."
5. RUNNING THE COURSE TO DEATHLESSNESS: See on 9 8.
6. IN HARMONY WITH THE PROMPTINGS OF THE SOUL: Ordinary Stoic doctrine, to which is added "prompted by . . . religion," to designate the added motivation and responsibility.

φώνως τοῖς τῆς ψυχῆς ἀφηγήμασιν κινοῦνται, οὕτως οἱ ἱεροὶ μείρακες ἐκεῖνοι ὡς ὑπὸ ψυχῆς ἀθανάτου τῆς εὐσεβείας πρὸς τὸν ὑπὲρ αὐτῆς συνεφώνησαν θάνατον. ⁷ὦ πανάγιε συμφώνων ἀδελφῶν ἑβδομάς. καθάπερ γὰρ ἑπτὰ τῆς κοσμοποιίας ἡμέραι περὶ τὴν εὐσέβειαν, ⁸οὕτως περὶ τὴν ἑβδομάδα χορεύοντες οἱ μείρακες ἐκύκλουν τὸν τῶν βασάνων φόβον καταλύοντες. ⁹νῦν ἡμεῖς ἀκούοντες τὴν θλῖψιν τῶν νεανιῶν ἐκείνων φρίττομεν· οἱ δὲ οὐ μόνον ὁρῶντες, ἀλλ' οὐδὲ μόνον ἀκούοντες τὸν παραχρῆμα ἀπειλῆς λόγον, ἀλλὰ καὶ πάσχοντες 10 ἐνεκαρτέρουν, καὶ τοῦτο ταῖς διὰ πυρὸς ὀδύναις· ¹⁰ὧν τί γένοιτο ἐπαλγέστερον; ὀξεῖα γὰρ καὶ σύντομος οὖσα ἡ τοῦ πυρὸς δύναμις ταχέως διέλυεν τὰ σώματα.

¹¹Καὶ μὴ θαυμαστὸν ἡγεῖσθε εἰ ὁ λογισμὸς περιεκράτησε τῶν ἀνδρῶν ἐκείνων ἐν ταῖς βασάνοις, ὅπου γε καὶ γυναικὸς νοῦς πολυτροπωτέρων ὑπερεφρόνησεν ἀλγηδόνων· ¹²ἡ μήτηρ

7–8 Freudenthal, Deissmann, Emmet interchange ευσεβειαν (7) and εβδο-   μαδα (8)   10 διελυεν] διελυσε A

---

7. SACRED HEBDOMAD: Several passages in Philo celebrate the virtues of the number seven, e.g., De opif. mundi 90: "I doubt whether anyone could adequately celebrate the properties of the hebdomad, for they are beyond all words." Philo then mentions some of these, properties and concludes (ibid. 128): "These and yet more than these are the statements and reflections of men on the number seven, showing the reasons for the very high honor which that number has attained in Nature, the honor in which it is held by the most approved investigators of the science of Mathematics and Astronomy among Greeks and other peoples, and the special honor accorded to it by that lover of virtue, Moses." Cf. also De spec. leg. 2.156; and see Bousset, Die Hauptprobleme der Gnosis, ch. 1, "Die Sieben." The index of Ginzberg's Legends has four columns of references to "seven."
MOVE IN CHORUS: I.e., with regularity and precision; but the figure of the "chorus" is used for the sake of the parallel use of "chorus" for the young men in v. 8. ABOUT RELIGION: Editors (see critical note) exchange the position of this word with that of "hebdomad" in v. 8, to the apparent improvement of the sense of both passages.
8. YOUTHS IN CHORUS CIRCLE: Their movement is as regular and as natural as that of the days of creation, and ("voiding") as irresistibly effective.
9. EVEN NOW: This suggests that the discourse was delivered or composed

ings of the soul, so did those holy youths, as if prompted by the deathless spirit of religion, harmoniously accept death on its behalf. ⁷O all-sacred hebdomad of brothers in harmony! For just as the seven days of creation move in chorus about religion, ⁸so do these youths in chorus circle about the hebdomad, voiding the fear of torment. ⁹Even now, we, when we hear of the agonies of those young men, must shudder; but they, not only in looking on, not only in hearing the utterance of the instant threat, but even in suffering, they endured with ¹⁰fortitude, and this in the burning agonies of fire—¹⁰than which what could be more painful? Sharp and incisive is the power of fire, and quickly did it destroy their bodies.

¹¹Nay, count it not a marvellous thing that reason prevailed over tortures in the case of those men, when the mind of even a woman despised torments even more manifold. ¹²For

in a tranquil period, with the horrors looked at in retrospect; but "now" need not imply a contrast of time, but may contrast the mood of the auditors with that of the participants.   WHEN WE HEAR ... SHUDDER: Probably our strongest indication that the discourse was intended for actual delivery; otherwise it would be more natural, and as effective, for our author to write "When we read ..." See Introd. 102.   NOT ONLY IN HEARING ... BUT ALSO IN SUFFERING: What is called the "*logo men ergo de*" antithesis ("in word, x; but in deed, y") is one of the oldest and commonest of rhetorical figures.

10. DID IT DESTROY: The reading of A, *dielusen* (gnomic aorist), is possibly preferable, as denoting a general truth: "does it destroy bodies." With the finality of complete physical destruction, the apostrophe to the brothers—and so the whole account of their martyrdom—is concluded; and the victory of—

11. REASON ... IN THE CASE OF THOSE MEN: Is made the basis for the transition to the more striking example of "even a woman." *Cf.* the transition in 2.1. The story of the mother's martyrdom (14.11–17.6) is an even stronger glorification of the power of reason.

12. THE MOTHER: Anonymous, like her sons in the older sources, and in the rabbinic sources called simply "the woman," or "a widow," or "Miriam daughter of Tanhum" (or Nahtum); in the Constantinople text of Josippon she is called Hannah, but not in the Mantua texts. Her death is mentioned, almost incidentally, in 16.1. Our author is chiefly concerned with her special and exquisite torment, which consists in having to witness the gruesome deaths of her sons. This is an artistic refinement over II Maccabees, where we are simply told (7.41) that after her sons the mother died also.

218   ΜΑΚΚΑΒΑΙΩΝ Δ'   15 1-2

γὰρ τῶν ἑπτὰ νεανίσκων ὑπήνεγκεν τὰς ἐφ' ἑνὶ ἑκάστῳ τῶν τέκνων στρέβλας. ¹³θεωρεῖτε δὲ πῶς πολύπλοκός ἐστιν ἡ τῆς φιλοτεκνίας στοργὴ ἕλκουσα πάντα πρὸς τὴν τῶν σπλάγχνων συμπάθειαν, ¹⁴ὅπου γε καὶ τὰ ἄλογα ζῷα ὁμοίαν τὴν εἰς τὰ ἐξ αὐτῶν γεννώμενα συμπάθειαν καὶ 15 στοργὴν ἔχει τοῖς ἀνθρώποις. ¹⁵καὶ γὰρ τῶν πετεινῶν τὰ μὲν ἥμερα κατὰ τὰς οἰκίας ὀροφοιτοῦντα προασπίζει τῶν νεοττῶν, ¹⁶τὰ δὲ κατὰ κορυφὰς ὀρέων καὶ φαράγγων ἀπορρῶγας καὶ δένδρων ὀπὰς καὶ τὰς τούτων ἄκρας ἐννοσσοποιησάμενα ἀποτίκτει καὶ τὸν προσιόντα κωλύει· ¹⁷εἰ δὲ καὶ μὴ δύναιντο κωλύειν, περιιπτάμενα κυκλόθεν αὐτῶν ἀλγοῦντα τῇ στοργῇ ἀνακαλούμενα τῇ ἰδίᾳ φωνῇ, καθ' ὃ δύναται, βοηθεῖ τοῖς τέκνοις. ¹⁸καὶ τί δεῖ τὴν διὰ τῶν ἀλόγων ζῴων ἐπιδεικνύναι πρὸς τὰ τέκνα συμπάθειαν, ¹⁹ὅπου γε καὶ μέλισσαι περὶ τὸν τῆς κηρογονίας καιρὸν ἐπαμύνονται τοὺς προσιόντας καὶ καθάπερ σιδήρῳ τῷ κέντρῳ πλήσσουσι τοὺς προσιόντας τῇ νοσσιᾷ αὐτῶν καὶ ἀπαμύνουσιν ἕως θανάτου; 20 ²⁰ἀλλ' οὐχὶ τὴν Αβρααμ ὁμόψυχον τῶν νεανίσκων μητέρα μετεκίνησεν συμπάθεια τέκνων.

15 ¹ῶ λογισμὲ τέκνων παθῶν τύραννε καὶ εὐσέβεια μητρὶ τέκνων ποθεινοτέρα. ²μήτηρ δυεῖν προκειμένων, εὐσεβείας καὶ τῆς ἑπτὰ υἱῶν σωτηρίας προσκαίρου κατὰ τὴν τοῦ

---

15 οροιφοιτουντα] οροιφυτουτα S, οροφοκοιτουντα Bekker, accepted by   Fritzsche, Deissmann, DuP-S

13. MATERNAL AFFECTION: This digression on maternal instinct, in its combination of "scientific" interest in natural history with sentimentality, is characteristic of Alexandrianism (not confined to Alexandria). Orators of the Second Sophistic frequently adorned their speeches with such bits of humanized learning. A comparable interest in natural history is indicated in Wis. 7.20.
14. UNREASONING ANIMALS: This technical expression recurs in v. 18; in Wis. 11.15; and frequently in Philo.
20. SYMPATHY FOR HER OFFSPRING DID NOT MOVE THE MOTHER: Though its natural power, as we have seen, is so great. This gives the point of the digression on maternal love, mastery over which is the greatest of all proofs of the dominance of reason; and so states the theme for ch. 15.

the mother of the seven youths endured the agonies of every one of her children. ¹³Consider how many-skeined is maternal affection, which draws all things to a feeling shared with her own inward parts. ¹⁴Even unreasoning animals have a sympathy and affection for those born of them, as have human beings. ¹⁵Of winged creatures, those that are tame protect their young by nesting in the roofs of houses; ¹⁶and those that build their nests on the peaks of mountains and in clefts of precipices and in the holes or tops of trees—these hatch their young, and repel any intruder; and even when they cannot repel them, they flutter about their nestlings in the anguish of love, and call to them in their own speech, and help their young in whatever way possible. ¹⁸But what need to demonstrate the sympathy of unreasoning animals for their offspring, ¹⁹when even the bees ward off intruders at the season of making honey, and pierce with their sting as with steel those that approach their young, and defend them to the death. ²⁰But sympathy for her offspring did not move the mother of the youths, whose soul was like Abraham's.

15 ¹O Reason of the children, master over the emotions! O religion, dearer to the mother than her sons! ²When two alternatives lay before her, religion, or the immediate salva-

ABRAHAM'S: Most appropriate in the present context, for Abraham is the prime example of mastery over love of offspring. Abraham's sacrifice is referred to also in 13.12, 15.28, 16.20; and in Wis. 10.5, where his fortitude is ascribed to wisdom.

1. O REASON: The greatest of all victories over the emotions is the mother's over maternal love. This is the climax of our author's eulogy of reason; and he expatiates upon it with all the resources of his rhetoric. OF THE CHILDREN: DuP-S correctly points out that this expression is out of place, for it is the mother's fortitude, not the children's, which is the subject of this chapter. *Teknon* may be a dittography from the phrase preceding or following; or better, the prefix *philo-* has dropped out. This would give the excellent sense, "O Reason, master over the emotions of maternal love!"

τυράννου ὑπόσχεσιν, ³τὴν εὐσέβειαν μᾶλλον ἠγάπησεν τὴν σώζουσαν εἰς αἰωνίαν ζωὴν κατὰ θεόν. ⁴ὦ τίνα τρόπον ἠθολογήσαιμι φιλότεκνα γονέων πάθη. ψυχῆς τε καὶ μορφῆς ὁμοιότητα εἰς μικρὸν παιδὸς χαρακτῆρα θαυμάσιον ἐναποσφραγίζομεν, μάλιστα διὰ τὸ τῶν παθῶν τοῖς γεννηθεῖσιν τὰς μητέρας τῶν πατέρων καθεστάναι συμπαθεστέρας. 5 ⁵ὅσῳ γὰρ καὶ ἀσθενόψυχοι καὶ πολυγονώτεραι ὑπάρχουσιν αἱ μητέρες, τοσούτῳ μᾶλλόν εἰσιν φιλοτεκνότεραι. ⁶πασῶν δὲ τῶν μητέρων ἐγένετο ἡ τῶν ἑπτὰ παίδων μήτηρ φιλοτεκνοτέρα, ἥτις ἑπτὰ κυοφορίαις τὴν πρὸς αὐτοὺς ἐπιφυτευομένη φιλοστοργίαν ⁷καὶ διὰ πολλὰς τὰς καθ' ἕκαστον αὐτῶν ὠδῖνας ἠναγκασμένη τὴν εἰς αὐτοὺς ἔχειν συμπάθειαν, ⁸διὰ τὸν πρὸς τὸν θεὸν φόβον ὑπερεῖδεν τὴν τῶν τέκνων πρόσκαιρον σωτηρίαν. ⁹οὐ μὴν δὲ ἀλλὰ καὶ διὰ τὴν καλοκἀγαθίαν τῶν υἱῶν καὶ τὴν πρὸς τὸν νόμον αὐτῶν εὐπείθειαν μείζω 10 τὴν ἐν αὐτοῖς ἔσχεν φιλοστοργίαν. ¹⁰δίκαιοί τε γὰρ ἦσαν καὶ σώφρονες καὶ ἀνδρεῖοι καὶ μεγαλόψυχοι καὶ φιλάδελφοι καὶ φιλομήτορες οὕτως ὥστε καὶ μέχρι θανάτου τὰ νόμιμα φυλάσσοντας πείθεσθαι αὐτῇ. ¹¹ἀλλ' ὅμως καίπερ τοσούτων ὄντων τῶν περὶ τὴν φιλοτεκνίαν εἰς συμπάθειαν ἑλκόντων τὴν μητέρα, ἐπ' οὐδενὸς αὐτῶν τὸν λογισμὸν αὐτῆς αἱ παμποίκιλοι βάσανοι ἴσχυσαν μετατρέψαι, ¹²ἀλλὰ καὶ καθ' ἕνα παῖδα καὶ ὁμοῦ πάντας ἡ μήτηρ ἐπὶ τὸν τῆς εὐσε-

XV 5 πολυγονωτεραι] –γονιμωτεραι V, φι-
4 των πατερων] A omits, S has των   λογωνοτεραι Grimm
παθων   7 ηναγκασμενη] –μενην A

3. TO ETERNAL LIFE: *Cf.* II Tim. 4.18.   ACCORDING TO GOD'S PROMISE:
An antithesis to v. 2, which justifies the word "promise" though it is not
repeated in the Gk.
4. SOUL AND OF FORM: The Stoics insisted on a physiological basis not
only for fraternal love (13.19–21), but also for spiritual heredity. Cleanthes
is quoted in Nemesius, *De natura hominum* (Pearson, *Fragments of Zeno
and Cleanthes* 263), as follows: "Cleanthes ... declares that we are similar
to our parents not only in respect to body but also in respect to soul, in
emotions, morals, dispositions." Plutarch, *Plac. Philos.* 7.11.3, says:
"The Stoics maintain that seed derives from the entire body and from the
soul and that likenesses in form and character is moulded from the same
origins, appearing to the beholder like an image painted with the same
colors."

15 3-12   THE FOURTH BOOK OF MACCABEES   221

tion of her sons according to the tyrant's promise, ³she loved religion better, which preserves to eternal life according to God's promise. ⁴In what terms can I describe the passionate love of parents for their children? Upon the tender mold of the child we impress a marvellous likeness of soul and of form; and especially mothers, for by reason of their travail ⁵they are more sympathetic to offspring than fathers. ⁵For mothers are not stalwart in spirit; and in the degree that their offspring is abundant their love of children is more abounding. ⁶But of all mothers the mother of the seven sons proved most abounding in love; for by seven travails she implanted in herself a deep affection for them, ⁷and because of the manifold pains in the birth of each she was constrained to cherish a deep bond with them; ⁸yet because of her fear of God she disregarded the temporal safety of her children. ⁹Nay, more: because of her very nobility, and their ready obedience to the Law, she cherished an even deeper affection for them. ¹⁰For they were just, and temperate, and courageous, and great-spirited, and united by fraternal love; and so loved their mother that in obedience to her they observed the Law even unto death. ¹¹Nevertheless, though so many considerations affecting maternal love drew the mother to sympathize with them, yet in the case of none of them did their manifold tortures avail to sway her reason; ¹²but each child severally and all together the mother urged on to death

---

5. IN THE DEGREE: In the Gk. this phrase precedes "mothers are not stalwart," but in sense the latter phrase is an independent generalization, to refute a possible supposition that maternal love decreases as the number of children rises.
9. BECAUSE OF HER VERY NOBILITY: The physical arguments for affection are reënforced by moral arguments.
10. JUST, AND TEMPERATE, ... : The Stoic cardinal virtues, with "Great-spirited" (*megalopsychoi*)—a quality peculiarly appropriate to martyrs—substituted for "prudence." FRATERNAL LOVE . . . MOTHER: The expressions *philadelphos* and *philometer* recur frequently in Jewish funcrary inscriptions, and testify to the closeness of family ties; *cf.* J. B. Frey, *Corpus inscriptionum judaicarum* I, Nos. 125, 152, 321, 363.
11. REASON: The essential point of the eulogy, in our author's view; and as such emphasized by the apostrophe—

βείας προετρέπετο θάνατον. ¹³ὦ φύσις ἱερὰ καὶ φίλτρα γονέων καὶ γένεσι φιλόστοργε καὶ τροφεία καὶ μητέρων ἀδάμαστα πάθη. ¹⁴καθένα στρεβλούμενον καὶ φλεγόμενον 15 ὁρῶσα μήτηρ οὐ μετεβάλλετο διὰ τὴν εὐσέβειαν. ¹⁵τὰς σάρκας τῶν τέκνων ἑώρα περὶ τὸ πῦρ τηκομένας καὶ τοὺς τῶν ποδῶν καὶ χειρῶν δακτύλους ἐπὶ γῆς σπαίροντας καὶ τὰς τῶν κεφαλῶν μέχρι τῶν περὶ τὰ γένεια σάρκας ὥσπερ προσωπεῖα προκειμένας. ¹⁶ὦ πικροτέρων νῦν πόνων πειρασθεῖσα μήτηρ ἤπερ τῶν ἐπ' αὐτοῖς ὠδίνων. ¹⁷ὦ μόνη γύναι τὴν εὐσέβειαν ὁλόκληρον ἀποκυήσασα. ¹⁸οὐ μετέτρεψέν σε πρωτοτόκος ἀποπνέων οὐδὲ δεύτερος εἰς σὲ οἰκτρὸν βλέπων ἐν βασάνοις, οὐ τρίτος ἀποψύχων, ¹⁹οὐδὲ τοὺς ὀφθαλμοὺς ἑνὸς ἑκάστου θεωροῦσα ταυρηδὸν ἐπὶ τῶν βασάνων ὁρῶντας τὸν αὐτὸν αἰκισμὸν καὶ τοὺς μυκτῆρας προσημειουμένους 20 τὸν θάνατον αὐτῶν οὐκ ἔκλαυσας. ²⁰ἐπί σαρξὶν τέκνων ὁρῶσα σάρκας τέκνων ἀποκαιομένας καὶ ἐπὶ χερσὶν χεῖρας ἀποτεμνομένας καὶ ἐπὶ κεφαλαῖς κεφαλὰς ἀποδειροτομουμένας καὶ ἐπὶ νεκροῖς νεκροὺς πίπτοντας καὶ πολυάνδριον ὁρῶσα τῶν τέκνων τὸ χωρίον διὰ τῶν βασάνων οὐκ ἐδάκρυσας. ²¹οὐχ οὕτως σειρήνιοι μελῳδίαι οὐδὲ κύκνειοι πρὸς φιληκοΐαν φωναὶ τοὺς ἀκούοντας ἐφέλκονται ὡς τέκνων φωναὶ μετὰ βασάνων μητέρα φωνούντων. ²²πηλίκαις καὶ πόσαις τότε ἡ μήτηρ τῶν υἱῶν βασανιζομένων τροχοῖς τε καὶ καυτηρίοις

---

13 γενεσι] γεννημασι S Fritzsche, γονευσι A, γενεσει V, on the basis of which Deissmann and Townshend read γενεσις / τροφεια] DuP-S regards dittography from φιλοστοργε

19 ουδε] Deissmann and DuP-S read συ δε following the Syriac / τον αυτον αικισμον] τ. εαυτων α. Fritzsche, Deissmann, DuP-S

20 αποκαιομενας] αποκεκομμενας SA

---

13. AH, SACRED NATURE, . . . : Which again calls attention to the forces which the mother resisted.   FILIAL YEARNING: A stop-gap translation for a dubious reading; so "nurture" is an anomalous form, which DuP-S may be justified in regarding as a dittography.
15. DISINTEGRATING . . . QUIVERING . . . FLAYED: The gruesome details are rehearsed (cf. 16.13) not for mere rhetorical sensationalism (cf. on 6.26), but to emphasize the mother's constancy, which is the paramount concern of this chapter. Hence the repeated apostrophes—
16. O MOTHER . . . : 17. O THOU WOMAN: Which give the impression of

for religion's sake. ¹³Ah, sacred nature, charm of parental love, filial yearning, nurture, the indomitable emotions of motherhood! ¹⁴One by one the mother saw her sons tortured and burned—and swerved not, for religion's sake. ¹⁵The flesh of her children she saw disintegrating in the fire; the fingers of their hands and the toes of their feet quivering on the ground; the flesh of their heads flayed down to the cheeks, exposed like masks. ¹⁶O mother, who did now experience anguish more bitter than in their birth pangs! ¹⁷O thou woman, who alone did bring perfect religion to birth! ¹⁸your first-born, breathing out his life, did not turn your resolution; nor did the second, gazing pitifully upon you in his torment; nor the third, as he breathed his last; ¹⁹nor, when you looked at the eyes of each one, as in his torments he gazed immovable upon the same savage cruelty; nor when you perceived their nostrils revealing the forebodings of approaching death, did you wail. ²⁰When you saw the flesh of your children burned over the embers of your children's flesh, and severed hands heaped on hands, and flayed skulls upon skulls, and corpses fallen upon corpses; and when you saw the place crowded with spectators of your children's torments, you did not weep. ²¹Not the sirens' melodies, nor the notes of the swan, so draw their hearers to the delight of hearing, as the voices of children in torment draw a mother's heart. ²²How numerous, then, and how great, were the tor-

involuntary ejaculations interrupting a calmer flow. 17. BRING . . . TO BIRTH: The notion of spiritual birth recurs in 16.13, and also in Wis. 3.13.
18. YOUR FIRST-BORN . . . SECOND . . . THIRD: The figure called climax; this and the following three vv. show our author's rhetoric at its most artistic and most effective.
19. GAZED IMMOVABLE: The Gk. *tauredon* means "like a bull," but the present usage has classical analogies.
20. FLESH OF YOUR CHILDREN . . . CHILDREN'S FLESH, . . . : The repetitions in variations of the chiastic order are effective in producing an impression of cumulative carnage.   CROWDED: *Polyandriu* frequently means "cemetery" in koine; the sense here is clearly "crowded," but a suggestion of the collateral meaning may be intentional.
21. SIRENS' . . . SWAN: Commonplaces for irresistibly attractive music.

ἐβασανίζετο βασάνοις. ²³ἀλλὰ τὰ σπλάγχνα αὐτῆς ὁ εὐσεβὴς λογισμὸς ἐν αὐτοῖς τοῖς πάθεσιν ἀνδρειώσας ἐπέτεινεν τὴν πρόσκαιρον φιλοτεκνίαν παριδεῖν. ²⁴καίπερ ἑπτὰ τέκνων ὁρῶσα ἀπώλειαν καὶ τὴν τῶν στρεβλῶν πολύπλοκον ποικιλίαν, ἁπάσας ἡ γενναία μήτηρ ἐξέλυσεν διὰ τὴν πρὸς θεὸν 25 πίστιν. ²⁵καθάπερ γὰρ ἐν βουλευτηρίῳ τῇ ἑαυτῆς ψυχῇ δεινοὺς ὁρῶσα συμβούλους φύσιν καὶ γένεσιν καὶ φιλοτεκνίαν καὶ τέκνων στρέβλας, ²⁶δύο ψήφους κρατοῦσα μήτηρ, θανατηφόρον τε καὶ σωτήριον, ὑπὲρ τέκνων ²⁷οὐκ ἐπέγνω τὴν σῴζουσαν ἐπτὰ υἱοὺς πρὸς ὀλίγον χρόνον σωτηρίαν, ²⁸ἀλλὰ τῆς θεοσεβοῦς Ἀβρααμ καρτερίας ἡ θυγάτηρ ἐμνήσθη. ²⁹ὦ μήτηρ ἔθνους, ἔκδικε τοῦ νόμου καὶ ὑπερασπίστρια τῆς εὐσεβείας καὶ τοῦ διὰ σπλάγχνων 30 ἀγῶνος ἀθλοφόρε· ³⁰ὦ ἀρρένων πρὸς καρτερίαν γενναιοτέρα καὶ ἀνδρῶν πρὸς ὑπομονὴν ἀνδρειοτέρα. ³¹καθάπερ γὰρ ἡ Νωε κιβωτὸς ἐν τῷ κοσμοπληθεῖ κατακλυσμῷ κοσμοφοροῦσα καρτερῶς ὑπέμεινεν τοὺς κλύδωνας, ³²οὕτως σὺ ἡ νομοφύλαξ πανταχόθεν ἐν τῷ τῶν παθῶν περιαντλουμένη κατακλυσμῷ καὶ καρτεροῖς ἀνέμοις, ταῖς τῶν υἱῶν βασάνοις, συνεχομένη γενναίως ὑπέμεινας τοὺς ὑπὲρ τῆς εὐσεβείας χειμῶνας.

24 απασας] Fritzsche, Rahlfs, ασπασασα A   32 υπερ] A omits

23. BUT DEVOUT REASON GAVE MANLY COURAGE: Our author never indulges in the sensationalism of his story so far as to neglect urging its moral at every appropriate juncture.
24. ALL THESE THINGS: Rendering the *hapasas* of our text; reading *aspasasa*, Emmet translates: "the noble mother bade them farewell and sent them forth in faith in God."
25. TRIBUNAL: The image of a council chamber and actual voting is an effective rhetorical device to make the mother's choice more vivid.
26. TWO BALLOTS . . . DOOM . . . SALVATION: A familiar figure in tragedy, e.g., Aeschylus, *Agamemnon* 815 f.: "They cast into the urn of blood their ballots for the murderous destroyers of Ilium; but to the urn of acquittal that no hand filled Hope alone drew nigh."
28. ABRAHAM'S: See on 13.12.
29. VICTOR: Lit. "prize-winner"; see 11.20 and 17.12 and notes. In the romances the image of the athletic victor is frequently used to praise a lover's fidelity and self control.

ments of the mother, as she suffered with her children as they were racked by the wheel and by fire! ²³But devout reason gave manly courage to her heart in the midst of these emotions, and nerved her to ignore the immediate claims of maternal affection. ²⁴And although she saw the destruction of seven children, and the manifold variety of their torments, that noble mother counted all these things as nought, because of her faith in God. ²⁵In the tribunal of her own heart, as it were, she saw clever advocates—nature, parentage, maternal love, the torment of children; ²⁶and she held in her discretion (a mother over her children!) two ballots: a doom of death, and salvation; ²⁷yet she did not choose that favorable course which would bring safety to her seven sons for a brief space, ²⁸but rather as a daughter of God-fearing Abraham bethought herself of Abraham's fortitude.

²⁹O mother of the nation, champion of the Law, defender of religion, and victor in the contest of the heart! ³⁰Or noble than men in endurance, O more heroic than heroes in perseverance! ³¹Like the ark of Noah, which, bearing the universe in the midst of universal cataclysm, bravely endured the buffetings of the waves, ³²so did you, guardian of the Laws, assailed on all sides in the midst of emotions' cataclysm by the powerful blasts of your sons' torments, with bold persistence withstand the tempests against religion.

---

30. NOBLER THAN MEN: Such heroism is more impressive when exhibited in a woman; the new point is thrown out for the summary to come (16.1). One may surmise that in our author's fashionable audience many of the ladies required and would be susceptible to so noble an example of the fortitude and the responsibilities of their sex.
31. ARK OF NOAH . . . WAVES: Such marine images as breasting a sea of troubles and the like are native in Gk. and frequent in tragedy. Here the fusion of the figure with Noah's ark is an interesting example of the intermingling of the two strains of tradition. In Alexandrian exegesis the ark of Noah is allegorically interpreted as resisting a flood of moral vices; *cf.* Philo, *Quaest. in Genesin* 2.18. For the ark as being the hope of the world, see Wis. 14.6.

16 ¹Εἰ δὲ τοίνυν καὶ γυνὴ καὶ γεραιὰ καὶ ἑπτὰ παίδων μήτηρ ὑπέμεινεν τὰς μέχρι θανάτου βασάνους τῶν τέκνων ὁρῶσα, ὁμολογουμένως αὐτοκράτωρ ἐστὶν τῶν παθῶν ὁ εὐσεβὴς λογισμός. ²ἀπέδειξα οὖν ὅτι οὐ μόνον ἄνδρες τῶν παθῶν ἐκράτησαν, ἀλλὰ καὶ γυνὴ τῶν μεγίστων βασάνων ὑπερεφρόνησεν. ³καὶ οὐχ οὕτως οἱ περὶ Δανιηλ λέοντες ἦσαν ἄγριοι οὐδὲ ἡ Μισαηλ ἐκφλεγομένη κάμινος λαβροτάτῳ πυρί, ὡς ἡ τῆς φιλοτεκνίας περιέκαιεν ἐκείνην φύσις ὁρῶσαν αὐτῆς οὕτως ποικίλως βασανιζομένους τοὺς ἑπτὰ υἱούς. ⁴ἀλλὰ τῷ λογισμῷ τῆς εὐσεβείας κατέσβεσεν τὰ τοσαῦτα καὶ τηλικαῦτα πάθη ἡ μήτηρ.

⁵Καὶ γὰρ τοῦτο ἐπιλογίσασθε, ὅτι δειλόψυχος εἰ ἦν ἡ γυνὴ καίπερ μήτηρ οὖσα, ὠλοφύρετο ἂν ἐπ' αὐτοῖς καὶ ἴσως ἂν ταῦτα εἶπεν ⁶ῶ μελέα ἔγωγε καὶ πολλάκις τρισαθλία, ἥτις ἑπτὰ παῖδας τεκοῦσα οὐδενὸς μήτηρ γεγένημαι. ⁷ῶ μάταιοι ἑπτὰ κυοφορίαι καὶ ἀνόνητοι ἑπτὰ δεκάμηνοι καὶ ἄκαρποι τιθηνίαι καὶ ταλαίπωροι γαλακτοτροφίαι. ⁸μάτην δὲ ἐφ' ὑμῖν, ὦ παῖδες, πολλὰς ὑπέμεινα ὠδῖνας καὶ χαλεπωτέρας φροντίδας ἀνατροφῆς. ⁹ὦ τῶν ἐμῶν παίδων οἱ μὲν ἄγαμοι, οἱ δὲ γήμαντες ἀνόνητοι· οὐκ ὄψομαι ὑμῶν

XVI
5 ταυτα] A adds οντως

1. IF, THEN: As in the philosophic summaries or digressions given in connection with Eleazar (6.31–35, 7.16–23) and with the seven sons (13.1–5), the author here restates his thesis; but whereas the former passages are in a dry, pedantic style, and can be suspected of being interpolations, the present passage conforms to the rhetorical ornateness of the whole context. Thus, "woman... elderly... mother" illustrates the figure of climax.
3. MISHAEL: In the Book of Daniel, Daniel in the lions' den (ch. 6) comes after the furnace (ch. 3); and this order is kept in I Mac. 2.59–60, III Mac. 6.6–7, and IV Mac. 18.12–13 (which may be an interpolation). But here and in v. 21 the Daniel episode is cited first. It is easier to explain the arrangement by the circumstance that Daniel is the principal personage in his book, than to suggest that our author's text of Daniel had a different order. INNATE: The Gk. is *physis*, and an intentional echo of the same word in 15.13 and 25.
4. QUENCH: The same figure (of extinguishing a fire) occurs in 3.17.
5. IF... SHE WOULD HAVE: As in the imaginary arguments ascribed to the brothers for yielding (8.16 ff.), the present imaginary speech of the

16 ¹If, then, a woman—elderly at that, and the mother of seven sons—endured seeing her children tortured to death, it must be acknowledged that religious reason is sovereign over the emotions. ²Thus I have demonstrated that not only men have shown mastery over the emotions, but that even a woman could despise the fiercest tortures. ³Not so savage were lions about Daniel; not so fiercely did Mishael's brazier burn with its greedy flame; as did innate maternal affection burn that woman, as she saw those seven sons of hers subjected to such manifold torments. ⁴But by reason which belongs to religion did the mother quench emotions so numerous and so intense.

5 ⁵This, too, you must consider: If the woman had been weak in spirit—being, as she was, a mother—she would have lamented over them, and perhaps have spoken as follows: ⁶"Ah, miserable woman that I am, repeatedly wretched time and again! Seven children have I borne, and I am the mother of none. ⁷In vain were my seven pregnancies; futile the ten-months burden borne seven times; fruitless the nursing, and wretched the suckling. ⁸In vain, my children, did I endure those many travails for you; and the harder anxieties of your upbringing. ⁹Alas for my sons—some unwedded, others mar-

---

mother puts the fairest face on yielding, and so makes her perseverance more admirable. The arguments (6–11) all turn on maternal love, which is the theme of the whole episode involving the mother.   BEING, AS SHE WAS, A MOTHER: It is hard to see the force of the concessive *kaiper* ("although") in this context; and none of the suggestions offered by commentators is wholly convincing. The translation is an effort to retain the sense of *kaiper* without making the difficulty too obvious.

6. AH, MISERABLE WOMAN: Like the imaginary discourse of the brothers, this speech has an elegiac character.   REPEATEDLY: the allusion is to the number seven.   TIME AND AGAIN: The Gk. has "thrice wretched" (*trisathlia*), but the *tris-* is a common prefix for indicating a large number.

7. IN VAIN ... FUTILE ... : Vv. 7–10 give the ordinary motives for enduring the discomfort of childbearing—the advantages and security of the parents.   TEN-MONTHS: Regularly cited by the ancients as the period of gestation, though they were aware of the correct figure.

9. OTHERS MARRIED: The first we hear of it, and perhaps inserted here for pathos; but it is to be noted that marriage is consonant with perfect virtue.

10 τέκνα οὐδὲ μάμμη κληθεῖσα μακαρισθήσομαι. 10ὦ ἡ πολύπαις καὶ καλλίπαις ἐγὼ γυνὴ χήρα καὶ μόνη πολύθρηνος· 11οὐδ' ἂν ἀποθάνω, θάπτοντα τῶν υἱῶν ἔξω τινά. 12Ἀλλὰ τούτῳ τῷ θρήνῳ οὐδένα ὠλοφύρετο ἡ ἱερὰ καὶ θεοσεβὴς μήτηρ οὐδ' ἵνα μὴ ἀποθάνωσιν ἀπέτρεπεν αὐτῶν τινα οὐδ' ὡς ἀποθνῃσκόντων ἐλυπήθη, 13ἀλλ' ὥσπερ ἀδαμάντινον ἔχουσα τὸν νοῦν καὶ εἰς ἀθανασίαν ἀνατίκτουσα τὸν τῶν υἱῶν ἀριθμὸν μᾶλλον ὑπὲρ τῆς εὐσεβείας ἐπὶ τὸν θάνατον αὐτοὺς προετρέπετο ἱκετεύουσα. 14ὦ μῆτερ δι' εὐσέβειαν θεοῦ στρατιῶτι πρεσβῦτι καὶ γύναι, διὰ καρτερίαν καὶ τύραννον ἐνίκησας καὶ ἔργοις δυνατωτέρα καὶ λόγοις εὑρέθης 15 ἀνδρός. 15καὶ γὰρ ὅτε συνελήμφθης μετὰ τῶν παίδων, εἱστήκεις τὸν Ελεαζαρον ὁρῶσα βασανιζόμενον καὶ ἔλεγες τοῖς παισὶν ἐν τῇ Ἑβραΐδι φωνῇ 16Ὦ παῖδες, γενναῖος ὁ ἀγών, ἐφ' ὃν κληθέντες ὑπὲρ τῆς διαμαρτυρίας τοῦ ἔθνους ἐναγωνίσασθε προθύμως ὑπὲρ τοῦ πατρῴου νόμου· 17καὶ γὰρ αἰσχρὸν τὸν μὲν γέροντα τοῦτον ὑπομένειν τὰς διὰ τὴν εὐσέβειαν ἀλγηδόνας, ὑμᾶς δὲ τοὺς νεανίσκους καταπλαγῆναι τὰς βασάνους. 18ἀναμνήσθητε ὅτι διὰ τὸν θεὸν

14 μητερ] πατηρ A / γυναι] γυνη A   17 νεανισκους] νεωτερους A

11. WHEN I DIE: The normal obligation of children; cf. Herodotus 1.87: "No one is so foolish as to prefer to peace war, which, instead of sons burying their fathers, fathers bury their sons." DuP-S cites an apposite inscription in J. B. Frey, *Corpus Inscriptionum Judaicarum* 1.68: *Mater dulcissimo filio suo fecit quod ipse mihi debuit facere*.
13. HER BROOD: Lit. "the number of her sons"; the thought being that she wished all to partake of immortality, and reserved none for her private satisfaction.
14. SOLDIER: A bold apostrophe for a woman, but our author elsewhere emphasizes her virility (15.30 and the end of this verse). The image of the soldier is frequent in the language of Hellenistic mysticism; cf. II Tim. 2.3, "soldier of Jesus Christ." In the *Crito* Plato has Socrates compare his obedience to the laws to a soldier keeping his assigned post. WOMAN: Translating the vocative *gunai;* the nominative *gune* would yield "though a woman."
15. WATCHED ELEAZAR: In II Maccabees the martyrdom of Eleazar is not connected with those of the mother and sons. Our author builds the nine into a single structure, in which each member involves the others, and all rise to a crescendo, with the agonies of the mother as the climax of pathos and heroism.

ried, but to no purpose; I shall never see your children, nor
10 shall I ever be blessed with the title of grandmother. ¹⁰I had
children, both numerous and handsome; and now am a
woman forsaken and solitary, with many sorrows. ¹¹Nor
when I die, shall I have any of my sons to bury me."

¹²Yet that holy and God-fearing mother lamented none of
them with such a dirge; nor did she urge any of them to
avoid death. Nor did she grieve, as they were on the point of
dying. ¹³On the contrary—as though her mind were of adamant, and as though she were again giving birth to her brood
of seven sons unto immortality—by her supplications she
rather encouraged them to death for religion's sake. ¹⁴Mother,
soldier of God through religion, Elder, woman! By your constancy you have vanquished even the tyrant; and by your
deeds and your words discovered yourself more stalwart than
15 a man. ¹⁵For when you were seized, along with your children,
you stood firm, as you watched Eleazar undergoing torture;
and you said to your children—speaking in Hebrew: ¹⁶"My
sons, noble is the contest; and since you are summoned to it in
order to bear testimony for your nation, strive zealously on
behalf of the Law of our fathers. ¹⁷'Twere shame indeed that
this old man should endure agonies for the sake of religion,
and you who are young should be terrified of torments. ¹⁸Remember that it is because of God that you have a share in the

---

16. NOBLE IS THE CONTEST: *Agon* ("contest") carries the connotation of athletic games (see on 6.10); but the word had been used in the classical period in senses precisely like the present; *cf.* Plato, *Republic* 10.608b: "Great is the issue [*agon*] at stake, whether a man is to prove excellent or base"; Euripides, *Medea* 235: "A fearful hazard [*agon*], whether we get a good husband or bad." The specialized meaning of *agonia* in the sense of "the passion" is illustrated in "you are summoned to it in order to bear testimony." If "martyrdom" is not the true reading at 12.16, this phrase (with *diamartyria*) is at least a close approximation of the meaning of bearing witness to faith in blood.
17. SHAME: The brothers themselves invoke the example of the old man, and their own greater obligation as young men, in 9.5-6.
18. SHARE . . . ENJOYED: In 8.23 the pleasures of life are proposed as a reason for shunning martyrdom; the present verse seems intended as a refutation.

τοῦ κόσμου μετελάβετε καὶ τοῦ βίου ἀπελαύσατε, ¹⁹καὶ διὰ τοῦτο ὀφείλετε πάντα πόνον ὑπομένειν διὰ τὸν θεόν, ²⁰δι' ὃν καὶ ὁ πατὴρ ἡμῶν Αβρααμ ἔσπευδεν τὸν ἐθνοπάτορα υἱὸν σφαγιάσαι Ισαακ, καὶ τὴν πατρῴαν χεῖρα ξιφηφόρον καταφερομένην ἐπ' αὐτὸν ὁρῶν οὐκ ἐπτηξεν. ²¹καὶ Δανιηλ ὁ δίκαιος εἰς λέοντας ἐβλήθη, καὶ Ανανιας καὶ Αζαριας καὶ Μισαηλ εἰς κάμινον πυρὸς ἀπεσφενδονήθησαν καὶ ὑπέμειναν διὰ τὸν θεόν. ²²καὶ ὑμεῖς οὖν τὴν αὐτὴν πίστιν πρὸς τὸν θεὸν ἔχοντες μὴ χαλεπαίνετε. ²³ἀλόγιστον γὰρ εἰδότας εὐσέβειαν μὴ ἀνθίστασθαι τοῖς πόνοις.

²⁴Διὰ τούτων τῶν λόγων ἡ ἑπταμήτωρ ἕνα ἕκαστον τῶν υἱῶν παρακαλοῦσα ἀποθανεῖν ἔπεισεν μᾶλλον ἢ παραβῆναι τὴν ἐντολὴν τοῦ θεοῦ, ²⁵ἔτι δὲ καὶ ταῦτα εἰδότες ὅτι οἱ διὰ τὸν θεὸν ἀποθνήσκοντες ζῶσιν τῷ θεῷ ὥσπερ Αβρααμ καὶ Ισαακ καὶ Ιακωβ καὶ πάντες οἱ πατριάρχαι.

17 ¹Ἔλεγον δὲ καὶ τῶν δορυφόρων τινὲς ὅτι ὡς ἔμελλεν συλλαμβάνεσθαι καὶ αὐτὴ πρὸς θάνατον, ἵνα μὴ ψαύσειέν τις τοῦ σώματος αὐτῆς, ἑαυτὴν ἔρριψε κατὰ τῆς πυρᾶς.

20 ισαακ και] και ισαακ Deissmann   XVII
24 αποθανειν] A omits   1 τις] τι A
25 ειδοτες] ιδοντες A

19. FOR THE SAKE OF GOD: The Gk. (dia ton theon) is an echo of the identical expression, rendered "because of God," in 18; but the force of the preposition is different, and hence the parallelism is lost in translation.
20. ISAAC: For the frequency of reference to his immolation, see on 13.12. FATHER OF A NATION: Ethnopatora, a hapax legomenon. The anomalous expression may be an elegant variant for the usual patriarches; or intended as a rhetorical antithesis to "son" in the preceding phrase.
21. DANIEL ... HANANIAH ... : As we have seen (16.3), along with Isaac the favorite exemplars for martyrdoms. For the order of names, see on 18.13. Other similar references to Daniel are I Mac. 2.60, III Mac. 6.7.
24. THE MOTHER OF THE SEVEN: The Gk. heptametor is a hapax, formed on the analogy ethnopator of v. 20.   DIE RATHER THAN TRANSGRESS: Cf. 9.1, II Mac. 7.2, and the rabbinic formula yehareg v'al ya'abor, "Let him suffer death rather than transgress." In the Talmud (Shebiit 84.5; see I. H. Weiss, Dor Dor 2.131) this principle is applied only to the sins of idolatry, adultery, and murder; if external pressure to transgress is ap-

world, and have enjoyed life: ¹⁹for this reason you are bound ²⁰to endure any hardship, for the sake of God. ²⁰For His sake also was our father Abraham zealous to immolate his son Isaac, the father of a nation; nor did Isaac flinch when he saw his father's hand, armed with a sword, descending upon him. ²¹Moreover, Daniel the righteous was thrown to the lions; and Hananiah, Mishael, and Azariah were flung into the fiery furnace, and they endured for the sake of God. ²²Do you, too, therefore, hold the same faith in God, and be not dismayed; ²³for it would be unreasonable for you, who know religion, not to withstand suffering."

²⁴With these words the mother of the seven encouraged each of her sons, and bade them die rather than transgress the ²⁵commandment of God; ²⁵and they too knew well that those who die for the sake of God live with God, as do Abraham and Isaac and Jacob and all the patriarchs.

17 ¹Certain of the guards declared that when she too was about to be seized and put to death, she flung herself into

---

plied, then only in the case of those three sins should martyrdom be preferred. In the present case the transgression is idolatry (involved in the eating of meats of which a portion was offered in sacrifice), aggravated by the public nature of the trial (*b'parhesia*), which in turn involves profanation of the divine name (*hillul ha-Shem*). In time of persecution even the slightest transgression must be avoided by martyrdom.

25. LIVE WITH GOD, AS DO ABRAHAM . . . : See on 7.19. This does not imply resurrection, even of the patriarchs, but rather the transformation of their incorruptible elements into angels, as in Philo (see Wolfson, 1.366 ff.). The loose grammatical connection of "knew well that" (*eidotes*) is not unexampled, and does not justify Freudenthal's (123 f.) rejection of the verse. There is no need, in language or meaning, to suspect a Christian gloss.

1. CERTAIN OF THE GUARDS: The suicide of the mother, as has been noted in 12.20, is probably our author's invention; hence this guarded statement of authority. Matt. 28.11 similarly attributes the account of the events at the Resurrection to "some of the guards." SO THAT NO ONE MIGHT TOUCH HER BODY: Any violation of chastity comes under the head of adultery, which (see on 16.24) is the second of the three sins requiring martyrdom.

² Ὦ μήτηρ σὺν ἑπτὰ παισὶν καταλύσασα τὴν τοῦ τυράννου βίαν καὶ ἀκυρώσασα τὰς κακὰς ἐπινοίας αὐτοῦ καὶ δείξασα τὴν τῆς πίστεως γενναιότητα. ³καθάπερ γὰρ σὺ στέγη ἐπὶ τοὺς στύλους τῶν παίδων γενναίως ἱδρυμένη ἀκλινὴς ὑπήνεγκας τὸν διὰ τῶν βασάνων σεισμόν. ⁴θάρρει τοιγαροῦν, ὦ μήτηρ ἱερόψυχε, τὴν ἐλπίδα τῆς ὑπομονῆς βεβαίαν ἔχουσα πρὸς τὸν θεόν. ⁵οὐχ οὕτως σελήνη κατ' οὐρανὸν σὺν ἄστροις σεμνὴ καθέστηκεν, ὡς σὺ τοὺς ἰσαστέρους ἑπτὰ παῖδας φωταγωγήσασα πρὸς τὴν εὐσέβειαν ἔντιμος καθέστηκας θεῷ καὶ ἐστήρισαι σὺν αὐτοῖς ἐν οὐρανῷ· ⁶ἦν γὰρ ἡ παιδοποιία σου ἀπὸ Αβρααμ τοῦ πατρός.

⁷Εἰ δὲ ἐξὸν ἡμῖν ἦν ὥσπερ ἐπὶ τινος ζωγραφῆσαι τὴν τῆς εὐσεβείας σου ἱστορίαν, οὐκ ἂν ἔφριττον οἱ θεωροῦντες ὁρῶντες μητέρα ἑπτὰ τέκνων δι' εὐσέβειαν ποικίλας βασάνους

3 τους στυλους] του στυλου A
5 ισαστερους] εις αστερας A / εστηρισαι] Dindorf and Bekker suggested ηστερισαι (from αστεριζω) which would suit the sense admirably and involves only a slight alteration, but the verb in the received reading is used in the sense acceptable here in Plutarch, *Moralia* 75d, 938a
6 πατρος] παιδος A
7 After τινος Deissmann, followed by Townshend, Emmet, DuP-S, sug- gests πινακος. Townshend cites a close parallel from John Chrysostom ... τους αγωνας και τα παλαισματα ωσπερ επι πινακος τινος της καρδιας υμων απογραψαντες, and DuP-S adds the paraphrase of Erasmus: Si possit in picturam aliquam manus humana describere ... sine lachrymis nemo transiret / της ευσεβειας σου ιστοριαν] ιστοριας σου ευσεβειαν A

2. WITH YOUR SEVEN SONS: In his peroration our author stresses the unity of the mother and her seven. The admirable figures of the pillars which support a single beam, and of the moon and stars (vv. 3, 5), emphasize this point.

3. PILLARS ... EARTHQUAKE: "Earthquake" is a suitable enough variant of waves for suggesting a cataclysmic force, but it is particularly appropriate to the figure of pillars supporting beams, and would be most meaningful in a city like Antioch, which was adorned with miles of colonnades which are known to have suffered in frequent earthquakes. See Introd. 111.

5. LIGHTING THE WAY: This is the first occurrence of this verb (*photagegosasa*), which apparently belongs to the vocabulary of mysticism. DuP-S cites such use of it in Clement of Alexandria 147 (*PG* 8.349) and Ammo-

the fire, so that no one might touch her body. ²O mother with your seven sons, who broke the violence of the tyrant, and rendered his evil devices futile, and demonstrated the nobility of faith! ³Nobly set as a beam upon the pillars of your children, unswervingly did you support the earthquake of the tortures. ⁴Be of good courage, then, mother of holy soul, who keep the hope of your endurance firm with God; ⁵not so majestic stands the moon in heaven, with its stars, as you stand; lighting the way to piety for your seven starlike sons; honored by God, and with them fixed in heaven. ⁶For your childbearing was of our Father Abraham.

⁷If it were possible for us to paint, as on a picture, the story of your religion, would not the spectators shudder when they saw the mother of seven children enduring manifold torments

---

nius, *Cat. Joann.* 1.4 (*PG* 85.1393): "The incarnation of the only begotten lights the way for men to true knowledge of God."   FIXED IN HEAVEN: As a star. The Stoics (Diogenes Laertius 7.145) and Plato (*Timaeus* 39e) regarded stars as living beings. Philo is ambiguous on the subject. At *De gigant.* 2.8 he says: "The stars are souls divine and unmixed," but from a comparison of other passages Wolfson (1.364 ff.) concludes that he did not consider the stars living beings.
6. YOUR CHILDBEARING: In 16.3 we are told that her bearing was of a spiritual order; hence in a mystic sense the begetter of her children is Father Abraham.
7–18.6. *The implications of the martyrdoms.*
7. IF IT WERE POSSIBLE: The conditional form of the sentence is most easily explained by the circumstance that the Second Commandment was interpreted as forbidding all forms of pictorial art, so that it was in fact not possible to paint. But the elaborate synagogue frescoes found at Dura Europus have provided dramatic evidence that painting was practiced (though sculpture, whether in relief or in the round, was probably forbidden) in the environs of Antioch; though the Dura paintings date from the 3d century they must have had predecessors. The conditional form, then, is due to the difficulty of the subject, which makes its visible representation impossible. In any case, the use of the pictorial analogy— even in a figure—indicates the influence of Hellenism.   AS ON A PICTURE: The word for picture (*pinakos*) is not in our text, but clearly seems to have fallen out; see critical note. The use of a painting to convey a moral story is familiar in later Greek literature; *cf.* the opening of *Tabula Cebetis,* and of Longus' *Daphnis and Chloe.* Descriptions of works of art and their effects were a regular department of rhetoric, called *ekphrasis.*

μέχρι θανάτου ὑπομείνασαν; ⁸καὶ γὰρ ἄξιον ἦν καὶ ἐπ' αὐτοῦ τοῦ ἐπιταφίου ἀναγράψαι καὶ ταῦτα τοῖς ἀπὸ τοῦ ἔθνους εἰς μνείαν λεγόμενα ⁹'Ενταῦθα γέρων ἱερεὺς καὶ γυνὴ γεραιὰ καὶ ἑπτὰ παῖδες ἐγκεκήδευνται διὰ τυράννου
10 βίαν τὴν Εβραίων πολιτείαν καταλῦσαι θέλοντος, ¹⁰οἳ καὶ ἐξεδίκησαν τὸ γένος εἰς θεὸν ἀφορῶντες καὶ μέχρι θανάτου τὰς βασάνους ὑπομείναντες.
¹¹'Αληθῶς γὰρ ἦν ἀγὼν θεῖος ὁ δι' αὐτῶν γεγενημένος. ¹²ἠθλοθέτει γὰρ τότε ἀρετὴ δι' ὑπομονῆς δοκιμάζουσα. τὸ νῖκος ἀφθαρσία ἐν ζωῇ πολυχρονίῳ. ¹³Ελεαζαρ δὲ προηγωνίζετο, ἡ δὲ μήτηρ τῶν ἑπτὰ παίδων ἐνήθλει, οἱ δὲ ἀδελφοὶ ἠγωνίζοντο· ¹⁴ὁ τύραννος ἀντηγωνίζετο· ὁ δὲ κόσμος καὶ
15 ὁ τῶν ἀνθρώπων βίος ἐθεώρει· ¹⁵θεοσέβεια δὲ ἐνίκα τοὺς ἑαυτῆς ἀθλητὰς στεφανοῦσα. ¹⁶τίνες οὐκ ἐθαύμασαν τοὺς τῆς θείας νομοθεσίας ἀθλητάς; τίνες οὐκ ἐξεπλάγησαν;

8 επιταφιου] ταφου DuP-S   16 θειας] αληθειας A
10 γενος] εθνος A

8. TOMB: This reference to a tomb and inscription has been taken as evidence that our discourse was intended for delivery at the actual site of the martyrs' tomb at a commemoration. The discourse was indeed probably so intended; but the mention of the tomb here cannot in itself be regarded as proof, in view of the rhetorical nature of the composition, and the proneness of rhetoricians to use such devices. The proposal of an imaginary epitaph is indeed classical; cf. Euripides, *Trojan Women* 1190 f., where Hecuba says of the slaying of Astyanax, "What will be the verse inscribed on your tomb? 'Within this grave a little child is laid, slain by the Greeks because they were afraid.' An inscription to make Greece blush" (Hadas and McLean, 285).

9. LIE BURIED: The usual formula in actual funerary inscriptions regularly uses a form of the verb *keimai* ("lie"); the verb *enkedeuo* here used is unusual, and denotes something like "discharge obligations due to the dead"—whence DuP-S deduces that a cult situation is involved.

AGED ... OLD ... SEVEN ... VICTIMS OF ... A TYRANT: The pathos of the victims and the inculpation of the persecutor are closely parallel to the "little child" and the "Greeks afraid" in the *Trojan Women* passage cited above.

11. CONTEST: See on 16.16. This peroration, almost a Pindaric ode in effect, is the most extended use of the figure of the athletic *agon*, and is carried on in—

unto death for the sake of religion? ⁸Indeed, it would be proper to inscribe upon their very tomb the words following, as a memorial to those [heroes] of our people: ⁹HERE LIE BURIED AN AGED PRIEST, AN OLD WOMAN, AND HER SEVEN SONS, VICTIMS OF THE VIOLENCE OF A TYRANT RESOLVED TO DESTROY THE POLITY OF THE HEBREWS. ¹⁰THEY VINDICATED THEIR RACE, LOOKING TO GOD, AND ENDURING TORMENTS EVEN TO DEATH.

¹¹Divine indeed was the contest of which they were the issue. ¹²Of that contest virtue was the umpire; and its score was for constancy. Victory was incorruptibility in a life of long duration. ¹³Eleazar was the prime contestant; but the mother of the seven sons entered the competition, and the brothers too vied for the prize. ¹⁴The tyrant was the adversary, and the world and humanity were the spectators. ¹⁵Reverence for God was the winner, and crowned her own champions. ¹⁶Who did not marvel at the athletes of the divine legislation, who were not astonished by them?

---

12. UMPIRE ... SCORE ... VICTORY: And sustained through v. 15.   INCORRUPTIBILITY: See on 9.22.   LIFE OF LONG DURATION: A noticeable anticlimax after "incorruptibility"; we should expect something like "eternal life," as in 15.3. DuP-S suggests that the expression may be a gloss by a reader who found "incorruptibility" too abstract, and preferred a Biblical phrase, like the citation from Deuteronomy in the second speech of the mother (18.19).

14. THE WORLD AND HUMANITY: A rhetorical effort to give cosmic significance to the event; somewhat like the cosmic effects (such as retarding the sun) of the crime of Thyestes in a play of Seneca or the like.   SPECTATORS: Essential to the rhetorician; in Lucan's *Pharsalia* 4.490 ff. a band of heroes ready to die in a desperate crossing of the Adriatic deplore only the lack of spectators. In the Greek romances the hero is regularly provided with a crowded arena or the like, in which to show his prowess and be justified in his claims.

15. CROWNED: DuP-S cites a figure from a Jewish tombstone (Frey, *Corpus Inscriptionum Judaicarum* 1.121) representing a Victory crowning a nude young man, and suggests that the young man may represent an athlete in the Law.

16. WHO DID NOT MARVEL: A characteristically deft transition to the particular reaction of—

¹⁷Αὐτός γέ τοι ὁ τύραννος καὶ ὅλον τὸ συμβούλιον ἐθαύμασαν αὐτῶν τὴν ὑπομονήν, ¹⁸δι' ἣν καὶ τῷ θείῳ νῦν παρεστήκασιν θρόνῳ καὶ τὸν μακάριον βιοῦσιν αἰῶνα. ¹⁹καὶ γὰρ φησιν ὁ Μωυσῆς Καὶ πάντες οἱ ἡγιασμένοι ὑπὸ τὰς χεῖράς σου. ²⁰καὶ οὗτοι οὖν ἁγιασθέντες διὰ θεὸν τετίμηνται, οὐ μόνον ταύτῃ τῇ τιμῇ, ἀλλὰ καὶ τῷ δι' αὐτοὺς τὸ ἔθνος ἡμῶν τοὺς πολεμίους μὴ ἐπικρατῆσαι ²¹καὶ τὸν τύραννον τιμωρηθῆναι καὶ τὴν πατρίδα καθαρισθῆναι, ὥσπερ ἀντίψυχον γεγονότας τῆς τοῦ ἔθνους ἁμαρτίας. ²²καὶ διὰ τοῦ αἵματος τῶν εὐσεβῶν ἐκείνων καὶ τοῦ ἱλαστηρίου τοῦ θανάτου αὐτῶν ἡ θεία πρόνοια τὸν Ἰσραηλ προκακωθέντα διέσωσεν.

²³Πρὸς γὰρ τὴν ἀνδρείαν αὐτῶν τῆς ἀρετῆς καὶ τὴν ἐπὶ ταῖς βασάνοις αὐτῶν ὑπομονὴν ὁ τύραννος ἀπιδὼν ἀνεκήρυξεν ὁ Ἀντίοχος τοῖς στρατιώταις αὐτοῦ εἰς ὑπόδειγμα τὴν ἐκείνων ὑπομονὴν ²⁴ἔσχεν τε αὐτοὺς γενναίους καὶ ἀνδρείους εἰς πεζομαχίαν καὶ πολιορκίαν καὶ ἐκπορθήσας ἐνίκησεν πάντας τοὺς πολεμίους.

17 συμβουλιον] συνεδριον αυτων A / την   υπομονην] S prefixes την αρετην και

17. THE TYRANT HIMSELF: The dramatic and intellectual character of our discourse are much more tastefully and convincingly maintained by showing the king impressed than by leaving him crushed and grovelling, as melodrama or mere chauvinism would have left him. A reasonably good but limited man is made to see the light by better and less limited men. Historically this attitude reflects a situation in which the Hellenized Jewish community could look forward to amicable relations with their environment, like Aristeas to Philocrates, and not to one where uncompromising persecution had made them desperate, like III Maccabees; on the expression and implication of these attitudes see my Aristeas 59 ff. AMAZED: In 1.11 and II Mac. 7.12 the amazement of the tyrant and his entourage at the constancy of his victims is also mentioned.
18. WHEREBY THEY NOW: An odd conclusion to a sentence which begins with the effects upon the king, and should properly continue with v. 23. Deissmann would therefore have v. 23 follow v. 17 immediately, and transpose vv. 18–22 to follow 18.3. Some displacement seems to be involved, but the transpositions suggested create more difficulties than they solve.   STAND BEFORE THE THRONE: *Cf.* Rev. 7.15.
19. MOSES SAYS: An exact quotation from LXX Deut. 33.3. The Heb. has, "All His holy ones—they are in Thy hand"; *hypo . . . kheiras* in the LXX means "under thy hands," *i.e.*, a gesture of protection.
21. RANSOM: See on 6.29 and Introd. 121. "Ransom" here puts the meaning

[17]The tyrant himself, and his whole council, were amazed at the constancy [18]whereby they now have their stand before the throne of God, and live the life of eternal blessedness. [19]For Moses says, "All the holy ones are underneath Thy hands." [20]These, then, having been sanctified by God, are honored not only with this distinction, but also by the fact that because of them our enemies did not prevail over our nation; [21]and the tyrant was chastised, and our land purified —they having become as it were a ransom for the sin of the nation. [22]It was through the blood of these righteous ones, and through the expiation of their death, that divine Providence preserved Israel, which had been ill used. [23]For the tyrant Antiochus, taking as a model the courage of their virtue, and their constancy under torture, advertised their endurance as a pattern to his own soldiers; [24]he thus got them noble and courageous for infantry battle, and for siege; and he ravaged and vanquished all his enemies.

of—
22. BLOOD OF THESE RIGHTEOUS ONES . . . EXPIATION: Beyond question. Otherwise merely a causal nexus but no vicarious atonement might be inferred.

23. ANTIOCHUS . . . ADVERTISED: Mention of Antiochus' victories seems not only inconsistent with but actually contrary to the doctrine of retribution which our book as a whole maintains. This consideration, and the fact that 23-24 are distinctly inferior in style leads DuP-S to regard the passage as an interpolation. But perhaps Antiochus' victories were too well known to be ignored, and our author ingeniously saves his case by attributing them to the infectious example of the martyrs. Antiochus' temporary successes would then make his ultimate fall (18.5) more sensational.

Up to this point the structure of our book is admirable; pathetic, expository, and hortatory sections alternate according to a well-conceived and intelligible plan. Ch. 18, by contrast, seems ill-organized, repetitious, even inconsistent, in part of different tone and inferior style; and critics from Grimm and Freudenthal on have been troubled by it, and have proposed various remedies or explanations, as will be noted below. On the other hand, we do not know how such commemorative discourses were composed or delivered. It may have been customary, after the main body of the discourse was delivered, and perhaps after a prayer or other liturgy, to resume the main points in a final exhortation, and even to include a mass of Scriptural citations (to which objection has been taken here).

18 ¹˚Ω τῶν Ἀβραμιαίων σπερμάτων ἀπόγονοι παῖδες Ἰσραηλῖται, πείθεσθε τῷ νόμῳ τούτῳ καὶ πάντα τρόπον εὐσεβεῖτε ²γινώσκοντες ὅτι τῶν παθῶν ἐστιν δεσπότης ὁ εὐσεβὴς λογισμὸς καὶ οὐ μόνον τῶν ἔνδοθεν, ἀλλὰ καὶ τῶν ἔξωθεν πόνων.

³Ἀνθ' ὧν διὰ τὴν εὐσέβειαν προέμενοι τὰ σώματα τοῖς πόνοις ἐκεῖνοι οὐ μόνον ὑπὸ τῶν ἀνθρώπων ἐθαυμάσθησαν, ἀλλὰ καὶ θείας μερίδος κατηξιώθησαν.

⁴Καὶ δι' αὐτοὺς εἰρήνευσεν τὸ ἔθνος, καὶ τὴν εὐνομίαν τὴν ἐπὶ τῆς πατρίδος ἀνανεωσάμενοι ἐκπεπόρθηκαν τοὺς πολεμίους. ⁵καὶ ὁ τύραννος Ἀντίοχος καὶ ἐπὶ γῆς τετιμώρηται καὶ ἀποθανὼν κολάζεται· ὡς γὰρ οὐδὲν οὐδαμῶς ἴσχυσεν ἀναγκάσαι τοὺς Ἱεροσολυμίτας ἀλλοφυλῆσαι καὶ τῶν πατρίων ἐθῶν ἐκδιαιτηθῆναι, τότε ἀπάρας ἀπὸ τῶν Ἱεροσολύμων ἐστράτευσεν ἐπὶ Πέρσας.

⁶Ἔλεγεν δὲ ἡ μήτηρ τῶν ἑπτὰ παίδων καὶ ταῦτα τὰ δικαιώματα τοῖς τέκνοις ⁷ὅτι Ἐγὼ ἐγενήθην παρθένος ἁγνὴ

XVIII

5 εθων] εθνων A

---

1. O DESCENDANTS . . . : An exhortation to heed the moral of the story seems highly appropriate at this point, but DuP-S finds vv. 1–5 repetitious of matter in the preceding chapter, the exordium, and the conclusion, and accordingly suspects their genuineness. He would reduce the concluding section from 41 vv. (17.7–24, 18.1–24) to 20, viz., 17.7–22, 18.2–24.   ABRAHAM . . . ISRAEL: Pointing to the unity of the audience with the heroes whose story they have heard.

2. RELIGIOUS REASON . . . EMOTIONS: Rehearsing the philosophical thesis of the discourse. Grimm thought this v. was the end of the discourse (but if the doxology at 1.12 is genuine, surely that at the end of the book is) and regarded as spurious everything from—

3. THOSE MEN: Actually this v. properly records the advantages which accrued to them personally, and to—

4. OUR NATION: Which through them "obtained peace" and "renewed the observance of the Law." By lifting the "enemies' siege" they illustrated divine retribution, for—

5. ANTIOCHUS WAS PUNISHED: The latter part of v. 5, from "For when he was by no means able," does seem to be a gloss on v. 4, and is, as Deissmann notes, a remarkable echo of the pagan view given in Tacitus, *Histories* 5.8: "King Antiochus strove to destroy the national superstition and to introduce Greek civilization, but was prevented by his war with

18 ¹O descendants of the seed of Abraham, children of Israel, obey this Law, and in every respect pursue religion; knowing that religious reason is master over the emotions, and over pains not only from within but also from without. ³Those men who yielded up their bodies to suffering for the sake of religion were in recompense not only admired by mankind, but were also deemed worthy of a divine portion. ⁴And it was because of them that our nation obtained peace; they renewed the observance of the Law in their country, and lifted their enemies' siege. ⁵But the tyrant Antiochus was punished upon earth, and is yet chastised after his death. For when he was by no means able to force the people of Jerusalem to change their race, and to depart from the usages of their fathers, he departed from Jerusalem and marched against the Persians.

⁶The mother of the seven children also uttered these righteous sayings to her children: ⁷"I was a chaste maiden,

---

the Parthians from at all improving this vilest of nations." If, as appears likely, the scene of our discourse is Antioch, mention of Jerusalem may seem strange; on the other hand, the tone is that of a speaker removed from the scene.

6–19. *The mother's discourse to her children.* Freudenthal condemned this passage as an interpolation because of its inferior style, its numerous citations, and its inconsistency with the thought of the remainder of the book. Deissmann is not wholly convinced by these objections, and thinks the passage may have been a continuation of the mother's speech at 16.16–23, from which it was transposed. That is indeed a suitable place; but, as has been suggested above, the peroration may have required the inclusion of some such passage. DuP-S regards the passage as an interpolation. Whether or not the passage is genuine, it presents a charming picture of domestic piety: the strict chastity of the maiden, the devotion of the wife to her husband, the love of children, the father reading Scripture to the family and instructing them in religion.

6. RIGHTEOUS SAYINGS: The variant would make "righteous" qualify "mother."

7. DID NOT DEPART FROM MY FATHER'S HOUSE: *Cf.* Philo, *De spec. leg.* 3.169: "The women are best suited to the indoor life which never strays from the house, within which the middle door is taken by the maidens as their boundary, and the outer door by those who have reached full womanhood." RIB FASHIONED INTO WOMAN'S BODY: Lit. "the built-up side," an expression unintelligible but for the plain allusion to LXX Gen.

οὐδὲ ὑπερέβην πατρικὸν οἶκον, ἐφύλασσον δὲ τὴν ᾠκοδομημένην πλευράν. ⁸οὐδὲ ἔφθειρέν με λυμεὼν ἐρημίας φθορεὺς ἐν πεδίῳ, οὐδὲ ἐλυμήνατό μου τὰ ἁγνὰ τῆς παρθενίας λυμεὼν ἀπάτης ὄφις. ⁹ἔμεινα δὲ χρόνον ἀκμῆς σὺν ἀνδρί· τούτων δὲ ἐνηλίκων γενομένων ἐτελεύτησεν ὁ πατὴρ αὐτῶν, μακάριος μὲν ἐκεῖνος, τὸν γὰρ τῆς εὐτεκνίας βίον ἐπιζήσας τὸν τῆς ἀτεκνίας οὐκ ὠδυνήθη καιρόν. ¹⁰ὃς ἐδίδασκεν ὑμᾶς ἔτι ὢν σὺν ὑμῖν τὸν νόμον καὶ τοὺς προφήτας. ¹¹τὸν ἀναιρεθέντα Ἀβελ ὑπὸ Καιν ἀνεγίνωσκέν τε ὑμῖν καὶ τὸν ὁλοκαρπούμενον Ισαακ καὶ τὸν ἐν φυλακῇ Ιωσηφ. ¹²ἔλεγεν δὲ ὑμῖν τὸν ζηλωτὴν Φινεες, ἐδίδασκέν τε ὑμᾶς τοὺς ἐν πυρὶ Ανανιαν καὶ Αζαριαν καὶ Μισαηλ. ¹³ἐδόξαζεν δὲ καὶ τὸν ἐν λάκκῳ λεόντων Δανιηλ, ὃν ἐμακάριζεν. ¹⁴ὑπεμίμνῃσκεν δὲ ὑμᾶς καὶ τὴν Ησαιου γραφὴν τὴν λέγουσαν Κἂν διὰ πυρὸς διέλθῃς φλὸξ οὐ κατακαύσει σε. ¹⁵τὸν ὑμνογράφον ἐμελῴδει ὑμῖν Δαυιδ λέγοντα Πολλαὶ αἱ θλίψεις τῶν δικαίων. ¹⁶τὸν Σαλωμῶντα ἐπαροιμίαζεν ὑμῖν λέγοντα Ξύλον ζωῆς ἐστιν τοῖς ποιοῦσιν αὐτοῦ τὸ θέλημα. ¹⁷τὸν Ιεζεκιηλ ἐπιστοποίει τὸν λέγοντα Εἰ ζήσεται τὰ ὀστᾶ τὰ ξηρὰ ταῦτα; ¹⁸ᾠδὴν μὲν γάρ, ἣν ἐδίδαξεν Μωυσῆς, οὐκ ἐπελάθετο διδάσκων τὴν λέγουσαν ¹⁹Ἐγὼ ἀποκτενῶ καὶ ζῆν ποιήσω· αὕτη ἡ ζωὴ ὑμῶν καὶ ἡ μακρότης τῶν ἡμερῶν.

10, 11 υμιν] ημιν A   18 μακροτης] μακαριοτης A

2.22, which employs the same words. Apparently, as Grimm suggests, "the built-up side" became a proverbial expression to designate a woman's body.
8. NO SEDUCER: In allusion to the belief that women are in danger of seduction by evil spirits; cf. Gen. 6, Jub. 4, 5, En. 6 ff., Sen. R. 24.6. OF THE DESERT: The special haunt of demons, generally and in Scripture; cf. Isa. 13.21, 34.14. It is remarkable that so philosophic a writer as our author should share these beliefs—unless he is putting dramatically suitable words into the mouth of a simple woman, or unless, with the "serpent" below, the whole verse is an allegorical and perhaps proverbial way of asserting that she remained chaste at home and abroad. IN THE FIELD: A clear allusion, as the language shows, to LXX Deut. 25.25.
9. THESE SONS: The Gk. has only "these," but the sons are clearly meant; and, as Grimm suggests, a word may have fallen out.
10. TAUGHT YOU: In accordance with the precept of Deut. 4.9, 6.7, 11.19.

and did not depart from my father's house; but I kept guard over the rib fashioned into woman's body. ⁸No seducer of the desert or spoiler in the field corrupted me; nor did the seducing and deceitful serpent defile the sanctity of my chastity. ⁹All the period of my maturity I abode with my husband. When these sons were grown up, their father died. Happy was he; for he was alive to enjoy the fair season of their birth, ¹⁰but was not grieved at the pangs of childlessness. ¹⁰He, when he was still with you, taught you the Law and the Prophets. ¹¹He read to you of Abel, done to death by Cain; of Isaac, offered as a holocaust; and of Joseph, in prison. ¹²He spoke to you of the zeal of Phineas; and taught you concerning Hananiah, Mishael, and Azariah in the fire. ¹³He also glorified Daniel, in the pit of lions, and called him blessed. ¹⁴He admonished you of the Scripture of Isaiah, which declares, 'When thou walkest through fire the flame shall not burn ¹⁵thee.' ¹⁵He chanted to you the psalm of David which says, 'Many are the ills of the righteous.' ¹⁶He recited the proverb of Solomon which says, 'He is a tree of life to them that do his will.' ¹⁷He affirmed the word of Ezekiel, 'Shall these dry bones live?' ¹⁸Nor indeed did he forget, in his instruction, the song that Moses taught, which says, ¹⁹'I kill and I make alive; for that is thy life and the length of thy days.' "

THE LAW AND THE PROPHETS: The customary designation in Gk.
11. HE READ TO YOU . . . : The examples of Isaac, Daniel, and the Three Children are cited in the mother's first discourse (16.20–21). Here Abel (Gen. 4), Joseph (Gen. 39), and Phineas (Num. 25.6 ff.) are added, and other texts are heaped up to strengthen the hope of the martyrs.
14. ISAIAH: 43.2 (LXX).
15. PSALM: 34.20.
16. PROVERB: Adaptation of Prov. 3.18: "She [*i.e.*, Wisdom] is a tree of life to them that lay hold upon her." The "She" is naturally not expressed in the Gk., and our author deliberately understands the subject to be God.
17. EZEKIEL: 37.3, with the "dry" taken from the preceding verse.
18–19. MOSES: Deut. 32.39, 30.20. The reading of A (*makariotes* for *makrotes*) gives "blessedness" for "length of days." DuP-S is disturbed at what he considers an illogicality in the order, Moses being put after the prophets, and suspects these verses also on grounds of poor connection. But the appropriateness of v. 19 is sufficient to explain a desire to conclude with it.

20 ²⁰ˀΩ πικρᾶς τῆς τότε ἡμέρας καὶ οὐ πικρᾶς, ὅτε ὁ πικρὸς Ἑλλήνων τύραννος πῦρ πυρὶ σβέσας λέβησιν ὠμοῖς καὶ ζέουσι θυμοῖς ἀγαγὼν ἐπὶ τὸν καταπέλτην καὶ πάλιν τὰς βασάνους αὐτοῦ τοὺς ἑπτὰ παῖδας τῆς Ἀβρααμίτιδος ²¹τὰς τῶν ὀμμάτων κόρας ἐπήρωσεν καὶ γλώσσας ἐξέτεμεν καὶ βασάνοις ποικίλαις ἀπέκτεινεν. ²²ὑπὲρ ὧν ἡ θεία δίκη μετῆλθεν καὶ μετελεύσεται τὸν ἀλάστορα τύραννον. ²³οἱ δὲ Ἀβραμιαῖοι παῖδες σὺν τῇ ἀθλοφόρῳ μητρὶ εἰς πατέρων χορὸν συναγελάζονται ψυχὰς ἁγνὰς καὶ ἀθανάτους ἀπειληφότες παρὰ τοῦ θεοῦ. ²⁴ᾧ ἡ δόξα εἰς τοὺς αἰῶνας τῶν αἰώνων· αμην.

20 σβεσας] φλεξας AS / παλιν] πασας inferior MSS	23 συναγελαζονται] ευαγγελιζ. S / αθανατους] αθλοφορους S

20–24: *Conclusion*.
20. BITTER: For its sufferings.   NOT BITTER: Because it initiated life eternal.   BITTER TYRANT: The repetition of the epithet—objectionable in English—is intentional, for rhetorical effect.   QUENCHED: More startling, but perhaps more effective, than the alternative "kindled."   CRUEL CALDRONS . . . SEETHING FURY: DuP-S would transpose these intentionally strained expressions, and read the normal "Seething caldrons . . . cruel fury"; but this is the same as emending Shakespeare to read "Sermons in books, stones in running brooks."   AGAIN: A variant reading gives "to all his tortures."   HIS: Attributing ingenuity to the tyrant makes him more fiendish.
21. THE PUPILS . . . PIERCED: This detail is not mentioned in the description of the tortures.

20 ²⁰Ah, that day—at once bitter and not bitter, when that bitter tyrant of the Greeks quenched fire with fire in his cruel caldrons, and in seething fury brought to the catapults and again to his tortures those seven sons of the daughter of Abraham; ²¹the pupils of their eyes he pierced, their tongues he cut off, and he slew them with manifold torments. ²²For these deeds divine justice has pursued that accursed tyrant and shall pursue him. ²³But the children of Abraham, with their mother, who bore off the prize, are ranged in the choir of their fathers; having received souls pure and deathless from God, ²⁴to whom be glory for ever and ever. Amen.

22. JUSTICE . . . PURSUED . . . SHALL PURSUE: Our author appropriately returns, in his epilogue, to his belief in divine justice and retribution here and hereafter; *cf.* 18.5, and Introd. . 121

23. BUT THE CHILDREN OF ABRAHAM: Grimm thinks the reference is to Jews in general, but the context surely implies that the martyrs are intended. Reward for the just is the obverse of the promise of retribution for the tyrant.   RANGED: The variant would yield "celebrated," but "ranged" is suitable for "choir"—for which the variant is "place." SOULS: The immortal souls, or spiritual essences to which physical bodies are transformed at death.

24. GLORY: The liturgical formula would prove that IV Maccabees is a religious, not an academic, discourse. Concluding doxologies are common in Jewish religious literature (*e.g.*, the Books of Psalms; III Mac. 7.23; Sir. 51.30; Tob. 14.15), whence the usage was taken over into Christian literature.

INDEX

Abot, 151, 173
adultery, 120
Aeschylus, 121, 211, 224
aetiology, 15, 24, 77
Aha, R., 112
Alexandria, 44 f., 57, 110
Ambrose, 123 f.
angelology, 2, 25 f., 75, 184
Antioch, 96, 110 ff., 127
Antiochus III, 1, 30
Antiochus Epiphanes 94, 165 f., 237
apocalyptic, 12, 122
Apollonius, 162 f.
Arabic, 113
Aristeas, 8, 24, 98, 147, 237
Aristotle, 145
Arsinoe, 33
Arze ha-Lebanon, 109
Asarah Haruge Malkhut, 107
athletic metaphors, 178, 197, 208, 224, 229, 235
Atonement, Day of, 107
Atthides, 16
Augustine, 112, 115, 123, 125

Bacon, B. W., 103
banquets, 6, 77
Barlaam and Joasaph, 127
Bauer, K., 112
Benjamin of Tudela, 109
Berossus, 13
bibliographies, 27, 139 ff.
Bickermann, E., 7 f., 10, 19, 95
b'parhesia, 119 f., 168, 231
Braun, M., 13
Bréhier, E., 154
brides, 55 f.
brotherhood, power of, 213

Caligula, 21, 96
Campenhausen, H. v., 201
canonicity, 26, 136
Cebetis tabula, 233
Chariton, 14
Christ-Schmid, 15
Christians at Antioch, 111 f.
Chrysippus, 172
Chrysostom, John, 112, 123
Cicero, 102, 149, 172, 175 f.
circumcision, 167
civic rights of Jews, 20 f., 45 f.
Claudius, 21
Cleanthes, 220
Clement of Alexandria, 233
Cleopatra, 8, 20
Cohen, J., 8, 44
Cologne, 127
Constantinople, 127

daimones, 25
Daniel, 19, 73, 211, 227, 230
dating, 21 ff., 95
David, temptation of, 158 f.
degrees in sin, 173
Delehaye, H., 112
deposits, sacred, 163
diatribe, 101
dietary laws, 175
Dio Chrysostom, 5, 14
Dionysius of Halicarnassus, 163
Dionysus, 1, 17 f., 45
Dositheus, 33
doxology, 85, 149, 243
Dura Europus, 233

earthquake, 233
Easter, 112

245

Edessa, 113
editions, 27, 137
Egypt, Jewish settlement in, 51 f.
Eleazar, 2, 71, 116, 126, 169
Eleh Ezkerah, 107
elephants, 59 f.
emotions, 144
Epictetus, 171, 176, 194
Epicurus, 170
epistolary forms, 6, 51, 79 f.
epitaph, 235
Erasmus, 127, 137
Eratosthenes, 17
Esther, 6 f., 24, 32, 71
Euripides, 97, 106, 229, 234
Eusebius, 114, 207
Ewald, H., 103
expiation, 121, 181, 237
Ezekiel, 121

Farag-book, 134
Felicitas, 127
festivals, 24, 77 f., 83
Février, J. G., 10
Finkelstein, L., 120
Friends (title), 45, 207

Gedaliah, 107
gentiles, relations with, 49, 55, 81, 97 f., 123, 133
Goodenough, E. R., 83, 185
Greek language, 22 f.
Greene, W. C., 97
Gregory Nazianz, 112, 123
Gutman, J., 96
gymnasium in Jerusalem, 167

Hadrian, 97, 128
Hannah, 134
Hanukkah, 104
Heinemann, I., 103
Heliodorus, 14
Hermon, 59, 63 f.
heroes, commemoration of, **105 ff.**
highpriesthood, 161 f.
hillul ha-Shem, 119, 173, 179, 184, 231

idolatry, 119
Ignatius, 208
immortality, 118, 121
Indian sages, 177
influence, 123
inscriptions, 221, 228, 235
intellect, 157
Isaac, 185, 211
Isaiah, 24

Jason of Cyrene, 93
Jason, highpriest, 167
Jeremiah, 121
Jerome, 114
Jerusalem, 110, 135
Job, 150
Joseph, 153
Josephus, 9 f., 96, 114, 155
Josippon, 134, 147
Jubilees, 108
Juvenal, 170

kapparah, 134, **181**
Kerateion, 112
Kerenyi, K., 14
kiddush ha-Shem, 119, 168, 175
Kiddushin, 173
Kinsmen (title), 67
Kraeling, E., 112

language, 22, 33, 37, 95, 207
laographia, 17 ff.
Law, 120, 171
Libanius, 124
Liebesny, H., 10
liturgy, 85
Livy, 31, 163
Longus, 233
Lucan, 103, 181, 235

mar'it ayin, 119, 172
Maas, M., 112
Maccabees (title), 5, 114 f.
Maccabees II, 11, 92 ff.
Manetho, 13
manuscript tradition, 26, 135
Marcus, R., 9, 38
martyrdoms, 101 f., 107 f., 124 ff.

maternal instinct, 219
Meecham, H. G., 9 f.
Motzo, B., 7

Nappaha, Isaac, 112
New Testament, 122, 147, 172, 185, 187, 194, 197, 199, 208, 220, 229, 231
Ninth Ab, 128
Ninus romance, 13
Nissim ibn Shahin, 135
Noah's Ark, 225
Norden, E., 98, 102

Obermann, J., 129
Onias, 161
Ovid, 16

paper, exhaustion of, 59
Passio SS. Machabaeorum, 127, 136
Passover, 113
Paul, 112, 175
Perdrizet, E., 44
Persians, 7
Peshitto, 136
Phalaris, 63, 67
Philo, 96, 118, 145, 149, 171, 173, 175 f., 185, 187, 196, 225, 229, 233, 239
philosophy, 115 f.
Phylarchus, 31
picture, 233
Pithom stele, 30, 33
Plato, 25, 101, 116 f., 144, 151, 171, 194, 196
Pliny, 125
Plutarch, 5, 149, 155, 172, 221
Polybius, 17, 30, 33, 83
Polycarp, 126, 208
Pompey, 34
prayers, 37 ff., 71, 134
proselytization, 25
proskynesis, 168
Providence, 23, 26, 118, 171
Ptolemy IV Philopator, 1, 3 f., 9, 16, 30 f.
Ptolemy IX Physcon, 11
Ptolemy XII Auletes, 8

Ptolemy Megalopolitanus, 31
Purim, 8

rabbinic versions, 129 ff.
Rampolla, Cardinal, 104 f.
Raphia, 1, 17, 30
Rashi, 107
Rattenbury, R. M., 13
Reitzenstein, R., 14
religious ideas, 25 f., 118 ff.
retribution, 25, 176
rhetoric, 5 f., 55, 98, 102, 150 f., 168, 175, 183
Rohde, E., 15
romances, Greek, 13, 55
Rome, 3, 19, 127

sabbatical year, 153
Schedia, 57
Schürer, E., 5
Scriptural texts, use of, 239 ff.
Scythians, 8, 200
Seleucus Nicanor, 161
Seleucus IV Philopator, 94, 161
Seneca, 5, 61, 103, 149, 155, 181, 208, 235
Sennacherib, 71
sermons, 103, 112
seven, significance of, 216
Shakespeare, 208
Shamuni, 135
Sifra, 151
Simon, 161
Simon, highpriest, 39
sins, cardinal, 230 ff.
Slavic, 136
sleep, 61
Socrates, 101, 116 f., 173, 179 f.
Sophocles, 207
Sosibius, 20, 30
spiritual birth, 223, 233
Statius, 61
status of Egyptian Jews, 4
Stoics, 117 f., 144, 151, 159, 170, 173, 208, 215, 221
Strabo, 57
Surkau, H. W., 124, 201
Syriac, 113

Tacitus, 238
Tanhuma, R., 112
Tcherikover, V., 19
Temple, 1, 25, 35, 95, 164 f.
Theodotus, 31
Thucydides, 14
Torrey, C. C., 7, 11, 102
torture, instruments of, 189 f.
Tracy, S., 9
tragic imagery, 101, 188, 192, 197, 211, 217, 224 f.
Trajan, 125
Tyrtaeus, 193

Varro, 16

Virgil, 31
versions, 27, 137 f.
virtues, 158, 173

Wallace, S. L., 16, 21
Westermann, W. L., 10
Wilcken, U., 9
Willrich, H., 21, 92
Wolfson, H. A., 118, 149, 233

Xenophon, 173, 213

Yoma, 151

Zeitlin, S., 5, 38, 108, 113